STUDIES ON THE TESTAMENT OF ABRAHAM

SOCIETY OF BIBLICAL LITERATURE
SEPTUAGINT AND COGNATE STUDIES

edited by
Harry M. Orlinsky
Number 6

STUDIES ON THE TESTAMENT OF ABRAHAM

edited by
George W.E. Nickelsburg, Jr.

STUDIES ON THE TESTAMENT OF ABRAHAM
edited by
George W.E. Nickelsburg, Jr.

The Society of Biblical Literature

STUDIES ON THE TESTAMENT OF ABRAHAM

Edited by
George W.E. Nickelsburg, Jr.

Copyright © 1976
by
The Society of Biblical Literature
Copyright © 1972
by
The Society of Biblical Literature

Daniel J. Harrington: Abraham Traditions in the Testament of Abraham and in the "Rewritten Bible" of the Intertestamental Period
Roy Bowen Ward: Abraham Traditions in Early Christianity
George W. E. Nickelsburg, Jr.,: Eschatology in the Testament of Abraham: A Study of the Judgment Scenes in the Two Recensions

Library of Congress Cataloging in Publication Data
Main entry under title:

Studies on the Testament of Abraham.

(Septuagint and cognate studies ; no. 6)
Revised papers of the Society of Biblical Literature Pseudepigrapha Seminar held at the International Congress of Learned Societies in the Field of Religion, held in 1972, and published as part II of the 1972 proceedings, compiled by R. A. Kraft.
Bibliography: p.
1. Bible. O. T. Apocryphal books. Testament of Abraham—Criticism, interpretation, etc.—Addresses, essays, lectures. I. Nickelsburg, George W. E., 1934-   II. Kraft, Robert A   comp. 1972 proceedings. III. Pseudepigrapha Seminar, Los Angeles, 1972. IV. International Congress of Learned Societies in the Field of Religion, Los Angeles, 1972. V. Series.
BS1830.T32S88 1976   229'.914   76-44205
ISBN 0-89130-117-8

CONTENTS

List of Contributors — vii

Preface — ix

Introduction — 1

PART ONE: ON THE TESTAMENT OF ABRAHAM

Review of the Literature — 9
George W.E. Nickelsburg, Jr.

The Recensional Problem

Eschatology in the Testament of Abraham:
A Study of the Judgment Scene in the Two Recensions — 23
George W.E. Nickelsburg, Jr.

The Two Recensions of the Testament of Abraham:
In Which Way did the Transformation Take Place? — 65
Francis Schmidt

Structure and Message in the Testament of Abraham — 85
George W.E. Nickelsburg, Jr.

Syntax Criticism of the Testament of Abraham — 95
R.A. Martin

Reassessing the "Recensional Problem"
in Testament of Abraham — 121
Robert A. Kraft

Miscellanea

The Genre Testament and the Testament of Abraham — 139
Anitra Bingham Kolenkow

The Angelology of the Testament of Abraham — 153
Anitra Bingham Kolenkow

PART TWO: ON PARALLEL TRADITIONS

Abraham Traditions in the Testament of Abraham and in
the "Rewritten Bible" of the Intertestamental Period   165
Daniel J. Harrington

Abraham Traditions in Early Christianity   173
Roy Bowen Ward

The Death of Moses   185
Samuel E. Loewenstamm

The Testament of Abraham and the Texts
Concerning the Death of Moses   219
Samuel E. Loewenstamm

The Pierpont Morgan Fragments of
a Coptic Enoch Apocryphon   227
Birger A. Pearson

The Judgment Scene in the Coptic Apocalypse of Paul   285
George MacRae

Summary and Prospects for Future Work   289

APPENDICES

The Church Slavonic Testament of Abraham   301
Donald S. Cooper and Harry B. Weber

The Coptic Testament of Abraham   327
George MacRae

LIST OF CONTRIBUTORS

Donald S. Cooper
   3016 Raven
   Iowa City, Iowa 52240

Daniel J. Harrington, Weston College School of Theology
   3 Phillips Place
   Cambridge, Massachusetts 02138

Anitra Bingham Kolenkow, University of California
   Faculty Apt. A
   Cowell College
   Santa Cruz, California 95064

Robert A. Kraft, University of Pennsylvania
   Box 36, College Hall
   Department of Religious Thought
   Philadelphia, Pennsylvania 19104

Samuel E. Loewenstamm, The Hebrew University
   Jerusalem, Israel

George W. MacRae, Harvard Divinity School
   45 Francis Avenue
   Cambridge, Massachusetts 02138

Raymond A. Martin, Wartburg Theological Seminary
   333 Wartburg Place
   Dubuque, Iowa 52001

George W.E. Nickelsburg, Jr., University of Iowa
   School of Religion
   Iowa City, Iowa 52242

Birger A. Pearson, University of California
   Department of Religious Studies
   Santa Barbara, California 93106

Francis Schmidt, École Pratique des Hautes Études
   10, place Durutte
   57000 Metz, France

Roy Bowen Ward, Miami University
   Department of Religion
   Oxford, Ohio 45056

Harry B. Weber, University of Iowa
   Department of Russian
   Iowa City, Iowa 52242

PREFACE

The Testament of Abraham and Related Problems was the title of a symposium sponsored by the Pseudepigrapha Seminar (now Pseudepigrapha Group) of the Society of Biblical Literature at the *International Congress of Learned Societies in the Field of Religion*, held in Los Angeles California, 1-5 September, 1972. The Chairman of the Seminar was Walter Harrelson. The symposium program was prepared by Robert A. Kraft. The session was chaired by John Strugnell, and the respondent was J. Smit Sibinga. Papers for this and an earlier session of the Seminar were pre-published as Part Two in *1972 Proceedings*, edited by Robert A. Kraft for the International Organization for Septuagint and Cognate Studies and the Society of Biblical Literature Pseudepigrapha Seminar (Septuagint and Cognate Studies 2; SBL, 1972).

At the close of the session, it was generally agreed that many issues had been left unresolved and even undiscussed. Opportunity to take up these issues once more arose when the first printing of S.C.S 2 went out of print. At that time it was decided to divide the revised edition into its two logically separable parts. Part One, which contained the papers of an IOSCS Symposium on *The Methodology of Textual Criticism in Jewish Greek Scriptures, with Special Attention to the Problems in Samuel-Kings*, will reappear in somewhat updated form under the editorship of Robert A. Kraft. To the undersigned was delegated the responsibility of editing an expanded version of Part Two. Since it seemed most feasible that this revision be a monograph on the Testament of Abraham, two papers from Part Two have been deleted: James H. Charlesworth, *"De Pseudepigraphorum Studio;"* and Robert B. Wright, "The Psalms of Solomon, the Pharisees, and the Essenes."

The nucleus of the present volume consists, then, of more or less revised versions of the papers read in 1972. To these a number of other papers and translations of texts have been added according to a rationale explained in our introduction.

Responsibility for all editorial decisions and for the final shape and format of the volume rests with the undersigned.

I should be remiss, however, were I not to acknowledge my debt and express my thanks to the many persons whose cooperation made the book possible.

Robert A. Kraft planned the original symposium, and the blueprint for this volume evolved from our discussions and correspondence since 1972. Moreover, his advice and collaboration were readily forthcoming whenever they were sought.

This volume is, in many ways, the product of an excellent working relationship among the members of the Pseudepigrapha Group. Thanks are in order not only to members of the Group who have contributed papers--old and new--but especially to those scholars who are not members of the Pseudepigrapha Group: Drs. Cooper, Loewenstamm, Pearson, Ward, and Weber. Their contributions have added a valuable dimension to the discussion.

Preparation of this volume was authorized and encouraged by the Committee on Research and Publications of the Society of Biblical Literature. Its chairman was Harry M. Orlinsky, who also serves as editor of the series, Septuagint and Cognate Studies.

Among the staff of Scholars Press I have received help from director Robert W. Funk, production manager Helen L. Melnis, and from Joann Burnich, who typed in excellent form some incredibly difficult manuscript pages.

At the University of Iowa, Georgiane Perret typed sizable portions of the manuscript, Stanley Bomgarden, my graduate assistant, proofread most of it, and James C. Spalding, the Director of the School of Religion has lent his support.

Grateful acknowledgement is made to the Magnes Press in Jerusalem for permission to reprint a revised version in English of Prof. Loewenstamm's Hebrew article on "The Death of Moses," and to the Pierpont Morgan Library in New York for facilitating Prof. Pearson's work in the fragments of a Coptic Enoch Apocryphon and for their permission to publish them.

For understanding and some sacrifice during an extended period of editing, my personal thanks to Marilyn, Jeanne, and Michael.

Iowa City, Iowa   George W.E. Nickelsburg, Jr.
July, 1976

INTRODUCTION

George W.E. Nickelsburg, Jr.

In an article published in 1957, Émile Turdeanu remarked that since Montague Rhodes James' publication of the *editio princeps* of the Greek Testament of Abraham, the scholarly discussion of that apocryphon had not made "any notable progress."[1] It is uncertain whether Turdeanu was aware of the articles by Kohler (1895) and McCurdy (1942), the translations of the Coptic and Ethiopic versions by Andersson (1903) and Leslau (1951), and the dissertation and article by Turner (1953, 1955),[2] since he cites none of them. However that may be, in direct or indirect response to Turdeanu's appeal for new study of the Testament--or independent of that appeal--the past decade has witnessed the appearance of no less than twelve articles, two dissertations, and two books on the subject.

This recent proliferation of "Abrahamica" rightly gives pause to the editor who considers expanding a collection of four articles into yet another monograph. We have, accordingly, narrowed the scope of our presentation to two areas: a) a discussion of issues that have not yet been settled; b) the publication of some primary sources relevant to this discussion, but for the most part not readily available. Moreover, we have been governed by the contents and concerns of the original seminar papers and the interests of the members of the Pseudepigrapha Group.

The papers discussed at the 1972 seminar were the following:

    D.J. Harrington, "Abraham Traditions in the Testament of Abraham and in the 'Rewritten Bible' of the Intertestamental Period"

---

[1] É. Turdeanu, "Notes sur la tradition littéraire du Testament d'Abraham," in *Studi biz. e neoell.* 9 = *Silloge bizantina . . . S.G. Mercati* (Rome, 1957) 405.

[2] For the bibliographical data, see below, pp. 9f. Turdeanu does cite Box's *"vulgarisation,"* *ibid.* 405, n.1.

1

A.B. Kolenkow, "The Angelogy of the Testament of Abraham"

G.W.E. Nickelsburg, "Eschatology in the Testament of Abraham: A Study of the Judgment Scene in the Two Recensions"

R.B. Ward, "Abraham Traditions in Early Christianity"

The purpose in assigning these topics was to cover major elements in the contents of T Abr. These were: its *narrative traditions* and the light which contemporary Jewish and Christian documents might shed on them; its *angelology*; its *eschatology*. In his invitation to participate in the seminar, Prof. Kraft had also requested papers on "the complex textual and recensional history of T Abr" and "the formal relationship of T Abr to other so-called 'testament' literature (question of genre, forms)." Consideration of the recensional question was a byproduct in the present writer's study of eschatology. The question of testamental genre has continued to surface in the Pseudepigrapha Group's subsequent discussions of the Testaments of Moses, Job, and Joseph. In consequence, Prof. Kraft's original agenda has returned to shape the contents of the present volume.

Part One of the book deals with issues in T Abr itself. We have prefaced the papers with a review of the literature on T Abr since Moses Gaster's publication of the Roumanian version in 1887. This includes an annotated bibliography of all known books, unpublished dissertations, and articles (excepting those in dictionaries and encyclopedias) and reviews of the recent works by F. Schmidt, M. Delcor, and E. Janssen.

The first five papers on T Abr deal with the recensional problem. The present writer, in his 1972 paper, wrote in conscious dialog with the 1971 dissertation of Francis Schmidt,[3] particularly with reference to the history of religions background of the judgment scene and the recensional question. Schmidt had, on new grounds, maintained the priority of the short recension, and this paper argued for the priority of the long recension in the case of the judgment scene and the chariot ride sequence. Considerable seminar time was spent on the

---

[3] *Le Testament d'Abraham*; see below, pp. 12-16.

issue, but no consensus was reached. In this volume, Dr. Schmidt responds to the critique of his dissertation, as well as to M. Delcor's arguments regarding recensional history.[4] In a brief addendum, the present writer has clarified his arguments vis-à-vis those of Schmidt. Since the evidence of the Slavonic and Coptic (Bohairic) versions is crucial in the aforementioned discussion, we have appended English translations of these two versions at the end of this volume. The translation of the Slavonic by Donald S. Cooper and Harry B. Weber is, to our knowledge, the first translation of this version into any modern language. George MacRae has retranslated the Bohairic ms. first translated into German by Andersson (1903) and then into French by M. Chaîne.[5]

R.A. Martin has taken a different approach to the recensional question in his paper "Syntax Criticism in the Testament of Abraham," where he seeks to isolate the comparative evidence for a Semitic *Vorlage* behind the two recensions. He concludes that in most, though not in all cases, the language of the long recension is less Semitic than that of the short recension in the corresponding section.

The present writer in his 1972 paper had attempted to establish the structure and function of the chariot ride sequence and of the judgment scene within it. Arguments for the priority of the long recension had developed from the results of this approach. In a brief additional paper ("Structure and Message in the Testament of Abraham"), we have sketched a tentative extension of this approach for the whole of the long recension, and again have suggested that, by comparison, the structure and logic of the short recension looks secondary.

It would have been desirable and proper to have had Dr. Schmidt respond to our addendum and second paper. However, deadlines have not permitted this, and we must leave further discussion beyond the covers of this book.

"Reassessing the 'Recensional Problem' in Testament of Abraham" is the title of a sweeping, two-edged article by Robert A. Kraft, which cuts to the heart of the various

---

[4]M. Delcor, *Le Testament d'Abraham* (Leiden: Brill, 1973) 5-14.

[5]Published in *ibid*. 186-96.

approaches to the recensional problem. Given the present state of our knowledge, claims of a solution are premature. We need new data and revised criteria.

Although our apocryphon has come to us with the designation "Testament," commentators with an eye for questions of genre (Denis, Schmidt, Delcor *inter alii*) agree that the Testament of Abraham does not fit the Jewish literary genre "Testament." Two papers below attempt to deal with this non-testamentary character of T Abr. The present writer argues that T Abr was composed as a parody on the genre, intended to describe, among other things, the futility of Abraham's stubborn refusal to accept inevitable death ("Structure and Message..."). For Anitra Bingham Kolenkow the source of the non-testamentary character of T Abr is the lack of a biblical reference to Abraham's making a testament. From this biblical datum, our author constructed a narrative which conveys his own parenetic intentions.

Angelology is an integral part of T Abr. In a revised version of her 1972 paper on "The Angelology of the Testament of Abraham," A.B. Kolenkow reviews and critiques earlier work on this subject, sets T Abr's angelology within the context of biblical and Hellenistic Jewish angelology, and seeks the literary and theological functions of the author's specific angelology.

Part Two of the volume contains papers dealing with traditions parallel to T Abr. Two of these papers--both of them slightly revised versions of 1972 seminar papers--discuss traditions which are tied to the figure of Abraham. Daniel J. Harrington delineates the (relatively few) parallels to T Abr in Jubilees, the Genesis Apocryphon, Pseudo-Philo, Philo, and Josephus. Roy Bowen Ward searches the literature of the New Testament and Apostolic Fathers. The early Christians interpreted the figure of Abraham according to their specific needs. There are, however, some indications that some of these writers knew traditions common to T Abr, if not the apocryphon.

Like the ancient Patriarch himself, traditions about Abraham have pursued a nomadic existence, wandering not only from place to place, but also from person to person.

Already in his *editio princeps*, M.R. James called

attention to the close similarities between T Abr and *midrashim* describing Moses' refusal to accept death.[6] He suggested that the Moses *midrashim* (and other similar traditions) had as their source the now-lost Assumption of Moses,[7] but he refrained from drawing any conclusions about the relationship between T Abr and the Assumption of Moses. Subsequent scholarship has taken sporadic note of James' finding, but no commentator has subjected the obvious relationship between these traditions to rigorous examination. The biblical and post-biblical Jewish traditions about the death of Moses were the subject of a lengthy Hebrew article by Samuel E. Loewenstamm (1958). A revised and expanded version of that article appears in this volume in English translation. Although Prof. Loewenstamm discussed in detail the Moses *midrashim* mentioned above, as well as the Assumption of Moses, he did not discuss parallels to T Abr. He has assumed that task in a second article below, "The Testament of Abraham and the Texts Concerning Moses' Death," where he argues that the traditions in question were originally Mosaic and have been only secondarily attached to Abraham.

Among venerables that populate the judgment scene in the short recension is Enoch, "the scribe of righteousness." While commentators have consistently and correctly cited parallels in 1,2,3 Enoch, the Enochic tradition that most closely parallels T Abr appears to have alluded everyone. Written in Coptic and first published by W.E. Crum in 1913, it combines details of the judgment scenes of both recensions of T Abr. Birger A. Pearson presents below the first thorough investigation of the contents of this remarkable document, "The Pierpont Morgan Fragments of a Coptic Enoch Apocryphon." His new transcription and translation are based on fresh examination of the papyrus fragments under ultraviolet light. He discusses the contents in their own right, but with a particular eye toward their relationship to T Abr. He concludes that the document is a Christian work, composed in Sahidic in 5th century Egypt, and influenced mainly by the short recension, but

---

[6]M.R. James, *The Testament of Abraham* (T&S 2:2; Cambridge: The University Press, 1892) 64-70.

[7]*Ibid.* 68.

also by the long recension of T Abr.

M.R. James' intimate acquaintance with early Christian as well as Jewish apocryphal literature led him to cite as a parallel to T Abr the Greek *Apocalypse of Paul*, first published by Tischendorf.[8] A Coptic apocalypse of Paul, different from the Greek,[9] has been identified among the Nag Hammadi codices, and George MacRae provides us with a translation of the relevant section, a judgment scene with striking similarities to that of the short recension of T Abr.

In our conclusion, we have attempted to summarize and synthesize the results of the papers in this volume and on the basis of these papers and the other literature, to delineate the state of the discussion and prospects for its pursuit.

---

[8] See below, p. 291, n. 1.

[9] See below, p. 291, n. 2.

PART ONE

ON THE TESTAMENT OF ABRAHAM

REVIEW OF THE LITERATURE

George W.E. Nickelsburg, Jr.

This review consists of two parts: A. a chronologically arranged annotated bibliography of all known modern discussions of T Abr (excepting encyclopedia and dictionary articles); B. reviews of the recent major works by F. Schmidt, M. Delcor, and E. Janssen.

A. Annotated Bibliography

Gaster, Moses. "The Apocalypse of Abraham: From the Roumanian Text, Discovered and Translated," *Transactions of the Society of Biblical Archaeology* 9 (1887) 195-226. Reprinted in Gaster's *Studies and Texts in Folklore, Magic, Medieval Romance, Hebrew Apocrypha and Samaritan Archaeology*. London: Maggs, 1925-28. Vol. 1, 92-124 (Now also in KTAV reprint).

Reconstructs "critical Roumanian text" from three mss. and provides Engl. translation. Version closely related to long Gk. recension.

James, Montague Rhodes. *The Testament of Abraham*. T&S 2:2. Cambridge: The University Press, 1892.

Editio princeps of Greek. Critical edition of the two recensions. Lengthy introduction. Long recension is original; short recension is an abridgement; Arabic is an independent abridgement. It is a second century Jewish-Christian writing composed in Egypt. W.E. Barnes contributes extracts of the Arabic version of the Testaments of Abraham, Isaac, and Jacob in an appendix.

Kohler, K. "The Pre-Talmudic Haggada II C: The Apocalypse of Abraham and its Kindred," *JQR* 7 (1895) 581-606.

Disputes James' hypothesis of Christian origin. Musters many parallels from Jewish (primarily rabbinic) sources and argues for Essene origin.

Andersson, Ernst. "Abraham's Vermächtnis," *Sphinx* 6 (1903) 220-35.

Translation of Bohairic version. See below, pp. 327-40, for new Engl. translation of the same ms.

Box, G.H. *The Testament of Abraham: Translated from the Greek Text with Introduction and Notes*. TED Series 2. London: SPCK, 1927.

Engl. translation of the two recensions, with brief notes. Introduction: long recension is original, though some original details in short recension; Alexandrian Jewish writing, perhaps from the first century C.E.; no firm position on its possible Essene character; highly probable that a Hebrew form of the book in some shape originally existed (following Kohler). Appendix contains S. Gaselee's translation of the Bohairic Testaments of Isaac and Jacob.

McCurdy, G.H. "Platonic Orphism in the Testament of Abraham," *JBL* 61 (1942) 213-26.

See below, pp. 27,31,33.

Leslau, Wolf. "The Testament of Abraham," in *Falasha Anthology: Translated from Ethiopic Sources with an Introduction. Yale Judaica Series* 6. New Haven: Yale University Press, 1951. Pp. 91-102, 176-80.

Engl. translation of Ethiopic Falasha text, with brief introduction and notes.

Turner, Nigel. *The Testament of Abraham: A Study of its Origin, Date and Language.* Diss. University of London, 1953.

See below, pp. 125f.

-----. "The 'Testament of Abraham': Problems in Biblical Greek," *NTS* 1 (1955) 219-23.

See below, pp. 125f.

Turdeanu, Émile. "Notes sur la tradition littéraire du *Testament d'Abraham*," in *Studi biz. e neoell.* 9 = *Silloge bizantina* ...*S.G. Mercati.* Rome, 1957. Pp. 405-9.

The Slavonic version, represented most faithfully by ms. P, is closest to James' Gk. ms. A of the short recension. Omissions common to A and Slav. indicate interpolations in Gk. mss. B and C. Turdeanu questions James' claim regarding the priority of the long recension.

Piattelli, Elio. "Il Testamento di Abramo (Testo apocalittico del I secolo dell' E.V.)," *Annuario di Studi Ebraici* (1964-65) 111-21.

Mainly a summary of the contents of T Abr. A few general comments.

Gaguine, Maurice. *The Falasha Version of the Testaments of Abraham, Isaac and Jacob: A Critical Study of Five Unpublished ms. with Introduction, Translation and Notes.* University of Manchester unpublished dissertation, 1965.

This dissertation was unavailable for study. Delcor summarizes it (*Testament* 19-22): Gaguine indicates the existence of numerous Eth. mss. One of these may indicate a 4th century date for the translation. It was made from the Arabic. The Falasha text is almost certainly a recension of the Christian-Ethiopic Version.

Delcor, M. "De l'origine de quelques traditions contenues dans le Testament d'Abraham," *Proceedings of the Fifth World*

Congress of Jewish Studies, ed. P. Peli. Jerusalem: World Union of Jewish Studies, 1969. Vol. 1, 192-200.

> Treats three items in T Abr: Abraham the farmer; Abel the judge; the glory of Adam. The first two developed from the Palestinian Targum, and the third is probably pre-Christian in content. These provide a *terminus a quo* for the dating of T Abr.

-----. "La portée chronologique de quelques interprétations du targoum Neophyti contenues dans le cycle d'Abraham," *JSJ* 1 (1970) 105-19.

> Abraham traditions in Targum Neophyti date ca. 100 C.E. but show similarities to traditions contained already in the LXX.

Denis, Albert-Marie. "Le Testament d'Abraham," in *Introduction aux Pseudépigraphes grecs d'Ancien Testament*. SVTP 1. Leiden: E.J. Brill, 1970. Pp. 31-37.

> Most complete *published* catalogue of Gk. mss. T Abr was written in Egypt either by a Jewish Christian or a Jew. Two recensions derive independently from the original. Original language was doubtless Hebrew. The date: 1st or 2nd century C.E.

Fishburne, Charles W. "I Corinthians III.10-15 and the Testament of Abraham," *NTS* 17 (1970) 109-15.

> The Pauline passage shows remarkable verbal parallels to T Abr 13. These and other parallels suggest dependence on T Abr, though Paul makes his own alterations.

Schmidt, Francis. *Le Testament d'Abraham*. Thèse Strasbourg, 1971. 2 Vols.

> See review below, pp.12-16.

Stone, Michael E. *The Testament of Abraham: The Greek Recensions*. T&T 2: Ps. Series 2. Missoula: SBL, 1972.

> Reprint of James' texts and apparatus of two recensions with facing Engl. translation.

Harrington, Daniel J. "Abraham Traditions in the Testament of Abraham and in the 'Rewritten Bible' of the Intertestamental Period," *SCS* 2 (1972) 155-64.

> In slightly revised form, below, pp. 165-71.

Kolenkow, Anitra Bingham. "The Angelology of the Testament of Abraham," *SCS* 2 (1972) 228-45.

> In revised form, below, pp. 153-62.

Nickelsburg, George W.E. Jr. "Eschatology in the Testament of Abraham: A Study of the Judgment Scene in the Two Recensions," *SCS* 2 (1972) 180-227.

> In slightly revised form, below, pp. 23-64.

Ward, Roy Bowen. "Abraham Traditions in Early Christianity," *SCS* 2 (1972) 165-79.

In slightly revised form, below, pp. 173-84.

Schmidt, Francis. "Conférence de M. Francis Schmidt: Année 1972-1973," *Annuaire de l'École Pratique des Hautes Études, 5e section (Sciences Religieuses)* Tomes 80-81:3 (1971-73) 321-25.

The Dream of Isaac (short rec. ch. 7) is paralleled in M. *Pesaḥim* 10:5 and Melito's Homily on the Passover 489-93. T Abr with its individual eschatology uses a portion of the Passover liturgy to describe the passing of the soul from narrowness (i.e., from the "Egypt" of the body) to the vastness of heaven, where it will await the resurrection.

-----. "Le monde à l'image du bouclier d'Achille: sur la naissance et l'incorruptibilité du monde dans le 'Testament d'Abraham,'" *Bulletin de la Société Ernest-Renan* N.S. 22 (1973) 14-18 = *RHR* 185 (1974) 122-26.

In the long recension ch 10, the description of the world as Abraham sees it imitates descriptions of the Shield of Achilles in Homer and Lucian of Samosata. Ps.-Heraclitus allegorically interpreted Hephaestus' forging of Achilles' arms as a cosmogonic myth. T Abr reflects this interpretation, but moves from macrocosm to microcosm. God has created man and does not wish his destruction.

Delcor, Mathias. *Le Testament d'Abraham.* SVTP 2 (Leiden: E.J. Brill, 1973).

See review, below, pp. 17-21.

Kolenkow, Anitra Bingham. "What is the Role of Testament in the Testament of Abraham?" *HTR* 67 (1974) 182-84.

T Abr was written to explain why Abraham did not give a testament (according to the Bible) and enabled the author to put forth his view of what Abraham would have revealed to his children if he had actually made a testament.

Janssen, Enno. "Testament Abrahams," *JSHRZ* 3:2. Gütersloh: Verlagshaus Gerd Mohn, 1975. Pp. 192-256.

See review below, p. 21f.

B. *Recent Major Works*

FRANCIS SCHMIDT. *Le Testament d'Abraham: Introduction, édition de la recension courte, traduction et notes.* Thèse Strasbourg (typescript), 1971. 2 Vols. Pp. 132 & 164.

In his introduction (Vol. 1), Schmidt deals in Part One with textual matters. He provides what is to date the most complete list of Gk. mss. He then reviews the versions. The *Slavonic* is most closely related to Gk. ms. E of the short recension. Manuscripts of the *Roumanian* are relate severally to both recensions. The *Ethiopic* derives from the Arabic, and the *Arabic*, from the *Bohairic*. In his chapter on the textual tradition of the short recension, he divides the Gk. mss. into three sub-groups. The latest of these is B F G. Manuscripts A D C form a second sub-group, though C has its own peculiar additions and variants, some of them related to the long recension. The third and most reliable sub-group is comprised of ms. E alone. However, Schmidt argues on the basis of a lengthy collation that Slavonic mss. P and T represent a translation made from an exemplar of this sub-group. A number of readings in the Bohairic indicate a similar derivation.

In Part Two of his introduction, Schmidt deals with the contents of T Abr, particularly those items which shed light on the structure, genre, date, and provenance of T Abr. His perspective and emphasis are primarily those of an historian of religions.

1. *The Place of T Abr in Intertestamental Jewish Literature*. Schmidt discusses the genre of the Jewish Testament. Although T Abr has the typical testamentary setting and the explicit command that Abraham make his testament, the writing lacks crucial features of the genre: the father's drawing an example from his personal experience (though T Abr does exemplify the virtue of hospitality); ethical commands; the transmission of a material or spiritual inheritance to the son; a revelation to Isaac of the heavenly mysteries to which Abraham was initiated. Only in one sense might we call T Abr a Testament: the author transmits his legacy to his reader.

2. In *the Dream of Isaac*, a solar myth of Iranian origins, attested also in 2 Enoch 14 and 3 Baruch 6-8, has been utilized to depict the separation of Abraham's soul from his body until the *eschaton*. This particular eschatological belief is most closely paralleled in 4 Ezra 7, and, if we may judge from the hypothetical source behind Josephus and Hippolytus, and it was at home among the Essenes.

3. *Abel and Enoch: the Judgment in the Short Recension*. Abel's function as judge stems from his status as first martyr and first accuser (Gen 5:10; cf. 1 Enoch 22:7) and reflects the belief that the righteous will execute judgment against their

oppressors (cf., e.g., Wisd 5). It is possible that reference to Abel may have been in the original Hebrew text of T Abr, or it may have resulted from a translator's interpretation of the Hebrew בן אדם (Son of Man) as "son of Adam," an interpretation that would have been facilitated by the presence of Adam in the text. Enoch's functions as Scribe and as proponent of the mercy of God have counterparts in the Enochic corpus. His triple crown refelcts rabbinic rather than Egyptian conceptions.

4. *The Balance and the Fire: the Judgment in the Long Recension.* Schmidt attributes most of the unique elements in this judgment scene to Egyptian influence, and he cites parallels in the Book of the Dead (for details, see below, pp. 32-36).

5. *Michael, the First of the Angels.* The portraits of Michael in the two recensions correspond to their differing angelologies. The short recension places the man Enoch in the heavenly court and states that Abraham has no peer among the angelic ranks (cf. 13:10 Slav., following Gk. E). In the long recension, the heavenly witnesses are angels, a higher and more developed angelology is evident, and there is an expressed incompatibility between heavenly and earthly beings. Similarly, the eschatology of this recension has no room for a resurrection of the body. In discussing Michael's ascent to heaven for the hour of prayer, Schmidt suggests that this may reflect Essene practices.

6. *Death in its Beauty and Death in its Rottenness.* These two alternative aspects of death reflect the Iranian daênâ-- the personification of the individual's good or evil deeds, which meets the soul three days after death. The conception is somewhat more developed (in accordance with Iranian ideas) in the long recension. The two faces of death described in the short recension (Gk. ms. E and Slav.) may be the result of a midrashic exposition of the Hebrew text of Job 20:15-16, 23-25.

7. *The Seven Faces of Death.* The variety of faces which the long recension attributes to death correspond to Egyptian astrological speculations about violent death, and they are reminiscent of the polycephalic Egyptian god Tithoes.

8. *The Date and Provenance of T Abr.* The evidence from ms. E of the short recension supports N. Turner's claim that the Greek of this recension is older than the Greek of the long recension. With respect to extra-Jewish influences, only the long recension reveals Egyptian influence, whereas both recensions contain the same Iranian influences. Schmidt concludes: a document originally created in Palestinian Jewish circles which were open to Iranian influence (short recension) was revised in Egyptian Jewish circles (long recension). Cumulative evidence suggests a date ca. 115 C.E. for the long recension. Similar evidence points to "popular Essenism" ca. 50 C.E. for the short recension.

9. *Sinfonia.* In his final chapter, Schmidt seeks to produce a "homogenous reading" of T Abr through the tools of structural analysis. He compares and contrasts two "isotopes," which correspond to the earthly and heavenly views of reality. The writing begins with the decree of Abraham's death and ends with the translation of his soul to eternal life. The point of the story is that no one can escape death, but that in the light of heavenly reality, this death is, in fact, the transition from death (earthly existence) to life (thus, Isaac's dream).

Volume 2 consists of texts, translations, and notes. Schmidt reproduces the text of Gk. ms. E, occasionally emended after the Slavonic and other Greek witnesses. He then prints the texts of A D C and B F G. There follow annotated translations of the two recensions, with special attention to the short recension.

Schmidt has rendered an important service to students of T Abr and related literature. He has shown that Gk. ms. E and the Slavonic version are indispensible to the interpretation of the short recension.

At many points his history of religions parallels are illuminating and convincing. More controversial are some of the conclusions he draws from them. Discussions of his resolution of the recensional question appear elsewhere in this volume (below, pp. 32-36 and 126-30) and need not be repeated here. We might note one example of the problems involved in tying particular ideas to certain geographical locations.

Schmidt sees the reflex of Iranian myth in 2 Enoch 14, a writing which scholarly consensus has tended to place (for good or bad reasons) in Egypt.

Schmidt's attribution of documents and ideas to Essene circles is not always convincing. The presence of a given writing in the Qumran library does not prove Essene origin, nor does the presence of an idea in an Essene writing necessarily indicate that the idea was uniquely Essene. Schmidt's argumentation regarding the Essene character of the short recension's view of body and soul is tenuous to say the least. As he himself notes, there is no reference to resurrection of the body in the Josephus passage (*JW* 2:154) which parallels Hippolytus' statement on this subject (*Ref*. 9:27). Moreover, no passage in the published Qumran corpus asserts such a resurrection. Furthermore, it certainly cannot be assumed that we would find a peculiarly Essene idea in 4 Ezra. These questions are important, because, to no small extent, Schmidt builds his case for Essene provenance on the accumulation of his findings in these areas.

Schmidt's quest for a holistic interpretation of T Abr marks an important methodological shift in "intertestamental" studies. We have not and cannot here do justice to the details of his structural analysis. We can only raise some questions. Is the contrast between the earthly and heavenly spheres central to the whole of T Abr (as central as it is, e.g., in T Job)? If the function of Abraham's trip to heaven is primarily to receive the knowledge that the righteous are taken to eternal life, why do we have such a lengthy description of the judgment of the *sinner*?

However we may judge Schmidt's conclusions in specific issues, he has raised new questions, and he has brought new data to bear on old questions. For this we are in his debt.

MATHIAS DELCOR. *Le Testament d'Abraham: introduction, traduction du texte grec et commentaire de la recension greque longue suivi de la traduction des testaments d'Abraham, d'Isaac et de Jacob d'après les versions orientales.* SVTP 2. Leiden: E.J. Brill, 1973. Pp. x + 282. Indices.

This volume is divided into three major sections: an introduction; a translation of the long Greek recension with commentary; translations of the short Greek recension and of the Bohairic, Ethiopic, and Arabic versions of the Testaments of Abraham, Isaac, and Jacob.

Recensions. Delcor presents a summary synopsis of the two recensions of the Greek in parallel columns and then enumerates the major differences between them. He concludes that the two recensions are the result of diverse (oral) developments and expansions of a common original, elements of which are preserved in both recensions. The Slavonic and Roumanian versions follow the long recension, while the Coptic, Arabic, and Ethiopic follow the short recension.

Linguistic matters. The influence of the LXX is evident throughout T Abr. Unusual vocabulary in the long recension has parallels in the unique usage of the Wisdom of Solomon and 2,3,4 Maccabees. Other rare words are paralleled in patristic usage. "Semiticisms" do not indicate translation from Hebrew or Aramaic, but rather an author at home in biblical Greek.

Sources for special ideas. The portrait of Abraham as a farmer rather than a herdsman stems from the LXX translation of Gen 21:33 (ἄρουρα ["field"] for אשל ["tamarisk tree"]). The emphasis on Abraham's hospitality derives from two sources: the Palestinian Targum (see T Neophyti Gen 21:23), from which the rabbinic sources derive the same motif; and the Testament of Job. For Abraham's trip to heaven, Delcor cites parallels from "intertestamental" literature (listed below, pp. 23-24) and rabbinic sources. Here again he sees the Palestinian Targum as the source of this speculation (see T Neophyti Gen 15:5; cf. 15:1).

Literary problems. T Abr is not really a Testament, for it lacks the parenetic element typical of that genre. The T Isaac and T Jacob fit the category better, although neither of these present the protagonist as a model for future generations, as is the case in other Jewish Testaments. The *Sitz im Leben* of T Abr is uncertain. The Christian exhortation and doxology at the end of the long recension may reflect earlier Jewish counterparts and indicate that the work was originally composed as a synagogue homily. Similarities between T Abr and T Job are particularly noteworthy. It appears that our author has intentionally transferred to Abraham certain virtues or qualities applied to Job in T Job. Late vocabulary and apocalyptic ideas in chs. 10-14 of the long recension (ideas which have no necessary relationship to the rest of the writing) perhaps indicate that this section is an interpolation.

Eschatology. Delcor discusses "entities" related to Abraham's death. The portrait of Michael is unusual. There is no dispute between him and Satan over Abraham's soul or body. There is no reference to his sounding the trumpet at the resurrection. His role in transporting the soul of Abraham to Paradise is paralleled only in Par Jer and 3 Baruch, both of which are relatively late. Enoch 71:1-3 provides a parallel to the idea of the assumption of the soul to heaven. The evident Essene or essenizing character of this book accords well with Josephus' description of Essene eschatology (*JW* 2:154-55) and suggests such a background for the same idea in T Abr. Michael's functions as chief angel and high priest in the short recension have various parallels in Jewish literature. The descriptions of Death reflect some widespread Semitic ideas, but also some themes peculiar to Egypt, as James already noted. Although Abraham's heavenly vision was drawn from the Palestinian Targum, the mediation of the vision by Michael is closely paralleled by the latter's function in 1 Enoch 24-25. Abel's function as judge derives from traditions attested in T Neophyti Gen 4:8 (see Delcor, "De l'origine...in bibliography above, p. 10). The triple judgment is modelled after the three degrees of jurisdiction in Roman Egypt.

Provenance. Delcor discusses at some length and rejects a Christian origin for the book. There is no Christology, and traces of christianizing are few and superficial. A number of elements point to Egypt as the place of origin (for both recensions): the psychostasia; the triple judgment; the portrayal of death. In addition, the book's vocabulary is most closely related to such "Alexandrian" works as Wisdom of Solomon, 2,3,4 Maccabees (4 Maccabees is placed at the time of the glory of Alexandrian literature). A more precise context is indicated by a number of "more or less Essene characteristics": Abraham's hospitality (cf. Josephus *JW* 2:134 on the Essenes, so Delcor, p. 34); Abraham's continuous communion with Michael is reminiscent of the Qumran community's consciousness of the angelic presence; Abraham's trip to "the River Ocean" (short recension ch. 8) accords with Essene beliefs attested in Josephus *JW* 2:155. Reference to Abraham's ascent on the chariot parallels Qumran speculations on the Chariot. Certain elements in T Abr do not fit well with Essenism: Abraham's sumptuous banquet does not accord well with Essene asceticism. Also lacking are a doctrine of fatalism and the numerous ablutions. Thus it is better to seek a place of origin among the Therapeutae, which would explain the many similarities to T Job, thought to be a Therapeutic writing.

Date. The existence in the fourth or fifth century C.E. of a copy of the Testaments of Abraham, Isaac, and Jacob provides a *terminus a quo.* Other factors suggest a date around the turn of the era. T Abr appears to be a polemic against T Job, which Delcor dates in the first century B.C.E. (p. 51). T Abr draws some of its traditions from the Palestinian Targum, which has its roots before the turn of the era. Linguistic parallels are to Wisdom of Solomon, 2,3,4 Maccabees, all of which are to be dated in the first century B.C.E. to first century C.E.

We have then, at the heart of T Abr, a midrashic account, developed in Egypt from the LXX, embellished by traditions from the Palestinian Targum, written in Therapeutic circles around the turn of the era.

In an appendix, Delcor suggests that the T Isaac is Jewish in origin, with Essenizing characteristics. It may have been composed at the same time and in the same circles as T Abr, though it presumes the latter.

In his commentary on the long recension, Delcor includes material mainly of three types: explanatory notes; linguistic data (e.g., cross references to the Greek Bible and to other

Jewish literature; copious reference to Jewish literature which illuminates the text at hand, and to secondary literature.

Delcor's translation of the short Greek recension is based on ms. A (rather than on the eclectic text published by James). The translation of the Bohairic Testaments of Abraham, Isaac, and Jacob duplicates material already published (Abraham, Anderssen, 1903; Isaac and Jacob, Gaselee in Box, 1927). Delcor prints a translation of two mss. of the Ethiopic T Abr. The first of these is the defective ms. translated by Leslau (1951). The second ms. begins with T Abr 6 and makes it clear that the Ethiopic version of T Abr is not as abbreviated as one might have supposed from the ms. which Leslau translated. This second ms. also contains the Testaments of Isaac and Jacob, hitherto unpublished. In his introduction, Delcor discusses the Ethiopic tradition at length (pp. 17-22). In James' edition, Barnes had provided extracts of the Abrabic versions of the Testaments of Abraham, Isaac, and Jacob. Here Delcor publishes a full translation of the same manuscript.

The strengths of Delcor's volume lie in several areas. He has made new versional material available to us. Although he does not discuss the Testaments of Isaac and Jacob at great length, he at least makes us aware that, at some point, T Abr must be discussed within this context. Most important, Delcor brings to bear on the interpretation of T Abr a wide knowledge of Jewish and patristic literature. He has dug deeply and has made a wealth of material available to the interpreter.

At a number of points, however, Delcor's conclusions will be questioned. His reasons for a Therapeutic (i.e. Essene-related) provenance are not without their problems. Hospitality was a virtue not limited to the Essenes, and Delcor's citation of rabbinic sources probably tells against this theory (pp. 36-38). Abraham's associations with Michael are of a totally different order from the eschatologically charged angelology of Qumran. Chariot speculation was not limited to the Essenes. To some extent Delcor's arguments regarding the date of T Abr are based on unknown quantities. He posits a dependence on T Job, a writing as difficult to date as T Abr. He posits a dependence on difficult-to-date targumic traditions (see also below, pp. 296f.). Delcor takes no real stand on the specifics of the recensional question. At a couple of points, however, his statements are incorrect or partly so. The Slavonic version represents the short, not the long recension. Evidently there are manuscripts of the Roumanian version which follow the short recension. These data raise problems with Delcor's geographical conclusions about the recensions, as Schmidt has noted (below, p. 66). Delcor's suggestion that the chariot ride sequence may be an erratic block in the long recension does not take sufficient account of its function in that recension (see below, pp. 25-27). Delcor suggests a Septuagintal origin for the idea that Abraham was a farmer, although he notes that the idea was present in the Palestinian Targum (p. 36) and in Jubiless 11 (p. 95). Given these latter two sources, derivation from the Greek Bible is perhaps too narrow an hypothesis. The Greek translations could reflect haggadic traditions spelled out in Jubilees and the Targum.

The works of Schmidt and Delcor complement one another rather well. First, and most obviously, each of them concentrates on a different recension. Where Schmidt does deal with the long recension (mainly the judgment scene and the faces of death), he marshals evidence to which Delcor hardly alludes. Here, too, we see the complementarity of the two works. Schmidt's strong suit is non-Jewish history of religions material. Delcor, on the other hand, discusses the wide span of Jewish literature. His linguistic data also goes beyond that supplied by Schmidt. On the other hand, Schmidt has happily supplied us with the text of the Greek ms. E of the short recension, which renders Delcor's translation of ms. A obsolete.

ENNO JANSSEN. "Testament Abrahams," in *Unterweisung in lehrhafter Form, Jüdische Schriften aus hellenistisch-römischer Zeit* 3:2. Gütersloh: Verlagshaus Gerd Mohn, 1975. Pp. 192-256.

Janssen follows the typical format of this series: a short introduction with bibliography, followed by a briefly annotated German translation.

According to Janssen, neither recension of T Abr is directly dependent on the other, but each contains both primitive elements and later additions. The writing was composed in Greek in Palestine during the Roman period of the Common Era. It is a Jewish composition that has passed through Christian hands.

A novel feature of this introduction is Janssen's attempt to correlate Abraham's attitudes toward his impending death with Elizabeth Kubler Ross' five stages of the attitude of the dying toward their own death (*Interviews mit Sterbenden* [Stuttgart, 1971]): denial (chs. 1-4); anger (ch. 7); bargaining (ch. 9); depression (ch. 16); acceptance (ch. 20). While this is an interesting attempt at cross-disciplinary study, Janssen appears to stretch the evidence. In ch. 16 Abraham evidences denial rather than depression. In ch. 20 the patriarch does not assent to his death; he is tricked into it.

In his translation, Janssen has done us the useful service of setting the translations of the two recensions side-by-side in parallel columns. His notes, though brief, provide useful information not always found in the works of Schmidt and Delcor. There are multitudes of cross-references to Jewish and Christian literature. He is particularly strong in rabbinic references (he criticizes Schmidt for paying too little attention to these sources in his development of an Essene hypothesis). He also provides a certain amount of linguistic information and helpful references to explanations of ideas and customs alluded to in the text of T Abr.

While Janssen's work is not intended to be of the scope and depth of Schmidt's thesis and Delcor's commentary, it does provide a useful and helpful supplement to these longer works.

ESCHATOLOGY IN THE TESTAMENT OF ABRAHAM
A STUDY OF THE JUDGMENT SCENES IN THE TWO RECENSIONS*

George W. E. Nickelsburg, Jr.

This paper will address itself to significant aspects of the judgment scene in the T Abr. The problem presented by the Long and Short Recensions (A & B) is especially magnified in this section, where, aside from some broad similarities, there are a multitude of important differences between A and B.[1] Indeed, these differences are so numerous and significant that it is unfeasible to discuss the two recensions in parallel. My discussion will be confined mainly to Rec. A, with a concluding section on the relationship between A and B.

A. The Context and Function of the Judgment Scene

The tradition that Abraham travelled through the heavens and received an eschatological revelation is not unique to T Abr. According to 4 Ezra 3:13f.,

> . . . you chose . . . Abraham . . . and to him only you revealed the end of the times secretly at night . . .[2]

---

*This paper is reproduced here in substantially the same form in which it first appeared in 1972 (SCS 2. 180-227). It was simply not possible to prepare a thorough-going revision in time to allow for the responses that follow. Some additional notes have been added, which are enclosed in square brackets In addition, I have discussed briefly in an addendum aspects of F. Schmidt's critique of this paper (below, pp. 62-64).

[1] The text of the Grk. recensions used here is that edited by M. R. James, *The Testament of Abraham*. Texts and Studies II.2 (1892), reprinted in *The Testament of Abraham: The Greek Recensions*, ed. by M. E. Stone, T. & T. 2. Ps. Series 2 (1972).

[2] Transl. after G. H. Box in *AP* II, ed. R. H. Charles (1912) *ad loc*. For the textual problem, see the apparatus *ad loc*.

Again in 2 Bar 4:5:

> And after these things *I showed it* (Paradise) *to my servant Abraham* by night among the portions of the victims.[3]

In Pseudo-Philo's *Liber Antiquitatum Biblicarum* 18:5, the Lord says,[4]

> Was it not concerning this people that I spoke to Abraham in a vision saying, your seed shall be as the stars of heaven, *when I raised him up above the firmament and showed him all the orderings of the stars*, and required of him his son for a burnt offering?

Finally, the Apocalypse of Abraham offers a lengthy description of Abraham's trip to heaven (chs. 9-32).[5] Among the objects of this vision are: the divine throne; Paradise; the fall of man; the actions of people on earth below; the events leading up to the end time. With the apparent exception of Pseudo-Philo, all of these texts specify as the time of the revelation the sacrifice described in Gen 15, perhaps because the divine word in Gen 15:13-16 is a revelation of events to come.[6]

In T Abr, the timing of the patriarch's heavenly journey fits the theme of the book. The journey is granted in response to a request that is one more procrastinating attempt to avoid death,

> ... while I am still in this body, *I wish to see the whole world and all the created things* which you established through one word ... (IX: 87.3-5).[7]

---

[3]Transl. by R. H. Charles, *AP* II *ad loc.*

[4]Passage cited by D. J. Harrington, "Abraham Traditions in the Testament of Abraham and in the 'Rewritten Bible' of the Intertestamental Period," below, p. 168. Transl. by M. R. James, *The Biblical Antiquities of Philo* (1917) *ad loc.*

[5]See G. H. Box, *The Apocalypse of Abraham* (1919).

[6]Cf. also Jub 14:13, which may know of such a tradition. [The Targum Neophyti Gen 15:17 also records a vision of Gehenna, see M. Delcor, *Le Testament d'Abraham* (Leiden, 1973) 39.]

[7]Citations give the chapter numbering (Roman numerals) of James and of Box's translation (*Testament of Abraham* [1927]) and the page and line numbers in James' text (Arabic numerals). [To reconcile the page numbers of the Stone edition with those of James' text, renumber the Greek pages of Stone consecutively from 77-119.]

The wording of the request suggests a trip of considerably greater scope than what T Abr describes and probably indicates familiarity with the traditions found in the texts cited above.[8] As Rec. A now stands, Abraham's view of the earth is limited to certain sins which he sees committed,[9] and his vision of the heavens centers on matters concerned with the judgment.[10]

The pericope forms a separate unit with a theme of its own. As he rides through the heavens viewing the sins of mankind, righteous Abraham becomes so zealous in calling down punishment on sinners (X: 87.28-88.15) that God orders Michael to cancel the tour, lest Abraham

> . . . destroy every existing thing. For behold, Abraham has not sinned, nor does he pity sinners (X: 88.19-21).

God then commands Michael to bring Abraham into heaven, so that he can see the judgment and repent of his actions concerning the souls of the sinners which he destroyed (X: 88.23-26).[11] The scene with Adam and the two ways stresses the large ratio of sinners to be destroyed over against the few righteous who will be saved (XI: 88-90). In the judgment scene that follows, attention focuses on one soul whose sins and merits are equally balanced (XII-XIV: 90-95). In compassion for the soul's unsettled fate, Abraham bids Michael to intercede with him in behalf of the soul; and when they arise from prayer, they find that the soul has been taken to Paradise (XIV: 93.19-94.12). God has accomplished his purpose in showing Abraham the judgment; for the patriarch now wishes to intercede also in behalf of the sinners whom he had previously condemned, and he admits his own sin in this respect:

> Now I know that I have sinned before the Lord our God. Come, Michael . . . let us call upon God with tears that he may forgive me the sin . . . (XIV: 94.19-23).

---

[8] One might, of course, argue that Abraham's actions force God to cut short the proposed grand tour of creation.

[9] Here T Abr shows some affinities with the Apocalypse of Abraham.

[10] His viewing of the judgment scene has its closest counterpart in the Similitudes of Enoch.

[11] Box translates "may change his mind," which in context is probably too weak for the Grk. μετανοήσῃ.

After considerable prayer, a voice from heaven says,

> Abraham, Abraham, I have heard your voice and your prayer, and I forgive you the sin; and those whom you think I have destroyed, I have in extreme goodness recalled and led into life (XIV: 94.26-95.3).

Thus, the judgment scene is not intended to convey eschatological information for its own sake. It plays a crucial role within a pericope (chs. 9-14) that has an ethical, didactic function. Much contemporary literature about Abraham presents the patriarch as an example to be emulated.[12] A similar motivation surfaces frequently in T Abr. The early part stresses his hospitality. At points, chapter I in Rec. A sounds like a veritable catalog of virtues (77.3,5-9; 78.4). But in his tour of the heavens, the patriarch's much acclaimed righteousness issues in a kind of self-righteous indignation that leads him to condemn a multitude of sinners. This is labelled as sin, and at this point Abraham is a negative example. But as he views the judgment, he is led from indignation to that compassion which is in the heart of God. The righteous one's sin is forgiven, and the problem created during his tour over the earth is resolved. We see the biblical motif of Abraham the intercessor (Gen 18), and the patriarch emerges again as a model to be emulated.

Two points are of importance for the analysis that will follow. First, the judgment scene has a key function in the whole chariot ride sequence as it is now extant in Rec. A (chs. 9-14). Secondly, within that judgment scene, the single soul, its plight and its fate, is the device by which Abraham is brought from indignation to compassion. These references are an integral part of, and absolutely indispensable to the whole pericope (chs. 9-14) as it now stands in Rec. A.[13]

---

[12] See, e.g., Jub 17:17f.; 19:3f.,8f.; Sir 44:19-22; 1 Macc 2:51f.; 4 Macc 15:28; 16:18-23.

[13] This is true not only for the Grk., but also for the Roumanian translation of Rec. A, translated into English by M. Gaster and printed with text in *Transactions of the Soc. of Bibl. Arch.* 9 (1887) 195-226. Translation reprinted in Gaster's *Studies and Texts in Folklore, Magic, Medieval Romance, Hebrew Apocrypha and Samaritan Archaeology* (KTAV, 1971).

Without the references, the narrative would crumble.

B. Adam and the Two Ways (XI-XII: 88.27-90.21)

G. H. McCurdy calls attention to the similarity between Rec. A XI-XIII and certain elements in Greek religious and philosophical writings.[14] Of interest here is the parallel between the two way scene and the Myth of Er in Book X of Plato's *Republic* (614-21).[15] The soul of Er is brought to the place of judgment. There are two openings in the earth and, above them, two in heaven. The judges sit between the two sets of openings, and the souls of the righteous and the wicked depart through one of the openings in the heaven and the earth respectively. The other two openings are the exits from heaven and Tartarus (614CD). Certain fierce fiery men drive the condemned souls to Tartarus, beating them with thorn branches. McCurdy does not posit a direct dependence of T Abr on the *Republic* but suggests that the philosophical and religious ideas of Plato (including the immortality of the soul) have influenced Jewish religious thought and T Abr in particular.[16]

Before appraising McCurdy's argument, we must look at the two way material in Jewish theology. The theme is an old one, and we need touch only on those aspects germane to the present text.[17] According to Jeremiah,

---

[14] G.H. McCurdy, "Platonic Orphism in the Testament of Abraham," *JBL* 61 (1942) 213-26.

[15] *Ibid.* 216f.

[16] *Ibid.* 225f. Other parallels to the judgment scene are cited below in section C. See below, note 30, for references to Platonic judgment scenes.

[17] On the broader subject of the two ways, see F. Nötscher, *Gotteswege und Menschenwege in der Bibel und in Qumran*. BBB 15 (1958). Emphasis on the Jewish background should not obscure the fact that the image also occurs in Greek sources, e.g., Xenophon, *Mem.* II.1.20-34 and Hesiod, *Works* 287-92. Material in the section that follows here has been worked out in greater detail in G. W. E. Nickelsburg, Jr., *Resurrection, Immortality, and Eternal Life in Intertestamental Judaism*. HTS 26 (1972) 156-65.

> Thus says the Lord: Behold I set before you the way of
> life and the way of death (21:8).

While the prophet's reference is to the choice between fighting and surrendering to the Chaldaeans, the image is elsewhere used primarily in ethical contexts. When Moses summarizes his great address on the covenant, and the blessings and curses to be meted out to those who obey and those who disobey the commandments of the covenant, he concludes,

> . . . . I have set before you life and death, blessing
> and curse . . . (Deut 30:19).

Later Jewish and Christian two way documents spell out the deeds that comprise the way of life and the way of death, and they detail the rewards and punishments with various degrees of specificity.[18] Moreover, the documents often state that there is an angelic guide along the way: the angel of truth (perhaps Michael or a personal guardian angel) along the way of life; an evil angel (either Satan or one of his cohorts) along the way of death and destruction.[19] The function of a way or road is to lead to an end or goal -- in our literature, eternal life or eternal death or destruction.[20] Concerning these, the Testament of Asher, a two way document, tells us,[21]

> For the ends of men show their righteousness, when
> they meet the angels of the Lord and of Beliar. For
> when the soul departs troubled, it is being tormented
> by the evil spirit which it also served in desires
> and evil deeds. But if it is peaceful, it is meeting
> the angel of peace, and he leads him to eternal life.
> (6:4-6)

At the moment of death, the soul of the individual, who has followed either the good or the evil angel on the way of life or the way of death, is conducted by his respective angel

---

[18] See, e.g., 1QS 3:13-4:26; T Asher 1-5; Did 1-6; Barn 18-20; Doct Apost 1-5; Herm Man.

[19] 1QS 3-4; T Asher; Herm Man; Barn 18:1f.

[20] The ways are both modes of living and roads that lead to an end or goal, viz., life or death. The light/darkness language appears in 1QS 3-4 and in Barn 18:1.

[21] On the textual problems in this passage, see R. H. Charles, *The Greek Versions of the Testaments of the Twelve Patriarchs* (1908) *ad loc.*

through the portal to his eternal destiny -- life or torment.[21a]

The imagery in this passage is reminiscent of another Platonic description of the judgment. Phaedo 107D-108C describes the plight of the soul after death. The *daimon* to which the person was allotted in life leads the soul to the gathering place of the dead, where judgment is executed. If the soul is too desirous of the body, the *daimon* must drag it away by force. Plato here seems to be reflecting popular Greek religious belief (λέγεται δέ, 107D). "Asher" appears to be reading Jewish two way materials in the light of popular Greek religious belief -- also reflected in Plato.[22]

A similar explanation may be given to the section of T Abr under consideration. The explicit references to the two ways leading to life and destruction reflect Jewish ideas and language about the two ways. The positioning of the judge (Abel in ch. XII) between the two gates and the *description* of the two punishing angels may reflect Greek beliefs. However, it should be noted that punishing angels (with scourges) are part of such Jewish writings as 1 Enoch and the *Manual of Discipline*.[23] Similarly, the angels who bear the souls of the righteous to paradise (Rec. A XI: 89.7f.,26-90.1) have their counterpart in T Asher.

C. The Judgment Scene (XII-XIII: 90.21-93.18)

Rec. A presents the following judgment scene. Abel, the judge of all, is seated on a glorious throne (XII: 90.21-24; 91.9f.; XIII: 92.3-16. Before him is a table, and on it, a gigantic book containing a record of men's deeds (XII: 90.24-91.2,22-26). To the right and left of the table are two angels, holding paper, ink, and pen; they record the righteous deeds and sins (XII: 91.2-4,10-13; XIII: 92.24-93.3). Before

---

[21a]The figures of these two angels, as they meet the soul, may be reflected in the two modes of death's appearance, described in Rec. B XIII. See especially the Grk. E, and the Slavic text, below, pp. 324f.].

[22]T Asher looks like a composition based on Pss 73-74. Parallels cited in Nickelsburg, *Resurrection*, pp. 161f., n.108.

[23]1 Enoch 56:1f.; 63:1; 1QS 3:23.

the table are two other angels (XII: 91.4-9). Dokiel weighs
the souls and/or their sins and righteous deeds in the scale
which he holds in his hand (XII: 91.13f.; XIII: 93.4-7).
Puriel tests the souls with the fire in the trumpet which he
holds (XII: 91.14f.; XIII: 93.7-18).

We are given only one glimpse into the actual judgment
process:

> And behold the angel who was holding the soul in his
> hand brought it before the judge. And the judge said:
> . . . Open this book for me and find me the sins of
> this soul. And he opened the book and found its sins
> and righteous deeds equally balanced. And he gave it
> neither to the tormenters nor to the saved, but set
> it in the middle   (XII: 91.19-26).

The passage, sketchy as it is, raises two problems within the
broader context of the whole judgment scene. Although we have
been told that "all (deeds) among all men are tried by fire and
the balance" (XIII: 93.17f.), no allusion is made here to Puriel and
the test by fire. This is perhaps because the author wishes
to show the equality of sins and righteous deeds -- a fact easily demonstrable by the trial by balance, but presumably not by
the trial by fire. A second problem involves the precise roles
of the two recording angels. What is the relationship between
the paper on which they record the sins and righteous deeds and
the book that contains the record of deeds? In the passage
under consideration, the record found in the book fits into the
judgment process. Perhaps the author intends to say that the
two angels copy out the record of the sins and righteous deeds
and lay the two sheets in the two pans of the balance. A less
likely explanation is that the angels' records are entered as
loose leaves into the book and are taken out and weighed at the
time of judgment.

According to Rec. A, the judgment before Abel is only the
first of three universal judgments (XIII: 92.10-24).

> And at the second coming (παρουσία), they will be judged
> by the twelve tribes of Israel, both every spirit and
> every creature. The third time they will be judged by
> the God of all.[24]

---

[24]Translation follows text of A. BCE: twelve tribes will
be judged by the (12) apostles. D and Roum.: the whole world
will be judged by the 12 apostles. If the reference to the
apostles is original, then A appears to be a de-christianizing

The rationale for this threefold judgment is that every matter must be established by three witnesses.

Although the author of Rec. A is not primarily concerned to make the judgment scene a revelation of eschatological information, the section does present a wealth of eschatological material. Some of it is paralleled in other Jewish texts. Some, it has been suggested, finds closer parallels in Egyptian and Greek religion.

Already in his critical edition, James suggested an Egyptian provenance for the writing, partly on the basis of Egyptian parallels to the weighing of souls and the recording angels.[25] McCurdy takes note of this and adds other parallels in Jewish, Christian, and Greek literature. For the *psychostasia*, he cites a play of that name by Aeschylus, the Iliad, and examples in Greek art.[26] For the angels and the book, he cites Aeschylus and Euripides, as well as Jewish and Christian writings.[27] For the golden throne of Adam and the crystal throne of Abel, he refers to the gold throne of Zeus and the great white throne in Revelation.[28] As a parallel to the enthronement of Abel, he cites the enthronement of Moses in a passage from Ezekiel the Tragedian. The description of the glorious appearance of Abel is reminiscent of the theophany in 1 Enoch 14.[29] He concludes that judgment scenes such as 1 Enoch 14 and Dan 7 in which

> there appears the Judge who sits upon the throne with the books of judgment open before him, seem to me to have their origin in the Greek conceptions so prevalent in the second century B.C. when Jewish apocalyptic was developing, and to go back ultimately to such grand Orphic judgment scenes as are found in Plato's *Gorgias* where the sons of Zeus judge souls, and in the *Republic*.[30]

---

reading. More likely, A is original, and the others represent a Christianizing of the passage.

[25] James, *Testament* 76.

[26] McCurdy, "Platonic Orphism" 218.

[27] *Ibid.* 218-20.

[28] *Ibid.* 222f.

[29] *Ibid.* 224.

[30] *Ibid.* 225. The Platonic passages to which he refers are *Gorgias* 523ff. (n. 59) and *Rep.* 614Cff. (n. 60).

He does not posit direct dependence on these dialogues, but suggests that the ideas have sifted down and have been assimilated in Jewish writings.[31]

Most recently the suggestion of Egyptian origin has been spelled out in considerable detail in a Strasbourg doctoral dissertation by Francis Schmidt.[32] Schmidt compares T Abr with judgment scenes in two late Egyptian documents: *The Book of the Dead of Pamonthes* (A.D. 63) and *The Tale of Satni-Khamois* (A.D. 50-100).[33] Osiris is seated on a throne of fine gold. Flanking him are the 24 "assessors." Before him is a table laden with lotus flowers. In the middle of the room is a balance in which good and evil deeds are weighed. Anubis watches the oscillation of the needle, and Thot records the result of the weighing (in Pamonthes, he reads a book). The monster of Amente waits to devour the wicked.

Schmidt notes the following parallels in Rec. A. Like Osiris, Abel presides over the judgment, seated on a glorious throne. The parallel is made closer by the fact that both were victims of the jealousy of their brother and were the first among the gods and among men to experience death. In both accounts a table stands before the throne. The recording angels in T Abr are the counterparts of Thot. Dokiel has the same function as Anubis. The counterbalancing of good and evil deeds is found in both T Abr and the Egyptian texts. Missing in T Abr are the monster of Amente (although the tormentors to whom the wicked souls are delivered may have this function, XII: 91.25) and the "negative confessions" and the twenty-four assessors characteristic of ch. 125 of *The Book of the Dead* and the vignettes that accompany it. Moreover, clear counterparts

---

[31]*Ibid.* 226.

[32]Francis Schmidt, *Le Testament d'Abraham: introduction, édition de la recension courte, traduction et notes*. Diss. Strasbourg, 1971.

[33]*Ibid.*, vol. I, 71-74. The texts he cites are: Pamonthes in F. Lexa, *Das demotische Totenbuch der pariser Nationalbibliothek* (Leipzig, 1910) ix and 6-8; Satni-Khamois in G. Maspero, *Les contes populaires de l'Egypte ancienne* (3rd ed., n.d.) 135-38.

to the two gates and the angel Puriel are missing in the Egyptian texts.[34]

In this aggregate of parallels, Schmidt finds evidence for a tentative conclusion that T Abr used an Egyptian judgment scene as its model. However, his clinching argument for dependence is the figure of Dokiel. Here he follows a suggestion by M. Schwab.[35] Dokiel, who weighs the sins and righteous deeds ἐν δικαιοσύνῃ θεοῦ (XIII: 93.6f.), is in reality $Ṣedeqiel$ = "the righteousness of God." This angel's name, in the form SATQVIEL, is among the names found on an engraved gem with an image of Anubis. Thus Dokiel=$Ṣedeqiel$=SATQVIEL was identified in Egypt with Anubis, the guardian of the scales. This function of Anubis is attributed to Dokiel in Rec. A and serves as confirmation of the Egyptian origin of the judgment scene.

The suggestions of McCurdy and Schmidt are of two sorts. McCurdy cites James' suggestion about the Egyptian provenance of the $psychostasia$ and the recording angels (and seems to agree with it).[36] However, he then moves on to cite Greek parallels to these elements, as well as many other points in chs. XI-XIII. Moreover, he cites Jewish and Christian parallels. He suggests that these latter, as well as T Abr, may be indebted to Orphic judgment scenes such as are found in the Platonic dialogues. It should be noted, however, that the Platonic judgment scenes contain very few of the elements found in T Abr[37] and that the Greek parallels which he does cite come from a wide variety of sources.

Schmidt, to the contrary, finds counterparts to most of the elements in T Abr in a single Egyptian source. In both of the documents that he cites, he finds: the judge on a throne of gold; a table before him; the weighing of the souls/deeds by a counterpart of Dokiel; the divine scribe; and possibly a

---

[34]Schmidt, $Testament$ I, 74. Schmidt cautiously suggests parallels to the two gates and Puriel but strains the evidence, I think.

[35]M. Schwab, $Vocabulaire\ de\ l'angélologie$: Mémoires présentés par divers savants à l'Académie des Inscriptions et Belles-Lettres (1897) 340f., 419, cited by Schmidt I, 78, nn. 36 and 41. Discussion, I, 75f.

[36]McCurdy, "Platonic Orphism" 218.

[37]Only the judges and the position between the two gates.

counterpart to the punishing angels. Thus, with the exception of the two gates and the positioning of the judge between them, Schmidt finds all of the elements mentioned by McCurdy in a single Egyptian source. This makes his case more plausible than McCurdy's. However, it is not without its problems.

In T Abr, *two* angelic scribes record the *sins* and *righteous deeds* of the soul, whereas in the Egyptian documents, there is *one* scribe, Thot, who records the *result* of the verdict.[38] The table in T Abr holds the *book of deeds* (for which there is perhaps a counterpart in the hand of Thot in Pamonthes), whereas the Egyptian texts describe a votive table with *lotus flowers* on it. The monster of Amente may have the same function as the punishing angels in T Abr, but he surely creates a different image. Finally, there is the figure of Abel. Schmidt presses the similarity between Abel and Osiris by noting that each was a victim of his brother's jealousy, and that they were the first martyrs among men and gods respectively. At the same time, Schmidt argues that Rec. A is an Egyptian-Jewish recension of the Palestinian Recension B.[39] Since the latter already has the figure of Abel in its judgment scene (VIII-XI),[40] one cannot press the similarities between Abel and Osiris, unless one argues that such similarities are what caused Rec. B to be revised according to the Egyptian model. It is more likely that if such revision did take place, it was because one judgment scene was being reshaped on the basis of another judgment scene.

Since the Egyptian model does not account for all of the elements in the T Abr judgment scene, we may look elsewhere for their source. The most obvious place is in Jewish writings, for we have already seen similarities between Jewish two way theology and chapters XI-XII of Rec. A.

Most enigmatic is Abel's function as judge of all creation. The attribution is, to my knowledge, unique among Jewish

---

[38] In Pamonthes, Thot is depicted twice, evidently representing the double functions of defender and accuser.]

[39] *Ibid.* I, 115-21.

[40] Abel is judge in Rec. B$^{Grk.-Slav.}$ but not in Rec. B$^{Arab.-Copt.-Eth.}$ I take the former to be original. See discussion below in section E.

writings.[41] Schmidt suggests a probable explanation for the development of the idea.[42] Its roots are in Gen 4:10, where Abel the persecuted righteous one becomes accuser of his murderer. In 1 Enoch 22:5-7, he is singled out as the accuser of all the descendents of Cain--presumably a kind of advocate for all the murdered righteous and the accuser of their persecutors. Elsewhere in 1 Enoch, as well as in Wisdom of Solomon 5, one finds the idea of the persecuted righteous functioning as judges, or executors of God's vengeance against their oppressors.[43] Indeed, the idea is fairly widespread in Jewish literature of this period.[44] There is, however, a significant difference between T Abr and these other texts. Early Jewish texts that attribute a judicial function to the righteous do so because the persecution of the righteous is a problem and the judgment is seen as the adjudication of the injustice perpetrated on the righteous.[45] In later texts, the judgment is universalized, and its function is not to bring retribution to the persecutors of the righteous (and vindication to the persecuted), but to dispense reward and punishment to all men, according to their deeds. In T Abr judgment is of this latter sort; however, the traditional idea of the righteous man as judge has been retained.[46]

---

[41]The problem is noted by James, *Testament* 125f.

[42]Schmidt, *Testament* I, 63-65.

[43]Schmidt cites 1 Enoch 95:3; 97:5; 98:12 and Wisd 5:1 and refers to P. Volz, *Eschatologie* 275f., *Testament* I, 68, nn. 19 and 20.

[44]E.g., Esth 9:5-10; 3 Macc 7:10-15; 1QH 4:22; 1 Enoch 38:5; 48:9.

[45]Thus Wisd 2,4-5; 1 Enoch 37-63 and 94ff. Other texts presupposing a similar situation and attributing the judgment to God or his angelic agent include Dan 12 and T Mos.

[46]Cf. Wisdom of Solomon, where the story of the persecution and exaltation of the righteous man (chs. 2,4-5) has been set in a context whose main concern is not persecution (chs. 1-6).

Whether such a tradition named Abel as judge, must be left undecided.[46a] Schmidt suggests one hypothesis.[47] Working again with the assumption that Rec. B is prior, he suggests that in the Hebrew original of this recension, it was "the son of man" who was judge. The Greek translator understood בן אדם to mean "son of Adam" (perhaps prompted by the presence of Adam in the two way scene), identified him with Abel, and added the gloss, "who first testified" (Rec. B XI: 115.13-16). Against this conjecture is the lack of any substantial similarities between the judgment scene in Rec. B and the son of man scenes in Dan 7 and 1 Enoch 46-49, 62-63.[48] On the other hand, it should be noted that in Rec. A, which Schmidt considers secondary, Abel is identified as υἱὸς Ἀδὰμ τοῦ πρωτοπλάστου (XIII:92.5f.).

The two angels who record the sins and righteous deeds find their counterparts in Jewish literature. Zech 3 describes the trial of Joshua, in which the high priest is flanked by the angel of the Lord, who serves as his advocate, and השטן, the angelic accuser. When Jubilees recounts the trial of Abraham (17:16-18:16), the story is set within the framework of a pair of scenes in the heavenly courtroom, in which the angel of the presence and the prince of *mastēmā* are juxtaposed. The latter appears as accuser, controverting the voices from heaven which

---

[46a] A midrash in the Targum Neophyti Gen 4:8 is significant here. Cain and Abel argue over whether there is judgment, a judge, another world, and reward and punishment. Cain's challenge here is precisely that of the wicked persecutors of the righteous man in Wisd 2:1-12. In ch. 5, they face the righteous man, who is their judge, and learn that they were in error. Thus the Targum appears to reflect knowledge of Wisd 2-5 and at least suggests that Abel may fill the role of the persecuted righteous man--turned judge. On this midrash, see M. Delcor, "De l'Origine de quelques traditions contenues dans le Testament d'Abraham," in *Proceedings of the Fifth World Congress of Jewish Studies*, ed. P. Peli (Jerusalem, 1969) vol. I 194-98; cf. also *ibid.*, *Le Testament d'Abraham* (1973) 143-45.]

[47] Schmidt, *Testament* I, 64f.

[48] The only parallels are: the soul's plea for mercy (cf. 1 Enoch 62:9); her reaction to the judgment (cf. 1 Enoch 62: 4f.); and her deliverance to the punishing angels (cf. 1 Enoch 62:11); and the books in Dan 7:10. Lacking is a convincing formal similarity with either of these texts.

speak in behalf of the patriarch's faithfulness. When Abraham remains faithful, the prince of *mastēmā* is put to shame, i.e., banished from court. Later, the story of the attempt on Moses' life is also revised (48:1-4). It is the prince of *mastēmā* who attempts to kill him (because of his guilt in not circumcising his son?); the angel of the presence delivers Moses from the satanic figure.

The angelic attorneys also function as scribes. In the animal apocalypse of 1 Enoch, an angel records in a book the wicked deeds perpetrated against the righteous. He then reads the book before the great judge, pleading the case of righteous Israel and bringing accusation against their persecutors (1 Enoch 89:59-77). 1 Enoch 104:7 also indicates that certain heavenly scribes are recording the wicked deeds of the oppressors of the righteous. This same chapter tells of the angels who remember the righteous before the divine throne, thus pleading for their vindication and the punishment of their oppressors in the coming judgment (104:1-4).[49]

The two angelic scribes in T Abr emerge out of this background. They fill the roles of advocate and accuser, writing down the righteous deeds and the sins respectively and testifying to these.

Is there any substantial relationship between the judgment scene in Rec. A and other Jewish texts in which the two angels appear? In this respect two texts come to mind. The first is T Judah 20.

> Two spirits wait on man--
>   the spirit of truth and the spirit of deceit . . .
> There is no time when the works of men can be hidden.
> For they are written on his heart before the Lord.
> And the spirit of truth witnesses all things and accuses all,
> And the sinner is burnt up by his own heart,
> And is not able to lift his face before the judge.

The passage presumes a judgment situation. The *two spirits* are juxtaposed--although the spirit of truth appears to function both as advocate and accuser. Mention is also made of the works of men being *written* on their hearts. Although the language appears to reflect Jer 31:33, here it is not the Torah,

---

[49]The last chapters of Enoch are mainly exhortations to the righteous and woes against their oppressors. They culminate in the announcement of the judgment in chs. 102-104.

but one's works which are written on the heart. The passage presupposes the idea of a *book of deeds*, which is here internalized, as are the two spirits. The last line makes mention of the *judge*. The previous line speaks of the sinner being "burnt up," as he stands before the judge. While the verb ἐμπυρίζειν might connote blushing here, it is reminiscent of trial by fire. Ch. 25, which may originally have belonged with ch. 20, mentions resurrection and the vindication of the righteous.[49a]

A second passage is Daniel 12:1-3. *Michael*, the angelic patron of Israel, arises in court. By analogy with 10:13-21, we may assume *his angelic opponent*, the angelic prince behind the Seleucid throne.[50] A *book* is opened--in this case the register containing the names of the righteous. The dead are raised. The results of the judgment are mentioned: eternal life and eternal contempt.

These two texts, among others, are, I believe, witnesses to a traditional Jewish description of the final judgment.[51] Elements in this judgment scene included: the two witnesses; the book; a reference to judgment for the dead (sometimes, though not always, resurrection); the two results of judgment: vindication and condemnation. Now all of these elements occur in the judgment scene in T Abr.[52] Those major elements in the Rec. A judgment scene not found in the above-mentioned tradition are the figure of the judge, the trial by fire, and the trial by the balance. The trial by fire may be alluded to in T Judah. This same text mentions the judge, and others surely presume him.

There are a few Jewish texts that use the metaphor of weighing in the context of judgment.[53] God weighs the spirit

---

[49a] Chs. 21-25:2 are a *florilegium* of materials found elsewhere in the *Testaments*.

[50] See Nickelsburg, *Resurrection* 14-15.

[51] Parallel texts are found in T Mos 10; Jub 23:27-31; 1 Enoch 104. The argument for the existence of this tradition is worked out in Nickelsburg, *Resurrection*, chs. I,IV,V.

[52] For the alternatives of vindication and punishment, see the section on Puriel, XIII: 93.10-16.

[53] Job 31:6; Ps 62:9; Dan 5:27. These and the texts in nn. 54 and 55 are cited by Schmidt, *Testament* I, 76, nn.3 and 4.

and the heart of man.[54] Enoch sees the actions of men weighed in the balance.[55] Whether 2 Enoch 49:2B and 52:15f. are to be taken literally is difficult to say.[56] In any event, aside from the T Abr we have no full-scale judgment scene with such a weighing process.[56a]

Our analysis has suggested that the core of the Rec. A judgment scene may be found in older Jewish texts: the two angels; the book; the results of judgment--which also extends to the dead. The judge is presumed in these texts and explicitly mentioned in T Judah 20. The identification of the judge with Abel can be adequately explained from a Jewish background. While the trial by fire is not explicit in T Judah 20, it cannot be adequately explained from Egyptian sources. The trial by balance is not to be found in the Jewish texts; however, it is explicit in the Egyptian texts. These texts, on the other hand, do not explain the presence of the two scribes nor of the book.

We offer the following explanation of these data. What was originally a traditional Jewish judgment scene has been expanded and fleshed out with details from a comparable Egyptian piece. The judge is given a glorious throne. The description of the scribes includes mention of their writing instruments àla the Egyptian texts and the vignettes in copies of the Book of the Dead. The book is placed on a table before the throne.[57]

---

[54]Prov 16:2; 21:2; 24:12. Cf. Ps Philo, *LAB* 40:1.

[55]1 Enoch 41:1; cf. 61:8. 2 Enoch 49:2B; 52:15f. The last of these mentions a scale and books. However, the dating of this book and these passages is problematical.

[56]On the question of the metaphorical or literal understanding of the references to weighing, see James, *Testament* 70f. and Schmidt, *Testament* I, 71f.

[56aFragmentary remains of such a text have been preserved in a Christian papyrus about Enoch. For a text, translation, and discussion of this papyrus and its parallels to T Abr, see the article by B.A. Pearson below, pp. 227-83.]

[57]Mention of the table is perhaps more significant than one might at first suppose. Although one might presume such a prop to hold up the book(s), it is never mentioned in other Jewish judgment texts.

The trial by balance assumes the crucial and central significance that it has in the Egyptian texts.[58]

Within the judgment scene in Rec. A, reference is made to a second and third judgment (XIII: 92.10-24). In the second judgment, *every spirit* and *every creature* will be judged by the twelve tribes of Israel.[59] Perhaps we are dealing here with a combination of the motif of the righteous judging their enemies (discussed above in connection with Abel's judgment) and the picture of Israel exalted over the nations, expressed in such passages as Daniel 7 and 1QM 17:6-8.[60] Moreover, the apostle Paul asserts that the righteous will judge *the world* and *the angels* (1 Cor 6:2f.). As to the third judgment, is is commonplace in Jewish literature that God himself will preside over the great judgment. However, the idea that there will be three separate universal judgments has no sure parallels in Jewish literature.[61] Indeed, the duplication in these three judgments is somewhat strange. The assertion of a second and a third universal judgment comes somewhat as a surprise after the clear statement that Abel will judge *everyone*. It raises the question as to whether there are double traditions, interpolations, and/or literary seams in the text. This would fit with our identification of an earlier traditional judgment scene.

---

[58] Is the weighing "by the *righteousness* of God" at all reminiscent of the Egyptian weighing of the soul against the feather of *truth (maat)*?

[59] On the text of this passage, see above, n. 24.

[60] In the two passages cited, however, Israel's exaltation is not for the purpose of judgment, but subsequent to that judgment.

[61] Schmidt cites some doubtful rabbinic parallels to the idea of such a judgment, based on Is 3:14, *Testament* II, 142, nn. on XIII, 4-8 and XIII, 6. Cf. Billerbeck, *Komm.* IV 1103f. [The Apocalypse of Weeks in 1 Enoch appears to presume three judgments, but they do not correspond to the three universal judgments here (see 1 Enoch 91:12,14,15, as translated from the Aramaic by M. Black, "The Fragments of the Aramaic Enoch from Qumran," in *La littérature juive entre Tenach et Mischna*, ed. by W. C. Van Unnik, *Rech Bib* 9 (Leiden, 1974) 24f.]

D. Literary Analysis

Two literary problems appear in the two way scene. First, there is a contradiction between this scene and the judgment scene that follows. The two way scene states explicitly that the two ways lead respectively to eternal life, i.e., Paradise (XI: 89.26-90.1) and to destruction and eternal punishment (XI: 90.6-8). However, when Abraham and Michael follow the two angels through the broad gate, they enter not Gehenna but an area in which Abel's judgment throne stands, once more between the two gates (XII: 90.19-24). Thus, although the departure of the souls through the one or the other gate presumes that judgment has already taken place, we find the judge of all seated on the other side of the two gates. In view of this contradiction, it seems unlikely that the same author has created both scenes *de novo* and then juxtaposed them. Rather, each scene has an integrity of its own, offering the seer a view of the judgment process, either in the channeling of the souls through the two gates or in the more elaborate rituals before Abel's throne. Perhaps an editor or author has juxtaposed two blocks of existing traditional material, or perhaps he has added a scene of his own composition to a traditional piece.

A second literary problem occurs in the reference to the one soul:

> . . . behold *two angels* fiery in visage and pitiless in intent and harsh in looks, were even (now) driving myriads of souls, pitilessly beating them with fiery lashes. [And *one soul the angel seized.*] And *they drove all the souls* into the broad gate toward destruction (XII: 90.14-19).[62]

The passage begins with *two* angels driving a *herd* of souls. Then we are told that *one* soul is seized by *the* angel--as if there were only one angel. The passage then reverts to a plural pronoun, *they*, as if the immediate antecedent were more than one angel, and states that *all* the souls are being driven to destruction. This double shift in number is explained if we

---

[62] Translation follows the reading of A. Only A and D mention the one soul, if I understand James' apparatus correctly. According to D and the Roum. translation (29), the angels (pl.) hold the soul in their hands. I accept as original the reading of A with its reference to the one angel because this is presupposed in XII: 91.19f. according to the reading of all mss.

assume that the reference to the single soul is an interpolation. With the excision of the bracketed sentence, the text reads smoothly.

The judgment scene is composed mainly of four parallel sections. A) The *dramatis personae* and the props are introduced (XII: 90.20-91.9). B) The actions of the various functionaries are briefly described (91.9-15). C) Abraham inquires as to the identity of the figures (XIII: 91.27-92.3). D) Finally, Michael answers Abraham's question (92:3-16,24-93.18). The four parallel sections include the following items:

A.	B.	C.	D.
Introduction	*Description*	*Question*	*Answer*
Throne, judge	Man judges	Who is judge	He is Abel
Table, book	-	-	-
Two angels	They record sins, righteous deeds	Who are recording angels	They record sins, righteous deeds
Angel with balance	Weighs souls	Who is angel with balance	He is Dokiel, weighs sins, r. deeds
Angel with fire to test sinners	Tests souls	Who is one holding fire	He is Puriel, tests works

Furthermore, these four sections are broken into at two points by additional blocks of material. Between B and C are a question and answer about the nature of the scene (XII: 91.15-19) and a short description of the weighing of the sins and righteous deeds of the one soul (91.19-26). Secondly, in the middle of D, between the identification of Abel and that of the two angels is the block of material about the second and third judgments. The whole scene may be outlined as follows:

    A. Introduction of functionaries, etc. (XII: 90.20-91.9)

    B. Description of actions (XII: 91.9-15)

        [a. Question and answer on nature of scene (91.15-19)

         b. Judgment of one soul (91.19-26)]

    C. Abraham asks about identities (XIII: 91.27-92.3)

D. Michael answers (92.3-16,24-93.18)
      1. Abel (92.3-11)
         [a. Reference to final judgment (92.11-14)]
         Abel, cont'd (92.14-16)
         [b. The second and third judgments (92.16-24)]
      2. The recording angels (92.24-93.3)
      3. Dokiel (93.4-7)
      4. Puriel (93.7-18)

We have already noted that the second and third judgments duplicate the function of the first, since they are all universal judgments. Literary analysis now bears out the secondary nature of the references to these second and third judgments. The first reference to God's *parousia* (D.1.a) separates the first half of the explanation about Abel's judgment from the second half of that explanation. "For every man has sprung. . ." logically follows the statement about Abel and not a reference to the *later* judgment. The second reference to God's *parousia*, i.e., to the second and third judgments (D.1.b), breaks in between Michael's answer regarding Abel and his answer regarding the two recording angels and thus is clearly secondary to the passage.

The other important block of material to be found in the judgment scene alongside the four parallel passages is the description of the judgment of the one soul (B.b). We have already seen that the reference to the one soul in the two way scene is secondary to that section. Since the present passage presupposes that interpolation, we may assume that B.b is also secondary to the judgment scene. Abraham's question regarding the nature of the scene, and Michael's answer to that question (B.a) may be original to the judgment scene and may have led up to the question about the identities of the various functionaries.

Thus, when we have removed the two major interpolations from the judgment scene, we are left primarily with four parallel sections, listed above as A.B.C.D. As indicated by the four parallel columns, there are two problems in these sections. The first regards the table and the book. These are mentioned only in section A. Moreover, the book is mentioned in the interpolation about the judgment of the one soul. Is the book also an interpolation into the judgment scene? This need not be the case. After the section on the judgment of the one soul was included in the scene--with its mention of the function of the book--there would have been no need for a question about its function and an answer to that question (sections C,D). If they had been in sections C and D, we can reasonably suppose that an editor might have deleted them. The omission in section B is also understandable, either on the grounds that mention of the book was deleted by the interpolator because it was about to be described in B.b, or because it never was included in a passage (B) which otherwise describes persons and their *actions*.

A second problem occurs in section D. Abraham asks about the identity of each of the functionaries. Michael mentions *by name* Abel, Dokiel, and Puriel, but with reference to the two recording angels, he repeats the description from section B. They are the angels who record the sins and the righteous deeds. We can only guess as to why their names are deleted. If, as it appears, we are dealing with a traditional piece, it is not totally unlikely that the interceding angel in that piece would have been none other than Michael himself.[63] Rather than giving this angel a new name, the editor/author gives no name at all. In earlier Jewish materials, the accusing angel is named according to his function, השטן.[64] That the presence of Satan in heaven would have given an author some trouble is altogether understandable--as is the deletion of that name.

From the present text of Rec. A we have now extrapolated an earlier tradition--a judgment scene which included the following elements:

---

[63] For this function of Michael, see Dan 12:1 and 3 Bar 10-15. Rabbinic materials are cited by W. Lueckens, *Der Erzengel Michael* (1898) 30f. See also the discussions by A. S. van der Woude, "Melchizedek als himmlische Erlösergestalt in den neugefundenen eschatologischen Midraschen aus Qumran Höhle XI," *OTS* 14 (1965) 368-72; and M. de Jonge and van der Woude, "11Q Melchizedek and the New Testament," *NTS* 12 (1966) 305f. [See also now J. T. Milik, "Milkî-ṣedeq et Milkî-reša' dans les anciens écrits juifs et crétiens," *JJS* 23 (1972) 95-144, and literature cited in his n.3]

[64] The generic title is given in Zech 3:1f. and Job 1-2. The same figure appears in heaven under the title, prince of *mastēmā*, in Jub 17-18.

1. Abel the judge
2. The two recording angels
3. The book of deeds[65]
4. The angel with the balance
5. The angel with the fire

Other Jewish texts, to which we referred earlier (e.g., Dan 12 and T Judah 20) contain judgment scenes with similar elements. What is the road from the tradition represented by such scenes to the final redaction of Rec. A?

The earlier judgment scenes occur at the end of historical apocalypses, functioning usually as the resolution of a particular historical crisis;[66] they are described in the future tense. In distinction from these, the specific stage of the tradition utilized in Rec. A is cast in another typical apocalyptic form, viz., that of vision, question, and interpretation. It may presume some sort of ascent into heaven, and the seer may have been Abraham himself, to whom such ascents are attributed in non-Abrahamic literature.[67] Whether such a first-hand account is a later development of the descriptions set in the future tense, or whether the latter presuppose a first-hand account is a moot question and not demonstrable from the present text. The pre-T Abr tradition also includes certain elements not found in parallel examples of that tradition, added perhaps from contact with Egyptian sources.

At some point, the judgment scene has been prefaced by the two way scene (without the reference to the one soul). The two way scene was either an existing block of tradition--also a first-hand account of the judgment process--or it was created partly in analogy to the judgment scene, which may have been set at the place of the two ways.[68]

---

[65] Even if the book is secondary to the original form of the judgment scene, the element is present in the records being kept by the angelic scribes.

[66] For such a function, see Dan 10-12; Jub 23:11-31; T Mos 5-10. The case is different, e.g., in T Judah 25, where there is no such crisis.

[67] See above, pp. 23f.

[68] Both scenes begin in a similar way (outside/between the two gates; the throne; a glorious figure seated on it). Possibly the judgment scene originally began in that way, with the

This pair of scenes is now interpolated with the references to the single soul, which become the thread that holds together the entire section from ch. X-XIV, as we have shown above in section A. We have also suggested there that this whole journey-judgment sequence fits well with the general interests of T Abr. Therefore this stage in the redaction is best equated with the composition of Rec. A itself.

We are left with the interpolations referring to the second and third judgments and to a certain amount of Christian retouching.[69] If we accept the reading of ms. A, the interpolations were evidently made within a Jewish context. They could have been made at the time of the composition of Rec. A--unless the rationale of the three witnesses reflects the form of the material about the one soul found in Rec. B. In the latter case, the interpolations were made subsequent to the composition of the Testament. The third judgment is included evidently because the interpolator found it necessary to involve God himself in the judgment process. The second judgment also reflects traditional ideas and was included possibly because the author saw significance in the idea of *three* witnesses.

In summary, we suggest the following stages of tradition:

1. A traditional apocalyptic judgment scene
2. Combined with the two way material--without the reference to the one soul.
3. Interpolated with the references to the one soul and set in the context of the heavenly journey at the time of the composition of the Testament
4. Interpolated with references to the second and third judgment--perhaps also at stage 4
5. Some later Christian additions and touch-up

The T Abr has preserved within it a traditional revelation of

---

throne located between the juxtaposed entrances to Paradise and Gehenna (cf. 4 Ezra 7:36). A redactor could have developed the two way reference into a separate scene, bringing in the figure of Adam in connection with Abel.

[69]On these elements, see James *Testament* 50-55, who has surely overstated his case, citing NT parallels that could themselves reflect Jewish ideas and sources. He maintains that the book was composed by a Jewish Christian, *ibid.* 55.

the heavenly throne room that rivals many sections of a work like the Similitudes of Enoch. As in this latter work, the seer is given a view of the judgment process. The difference is that Enoch views what will happen in the future, "on that day." For the author of our scene, the judgment is going on now. Souls are judged immediately after death. There is no evidence that this judgment is preliminary. There is no hint of a future resurrection. It is the soul that is led to eternal life or destruction. In this respect, the theology of the tradition is of one piece with other Jewish works such as the Testament of Asher, Wisdom of Solomon, and 4 Maccabees. The judgment by Abel is universal. As Adam's son, he judges all the rest of Adam's progeny. A similar universality of judgment is perhaps implicit in most contemporary two way documents, which in effect divide all mankind into two groups, who will receive their ultimate reward and punishment. These same two way documents, although they sometimes maintain a kind of immortality or assumption theology, do not necessarily lose sight of history. They conclude with an eschatological section that describes God's final "visitation," his consummation of history and ultimate judgment (which need not involve resurrection and judgment of the dead already judged). Examples of this can be seen in T Asher 7:3; Wisd 5:17-23; 1QS 4:18-23. Perhaps something of this dynamic was at work when ch. XIII was interpolated with references to God's great and glorious *parousia*. We probably introduce a false category if we suppose that the interpolator was bringing the immediate eschatology of this judgment scene into line with "mainline" or "orthodox" eschatology. Yet the fact remains that he could have introduced a judgment by God without describing it as one great future assize. The interpolator, like many theologians after him, felt it necessary to posit that glorious *eschaton*, even if it had no necessary function. Over against a perennial heavenly judgment, there was something unavoidably attractive in the contemplation of a grand style *parousia* and judgment in the sight of all.

E. The Relationship between Recensions A and B

Scholars have reached a variety of conclusions regarding the relationship between the two recensions. According to

James, Rec. A is the more original, although its language has been somewhat medievalized. Rec. B is an abridgment of the longer recension, with a few elements more original than A and with more original linguistic features that also indicate that it is not an abridgment of A as we know it. The Arabic version represents an independent abridgment.[70] Box agrees substantially with this judgment.[71]

Nigel Turner studied the Greek of the two recensions and refined the linguistic aspects of James' observations.[72] As it now stands, Rec. B is to be dated around the 3rd century A.D., although it reflects the Greek of certain pre-Christian Jewish books. Rec. A, as it stands, cannot be earlier than the 5th or 6th century A.D.; however, it too has linguistic affinities with pre-Christian writings. These similarities reflect either earlier Greek sources or an earlier Greek version which has been interpolated by certain medieval Christian material. In comparing the earlier Greek strata in the two recensions, Turner disagrees with James and Box and argues for the priority of B. He argues that it betrays no knowledge of the LXX, whereas Rec. A does in the case of Genesis. Moreover, the Greek of Rec. B is similar to that of Tobit (Sinaiticus) and the Testaments of the Twelve Patriarchs, whereas Rec. A reflects the later Greek of 2,3,4 Maccabees. Schmidt takes up the observations of Turner and supports them with his own conclusions regarding extra-Jewish influences in the two recensions.[73] Egyptian influences occur in Rec. A, but not in Rec. B. On the other hand, Iranian influences in Rec. A are all found in Rec. B. Thus, he concludes, Rec. A was made in a Jewish milieu in Egypt on the basis of a document which issued from a Jewish circle that was

---

[70] James, *Testament* 35-49. The texts of the Coptic and Ethiopic, which substantially agree with the Arabic, were not used by James.

[71] Box, *Testament* xii-xv. He does not deal with the possibility of the independence of the Arabic from the Grk. mss.

[72] Nigel Turner, *The Testament of Abraham: A Study of the Original Language, Place of Origin, Authorship, and Relevance*. Diss. London, 1953. His conclusions appear in his article, "The 'Testament of Abraham': Problems in Biblical Greek," *NTS* 1 (1954-55) 219-23, from which this summary is taken (pp. 221f.)

[73] Schmidt, *Testament* I, 117f.

open to Iranian influences. The reverse hypothesis is unacceptable, viz., that a reviser would have systematically eliminated all Egyptian and no Iranian material from a document that contained both.

The development of the discussion regarding the Greek Bible raises a number of questions about Turner's method and conclusions which cannot be adequately discussed in the compass of this paper.[74] Schmidt's conclusion hinges in large part on his judgment that there are no Egyptian influences in Rec. B.[75] The discussion that follows will deal with this question within the context of a broader comparison of the contents of the judgment scenes in the two recensions.

Dissimilarities among the Greek, Slavonic, Arabic, Coptic, and Ethiopic versions of the short recension compound the difficulty of a comparison with the long recension.[76] These will

---

[74] Some qualifications regarding categorical statements about the LXX may be in order in view of the complex picture of the development of the text of the OT which has emerged since the discovery of the Qumran texts. Can one draw definite conclusions from the use or non-use of certain texts or text families of the OT? Could a later writer use a ms. of an earlier recension? Moreover, some question may also be raised regarding Turner's apparent early dating of the Testaments of the Twelve Patriarchs.

[75] Following his paragraph on the Egyptian and Iranian influences, he states, "L'antériorité de cette recension sur la longue est donc bien établie" (italics mine), *Testament* I, 118.

[76] For the Grk., the text of James was used. His apparatus cites mss. ABC. Schmidt divides these into two families, and adds to them three others: A D C / B F G. To these he adds another, E, which he takes to represent the earliest of three families, *Testament* II, 34. While I did not have recourse to his publication of E, I did use an English translation of one Slavonic text, which he relates closely to E (collation on pp. 31-33). Thus my references to B$^{Slav.}$ can probably most often be equated with Grk. E. The Coptic, Arabic, and Ethiopic were available to me only in translation: extracts of the Arabic, transl. by W. E. Barnes in James, *Testament*, pp. 135-39; Coptic, transl. by Ernst Andersson, "Abraham's Vermächtnis," *Sphinx* 6 (1903), 220-35; Ethiopic, transl. by Wolf Leslau, in *Falasha Anthology* (1951), pp. 92-102. The Slavonic was translated by my colleague, Harry Weber, from the text in N. S. Tikhonravov, *Pamiatniki otrechennoi russkoi literatury* (1863), I, 79-90. [All comments on the Coptic version are consonant with the English translation printed below, pp. 327-340. For a French translation of Eth., see Delcor, *Testament* 214-224.]

be taken into account shortly. We begin, however, with those points in which the long recension agrees with the whole of the short recension. The judgment portion of both is divided into two sections. The first describes the two ways and depicts Adam viewing the fate of the souls and reacting thereto (A XI-XII. B VIII-IX). Note is taken of the preponderance of the damned, dramatized by myriads being herded to destruction. One soul is singled out for special mention. The second section describes the judgment itself (A XII-XIII. B X-XI). Common to both recensions are the judge, the witness(es), the book(s). The judgment is exemplified in the trial of one soul. The process includes a call to check the book(s) for a record of the soul's deeds, and judgment is rendered on the basis of the finding. In both recensions, Abraham queries Michael on the identity of one or more of the functionaries. Beyond these similarities, there are numerous differences between the long recension, on the one hand, and all or parts of the short recension, on the other.

The following are points in which the whole short recension (with the exception of one omission in Eth.) agrees *against* the long recension. The two gates are situated at the place of the (River) Ocean (chart, App., #1).[77] There is a section in which Abraham expresses skepticism as to whether he can fit through the narrow gate and Michael encourages him (chart, 3). In all but the Eth., Michael and Abraham, at Michael's suggestion, go off in search of a single righteous soul (5). In connection with this (in all but Eth.), Abraham asks Michael whether "Death" is the angel who removes the souls from the bodies (6). The heavenly witness is not an angel, but Enoch the righteous scribe (28-29). The single soul who is judged is shown to be a gross sinner (12-14, 23-26). The condemned soul denies the charges against her (14, 26). The soul is cast into hell rather than left in the middle and eventually saved (27).

Over against these similarities among the versions of Rec. B, there are numerous points of difference. In Grk., Slav., Abraham's question about fitting through the narrow gate

---

[77]Barnes' extracts from the Arabic begin after this point.

precedes the appearance of the myriads of souls (3,4); Arab.,
Copt., Eth. have the reverse order. In Arab., Copt., Eth.,
Abraham and Michael discuss the number of souls that are born
and that die each day (7); Grk., Slav. record no such conversation. According to Grk., Slav., Abraham is transported from
the place of the two ways to Paradise, where he witnesses the
judgment (8). There is no such shift of scene in Arab., Copt.,
Eth. In Arab., Copt., Eth., the soul is brought by a multitude
of angels, who surround it and bring charges against it (Copt.,
Eth.) (10-11). Slav. mentions no escort. In Grk. the soul is
the same one mentioned in the two way scene and is escorted by
the same angel. On this last point, Grk. alone agrees with
Rec. A. The detailing of the indictment is found in two different places. In Grk., Slav., the scene opens with the soul
pleading for mercy. The judge responds with a series of charges
which the soul denies (12-14). In response to this, the judge
calls for the witness, and the books are read to present proof
positive (15-21). Arab., Copt., Eth. omit the indictment at
the beginning of the scene (12-14), and describe the summoning of
the witness, and the reading of the book (15-21). The soul responds with a denial (22), which then leads in Arab., Copt.,
Eth. to the summoning of three witnesses and their recitation
of the indictment (23-26=12-14).[77a] The mention of the three
witnesses corresponds to the same idea in Rec. A, where, however, it refers to the three judgments. In Grk., Slav., the
cherubim bring in the books (16). Arab., Copt., Eth. do not
mention the cherubim; it is Enoch himself who carries the books
(17-18). In Grk., Slav., Abraham queries about the identity of
the judge. He is Abel, as he is in Rec. A (28-29). The question is unnecessary in Arab., Eth., Copt., because the judge is
God himself. Grk. and Slav. agree against Arab., Copt., Eth.
in giving longer descriptions of Enoch and his functions (19,
30). Following the judgment section, Abraham is returned to
his home, according to Arab., Copt., Eth. In Grk., Slav. he is
given a tour through the lower heavens, where he sees the sinners on earth and calls down judgment on them. As a result of
this, he is taken home. This part of Abraham's trip is similar

---

[77a]This incident is missing in the ms. translated by W.
Lesau (see above, n. 76), but it is found in a second, fragmentary Eth. ms. translated by Delcor, *Testament* 221.]

to Rec. A, where, however, his actions lead to his being taken up to view the judgment.

To summarize our findings: 1) All the versions of Rec. B agree against Rec. A in some small points of detail but also in this major point that the judgment scene primarily involves the sentencing of a gross sinner. Also against Rec. A, they agree in identifying the heavenly scribe as Enoch. 2) There are also major points of difference among the versions of Rec. B themselves, which divide themselves into two groups: Grk.-Slav. and Arab.-Copt.-Eth. (see chart).

In view of these data, the two possible relationships between Rec. A and Rec. B can be further refined.

1) If B is a condensation of A, we must reckon with a single original abridgment, of which the two groups are two variations.[78]

2) If A is an expansion of B, it is an expansion of one of two forms of B.

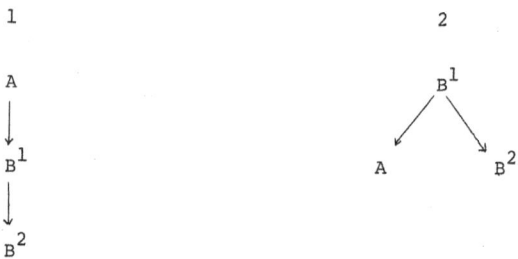

A choice between alternatives 1) and 2) would be simplified immensely if we knew whether B^1 was represented by the Grk.-Slav. group or the Arab.-Copt.-Eth. Unfortunately, there are sufficient variations even among these to make such a choice premature at this time, even though preliminary findings suggest a closer similarity between Rec. A and Rec. $B^{Grk.-Slav.}$ than between Rec. A and $B^{Arab.-Copt.-Eth.}$. Therefore, so that we do not prejudice our conclusions, we shall discuss alternatives 1 and 2, comparing Rec. A with both groups of B, wherever this is necessary.

---

[78] This against James, who argues that Arab. is an abridgment independent of Grk. B, *Testament* 48f.

In order to determine which recension is more likely to have developed from the other, we shall look at those places where both recensions have the same element. Which appears to be the more primitive? Are there cases in which the one cannot be understood except with reference to the other? Does one recension make more sense than the other? This does not mean accepting "the easier reading," but accepting a reading which makes sense over one which makes little or no sense. The agenda for our investigation will be the findings of the first part of this paper. Can we find evidence in Rec. B for the literary seams discovered in Rec. A? Have they been smoothed over? Do the traditions found in Rec. A occur here in more primitive or more developed form, or have they begun to break down?

In section D we saw that the appearance and trial of the one soul was a secondary interpolation, albeit one that becomes the central focus for that whole portion of Rec. A. A comparison of Rec. A XII: 90.14-19 with its counterparts in Rec. B$^{Grk.-Arab.-Copt.}$ indicates that all three have smoothed out the difficulty by excising the mention of the single angel with the one soul and bringing it in at a later point. This is not the case with the Slav. The text reads as follows:

> And while Abraham stood and marvelled, even at that very hour, *the angels* drive 70,000 souls; but one (soul) *he* was holding in *his* hand. And *he* drove the 70,000 into the gate leading to destruction, and they entered it.[79]

Of all the versions of Rec. B, this alone corresponds point by point to the same section in Rec. A. Here too we note the disjunction between the angels (pl.) and the sudden mention of one angel holding a single soul in his hand. Beyond this, the text has been smoothed over slightly beyond the accepted text of A; for it continues to speak of the single angel (rather than reverting to the plural), and it refers to the "70,000" going through the gate (rather than "all the souls"). In any event, the presence of this literary problem also in a text of Rec. B means that either recension could have been the source of the other.

If the references to the single soul are interpolations,

[79 Translation of Slavonic ms. T (see above, n. 76).]

then at one point the context existed without them. Moreover, there was a reason for the interpolations. Does the text of either recension indicate that: 1) it could have existed without mention of the single soul; 2) there was good reason for such a reference to have been interpolated? We have already seen that precisely this is the case in Rec. A. We isolated a two way scene in which the reference to the soul is not necessary and a judgment scene that has an integrity of its own without reference to the soul. Moreover, we saw that the single soul is the thread that runs through the entire section about Abraham's chariot ride and his repentance. It is a reasonable hypothesis that it was added at the time that this unit was composed. That is, the judgment scene can stand without reference to the one soul, but the whole of chs. 9-14 cannot.

The texts of Rec. B all differ in their treatment of the one soul and must be discussed separately.[80] In Grk., as in Rec. A, the same soul is mentioned in the two way scene and in the judgment scene. However, different from Rec. A, if we excise mention of the soul, the whole judgment scene collapses, for different from Rec. A, it is not mainly a description of the various functionaries and their duties, but rather a description of the process involved in the judgment of the one soul. In Slav., the soul mentioned in the first scene is different from the one in the second scene. We can excise mention of the first soul, and the judgment scene will remain intact. However, there appears to be no reason to have added the reference to the first soul. Michael and Abraham search for one righteous soul to save. They find only the one soul, whose sins and righteous deeds are equally balanced. They place it in the middle and nothing happens to it. Arab., Copt. agree with Slav. in that they describe two different souls. Again we can delete reference to the first without touching the integrity of the judgment scene. However, the first soul presents an enigma. As in Slav., Abraham and Michael search for a righteous soul and find only one whose sins and righteous

---

[80] For the sake of discussion, we shall grant that the literary difficulty at the point of the introduction of the one soul may have been smoothed over in what could otherwise be more primitive texts, i.e., Grk., Arab., Copt.

deeds are equally balanced. And *on these grounds* they take the soul to eternal life. This strange turn of events (though no stranger than Grk., where the soul with deeds equally balanced is damned) is most easily explained if we understand the text as a compression of the whole sequence in the Rec. A judgment scene, where the soul with deeds equally balanced is saved through the intercession of Abraham and Michael. The Eth. might appear to be the most primitive text since reference to the single soul is completely missing in the two way section. However, as we have seen, the addition of such a reference in the Arab. and Copt., to which it is most closely related, is not at all likely.[81] More likely, we have another example of the corruptions and deletions that mark other parts of this text.[82]

In summary: our study of the material about the one soul favors the priority of Rec. A.

We noted in our discussion of Rec. A the difficulty that emerges through the juxtaposition of the two way scene and the judgment scene. Souls are effectively judged when they are channelled through the two ways; yet the judgment throne is located on the other side of the two gates. It was suggested that either two judgment scenes had been juxtaposed or a two way setting of the judgment scene has been expanded into a scene of its own. Again it might appear that the Copt., Arab., and Eth. are more primitive in that they posit no change of scene from the two ways to the judgment. In such a case, we would have to presume that the one scene form in Arab., Copt., Eth. developed into two scenes in Rec. B$^{Grk.-Slav.}$ From this Rec. A developed, complicating the problem by moving the place of judgment from Paradise down to the other side of the two gates. Just as likely, Rec. A$^{Grk.}$ is the original--with its

---

[81] It is conceivable that a text form like Eth. could have been interpolated in the two way scene with the material about the one soul, but with this soul being identified with the soul in the judgment sequence, i.e., the pattern of Grk. However, at every other point, Eth. agrees with Arab.-Copt. against Grk. It would be too rash to suppose that Grk. develops from Eth.

[82] On these corruptions, see Leslau's translation, p. 95, and his notes, pp. 176-80.

difficulties. Grk., Slav. attempt to remove the difficulty by setting the place of judgment in Paradise. Copt., Arab. delete the change of scene, as does the Roumanian version of Rec. A. The evidence is uncertain. The same is true regarding the interpolation about the three judgments. There is no way to decide whether the interpolation in A or the reference to the three witnesses in Rec. B$^{Arab.-Copt.}$ is more original.

In Rec. A we isolated a form of a traditional judgment scene. Stemming from that tradition were the two angelic witnesses, the record of deeds, and possibly the judge and the trial by fire. The fire does not appear in Rec. B. The judge does. The place of the angelic witnesses is taken in part by Enoch, who is the heavenly scribe. However in B$^{Grk.-Slav.}$ there are also the cherubim, who are the guardians of the two books--presumably the records of good and evil deeds. One should perhaps not make too much of the presence of angels in the heavenly courtroom. However, the picture suggests the idea expressed more clearly in Rec. A, viz., the two angelic scribe-attorneys. In Rec. B$^{Grk.-Slav.}$ they have been demoted to guardians of the books, as their office is taken over by Enoch. In Rec. B$^{Arab.-Copt.-Eth.}$ mention of them is completely deleted. This explanation seems superior to the reverse, viz., that cherubim who happen to be carrying two books develop into the two recording and witnessing angels, who are already part of the traditional trappings of Jewish eschatology.

Schmidt argues that all Egyptian elements in Rec. A are missing in Rec. B, indicating the priority of the latter. Among these, he would include in the judgment scene: Abel's throne; the table; the writing tools of the scribes; and Dokiel and his balance. The absence of the throne and the table can be explained by the fact that the judgment scene in Rec. B is one of action rather than a description of the way that things are. But what of Dokiel and his balance? The idea of the weighing of deeds is present in the two way scene in Rec. B$^{Grk.-Slav.-Arab.-Copt.}$ Abraham and Michael find a soul whose deeds are equally balanced. According to Schmidt,

> cette allusion à la pesée, qui reste ici métaphorique, est le point de départ de la représentation de la psychostasie dans la rec. longue.[83]

---

[83]Schmidt, *Testament* II, 132, n. on IX,8.

But is the allusion metaphorical? Does not the specification "equally balanced" envision a weighing process? How do Abraham and Michael determine that the sins and righteous deeds are equally balanced? I would suggest that the "allusion" here is precisely to the weighing process which is explicitly referred to in Rec. A, where it and the equal balance are integral to the resolution of the problem presented by Abraham's inability to have compassion on the souls of sinners. On the other hand in the whole of the short recension, the *equal* balancing defies explanation. In Arab., Copt, it is the basis for saving the soul. In Grk. the soul is damned in spite of it. In Slav. it is just mentioned and nothing happens. This state of affairs is best explained if we are dealing with a vestigal remain of the scene in Rec. A.

But what of Dokiel? Is there no trace of him? Abraham asks Michael,

> And how is Enoch able to bear *the weight of the souls*, since he has not seen death? (XI: 115.21-23)

This reading occurs only in ms. A of the Grk., although it is probably presumed in C and the Slav.[84] The expression--if we take it to be the correct reading--is odd, that is, unless it reflects the picture of Dokiel at the judgment, weighing the souls.[85]

Finally, there is the question of the placement of Abraham's journey over the world. In Rec. A, it is an integral part of the entire section and raises the problem that is of prime concern for the author and is resolved only at the end of the section. In Rec. B, Abraham's judgmental attitude surfaces only after he has seen the judgment, indeed after Michael has stated that it is the Lord who gives sentence (XI: 116.1f.). It comes as an anti-climax and serves no real function.

---

[84] A reads βαστάσαι τὸ βάρος τῶν ψυχῶν . C reads μέρος for βάρος and is probably a corruption of the reading in A, caused by the confusion of the labials β and μ. Slav. reads *chas*=ὥρα. With a slight emendation to *chast'*, it would translate μέρος. [The reading conjectured by H. Weber is found in Slav. ms. P, see below, p. 322. The confusion of β and μ is probably paleographic rather than phonetic.]

[85] Surely that is not the meaning here. Note, however, that parallel to the expression is, "or how is he able to render sentence on the souls?"

It is best explained as the result of some radical surgery, perhaps motivated in part by the desire to remove the idea that the souls of the dead can be interceded for.[86] The inappropriateness of the placement of the section in Rec. B$^{\text{Grk.-Slav.}}$ is perhaps attested in Arab., Copt., Eth., where the final journey is deleted, quite probably by a later reviser of the recension.

In summary: evidence from the judgment scene and the shape of the pericope as a whole corroborates our earlier conclusion regarding the earlier form of the one soul material, viz., that Rec. A is prior to Rec. B.

This conclusion regarding the priority of Rec. A is put forward with some caution, since it is a conclusion drawn on the basis of evidence from only one section of the Testament. However, it seems well enough founded to call for further examination of these data and similar examination of the whole of the two recensions.

Having opted for this alternative, we can only briefly sketch possible alternatives as to the history of the short recension and its relationship to the long recension. A comparative study of the versions of Rec. B with Rec. A indicates that Grk.-Slav. agrees with Rec. A more often than does Arab.-Copt.-Eth. These agreements include the placing of the equally balanced soul "in the middle," the change of scene from the two ways to the judgment, the connection of the two books with the cherubim, the identification of Abel as judge, the inclusion of Abraham's journey over the world. The Grk. alone agrees with Rec. A in identifying the single soul in the two way scene with the one in the judgment scene. The Slav. alone retains the first difficult mention of the single soul in the hand of the one angel. On the other hand, the Arab. and Copt. correspond more closely to Rec. A in their mention of the three witnesses and in the fact that the soul with equally balanced deeds is finally saved.

With these facts in mind we can detail the history of the recension in three possible ways. In any event, it will be granted that the Slav. reflects the fact that the literary

---

[86] See James, *Testament* 47. For an assertion that death cuts off the last chance for repentance, see 4 Ezra 9:12. Cf. 2 Bar 85:12, which makes a similar statement and denies the possibility of intercession by the fathers.

difficulty caused by the insertion of the one soul into the two way scene was not totally smoothed over in the *Grundschrift* of Rec. B, even if it has been smoothed over in the present texts of Grk., Arab., and Copt.

1) The Arab.-Copt.-Eth. group most closely represents the original of Rec. B. a) The reviser has compressed the whole one soul sequence into the two way scene. The placing in the middle is unnecessary and is deleted. The judgment sequence, now set in the same place as the two way scene, becomes the locus for the trial of a second soul, so that we have a description of the fate of one righteous and one wicked soul. The identity of judge is changed from Abel to God himself. b) The Slav. follows this group by maintaining the separate identity of the two souls and by mentioning eternal life in connection with the first soul (and implying in spite of itself that the soul would be saved). However, if Slav. is essentially based on the Arab.-Copt. scheme, it and the Grk. after it have gotten secondarily from Rec. A all of those features which they share with A over against Arab.-Copt.

2) The form represented by Grk. is primary. a) It follows Rec. A at many points as indicated above; but of concern here, it identifies as one, the two single souls in the two scenes. The problem here is to explain why the author builds a whole scene to show up the gross sins of the soul whose deeds are equally balanced. This element is better understood as a remnant from a version in which there was a second soul (i.e., Slav. or Arab., Copt.). b) Slav. would follow from the Grk. Yet it is similar to Rec. A in hinting that the soul with equally balanced deeds will be saved. At this point it diverges from Grk. in separating the two souls. c) Copt. and Arab. carry the process one step farther, but their reference to the three witnesses also shows some secondary influence from Rec. A.

3) The form represented by Slav. is closest to the *Grundschrift*. a) A priori evidence in favor of this is its retention of the literary seam at the first mention of the one soul. The whole one soul sequence is compressed, the placing in the middle is mentioned, and the ultimate saving of the soul is hinted at, though we see the soul left suspended in the middle. With an interest in showing the fates of two kinds of souls,

the reviser creates the scene about the second soul. b) The form of the Grk. would be dependent on this version. The major difference is in the identification of the two souls, possibly from contact with Rec. A, or by influence from the ambiguities in Slav. c) Arab., Copt. are also dependent on Slav. They make specific reference to the saving of the first soul, perhaps by contact with Rec. A--though possibly they are simply explicating the hint in Slav. Since the soul is saved, mention of the placing in the middle is dropped. The only necessary point of contact with Rec. A is the reference to the three witnesses, unless this is original with this group and is interpolated back into Rec. A (together with mention of God as judge).

The last of these three alternatives (modified to allow the primitivity of individual readings in various mss.) brings us closest, I believe, to the complex history of the recension[87] and its relationship to Rec. A--a history that will be most nearly ascertained by a careful combination of text, literary, and form criticism of all the mss. of all the versions of both recensions.

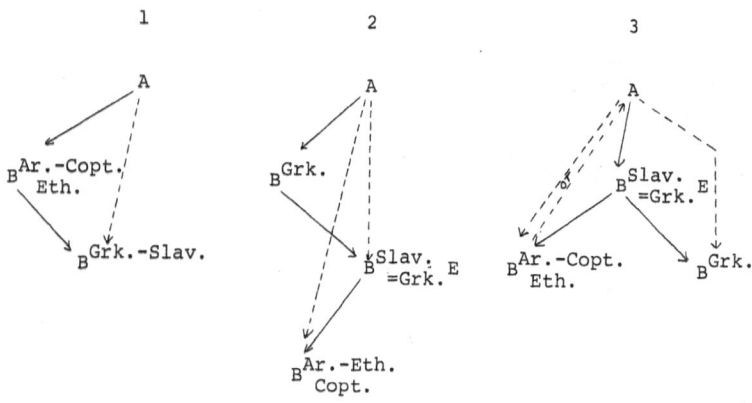

APPENDIX

The Short Recension

		Greek	Slavonic	Arabic	Coptic	Ethiopic
1.	Michael, Abr. to Ocean	x	x	–	x	x
2.	Two gates, Adam	x	x	x	x	x
3.	Abr. and 2 gates	x	x	[x]	[x]	[x]
4.	Myriads of souls	x	x	[x]	[x]	[x]
5.	Seek, find 1 soul	x	x	x	x	–
6.	Death who removes	x	x	x	x	–
7.	How many souls	–	–	x	x	x
8.	M., Abr. to Paradise	x	x	–	–	–
9.	One soul	x	x	x	x	x
10.	"Surrounded"	–	–	x	x	x
11.	Escorts address judge	–	–	–	x	x
12.	Soul's plea	⎧ x	x ⎫	–	–	–
13.	Judge's indictment	⎨ x	x ⎬	–	–	–
14.	Soul denies	⎩ x	x ⎭	–	–	–
15.	Judge summons witness	x	x	x	x	x
16.	Cherubim with books	x	x	–	–	–
17.	Man appears	x	x	x	x	x
18.	with books	–	–	x	x	x
19.	His description	x	x	–	–	–
20.	Man reads	x	x	x	x	x
21.	Judge responds	x	x	–	–	–
22.	Soul responds	x	x	⎧ x	x	x ⎫
23.	Judge responds	–	–	⎪ x	x	x ⎪
24.	Summons 3 witnesses	–	–	⎨ x	x	x ⎬
25.	Recite sins	–	–	⎪ x	x	x ⎪
26.	Soul's response	–	–	⎩ x	x	x ⎭
27.	Soul cast out	x	x	x	x	x
28.	Who is: judge	x	x	–	–	–
	old man	x	x	x	x	x
29.	Answer: Abel	x	x	–	–	–
	Enoch	x	x	x	x	x
30.	Longer description	x	x	–	–	–
31.	Journey	x	x	–	–	–

ADDENDUM

In his paper on the two recensions, Francis Schmidt offers counterarguments to those of Delcor and myself, and he presents his own positive arguments to support the priority of Rec. B. In this addendum, I shall limit myself to the clarifying of my own arguments vis-a-vis Schmidt's counterarguments and to the underscoring of those of my arguments which are relevant to Schmidt's counterproposals, but which he bypasses.

On pp. 69f., Schmidt presents four textual arguments against my position. Three of these arguments do not, I believe, touch the substance of my position as it was argued in my paper.

1. My wording "secondary interpolation" (p. 53) is misleading. By it I meant secondary to *a tradition* into which it was inserted, not secondary to Rec. A of T Abr (cf. pp. 45f.). I agree that the textual evidence cited by Schmidt proves that XII,2 was original to Rec. A.

2. In my footnote 76, I indicated on the basis of Schmidt's collation, which alone was available to me at the time of writing, that "my references to $B^{Slav.}$ can probably most often be equated with Grk. E." I agree with Schmidt that the reference to the single soul is most probably original to the Grk. text of Rec. B. The rest of the Grk. mss., as well as the Arab. and Copt., would still, according to my hypothesis, represent a smoothing out of the difficulty.

3. In the structure of my argument on p. 53, my reference to the Slavonic witness was intended only to admit that at least one witness to Rec. B does contain the literary problem found in Rec. A, thus indicating that "either recension could have been the source of the other" (p. 53). If we accept the reading of $Grk.^E$ and $Slav.^P$, as Schmidt does, the *whole* textual tradition of Rec. B reflects what I have called the smoothing over of the literary difficulty.

4. This alone of Schmidt's four points presents difficulties for my argument; for it maintains that in the original form of Rec. B, the single soul with sins and righteous deeds equally balanced is different from the soul that is judged in the following scene. Assuming that Schmidt is correct, a

comparison with Rec. A is still instructive. In Rec. B, the soul with equally balanced deeds is mentioned and then not referred to again. What is the purpose of introducing it in the first place? Evidently, it leads Abraham to request a view of the judgment process, although this connection is not explicit. But if this is the connection, why does the author introduce a soul with *equally balanced* deeds. We should expect that the judgment scene would depict the process of weighing; but this process is not depicted in Rec. B. On the other hand, in Rec. A, the equal balancing of good and evil deeds is a functioning and indispensible part of the judgment scene and its context. For this reason, it seems easier to explain Rec. B as a telescoping of Rec. A, than Rec. A as an expansion of Rec. B (thus above, pp. 56f.).

After Schmidt has defended the priority of Rec. B, he turns his attention to the distinctions within Rec. B between the Grk.-Slav. and the Arab.-Copt.-Eth. groups (pp. 76-78) and concludes that "the Coptic version is a witness of the short recension that is located between the tradition represented by ms. E and the Slavonic on the one hand, and the long recension on the other" (p. 78).

The difficulties raised by this position are serious. Over against Rec. $B^{Copt.}$, Rec. $B^{Grk.-Slav.}$ has the following items *in common with Rec. A*: there is a change of place between the two way scene and the judgment scene (Schmidt's point 2); there are angel(s)/Cherubim connected with the book(s) (Schmidt's point 3); Abel is depicted as judge (4); Abraham takes a journey over the world (5); there is an initial mention of the single soul (7). If with Schmidt we accept the priority of Rec. B., we can explain these unique similarities between Rec. A and Rec. $B^{Grk.-Slav.}$ on literary grounds only by positing that the author of Rec. A knew *both* families in Rec. B.

A second difficulty is Schmidt's point 1. Rec. A offers a good and cogent reason for the saving of the soul with equally balanced deeds. First it is placed in the middle; then it is saved through Abraham's and Michael's intercession. In Rec. $B^{Copt.}$, it is not placed in the middle, but it is saved for no apparent reason. This is most easily read as a compression of the narrative of Rec. A.

In the last part of my paper (pp. 54-60), I argued that the variations among the families of Rec. B can be explained as different attempts to smooth out difficulties in a common archetype. When Schmidt argues the priority of Rec. B, he must posit (though he does not do so in his paper) the dependence of Rec. A on both families of Rec. B. Moreover, the form of some of the elements in Rec. B is more difficult to understand than it is in Rec. A.

THE TWO RECENSIONS OF THE TESTAMENT OF ABRAHAM:
IN WHICH DIRECTION DID THE TRANSFORMATION TAKE PLACE?*

Francis Schmidt

In the wake of studies on the Testament of Abraham during the past four years, the main problems on which the discussion should now focus are that of the date and original milieu of the two recensions, and more precisely that of the direction in which the transition from one to the other took place. For M. Delcor[1] and E. Janssen[2] both recensions contain data useful for reconstituting an earlier Greek text. It is this original text which they propose to locate in time and space and not one or the other recension. Consequently neither Delcor nor Janssen takes a position on the issue of which is the older of the two recensions. But while Janssen thinks that the original was drawn up in Palestine during the Roman period, perhaps only in the second or third century A.D. (pp. 198-199), for Delcor, on the other hand, it is a production of the Jewish diaspora in Egypt, more exactly of the Therapeutae, in the first century B.C. or the first century A.D. (pp. 72, 76).

G. W. E. Nickelsburg, Jr. and I have attempted to locate the two recensions in a relative chronology, on the theory that one was in some fashion the transformation of the other. But our conclusions differ on the direction of this transformation. Nickelsburg thinks that the long recension presents a state of the text that is older than that of the short recension;[3] in my 1971 work, on the other hand, I saw in the long recension a development of the short text.[4] In addition I concluded that the short recension had a Palestinian origin, and the long an Egyptian origin.

The diversity of positions warrants a reexamination of the problem. I should like here to evaluate the arguments of Delcor and Nickelsburg, then to take up the question which seems to me the most important in the current discussion: Which is

---

* Translated from the French by George MacRae.

the older of the two recensions of the T Abr?

Delcor offers the following objection to my position: "If the short recension were of Palestinian origin, as Schmidt maintains, it would be more difficult to understand why the short recension is the prototype of the southern versions (Arabic, Coptic, Ethiopic). If on the contrary the short recension is also of Egyptian origin, this fact explains quite well why it is normally regarded as the origin of the southern versions" (pp. 77-78). This notion, expressed several times in Delcor's work, that the short recension is the prototype of the southern versions, rests on an erroneous conception. In reality it is wrong to state that "the Slavonic and Rumanian versions follow Recension A, while the Coptic, Arabic and Ethiopic versions are modeled in all likelihood on Recension B" (p. 14), or that "the long recension is the exclusive source of the northern versions (Slavonic and Rumanian), the short recension is the prototype of all the southern ones (Arabic, Coptic and Ethiopic)" (p. 23; see also the table on the same page). As a matter of fact, in the present state of the documentation available to us, only the Rumanian witnesses published by Gaster depend on the long recension, more exactly on the tradition attested by MSS D L M of this recension.[5] On the other hand, the short recension is at the origin of all the other versions: Coptic, Arabic, Ethiopic, and also Slavonic and Rumanian. In fact Codex Sturdzanus published by B. Petriceicu-Hăsdeu and MS 2158 of the Library of the Rumanian Academy of which N. Cartojan has furnished a brief résumé, are both Rumanian witnesses to the short recension.[6] The area in which the short recension was circulated in the course of its history is far from being limited to the southern Mediterranean region, and therefore one cannot derive an argument from the Coptic version to prove the Egyptian origin of the short Greek recension.

In addition, according to Delcor, the proofs for an Egyptian origin of the two recensions of T Abr are the following: (1) the Egyptian influences which mark the representation of the psychostasia, the notions relating to the three judgments (which would be a heavenly counterpart to the three degrees of jurisdiction inherited from the Ptolemaic administration), and the representation of Death (pp. 67-68); (2) the affinities in

vocabulary which T Abr shows with the Book of Wisdom and the
last three Books of Maccabees (pp. 29, 68-69). Whatever the
value of each of these arguments, on which I shall not take a
position here, one must observe that none of them applies to
the short recension; all deal with the long recension. The
only conclusion that is possible to draw from this line of argument is that the long recension is of Egyptian origin. The
problem of the origin of the shorter text remains intact.

With Nickelsburg, I should like now to take up the following question: In what direction did the transition from one
recension to the other take place?

This question presupposes that one maintain the distinction proposed by M. R. James between a short and a long recension. As a matter of fact, after reading a number of Greek MSS
of which James was not aware,[7] it seemed to me that the distinction could be maintained. It has always appeared to me
possible to classify a new witness either on the side of the
short recension or on that of the long. But within the two
distinct textual traditions the situation is far from being as
clear as James's edition would lead one to think. In my 1971
work I set forth the reasons why MS E (Milan, Ambrosian Greek
405, 11th-12th century) seemed to me to hold a completely
privileged place among the witnesses to the short recension.
The Coptic and Slavonic versions, independently of one another,
are each related to the Greek tradition attested by E.[8] Moreover, the vocabulary of this MS is markedly older than that of
the other witnesses to the short recension: while N. Turner[9]
enumerated about ten words attested only since the Christian
period in the MSS edited by James, the tradition represented
by E contains only four.[10]

As for the long recension, only a new edition will permit
us to clarify an entangled textual tradition. It seems that in
the totality of the MSS of this recension one must again distinguish between a long text (more or less the one which James
edited, relying upon A) and one or more short texts (e.g.
K N O, which, however, are not related to each other). One
must therefore wait for this new edition, on which J. Smit
Sibinga and I are currently working, to take a more precise
stand on the problem of the relationship between the two

recensions. Indeed, if the short recension (B) is a transformation of the long (A), does Rec. B result from a transformation of a short text or a long text of Rec. A? On the other hand, if Rec. A is a transformation of Rec. B, does the transition take place in the direction B--A (short text)--A (long text) or B--A (long text)--A (short text)?

The method that I shall follow is the following: if one of the recensions is the transformation of the other, it must be possible to find in the internal structure of the transformed recension traces (which might be contradictions or breaks in the continuity of episodes) of the structure proper to the recension that served as its model. One must begin therefore by uncovering the contradictions and breaks in the logical structure of each text. One must then try to show that these aporiae are the traces, within the recension (y) where they are discovered, of the structure proper to the other recension (x). Then the direction of the transformation is x--y; the reverse y--x is impossible.

For this purpose I shall begin with Nickelsburg's study on the judgment scenes in the two recensions. In a very convincing manner the author sets forth the logical structure proper to Rec. A, and he discovers certain contradictions within this text. The following are the results of his analysis: the heavenly journey of Abraham begins with his observing the inhabited world and the punishment of sinners (X,1-15; James 87, 16--88,26);[11] it ends with intercession for these sinners on the part of the patriarch (XIV,10-15; James 94,12--95,3). Between the initial and the final episodes there are two intermediary ones: that of the two ways (XI,1--XII,2; James 88,27--90,19) and that of the judgment (XII,3--XIV,9; James 90,19--94,12). These have as their function to bring Abraham from indignation to compassion; more exactly, "within that judgment scene, the single soul, its plight and its fate, is the device by which Abraham is brought from indignation to compassion" (p. 184). The treatment of the single soul (XII,1-3; James 90, 14-21. XII,16-18; James 91,19-26. XIV,1-9; James 93,19--94,12), therefore, holds a central place in the internal structure of the whole of this section of Rec. A (X-XIV). As Nickelsburg puts it, the single soul is "the thread that holds together the entire section" (p. 46).

On the other hand, the author points out in the scene of the two ways and in that of the judgment a certain number of difficulties or contradictions in which he sees the mark of literary seams. Up to this point I would agree with the essentials of Nickelsburg's analysis. But we separate over the conclusions that should be drawn from it. For Nickelsburg indeed these "literary seams" allow one to show that the long recension is the result of the combination of several texts or traditions which first had an independent existence (on the different stages of redaction of Rec. A see pp. 45-46). Then, moving on to examine the short recension, the author thinks that these seams have disappeared. The redactor of the short text, wishing to smooth over the literary difficulties found in his model, would have obliterated these seams. Thus we would have proof that Rec. B is a reworking of Rec. A. It seems to me, on the contrary, that one can treat this ingenious but too complicated explanation more economically by seeing in the seams traces of the reworking of the short recension on the part of the redactor of the long recension.

Yet if I do not retain Nickelsburg's line of argument, it is not only by virtue of the fact that it is too complex. It is also and especially because it seems to me to rest on several hypotheses which the MS tradition, particularly the material not known to James, does not confirm.

1. Nickelsburg writes: "We saw that the appearance and trial of the one soul was a secondary interpolation" (p. 53). This hypothesis, on which the author bases an important part of his demonstration, has as its point of departure an analysis of XII,1-2 (James 90,14-19; cf. Nickelsburg, pp. 41f.). This then permits the author to resolve the difficulty presented by the abrupt transition from plural to singular and from singular to plural. But it appears that Nickelsburg (cf. p. 62 , n. 62) has been led astray by an inaccuracy in the apparatus of James. In reality, not only do A and D mention the single soul, but also B C E, and to these witnesses we must now add H I J L M P Q. The hypothesis of the interpolation of XII,2 (James 90, 17-18) cannot therefore be supported by the MS tradition. Also it seems to me difficult to extend this hypothesis, as the author does (p. 43), to all of the episodes dealing with the single soul.

2. Nickelsburg states: "A comparison of Rec. A XII:90, 14-19 with its counterparts in Rec. B^Grk.-Arab.-Copt. indicates that all three have smoothed out the difficulty by excising the mention of the single angel with the one soul and bringing it in at a later point" (p. 53). Contrary to Greek MSS A C D and B F of the short recension, MS E does mention the single soul which the angel holds in his hand. The following is the text and translation of Rec. B IX,5 (James 113,22-24) according to E:

καὶ ἑστῶτος τοῦ Ἀβραὰμ καὶ θαυμάζοντος ἐν τῇ ὥρᾳ ἐκείνῃ καὶ ἰδοὺ ἄγγελος ἐλαύνων ψυχὰς ὡς μυριάδας ἕξ, μίαν δὲ ψυχὴν κρατῶν ἐν τῇ χειρὶ αὐτοῦ. καὶ ἀπήξεν τὰς μυριάδας τῶν ψυχῶν εἰς τὴν πύλην τὴν ἀπάγουσαν εἰς τὴν ἀπώλειαν.

While Abraham stood and looked with astonishment, at that hour, behold an angel driving some six myriads of souls before him, but holding one soul in his hand. And he guided the myriads of souls toward the gate that leads to perdition.

3. Next, comparing the Slavonic witness to the short recension edited by Tichonravov with the corresponding passage of the long Greek recension, Nickelsburg concludes: "Of all the versions of Rec. B, this alone corresponds point by point to the same section in Rec. A" (p. 53). Henceforth it is with MS E of the short recension that one must compare the Slavonic version. Moreover, the transition from plural to singular which Nickelsburg pointed out in the MS of Tichonravov ("The angels drive 70,000 souls; but one [soul] he was holding in his hand"), is absent from the MS edited by Polívka:[12] "Behold an angel driving [...lacuna...] carrying one soul in his hand."

4. Still in dependence on James's edition, Nickelsburg writes further: "In Rec. B Grk., as in Rec. A, the same soul is mentioned in the two way scene and in the judgment scene" (p. 54). This analysis corresponds to the tradition represented by MSS A C D and B F, which make clear in IX,8 (James 113,29) that the soul is that of a woman and in X,3 (James 114, 14) that it is this soul which was led before the judge. On the other hand, the tradition to which MS E bears witness, like the Slavonic, makes a clear distinction between the single soul of the two way scene (neither E nor the Slavonic note that the soul is that of a woman) and the soul of the sinful woman which appears only in the judgment scene.

Finally, Nickelsburg concluded: "Our study of the material about the one soul favors the priority to Rec. A" (p. 55).

The foregoing observations are enough to show, in my opinion, that the new MSS call into question this conclusion at which the author arrived on the basis only of the edition of James. The question must therefore be taken up again.

Let us examine now the contradictions of the long recension which call into question the general structure of the narrative. If we consider the three episodes that constitute Abraham's journey to heaven in this recension (the inhabited world, the two ways, the judgment) from the viewpoint of what happens to the sinful person, we note that the text hesitates between two different logical sequences. One can find either the sequence sin--<u>retribution</u>--judgment or the sequence sin--<u>court appearance</u>--judgment. This hesitation, which has a bearing on the episode of the two ways, is shown notably in two contradictions and a break in the narrative.

1. Certain data of the scene of the two ways indicate that Adam is present at the movement of the souls which have already been judged toward the place where the sentence will be carried out: "This narrow gate is that of the righteous which leads to life; those who go through it go to paradise" (XI,10; James 89,26--90,1); "the broad gate is that of sinners, which leads to perdition and to eternal punishment" (XI,11; James 90, 6-8); and Adam laments: "Many are those who are lost, but few those who are saved" (XI,11; James 90,10-11); finally, according to XII,1-2 (James 90,14-19), practically the total number of souls are led "toward the broad gate, to perdition."

On the other hand, at the end of the two ways scene, Abraham is present at the movement of a soul which has not yet been judged toward the place where the sentence will be pronounced.

2. Likewise, as Nickelsburg has noted (p. 41), there is a contradiction between the indications that the broad gate leads to perdition and to eternal punishment and the data of XII,3-15 (James 90,19-91,19), according to which the broad gate leads to the heavenly tribunal.

3. The hesitation which the text displays between a scene of retribution and one of court appearance is therefore particularly notable in XII,1-3. And it is precisely at this point that one finds the clearest trace of redactional activity. At XII,3 (James 90,19-21) there is a break in the narrative as it moves from third person to first person plural. Abraham and

Michael become for the time being the narrators: "We therefore followed the angels, we too, and we penetrated beyond this broad gate." This brief "we" sequence is very well attested in the MS tradition of the long Greek recension. In contrast, in XII,1 (James 90,14) the text established by James (ἔτι δὲ ἐμοὶ ταῦτα λαλοῦντος) is not acceptable. The MSS have the following readings: υμιν A; εμε C; εμαυτου E P; om. B H I J Q and G K N O; finally D L M have at this point ἔτι δὲ αὐτοῦ λαλοῦντος.

Let us relocate the two ways scene in the logical structure of the whole heavenly journey of Abraham as the long recension presents it. Nickelsburg has shown that the text made use of a device which enables Abraham to pass from indignation to compassion. Indeed, in order for Abraham to repent of his excessive severity, he must learn that the sentence pronounced in heaven is not definitive (a second and a third judgment must follow that of Abel), but especially that by intercession it is possible to modify the sentence of Abel in the direction of clemency. This device makes it necessary that the linking of sequences follow a chronological order: sin--<u>court appearance</u>--judgment--intercession. Having punished the sinners, Abraham accompanies the single soul from the two ways scene (where the angel is about to bring it before the tribunal) to the judgment scene; then the patriarch intercedes for it; only then is he able to become aware of his sin and to repent. In other words, the logical structure of the whole heavenly journey implies that the two ways scene is a scene of <u>court appearance</u> in which the souls are led to judgment, not a scene where souls already judged are led to the place of their respective retribution.

Yet we have seen that a certain number of other data make this sequence a scene of <u>retribution</u>. How shall we account for this contradiction within the long recension?

In the short recension the sequence of the two gates is a retribution scene (VIII,3--IX,11; James 112,17--114,8): the souls that Adam sees passing by have already been judged; they are going toward life or perdition. Likewise the judgment of the soul which the angel puts in an intermediary place has already taken place. In the course of his journey Abraham successively attends the sights of <u>retribution</u>, <u>judgment</u> (X, 1--XI,11; James 114,9--116,10), <u>sin</u> (XII,1-14; James 116,11--

117,3). From the viewpoint of the destiny of man as a sinner, these episodes unfold backwards, the opposite of chronological order. Moreover, each scene takes place in a different place in heaven (river Ocean, paradise, firmament), and in each place the actors are different (the soul which the angel holds in his hand; the soul of the sinful woman; the adulterous couple, the calumniators, the murderers).

The contradiction discovered within the long recension can only be explained, in my view, if the transformation took place in the following direction: from the order <u>retribution--judgment--sin</u> (Rec. B) to the order <u>sin--retribution/court appearance--judgment</u> (Rec. A). The initial retribution scene is modified in the process into a scene of court appearance. The hypothesis of the opposite transformation seems to me impossible. The limits imposed by the original text on the transformed text have caused the long recension to preserve traces of the structure of episodes that is proper to its model. Even though it makes the two ways episode a scene of court appearance, the text of Rec. A retains certain of the elements that had made it a scene of retribution. It is therefore the long recension which is a reworking of the short, and not the reverse.

Now I should like to take up the principal modifications which Rec. A makes on Rec. B in order to show that they hold together. In the short text Abraham's heavenly journey ended with the episode of the punishment of the sinners. By an excess of justice, the patriarch leans toward injustice; God orders Abraham's return. The long text displaces this episode and puts it at the beginning of the journey. This displacement, the function of which is to avoid having the patriarch's excessive severity tarnish his image as a Just One and Friend of God, upsets the structure of the whole heavenly journey and involves as a consequence a whole series of transformations. Let us examine their logical connections.

In the short recension the sinners punished by Abraham were an adulterous couple, calumniators and murderers. The sins were a repetition of those committed by the woman judged at the tribunal: she had slept with her son-in-law, calumniated and killed her daughter. The long recension, taking up the fifth, sixth and seventh commandments of the Decalogue, replaces the series adultery--calumny--murder--which no longer had its raison d'être in the continuity of the narrative (the single soul taking the place of the sinful woman) with the order: murder--adultery--theft.

Above all, Rec. A adds the treatment of human activities (X,2-3; James 87,20-28). The theological meaning of this description of the world compared to the shield of Achilles (*Iliad* XVIII,541-549) has been shown elsewhere.[13] It is enough to recall that this representation of the world was interpreted notably in the Hellenized circles of Egypt, as a cosmogonic narrative. It is the mythological translation of the statement that the world does not exist from all eternity but was born; having been born, it has a Father; since it has a Creator, he sees to the preservation of his creature. This episode of the long recension, therefore, sets the merciful benevolence of the Father in opposition to Abraham's indignation. In the following stages of the journey the device centered on the single soul will be placed, of which the function is to bring the patriarch from indignation to compassion. For that purpose Rec. A develops the story of the soul whose good and evil deeds balance out (B IX,5-8; James 113,22--114,3) in three episodes: court appearance (A XII,1-3; James 90,14-21), judgment (XII, 16-18; James 91,19-26), and intercession (XIV,1-9; James 93, 19--94,12).

1. In the short recension the soul had already been judged. In the long recension, in order for Abraham to follow the soul from its appearance before the tribunal to its judgment and then for him to intercede for it, it is necessary that the sentence should not yet have been pronounced. Rec. A, therefore, has to add to the angel who leads to perdition the many souls already judged, a second angel (XII,1-2; James 90, 14-19) who takes charge of the soul whose trial has yet to take place. The abrupt transition from plural to singular and then the return to the plural (Nickelsburg, p. 41) is a trace of this reworking.

In addition Rec. A has to shorten the distance between the two ways scene and the judgment scene in its model. Instead of the patriarch going from the river Ocean to paradise, it is enough for him to go through the broad gate. This modification also leaves a trace in the transformed text, namely the "we" passage.

2. Next the long recension substitutes the judgment of the single soul (XII,16-18; James 91,19-26) for that of the sinful woman in the short recension (X,3-16; James 114,15--115,12). Perhaps one should also include in this series of transformations the addition of the second and third judgments (XIII,6-8; James 92,16-24; cf. Nickelsburg, pp. 40-41 , 43), for this addition highlights the fact that the sentence given by Abel does not have a definitive character. Repentance or intercession can modify its severity.

3. Through his intercession for the single soul, which Rec. A (XIV,1-9; James 93,19--94,12) adds to its model, the patriarch becomes aware of the divine mercy. Hence he is able to understand that he sinned in not showing himself merciful. Finally, the displacement of the episode of the punishment of the sinners from the end of the journey (Rec. B) to the beginning (Rec. A) logically involves the addition of Abraham's intercession for those whom he has caused to die (XIV,10-15; James 94,12--95,3). This prayer along with this repentence wipes out his sin.

The problem posed initially is thus resolved: by the series of transformations which the long text makes of the short, Abraham the implacable Just One has become the merciful Just One. All these transformations, subject to the limits of a single logic, have therefore been made in sequence. It appears that on the opposite hypothesis of a reworking of the long recension by the short it is impossible to reconstitute the logical succession that governs the omissions and modifications which, in this case, would have affected the short text.

The global function of this series of transformations seems therefore to be to resolve the contradiction between the divine justice and mercy by giving primacy to the mercy of God the creator. For its part, the short recension insists on the incompatibility between an earthly, bodily mode of existence and a heavenly mode of existence: before the resurrection of the body, only the soul will dwell in the place of retribution. The scene in which Abraham finds it impossible to enter the narrow gate because of his body is particularly instructive for this dichotomy. The entire two ways scene (VIII,3--IX,11;

James 112,17--114,8), as is indicated by Abraham's final question about the angel who brings the souls out of bodies, teaches the patriarch that the separation of soul and body must of necessity precede the retribution, of sinners as well as of the righteous or of those whose good and evil deeds are equal.

This problematic has completely disappeared from Rec. A[14] and has been replaced by a different one, that of the contradiction between justice and mercy. In parallel fashion the long recension substitutes the doctrine of the immortality of the soul for that of the resurrection of the body.[15] Clearly we must see in these two substitutions an indication of the doctrinal differences which separate the original milieu of Rec. A from that of Rec. B.

Let us now examine the respective positions of the Slavonic and Coptic versions in relation to the two Greek recensions. Nickelsburg concludes his examination of this question thus: "A comparative study of the versions of Rec. B with Rec. A indicates that Grk.-Slav. agrees with Rec. A more often than does Arab.-Copt.-Eth" (p. 58). According to him the points of contact between the long recension and the Greek and Slavonic versions of the short recension are the following:

1. "The placing of the equally balanced soul 'in the middle.'". In the Coptic the soul whose good and evil deeds balance out is led to life. This point of contact can be explained only by the fact that Rec. A makes use of the corresponding data of Rec. B.

2. "the change of scene from the two ways to the judgment." In the Coptic it seems that the two scenes take place at the same place. Is this a point of contact between Rec. B Greek-Slavonic and Rec. A Greek, or on the contrary between Rec. B Coptic and Rec. A Greek? Indeed, neither of the two latter texts mentions the movement of Abraham on the cloud. This common omission helps relate the two scenes to each other spatially.

3. "the connection of the two books with the cherubim." In the Coptic, which does not mention the angel carrying the books, it is Enoch alone who fulfills this function. Same observation as in no. 1 above.

4. "the identification of Abel as judge." In the Coptic God judges the sinful woman. Same observation as in no. 1 above. It appears on the contrary that the Coptic should be compared with Greek Rec. A, which foresees that the third judge will be God.

5. "the inclusion of Abraham's journey over the world." This sequence is absent from the Coptic. Same observation as in no. 1 above.

6. "The Grk. alone agrees with Rec. A in identifying the single soul in the two way scene with the one in the judgment scene." We have seen above that MS E, like the Slavonic and the Coptic, distinguishes the single soul from that of the sinful woman.

7. "The Slav. alone retains the first, difficult mention of the single soul in the hand of the one angel." We have seen above that this mention is likewise found in E. It is absent from the Coptic. Same observation as in no. 1 above.

The points of contact observed by Nickelsburg may be explained solely by the fact that Rec. A made use of the elements of Rec. B. They do not prove that the Greek/Slavonic texts of the short recension are closer to the long recension than the Coptic version is. I believe on the contrary that of all the versions of Rec. B the Coptic is most closely related to Greek Rec. A. Indeed, Nickelsburg himself admits that "on the other hand, the Arab. and Copt. correspond more closely to Rec. A in their mention of the three witnesses" (p. 58 ; in the Coptic the three witnesses are perhaps a development of the three crowns of Enoch in Greek Rec. B "which are called witnesses"; cf. E X,8-9; James 114,22-25) and "in the fact that the soul with equally balanced deeds is finally saved." Besides the points of contact indicated above in 2 and 4, one must point out especially the following parallelism: in the Coptic as in the long Greek recension the narrative changes from the third to the first person: compare the "we" passage of Rec. A (XII,3; James 90,19-21) and the "I" passage of the Coptic which extends to the entire narrative of the heavenly journey (though the narrative returns temporarily to the third person in the passage in which the soul whose good and evil deeds are balanced is led into life).

In addition, in the last part of the Coptic version, when

Abraham has returned home, he sets his slaves free. Likewise in the long Greek recension the tradition attested by MSS D L M mentions the setting free. Yet this mention is not found before the coming of Death as in the Coptic, but immediately before Death asks the patriarch to kiss his right hand (XX,7; James 103, note on line 14).

Finally, according to a copy of the Sahidic fragments which M. Weber has kindly put at my disposition, the enumeration of the faces of Death seems to present points in common with that of Rec. A. The fragmentary text is uncertain, and one must await the publication of these fragments by Weber to be certain of the reading of this passage. It seems, however, that it is possible to recognize, in addition to the dragon face, the faces of the panther and the basilisk (cf. Rec. A XIX,14; James 102,12).

Thus it is the Coptic version, and not the tradition represented by the Greek and the Slavonic, which offers the closest affinity with the long Greek recension. The Coptic version is a witness of the short recension that is located between the tradition represented by MS E and the Slavonic on the one hand,[16] and the long recension on the other.

To place the two recensions in a relative chronology we have examined the question of whether it was possible to determine the direction in which the narrative transformations took place. Our conclusion coincides with that reached by a study of the influences external to Judaism with which each of the two recensions is marked.[17] We shall limit ourselves here to recalling the results of this study, first with respect to the long recension.

In chap. X the vision of the world compared to the shield of Achilles is the mythical translation of a philosophical problem debated notably in the Hellenised circles of Egypt (see above).

The description of the weighing of deeds at the heavenly tribunal (chap. XII-XIII) derives from the Egyptian representation of the psychostasia. This conclusion emerges in particular from a comparison of T Abr with the judgment scene of two late documents, the *Book of the Dead of Pamonthes* and the *Tale of Satni-Khamois*, both of which date from the second half of

the first century A.D. But especially in "the archangel
Dokiel, the just weigher," who weighs deeds "with the justice
of God" (XIII,10; James 93,4-7), we have seen the archangel
Sedekiel, whose name means precisely the "justice of God."
Sedekiel is associated with Anubis on a gem engraved with the
image of the Egyptian god with the scales.[18]

The representation of Thanatos with seven faces who strikes
sinners with violent forms of death (chap. XVII, XIX) is likewise
marked with Graeco-Egyptian influences: the various classes
of accidental forms of death which correspond to the different
faces of Thanatos are the very ones which the mathematici
enumerated in Egypt, and notably Claudius Ptolemaeus at Alexandria,
in their speculations on the biaeothanati. Moreover,
it has been proposed that one see in the representation of the
seven-headed Thanatos as agent of violent death an adaptation
of the likewise seven-headed deity, whose function also is to
bring premature and violent death, named Toutou by the Egyptians
and Tithoes by the Greeks. The diffusion of this god is
particularly attested in lower Egypt in the imperial period
under Trajan and Hadrian.[19]

All the episodes that bear the mark of these Greek and
Egyptian influences are proper to the long recension. On the
other hand, the passages of the short recension for which one
must have recourse to the hypothesis of an influence external
to Judaism find their explanation in the hypothesis of Iranian
influences.

The sequence that is most significant in this respect is
the description of Death adorned or corrupted, depending on
whether he approaches a just person or a sinner (chap. XIII).
This representation is inspired by that of the Iranian *Daena*,
"beautiful girl with white arms" or "woman of evil life, foul
and corrupted," who in reality is none other than the good or
evil deeds of the deceased. This development, which is likewise
found in the long recension (chap. XVI-XVII), suggests
that the short recension, which has no Egyptian features,
emerged from a Jewish milieu open to Iranian influences. One
would tend to think naturally of a Palestinian milieu.[20]

On the other hand, we have seen in the rhythmic passage of
the dream of Isaac (Rec. B VII,10-11; James 111,19-22), which
has no counterpart in Rec. A., a section of the Jewish Passover

liturgy (*Pesaḥim* X,5). This liturgical passage, attributed to Gamaliel I, inserted into the exposition of the destiny of the soul after death which is what Isaac's dream is, also suggests a Palestinian milieu.[21]

Thus all the Greek and Egyptian influences are proper to the long recension; the short recension bears no trace of them. In return, there is no Iranian influence that is peculiar to Rec. A; all the Iranian traits that one can point to are found likewise in Rec. B. The conclusion is obvious: the long recension is the reworking, done in the Jewish diaspora of Egypt, of an older document coming from a Palestinian Jewish circle that is open to Iranian influences. The opposite hypothesis is unacceptable, for how would one explain that the author of the reworking should have systematically eliminated all traces of Greek and Egyptian influence from an older document which contained elements of Hellenistic, Egyptian and Iranian character all at once?

The examination of the narrative transformations and that of the influences thus arrive at the same conclusion: the short recension is prior to the long, and not the reverse.[22] One should next review the totality of the material again to date the two texts in an absolute chronology. Without going over the arguments again in detail, here is the conclusion to which we have come: the T Abr was very likely written in the second half of the first century A.D.; it is possible that the original was composed in a Semitic language; in this case it would then have been translated into Greek,[23] forming the short recension. MS E and the Slavonic version are currently the best witnesses of this state of the tradition. It was further reworked in a Jewish community of lower Egypt in the second, or indeed at the beginning of the third century, forming the long recension. Perhaps one must suppose that between the short and long recensions of the Greek there existed an intermediary state of the Greek tradition of which the Sahidic Coptic would be the translation.

NOTES

[1] M. Delcor, *Le Testament d'Abraham* (Studia in Veteris Testamenti Pseudepigrapha 2; Leiden: Brill, 1973).

[2] E. Janssen, "Testament Abrahams," in *Jüdische Schriften aus hellenistisch-römischer Zeit* (Gütersloh: Mohn, 1975) III.2, 193-256.

[3] G. W. E. Nickelsburg, Jr., "Eschatology in the Testament of Abraham: A Study of the Judgment Scenes in the Two Recensions," in R. A. Kraft, ed., *1972 Proceedings* (SCS 2; Missoula: SBL, 1972) 180-227; reprinted above, pp. 23-61.

[4] F. Schmidt, *Le Testament d'Abraham: introduction, édition de la recension courte, traduction et notes* (unpublished dissertation; Strasbourg, 1971).

[5] M. Gaster, "The Apocalypse of Abraham. From the Roumanian Text, Discovered and Translated," *Transactions of the Society of Biblical Archaeology* 9 (1887) 195-226; reprinted in M. Gaster, *Studies and Texts in Folklore, Magic, Medieval Romance, Hebrew Apocrypha and Samaritan Archaeology* (London: Maggs, 1925) I, 92-123. Cf. F. Schmidt, *Le Testament d'Abraham*, I, 10-12.

[6] Schmidt, *Le Testament d'Abraham*, I, 9-10, 12. B. Petriceicu-Hăsdeu, *Cuvente den bătrâni, II, Cărțile poporane ale Românilor în secolul XVI în legătură cu literatura poporană cea nescrisă* (Bucarest, 1880) 189-194; N. Cartojan, *Cărțile populare în literatura românească* (Bucarest, 1880) I, 87-88.

[7] Cf. Schmidt, *Le Testament d'Abraham*, I, 1-5. The following is a list of MSS unknown to James of which I have been able to obtain copies:
   a. short recension
      D Milan, Ambrosian Greek 259 (D 92 sup.), f. 115^r-118^v, 11th c.
      E Milan, Ambrosian Greek 405 (G 63 sup.), f. 164^r-171^r, 11th-12th c.
      F Meteora, Library of the Metamorphosis 382, f. 123^r-130^v, 15th c.
      G London, British Museum Addit. 10014, f. 38^r-39^v, 16th c.
      H Athens, Society of History and Ethnology 254, f. 215^r-222^r, 16th c.
   b. long recension
      G Istanbul, Patriarchal Library Panaghias 127 (olim 130), f. 140^r-153^r, 17th c.
      H Andros, Hagia Monastery 9, f. 65^v-81^r, 16th c.
      I Ankara, Library of the Turkish Historical Society, Greek 60, f. 267-320, 16th c.
      J Montpellier, Section de Médecine, Greek 405, f. 61^r-83^r, 15th-16th c.

K Jerusalem, Patriarchal Library of Saint Sabas 373, f. 405^r-411^v, 16th c.
L Venice, Marcan Greek VII, 39 (coll. 1386) (olim Nanianus CLV), f. 359^r-378^v, 16th c.
M London, British Museum Addit. 25 881, f. 366^r-378^r, 16th c.
N Athos, Panteleimon 631, f. 49^r-67^v, 17th c.
O Jerusalem, Patriarchal Library of Saint Sabas 492, f. 33-44, 18th c.
P Bologna, University Library 2702 (olim 579), f. 129^r-152^v, 15th c.
Q Athos, Costamoni 14, f. 358-391, 15th c.
R Patmos, Monastery of Saint John 572, f. 186^r-190^r, 16th c.

[8] Schmidt, *Le Testament d'Abraham*, I, 29-34.

[9] N. Turner, *The Testament of Abraham: A Study of the Original Language, Place of Origin, Authorship, and Relevance* (unpublished dissertation; London, 1953) 49-54. Turner published his principal results in "'The Testament of Abraham': Problems in Biblical Greek," *NTS* 1 (1954-55) 219-223.

[10] Schmidt, *Le Testament d'Abraham*, I, 118.

[11] The division into chapters and verses is that of P. Riessler, *Altjüdisches Schrifttum ausserhalb der Bibel* (Augsburg, 1928) 1091-1103.

[12] Cf. G. Polívka, "Die apokryphische Erzählung vom Tode Abrahams," *Archiv für slavische Philologie* 18 (1896) 118-125. E. Turdeanu, "Notes sur la tradition littéraire du Testament d'Abraham," in *Studi bizantini e neoellenici a cura di Silvio Giuseppe Mercati* (Rome, 1957) IV, 409-410, has shown that this witness is "undeniably the best."

[13] F. Schmidt, "Le monde à l'image du bouclier d'Achille: sur la naissance et l'incorruptibilité du monde dans le *Testament d'Abraham*," *Bulletin de la Société Ernest-Renan* 22 (1973) 14-18; *RHR* 185 (1974) 122-126.

[14] Σῶμα is mentioned 13 times in Rec. B (IV,9, 12; VII, 14 [A D B F], 17, 19; VIII,2, 3, 13; IX,3, 10; XIII,1, 16, 17); unless I am mistaken, it is mentioned only 4 times in Rec. A (I,7; IX,6; XV,7; XX,11).

[15] Compare Rec. B VII,12-13, 17 (James 111,23-25, 112,1-3) with Rec. A VII,6, 8 (James 84,15, 20): in Rec. B Isaac wishes that the rays--which symbolize the body--be carried off at the same time as the sun; in Rec. A Isaac begs the man of light to leave him at least the moon, which represents Sarah.

[16] On the points of contact between the Coptic and MS E only see Schmidt, *Le Testament d'Abraham*, I, 33-34.

[17] *Ibid.*, I, 118.

[18] *Ibid.*, I, 74-76.

[19] *Ibid.*, I, 102-110.

[20] *Ibid.*, I, 94-95.

[21] I should like to express my thanks here to J. Smit Sibinga, who kindly drew my attention to this Mishnah text. On the meaning of this section of the Passover liturgy in the dream of Isaac, see *Annuaire de l'École Pratique des Hautes Études, 5e section (sciences religieuses)* 80-81.3, conference notes (1972-73) of F. Schmidt, pp. 321-322.

[22] To the examination of narrative transformations and of foreign influences, one should add also the study of the language of the two recensions, which also leads to the conclusion that the short recension is prior; see notes 9 and 10 above.

[23] The method established by R. A. Martin, *Syntactical Evidence of Semitic Sources in Greek Documents* (Septuagint and Cognate Studies 3; Missoula: SBL, 1974), should allow us to determine whether it is appropriate or not to retain the hypothesis of a Semitic original for Rec. B. The tradition to which MS E bears witness ought to be the point of departure for such a study. [See below, pp. 85-110, for Martin's application of this method to T Abr. See also pp. 133-35 for R.A. Kraft's critique. -Ed.]

STRUCTURE AND MESSAGE IN THE TESTAMENT OF ABRAHAM

George W.E. Nickelsburg, Jr.

In a previous paper, I discussed the structure and literary function of the chariot ride sequence in Recension A of T Abr (above, pp. 25-27). My purpose here is to sketch out the structure of *the whole* of Rec. A, with a view toward discerning in it the author's message. In the second section, I shall deal with related matters in Rec. B. Against this background, I shall raise the question of priority.

Recension A

The book is neatly divided into two parallel and symmetrical parts. Each begins as God summons the messenger of death and ends with Abraham on his bed, surrounded by his household, i.e., the typical testamentary situation.

Part I	Part II
Ch.	Ch.
1. God summons Michael: Go, tell Abraham he will die, so that he makes testament	16. God: summon Death Go, bring Abraham to me
2. Michael leaves, goes to Abraham who sits at Mamre	Death leaves, goes to Abraham who sits at Mamre
Abraham sees, rises to meet	Abraham sees, rises to meet
Michael greets: honored father, righteous soul, friend of God	Death greets: honored Abraham, righteous soul, friend of God
Abraham returns greeting, notes M's glory, beauty Whence are you?	Abraham returns greeting, notes Death's glory Who are you and whence?
Michael replies elusively re. mission	I tell you truth: I am Death
	Abraham contradicts, then refuses to follow
2-3. They go to his house, conversing	17. They go in the house Death is silent

Part I	Part II
The talking tree: a hint	
Isaac, Abraham wash feet	(Abr.'s sullen inhospitality)
4. Prepare room	
Michael returns to heaven	Death stays
5. They eat, go to bed	Abraham goes to bed, orders Death away
5-7. Isaac's dream, interpretation Michael reveals identity, mission	Are you Death? Discuss how Death comes to different people.
7. Abraham refuses to go	
8-9. Michael's ascent, return: Make Testament!	Death stays
9. Abr. asks to see all the world	Show me all your rottenness
10. Abraham sees, calls down various kinds of death	D. unmasks, shows Abr. various kinds of death; Servants die
11-13. Sees Judgment, Michael explains	
14. They pray for the dead; revived	18. They pray for dead; revived
	19. Further delays, refusal, Death explains vision
15. Michael returns Abr. to Sarah, Isaac, servants, who rejoice	20. Isaac, Sarah, servants mourn
Make your Testament! No! Michael returns to heaven	Abraham is suddenly taken Michael takes soul to heaven

Binding these two parts together is a double narrative thread: God's command that Abraham prepare for death and Abraham's refusal to do so. The plot line moves through the two parts from God's initial command to its fulfilment in Abraham's death. Each of the two parts has its own pace and tone, corresponding to its relative place in the development of the plot. Part I is lengthy and rambling, and it has more than its share of humorous touches: the double entendre in Michael's identification of himself (ch. 2); the picture of the disturbed patriarch, afraid to admit that he hears trees talking and sees teardrops turning to pearls (ch. 3); Michael, unable to cope with Abraham's repeated refusals, making repeated trips to the divine throneroom for new orders (chs. 4, 8, 9, 15). When Michael fails in his mission, we move to Part II, where a totally different pace and tone pervade. The divine messenger is "merciless, rotten Death." His identification of himself is quick and to the point. Abraham's continued refusals are met not by repeated trips to the throneroom, but by Death's pursuit of Abraham into the inner chambers of his house, right to his bed. This time Abraham's request for a revelation results in a fierce vision that strikes terror in the patriarch's heart, and he falls into "the faint of death." Again Abraham's family gathers around his bed, not to rejoice over his return, but to mourn over his imminent death. Now there is no command to make his testament, only the sudden, unexpected death about which he had inquired moments before. God's command is finally fulfilled. The plot is resolved.

The message of the book can be deduced from its plot line. The moment of death, and its inevitable consummation, are in the hands of the sovereign God, and there is none who can resist. So the author tells us in his first paragraph.

> Even upon him ("pious, all-holy, righteous, hospitable Abraham" [previous line]) there came the common, inexorable, bitter cup of Death and the uncertain end of life (ch. 1).

In order to make his point, the author has composed a startling portrait of Abraham. Although he ascribes to the patriarch some of the virtues traditionally attributed to him (righteousness, hospitality), the author has glaringly omitted the most celebrated of these, viz., Abraham's obedient faith.[1] Indeed, he has created a veritable parody on the biblical and traditional Abraham. He fears God's summons to "go forth" (cf. T Abr 1 and Gen 12:1), and his haggling with God takes on the character of disobedience.[2] Seven times he refuses to go with God's messenger (chs. 7, 9, 15, 16, 17, 19, 20). The

---

[1] I refer here not to the Pauline interpretation of Abraham's faith, but to his faithfulness which shows itself in his obedience to God's commands, the most celebrated example being the sacrifice of Isaac. For this motif, see Jub 17:15-18:16; 19:1-9; Sir 44:20; 1 Macc 2:52; 4 Mac 16:18-23; 18:2; Heb 11:8-9; 17-19 (in a context [11:1-12:3] where faith always involves obedient action); Jas 2:21-24 (*functionally* the same as the Hebrews passage, although the author separates Abraham's "faith" from his action in consequence of it). On the NT passages (including Paul) see the paper by R.B. Ward, below, pp. 173-84.

[2] Abraham's haggling with God is reminiscent of Gen 18:22-33, which also depicts the patriarch's intercession. In T Abr, however, Abraham's haggling is for his own benefit and specifically involves disobedience of God's command.

first line of the work might lead us to expect a testament. What we get is a parody on the genre -- a non-testament.[3] Abraham refuses to make his testament, for to do so is to concede that he must die.

Recension B Compared with Recension A

Recension B also has a bipartite structure. These two parts begin: "When the days drew near" for Abraham to die, and they end with the deaths of Sarah and Abraham respectively. Moreover, as our columns indicate, there are many similarities between the two parts, although this parallelism both of elements and of wording is not nearly as close or as frequent as it is in Rec. A.[4]

Part I	Part II
1. When the days drew near for Abraham to depart	13. When the days drew near of Abraham's death
	Death did not dare...
Lord said to Michael:	Lord said to Michael:
	Adorn Death in *beauty*
Go to Abraham, say...	Send D. to Abr. so he can see
2. Michael came to Abraham	Michael sends Death to Abraham
meets him *sitting* near oxen	
Abraham	Abr. *sees* D. sitting, frightened

---

[3] I use the term "genre" advisedly, to refer to works that have a deathbed setting, in which the father makes a dispensation to his children. This may be in the form of commands or of blessings and forecasts of the future (see A.B. Kolenkow, below, pp. 141-42). In some testaments, there is also a distribution of property (Jub 20:11; T Job 45-47). In T Abr, the command that Abraham dispose of his property is explicit five times (I:77.13-15; IV:81.26-28; VIII:86.5-8; XV:95.6-9,22-25). Clearly we have the testamentary situation and the command to make a testament. That the author has in mind more than distribution of property is evident in VIII:86.8, "so that you may bless Isaac your beloved son." Chs. I and IV appear also to imply this. God has "*blessed*" Abraham and prospered him. Presumably the passing on of his goods involved the passing on of this blessing. The author writes a story about how Abraham refuses to make his testament. This I take to be a parody on literature which describes the father making his testament, even if its contents do not involve the distribution of property.

[4] I have italicized words or elements which, in Rec. A, appear with a corresponding element in the other Part. Here they occur in only one Part.

	Part I	Part II
	greets Michael	says
	Whence are you?	Who are you?
	Abr.: come closer, stay	Go away
		I was frightened; you are spirit
		D.: There is none like you
	Michael: What is your name	Abr.: Do you dare lie; Whose beauty?
	Abr.: My name, Abram/Abraham	D. hints...finally, I am Death
2-3.	They go *to Abraham's house*	
	Talking tree: no clear hint	
	Abraham and Isaac wash feet	
4.	Michael ascends to heaven	
5.	They eat, *go to bed*	
6-7.	Isaac's dream, interpretation	
	M. reveals identity, mission	
		Discussion of how death comes to various people
	Make testament	
	Let me see *whole* creation	14. Show me your rottenness
8-11.	Sees judgment, M. explains	Death unmasks
12.	Sees world, calls down death	Servants die
	Returns home	
		Abraham intercedes, revived
	Sarah dies	Death takes Abraham's soul
	is buried	Abraham's burial

Although the cast of characters in Rec. B, the action in which they are involved, and the bipartite structuring of that action are roughly parallel to similar features in Rec. A, there are substantive and significant differences between the two recensions in all of these respects.

In Rec. A, Abraham's request for a tour of the heavens is one of a series of procrastinations and refusals to die. In Rec. B, Abraham's continual refusal to die is totally lacking. The request for a heavenly tour has no connotations of any such refusal. In Rec. A, the request is the motivation for a didactic section that parodies the traditional righteous Abraham in the same way that the rest of the book parodies the obedient

Abraham and the testament genre itself. In Rec. B, neither the chariot ride sequence nor any of the rest of the book indicates any such parody. In Rec. A, Abraham's refusal to make his testament is of the essence of the non-testamental character of the book. In Rec. B, Abraham is also told to make his testament (VII: 112:3-5), but his failure to do so is evidently unrelated to the rest of the story.

In Rec. A, Parts I and II are causally and logically related; in Rec. B, they are merely juxtaposed. In Rec. A, Abraham's trip to heaven is granted after he gives his word that he will concede death upon his return. This makes him the more culpable when, upon his return, he once more refuses to go. This refusal, and Michael's failure in his mission, are the cause for the beginning of Part II and the sending of Death, the appearance of whom has been hinted at in the very first lines of the story (I: 77.9-11). Rec. B begins with the statement that Abraham's death is near. God sends Michael with the message. Abraham's request for a tour of the heavens has no clearly delineated function, except, perhaps, to make it possible for him to see that his body cannot fit through the gate. In any event, it is not a delaying tactic, nor does it follow a promise, the breaking of which leads to Part II. Abraham asks to see the creation before he dies. He is granted the vision. He returns home, and--wonder of wonders--the part that began with the announcement of *Abraham's* imminent death ends with the death *of Sarah!* Part II begins as Part I did, "When the days of Abraham's death drew near," but there is no logical connection between the two parts, as there is in Rec. A. Death is dispatched to Abraham not because of any failure on the part of Michael, but because it is Death's responsibility to take human souls (Rec. B IX: 114.4-8).

In Rec. B, although Michael and Death play parallel roles vis-a-vis Abraham, the contrast between the two, developed with such finesse in Rec. A, is totally lacking. Since Abraham does not continually refuse to die, the contrast between Michael's trips to heaven and Death's remaining with Abraham is not evident--although Michael does make two trips to heaven and Death does stay with Abraham. Moreover, Abraham's conversation with Death, with its overtones of hostility and its refusal to accept Death's self-identification, has not been prepared for in

Part I, as it has in Rec. A.

Three final points of contrast between the two recensions are worthy of note. To the first we have already alluded. In Rec. B, Part I ends with Sarah's death. This is strange since the beginning of Part I would lead us to expect Abraham's death. In Rec. A, at the end of Part I, Sarah is mentioned together with Isaac and the servants, all of whom are present at Abraham's bedside to rejoice over his return. The scene is clearly intended as a foil to the end of Part II, where the same dramatis personae are present at his bedside to lament his imminent death. Moreover, their presence at the end of Part I is the proper setting for Michael's demand that Abraham make his testament--which he refuses to do. Sarah's death at the end of Part I in Rec. B is more consonant with the biblical narrative than is Rec. A, where Sarah outlives Abraham.

A second point of contrast between the two recensions involves Abraham's intercession for the dead. In Rec. A, the intercession of Death(!) and Abraham for the dead servants is strange, to say the least. The best explanation for the sequence appears to be that it is intended as an interesting and entertaining (comical) contrast to Part I, where Michael's and Abraham's intercession for the dead is an integral part of the whole chariot ride sequence. In Part II of Rec. B, Abraham, and he alone, intercedes for the dead servants. This act has no counterpart in Part I, nor does the sequence have any motivation or perceptible function in Part II. It just happens.

A final point of contrast involves the soul with equally balanced sins and righteous deeds. In Rec. A, the soul is the focus of the entire judgment scene and chariot ride sequence (see above, pp. 25-27). In Rec. B, if we are to trust the textual evidence of Grk. E and the Slavic version, the soul is mentioned and then no longer alluded to. This is especially odd since Abraham's sight of the soul leads to a request to see the judgment process. We should expect that judgment process to include the weighing of the souls, presumed by the evidence of the soul in question. However, this weighing is not part of the judgment scene in Rec. B, as it is in Rec. A.

The Relationship of the Recensions

This comparison of the two recensions raises some interesting and difficult questions about their relationship. Clearly Rec. A is the more artful of the two compositions. It has shape and plot, and out of these, a discernible point to make. Its parodies on a known genre and on traditional portraits of Abraham are evidence of the author's message. By contrast, Rec. B is a potpourri of incidents, elements, and characters, with little evident structure, plot, and relationships among the characters. It certainly falls short of Rec. A in this respect. One may, of course, argue that the author of Rec. A took the raw materials in Rec. B and gave them new and interesting shape and purpose. However, it is not simply a matter of shaping raw materials. Numerous elements, *which are simply present* in Rec. B, *with no clearly delineated function, are of the essence* of the structure and plot of Rec. A. These elements are not isolated items or characters. They are narrative sequences, implicit or explicit actions, and juxtaposed characters, unintegrated and non-functional in Rec. B, but developed in detail and functional and integral to the structure and plot of Rec. A.

This state of affairs suggests to me that *the structure* of Rec. A is more primitive than that of Rec. B, although the latter may contain some primitive elements and wording which were revised in Rec. A. If Rec. A is the more primitive of the two recensions, one must look for reasons for the revision in Rec. B. This is beyond the scope of the present paper. However, it is not impossible that some of this deviation is the result of a clumsy process of oral transmission, in which the storyteller(s) badly garbled the tradition.

By admitting into the argument the possibility of oral transmission, I also allow for a kind of flexibility which perhaps stands in tension with my judgments regarding the priority of Rec. A in specific cases. However, these judgments do not imply the *literary* priority of Rec. A *as a whole*. Rather, I am suggesting: a) *in the cases discussed*, Rec. A retains a more primitive form of the substance of the tradition; b) taken together, these elements constitute a form of the story that is more primitive than that in Rec. B. It may well be that our present literary remains do not allow us to reconstitute a primitive (oral or literary) form of the story. The *process* of transmission leading to our present texts is also open to question, as R.A. Kraft shows in the contribution that follows.[5]

---

[5] See below, especially pp. 127-29.

SYNTAX CRITICISM OF THE TESTAMENT OF ABRAHAM

R. A. Martin

While it has been most commonly held that the Testament of Abraham was originally written in a Semitic language[1], recently Turner[2] and Delcor[3] have suggested other possibilities.

Turner considers it to be "an excellent example of the 'Jewish' Greek language of the early Christian centuries"[4] but notes that since this 'Jewish' Greek "is usually so drenched in Semitic idioms and forms of syntax, it is extremely difficult to decide whether a book has been translated from Hebrew into Greek or whether it was originally composed in its present language."[5]

Finally he concludes that there are "a few cases of paranomasia and mistranslation which may point in the direction of direct translation from Hebrew in the case of the Testament of Abraham",[6] noting, however, that this is more likely to be true for Rec. B than for Rec. A.[7]

As an explanation for the obvious Semitisms in the Testament Delcor feels the choice is between translation from a Hebrew original or the unconscious influence of the Septuagint on the writer as he composes in Greek.[8] He finally opts for the latter.[9]

An interesting feature of the Testament of Abraham is its existence in two recensions which differ considerably from each other, both as to length and as to the Semitic quality of the Greek texts.[10]

---

1. Cf. e.g. B.J. Bamberger, "Abraham, Testament of" in IDB, Vol. 1, p. 21; also Delcor, Le Testament d' Abraham, SVTP, 2 (Leiden: Brill, 1973), pp. 32f.
2. N. Turner, "The 'Testament of Abraham': Problems in Biblical Greek," NTS I (1955), pp. 219-223.
3. Op. cit., pp. 32,34.
4. Op. cit., p. 220.
5. Ibid., p. 222.
6. Ibid., p. 223.
7. Cf. ibid., pp. 223 and 221f.
8. Op. cit., p. 32.
9. "Nous sommes apparemment en présence d'une situation assez généralement un ourvage composé directement en grec à Alexandrie par un auteur judéo-hellénistique. En di'autres termes, le grec du Testament est, semble-t-il, non celui d'un traducteur mais la langue d'un juif connaisant la Bible grecque et qui parle le grec." Op. cit., p. 34.
10. Cf. e.g., the detailed comparison in Delcor, op. cit., pp. 5-14 and the comments of Turner, op. cit., pp. 219 and 221f.

Turner considers Rec. B. to be "the more primitive" on the basis of its language and its non-use of the LXX.[11] Delcor notes that the recensions are related to different geographical areas[12] and feels neither is dependent on the other, but that both go back to an earlier form.[13]

While Syntax Criticism[14] of the Testament does not offer a final solution to these questions, it does isolate a number of features concerning each of the recensions which 1) indicate that Recension B is clearly more Semitic than A and 2) point in the direction that both recensions are probably ultimately related to an earlier translation of a Semitic original.[15] This appears to be Turner's position ultimately on the matter, also.[16]

Each Recension of the Testament of Abraham as a Whole

The 17 syntactical criteria of translation Greek[17] were calculated for both recensions of the Testament of Abraham.[18]

---

11. Op. cit., p. 221.
12. Recension A is related to the Slavonic and Rumanian versions; Recension B to the Coptic, Arabic and Ethiopic. Op. cit., pp. 13f.
13. Ibid.
14. The term "Syntax Criticism" is used to designate the analysis of a Greek document by means of the 17 syntactical criteria of translation Greek presented initially in R. A. Martin, Syntactical Evidence of Semitic Sources in Greek Documents (SBL Septuagint and Cognate Studies, 3; Missoula: Scholars Press 1974) and briefly summarized and applied to the "additions to Esther" in Martin, "Syntax Criticism of the LXX Additions to the Book of Esther", JBL 94 (1975), pp. 65-72. A brief summary of the methodology is found in Appendix 5 at the end of this paper.
15. One of the main objections to explaining the numerous Semitisms in the Testament of Abraham by positing either a special 'Jewish' Greek dialect (Turner) or unconscious influence of the language of the LXX (Delcor) is that in both cases (since we are dealing with the writers' natural style) one would expect a consistent distribution of the Semitisms throughout the work as a whole.
    The data isolated by Syntax Criticism as presented in the following pages shows that this is not the case in either recension. Mention may be made here of the fact that both of these solutions have been earlier suggested as an explanation for the Semitisms of Luke-Acts, but in both of those documents the distribution of Semitisms is even more spotty and are there best explained by translation of Semitic sources. Cf. Martin, Syntactical Evidence, espec. p. 101 for Acts, and a forth coming study Syntax Criticism of the Synoptics for Luke.
16. Op. cit., pp. 221f.
17. Cf. Appendix 5 for a summary presentation of these 17 criteria.
18. The edition of M.R. James was used, as reprinted in M.E. Stone, The Testament of Abraham: The Greek Recensions (T.&T. 2, Ps. Ser. 2; Missoula: S.B.L., 1972). References follow this edition (I.2.1 = ch. 1, p. 2, line 1 of edition).

The data are listed in Appendices 1-4 at the end of this paper. From those data it will be seen that Recension A taken as a whole consists of 793 lines[19] and has +4 net original Greek frequencies. Recension B, consisting of 360 lines, has -3 net translation Greek frequencies. Reference to Chart I which follows below will show that these net frequencies do not put either recension in the translated or the original Greek ranges of the scale, though Recension B is just a little shy of falling into the translated Greek range.

The above situation suggests that in both recensions some of the smaller units will appear as translation Greek and some will appear as original Greek. That this is in fact the case will appear from the data for smaller units of text which follows.

Subsections of Recensions A and B

The net frequencies of the smaller subsections were calculated for each recension, generally using the editor's divisions, but subdividing the longer ones. The data by chapter and subdivision are found in the charts in Appendices 1-4.

In my study, Syntactical Evidence (pp. 49,51 and 53) ranges were established for units of 31 to 50 lines, 16 to 30 lines and 4 to 15 lines in length in texts of both original and translated Greek.

Recension A and B Units of More Than 50 Lines in Length

Recension A had 3 such units and Recension B only 1. Chart I already referred to indicates that the single unit of Recension B falls into the translated Greek area (-5 net frequencies), whereas none of the Recension A units fall either into the translated or the original Greek areas, but somewhere in between these clearly defined ranges.

Recension A and B Units of 31 to 50 Lines in Length

There were 6 such units in Recension A and only 1 in Recension B. The one unit of Recension B again fell into the translated Greek range (0 net frequencies), as did one unit of Recension A (0 net frequencies)--Cf. Chart II below. The remaining 5 units of Recension A again fell neither in the translated nor original Greek ranges.

Recension A and B Units of 16 to 30 Lines in Length

In Recension A 12 such units occur and 6 in Recension B. As will be seen from Chart III below some of these units in both recensions fall into the area occuppied only by trans-

---

19. These are actual lines, since the length of the lines in Stone's edition are the same as the standard line length used in my original study (Cf. Appendix 1, p. 109f. of that study for details).

Chart I
Net Original Greek or Translation Greek Frequencies Appearing in Units of Text More Than 50 Lines in Length

Name	No. of Lines	Net No. of Frequencies Characteristic of Original Greek												Net No. of Frequencies Characteristic of Translation Greek											
		17	16	15	14	13	12	11	10	9	8	7	6	5	4	3	2	1	0	-1	-2	-3	-4	-5	-6	-7	-8	-9	-10	-11	-12	-13	-14
Genesis 1-4,6,39	382																			X													
1 Samuel 3,4,22	194																										X						
1 Kings 17	58																							X									
2 Kings 13	71																											X					
Dan. - Heb. -- LXX	482																								X								
Dan. - Heb. -- Theod.	460																									X							
Dan. - Aram. -- LXX	595																									X							
Dan. - Aram. -- Theod.	634																																X	
Ezra -- Hebrew	328																																	X
Ezra -- Aramaic	211																									X							
Plutarch-Selections	325	X																															
Polybius -- Bks I,II	192			X																													
Epictetus -- Bks III,IV	138	X																															
Josephus--Selections	215	X																															
Papyri--Selections	630	X																															
Entire Testament of Abraham........ Rec. A	793												X																				
Rec. B	360														X																		
Sub Units....... Rec. A	3											1	1		1																		
Rec. B	1																					1											

Chart II
Net Original Greek or Translation Greek Frequencies Appearing in Each Unit of Text 31 to 50 Lines in Length

Name	No. of Units	Net No. of Frequencies Characteristic of Original Greek																		Net No. of Frequencies Characteristic of Translation Greek											
		17	16	15	14	13	12	11	10	9	8	7	6	5	4	3	2	1	0	-1	-2	-3	-4	-5	-6	-7	-8	-9	-10	-11	-12	-13	-14
Genesis 1-4,6,39	4																			1	1		2										
1 Samuel 3,4,22	--																																
1 Kings 17	--																																
2 Kings 13	--																																
Dan. - Heb. -- LXX	1												1																				
Dan. - Heb. -- Theod.	1																							1									
Dan. - Aram. -- LXX	--																																
Dan. - Aram. -- Theod.	--																																
Ezra -- Hebrew	3																					1		1	1								
Ezra -- Aramaic	2																				1			1									
Plutarch-Selections	4					3	1																										
Polybius-Bks I,II	3						1	1	1																								
Epictetus-Bks III,IV	2				1		1																										
Josephus-Selections	1						1																										
Papyri-Selections	3				1		1		1																								
Testament of Abraham............ Rec. A	6									1	1	2		1		1																	
Rec. B	1											1																					

Chart III
Net Original Greek or Translation Greek Frequencies in Each Unit of Text 16 to 30 Lines in Length

Name	No. of Units	Net No. of Frequencies Characteristic of Original Greek																		Net No. of Frequencies Characteristic of Translation Greek											
		17	16	15	14	13	12	11	10	9	8	7	6	5	4	3	2	1	0	-1	-2	-3	-4	-5	-6	-7	-8	-9	-10	-11	-12	-13	-14
Genesis 1-4,6,39	5													1						2	1		1										
1 Samuel 3,4,22	4																			1	1	2											
1 Kings 17	--																																
2 Kings 13	1																			1													
Dan. - Heb. -- LXX	6															1				2	2	1											
Dan. - Heb. -- Theod.	4																			2			2										
Dan. - Aram. -- LXX	10									1	1	2								3	1		1		1								
Dan. - Aram. -- Theod.	13											1								1	2	1	3	2		1	1	1					
Ezra -- Hebrew	10																				1	1	1	5		2							
Ezra -- Aramaic	7																			1	1	1	2	2									
Plutarch-Selections	7					1	1		1	1			2		1																		
Polybius--Bks I,II	5							1	2	1	1																						
Epictetus--Bks III,IV	5							1		1	1	1	1																				
Josephus--Selections	5								1		3	1																					
Papyri-Selections	12							2	2	3	3	1				1																	
Testament of Abraham........... Rec. A	12												3		2	2	1	2	2														
Rec. B	6													1			2	1		1		1			1								

Chart IV
Net Original or Translation Greek Frequencies in Each Unit of Text 4 to 15 Lines in Length

Name	No. of Units	17	16	15	14	13	12	11	10	9	8	7	6	5	4	3	2	1	0	-1	-2	-3	-4	-5	-7	-8	-9	-10	-11	-12	-13	-14
Genesis 1-4,6,39	13															2	3	2	3			3										
1 Samuel 3,4,22	12																1	1	5		1	2	2									
1 Kings 17	5																1	1	1		1											
2 Kings 13	5																	1		1	1	1	1									
Dan. - Heb. -- LXX	35									1						1	3	2	5	7	8	4	3	1								
Dan. - Heb. -- Theod.	37																2	3	3	2	7	8	10	2								
Dan. - Aram. -- LXX	38											1	1		3	4	3	4	6	3	6	4	2		1							
Dan. - Aram. -- Theod.	36														2	5	1	4	6	3	6	5	3	1								
Ezra -- Hebrew	15															1		2	3	2	2	2	2	1								
Ezra -- Aramaic	6														2					1	2	1										
Plutarch-Selections	49							1	5	3	6	12	8	4	6	2	2															
Polybius--Bks I,II	12								1	3	2	1	2	3																		
Epictetus--Bks III,IV	2								1						1																	
Josephus - Selections	22									1	2	3	3	6	6	1																
Papyri-Selections	75			2	1	2	5	7	16	9	13	12	2	2	3	1																
Testament of Abraham Rec. A	113									1	2	1	9	11	17	26	15	16	8	2	3	1	1									
Rec. B	58											2	1	2	9	6	11	10	6	6	1	3	1									

99

ted Greek. Some (of both recensions) fall into the area shared by both original and translated Greek (net frequencies +2 to +4), similar, for example, to the LXX of the Aramaic sections of Daniel.

However, three Recension A units and one Recension B unit fell into the range only occupied by original Greek documents (having +6 net frequencies). These units are: Recension A: Chap. XI. 24.27-26.17a, 26.17b-28.13 and Chap. XV. 38.19b-40.15; Recension B: Chap. VII. 70.3-28b. Possible explanations for this phenomenon will be discussed below.

Recension A and B Units of 4 to 15 Lines in Length

Recension A had 113 such units and Recension B had 58. A study of Chart IV above indicates that some such units in both recensions fell into the translated area (-1 to -4 net frequencies) some also fell into the area shared both by original and translated Greek (0 to +7 net frequencies), again quite similar to the distribution of such units in the LXX translation of the Aramaic part of Daniel.

Only 3 units, all in Recension A, fell into the area occupied only by original Greek units. These units are: Chap. XVIII. 48.22b-28a and Chap. XIX. 50.17b-22a and 50.22b-29a.

As a result of studies on the Synoptic Gospels currently in progress[20], it appears likely that the producer of Recension A (and possibly also the producer of Recension B) is editing a Greek text which was earlier translated from a Semitic language. There may also be some additions to the text which do not go back to a Semitic original.[21]

---

20. The projected study *Syntax Criticism of the Synoptics* mentioned in note 15 above.

21. Cf. Bamberger, *loc. cit.* and perhaps also Turner, *op. cit.*, p. 221.

Chart V
Summary Comparison of Recensions A and B

TITLE	REC.	LOCATION	NO. OF LINES	NET FREQ.	CLEARLY ORIG.	AREA OF AMBIGUITY PROB. ORIG.	PROB. TRANS.	CLEARLY TRANS.	CHART
Michael to Announce Abraham's Death	A	I.2.1-4.10	25	+3		Rec A			III
	B	I.58.1-6	5	+4			Rec B		IV
Michael Meets Abraham in the Field	A	II.4.11-6.15	37	+6		Rec A			II
	B	II.58.7-62.4	33	0				Rec B	II
To House; Meet Isaac	A	III.6.16-8.14	33	+4			Rec A		II
	B	III.62.5-64.8	25	-5				Rec B	II
Isaac Prepares House	A	IV.8.15-28a	13	+3		Rec A			III
	B								IV
Sarah Questions Abraham	A								
	B	IV.64.9-15a	6	-1				Rec B	IV
Michael Dines, Ascends	A	IV.8.28b-10.29	37	+2			Rec A		II
	B	IV.64.15b-66.13	25	+3			Rec B		III
Michael Returns, Isaac Retires	A	V.10.30-12.9a	14	+5		Rec A			III
	B	V.66.14-26	12	-3				Rec B	IV
Isaac Dreams	A	V.12.9b-14.2	25	+1			Rec A		III
	B	VI.66.27-68.11a	15	+1			Rec B		IV
Sarah Recognizes the Angel	A	VI.14.3-29	26	0			Rec A		III
	B	VI.68.11b-70.2	16	-2				Rec B	III
Isaac Relates His Dream	A	VII.14.30-16.18a	23	0			Rec A		III
	B	VII.70.3-28b	26	+6	Rec B				III
Michael Interprets the Dream	A	VII.16.18b-25	8	+1			Rec A		IV
	B	VII.70.28c-72.5	6	+4			Rec B		IV
Michael Identifies Self and Abraham Refuses	A	VII.16.26-18.5	9	0			Rec A		IV
	B								
Michael Ascends and Is Commissioned	A	VIII.18.6-20.13	39	+4			Rec A		II
	B								
Michael Returns & Abraham Requests Vision	A	IX.20.14-22.6a	23	+4		Rec A			III
	B	VII.72.6-12	7	+2			Rec B		IV
Michael Ascends, Returns	A	IX.22.6b-15	9	+3			Rec A		IV
	B	VIII.72.13-17b	5	0				Rec B	IV
Abraham Sees Sinners and Condemns Them	A	X.22.16-24.15a	30	+1			Rec A		III
	B	XII.80.11-28b	17	+2				Rec B	III

TITLE	REC.	LOCATION	NO. OF LINES	NET FREQ.	CLEARLY ORIG.	AREA OF AMBIGUITY PROB. ORIG.	PROB. TRANS.	CLEARLY TRANS.	CHART
God's Reaction	A	X.24.15b-26	11	0			Rec A		IV
	B	XII.80.28c-82.15	6	0				Rec B	IV
Two Ways - Adam	A	XI.24.27-26.17a	21	+6	Rec A				III
	B	VIII.72.17c-24	7	0				Rec B	IV
Abraham's Inquiry; Michael's Interpretation	A	XI.26.17b-28.13	22	+6	Rec A				III
	B	VIII.72.25-74.13	19	+3			Rec B		III
Abraham's Fears re Narrow Gate	A								
	B	IX.74.14-22a	9	+7	Rec B				IV
Souls Driven	A	XII.28.14-19a	6	+5		Rec A			IV
	B	IX.74.22b-27	5	+2			Rec B		IV
The Judgment	A	XII.28.19b-34.25a	82	+3		Rec A			III
	B	IX-XI.74.28-80.10	60	-5				Rec B	I
Abraham's Intercession and Consequences	A	XIV.34.25b-38.3	35	+3		Rec A			II
	B								
Abraham's Return	A	XV.38.4-19a	16	+2			Rec A		III
	B	XII.82.1a-6	5	+5		Rec B			IV
Abraham's Refusal to Die	A	XV.38.19b-40.15	26	+6	Rec A				III
God Sends Death in Disguise	A	XVI.40.16-42.12a	22	+4		Rec A			III
	B	XIII.82.7-16a	9	-4				Rec B	IV
Death Appears; Abraham Greets Him	A	XVI.42.12b-26	14	+5		Rec A			IV
	B	XIII.82.16b-28b	12	+2			Rec B		IV
Death Speaks; Abraham Responds	A								
	B	XIII.82.28c-84.4b	6	-1				Rec B	IV

TITLE	REC	LOCATION	NO. OF LINES	NET FREQ.	CLEARLY ORIG.	AREA OF AMBIGUITY PROB. ORIG.	PROB. TRANS	CLEARLY TRANS	CHART
Death Reveals Self; Abraham Refuses	A	XVI-XVII.42.27-46.5a	34	0			Rec A		II
	B	XIII.84.4c-16	12	+1			Rec B		IV
Death Reveals Its Ugliness	A	XVII-XVIII.46.5b-48.32	56	+6		Rec A			I
	B	XIV.84.17-25a	8	+4			Rec B		IV
Further Delays	A	XIX-XX.48.33-54.14a	75	+7		Rec A			I
	B								
Abraham's Death; Michael Takes His Soul	A	XX.54.14b-56.5a	22	+3			Rec A		III
	B	XIV.84.25b-86.2	4	+3			Rec B		IV

Another possibility might be that Recension B is a translation of a Semitic text and Recension A a reworking of the Greek text of Recension B. To decide that matter would require a more detailed comparison of the texts than is possible at this time.

Summary Comparison of Recensions A and B

In Chart V above a comparison of the net frequencies in parallel subdivisions of Recensions A and B is given.[22]

It will be noted from that chart that while in most cases where Recensions A and B have parallel material B is more Semitic than A by the 17 criteria of Syntax Criticism, in 7 instances it is less Semitic than A (Michael Dines; Isaac Dreams; Isaac Relates His Dream; Michael Interprets the Dream; Abraham Sees Sinners; Abraham's Return; Death Reveals Self). In all but one of these cases (Isaac Relates His Dream) Rec. A is considerably longer than Rec. B, and usually the content differs considerably as well. This may indicate a Semitic source behind the additional material found in Recension A, though again this would require more detailed investigation than can be undertaken at this juncture.

It would appear that one or other of the diagrams below most nearly approximates the history of the text of the Testament of Abraham.

---

22. I am here following the subdivisions suggested by Dr. G.W. Nickelsburg.

A. <u>Direct Dependence of Recension A on Recension B</u>

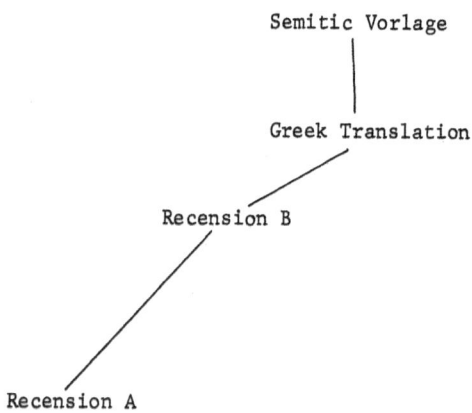

B. <u>No Direct Dependence of Recensions A and B</u>

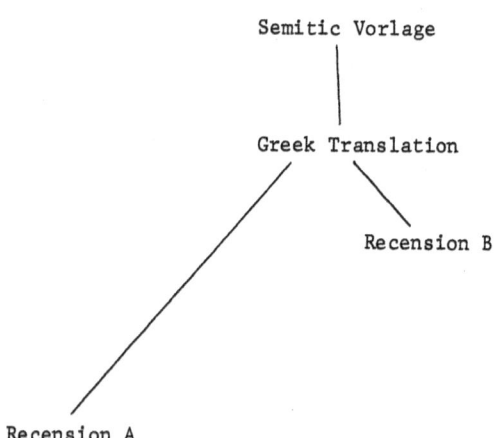

Appendix 1
Frequencies of the 17 Criteria in Testament of Abraham - Recension A

Translation Frequencies	No. of lines of Greek text	No. of occur. of all	dia	kata	W. accus	eti	W. all cases	Para w. all cases	Prep. w. dative	Megas w. genitive	No. of occur. of hoi for each occur. of tēs	Percent. of super. articles	No. of dep. gen. prep. prec.	No. of dep. gen. prec. gov.	Linea/sa gen. dep. prec. gov.	No. of prec. attr. adj. for each attr. adj. post position	No. of linea/sa. prec. adjs.	No. of linea/sa adverbs participle	No. of lines of travel for each occur. of ex.	Tot. no. of travel Grk. frequencies	Tot. no. of orig. Grk. frequencies	No. of instances where occur. of criteria are less than to be indic.	Net original Grk. frequencies	Net translation Grk. frequencies
			.06+ .01	.18- .01	.49- .01	.18- .01	.19- .01	.27- .01	.024 .01	.07- .01	2.1+	.05-	22+	9-	77-	.35-	10.1+	6+	2-	17	-	-	17	
Entire Rec A	793	95	.17	.29	.56	.02	.06	.12	-	.12	1.8	.15	9.6	4.0	33.0	.93	3.0	4.5	1.4	6	10	1	+4	
I.																								
2.1-9a	8	2	-	-	-	-	-	-	-	-	-	.00	.10	7	2.7	-	4.0	2.0	4.0	1.0	3	6	8	+3
2.9b-15a	6	-	-	-	-	-	-	-	-	2	-	1.0	.25	1.0	3.0	-	4.0	1.5	6.0	-	2	6	9	+4
2.15b-4.5a	5	2	-	-	-	-	-	-	-	-	-	2.0	-	5	5.0	-	-	5	5	.00	3	4	10	+1
4.5b-10	6	2	-	-	-	-	-	-	.50	-	-	2.0	.43	1.0	6.0	-	2.0	3.0	6	.50	3	6	8	+3
2.1-4.10	25	6	-	-	-	-	-	.50	-	-	-	1.3	.19	5.0	3.6	-	10.0	2.5	8.3	.50	3	6	8	+3
II.																								
4.11-15	5	-	-	-	-	-	-	-	-	-	-	1.0	.11	3	-	-	-	2.5	2.5	-	-	5	12	+5
4.16-23a	7	-	-	-	-	-	-	-	-	-	-	.50	.13	3	-	-	.67	1.4	1.4	-	-	6	11	+6
4.23b-29b	6	-	-	-	-	-	-	-	-	-	-	1	.38	3	6.0	-	.50	2.0	6	-	2	5	10	+3
4.29c-6.1b	5	-	-	-	-	-	-	-	-	-	-	1.0	.50	4	1.7	2.5	3.0	1.0	5	-	2	6	9	+4
6.1c-7a	6	1	-	-	1.0	-	-	-	-	-	-	1.0	-	4	6.0	-	.00	2.0	6.0	.00	4	4	9	0
6.7b-15	8	1	-	-	-	-	-	-	-	-	-	-	.20	2	4.0	8.0	.33	2.0	2.7	2.0	5	4	8	-1
4.11-6.15	37	2	-	-	.50	-	-	-	-	-	-	1.0	.20	19	5.4	12.3	.50	1.8	3.4	2.5	2	8	7	+6
III.																								
6.16-22b	7	-	-	-	-	1	2	-	-	-	-	.50	-	3	7.0	-	1.0	3.5	3.5	-	1	7	9	+6
6.22c-27b	5	1	-	-	-	-	-	-	-	-	-	1.0	-	5	1.7	5.0	-	5	2.5	.00	4	4	9	0
6.27c-33b	6	-	-	-	-	-	-	-	-	-	-	b	.10	8	1.3	-	1.0	6.0	6	-	3	5	9	+2
6.33c-8.3b	4	-	-	-	-	-	-	-	-	-	-	.00	-	1.0	4.0	-	1.0	2.0	4.0	-	1	5	11	+4
8.3c-7	4	-	-	-	-	1	-	-	-	-	-	.67	-	2	-	-	-	4	2.0	-	-	5	12	+5
III. 8.8-14	7	1	-	-	1.0	-	-	-	-	-	-	1.0	-	3.5	-	-	7.0	1.0	.00	2	5	10	+3
6.16-8.14	33	2	-	-	1.0	.50	1.0	-	-	-	-	1.2	.02	23.0	2.8	33.0	1.0	5.5	2.4	4.0	4	8	5	+4
IV.																								
8.15-22a	7	1	-	-	1.0	-	-	-	-	-	-	.67	-	5	3.5	7.0	-	7.0	7	3.0	3	5	9	+2
8.22b-28a	6	-	-	-	-	-	-	-	-	-	-	-	-	3	3.0	-	1.0	1.5	6.0	-	2	3	12	+1
8.15-28a	13	1	-	-	1.0	-	-	-	-	-	-	1.0	-	8	3.3	13.0	.67	2.6	13.0	4.0	3	6	8	+3
8.28b-35b	7	3	-	-	.33	-	-	-	-	-	-	1.3	.13	3	-	-	1.0	3.5	3.5	.33	2	6	9	+4
8.35c-10.6b	6	-	-	-	-	-	-	-	-	-	-	-	.29	2	-	-	.60	.75	6	-	1	4	12	+3
10.6c-14b	8	1	-	-	1.0	-	-	-	-	-	-	1.0	.08	9	1.3	-	-	8.0	8	.00	3	5	9	+2
10.14c-20b	6	2	-	-	-	-	-	-	-	-	-	3.0	.33	1	-	-	-	.50	2.0	6.0	.50	4	4	9	0
10.2c-29	10	1	1.0	1.0	-	-	-	2.0	-	-	-	3.0	.21	3.0	3.3	-	1.0	5.0	10.0	1.0	4	7	6	+3
8.28b-10.29	37	7	.14	.14	.29	-	-	.29	-	-	-	1.7	.18	10.5	4.1	-	.77	2.3	9.3	.43	5	7	5	+2
V.																								
10.30-12.1a	5	1	-	-	2.0	1.0	1.0	-	-	-	-	1.5	.13	2	5.0	-	-	5.0	5	1.0	2	8	7	+6
12.1b-9a	9	4	-	-	-	-	-	-	-	-	-	1.0	.25	2	2.3	-	3.0	3.0	4.5	.25	3	6	8	+3
10.30-12.9a	14	5	-	-	.40	.20	.20	-	-	-	-	1.3	.20	9	2.8	-	3.0	4.7	4.7	.40	3	8	6	+5
12.9b-18a	8	2	-	-	.50	-	-	.50	-	-	-	2.0	-	6	2.7	-	8	2.7	.50	2	6	9	+4
12.18b-25a	8	1	-	-	-	-	-	-	-	-	-	1.0	-	3	2.6	-	8.0	1.0	3.0	-	2	5	10	+3
12.25b-14.2	9	-	-	1	-	-	-	1	-	-	-	3.0	-	4	2.3	4.5	-	9.0	3.0	-	4	3	8	-1
12.9b-14.2	25	3	-	.33	.33	-	-	.67	-	-	-	1.6	.00	13	2.5	12.5	-	25.0	1.8	2.7	5	6	6	+1
VI.																								
14.3-8a	5	-	-	-	-	-	-	-	-	-	-	.50	-	4	5.0	5.0	-	5	5.0	-	2	4	11	+2
14.8b-17a	9	2	-	-	-	-	-	-	-	-	-	.50	.14	5	2.3	4.5	.33	2.3	9.0	2.0	2	6	4	7	-2
14.17b-24	8	3	-	-	-	-	-	-	-	-	-	2.0	.18	5	2.0	-	-	8.0	4.0	.67	3	5	9	+2
14.25-29	4	1	-	-	-	-	-	-	-	-	-	1.0	-	2	4.0	4.0	-	4	4.0	2.0	4	4	9	0
14.3-29	26	6	-	-	-	-	-	-	-	-	-	.83	.11	.16	2.6	6.5	5.2	5.2	.83	5	5	7	0	
VII.																								
14.30-33	4	1	-	-	-	-	-	-	-	-	-	2.0	-	1	4.0	4.0	-	4.0	4.0	1.0	4	4	9	0
14.34-16.5a	6	-	-	-	-	-	-	-	-	-	-	2.0	-	3	2.0	6.0	-	6.0	.75	-	2	4	11	+2
16.5b-11a	5	-	-	-	-	-	-	-	-	-	-	4.0	-	2	3.0	-	-	6.0	1.5	-	2	4	11	+2
16.11b-18a	7	-	-	-	-	1	-	-	-	-	-	1.7	.29	2	3.5	7.0	-	7.0	7	-	3	4	10	+1
14.30-16.18a	23	1	-	-	-	1.0	-	-	-	-	-	2.5	.07	8	2.9	7.7	.00	5.8	1.8	2.0	5	5	7	0
16.18b-25	8	1	-	-	-	-	-	-	-	-	-	1.0	.29	3.0	2.7	-	4.0	1.6	8.0	.00	4	5	8	+1
16.26-18.5	9	-	-	-	-	-	-	-	-	-	-	4.0	.10	4.0	4.5	-	-	9.0	9	-	3	3	11	0
VIII.																								
18.6-13a	7	-	-	-	-	2	-	-	-	-	-	1.0	.18	2	7.0	-	.50	2.3	3.5	-	1	7	9	+6
18.13b-23a	10	2	-	-	-	-	-	-	-	-	-	1.0	-	9	2.5	-	-	10.0	5.0	.50	3	4	10	+1
18.23b-20.4a	12	2	-	-	-	-	-	-	-	-	-	2.0	.27	1	12.0	-	-	12.0	12	3.5	3	5	9	+2
20.4b-13	10	-	-	-	-	-	-	2	-	-	-	3	.20	3.0	3.3	-	.50	3.3	10.0	3	3	6	8	+3
18.6-20.13	39	4	-	.50	-	-	-	.50	-	-	-	2.0	.15	15	3.0	4.3	-	.33	4.9	7.8	2.5	3	7	7	-4
IX.																								
20.14-18a	4	-	-	-	-	1	-	-	-	-	-	.50	.11	2	-	-	4	2.0	-	-	6	11	+6
20.18b-25	8	-	-	-	-	-	-	-	-	-	-	-	.38	4	4.0	-	4.0	2.0	4.0	-	1	5	11	+4
20.26-22.6a	11	2	.50	.50	-	-	-	-	-	-	-	4	.25	5.5	11.0	2.0	5.5	11.0	1.0	5	6	4	+1	
20.14-22.6a	23	2	.50	.50	.50	-	-	-	-	-	-	3.0	.24	9.0	5.7	23.0	6.0	3.8	4.6	2.0	4	8	5	+4
22.6b-15	9	1	-	-	1.0	-	-	-	-	-	-	5.0	.13	4	4.5	-	1.0	4.5	3.0	1.0	3	6	8	+3
X.																								
22.16-20a	5	-	-	-	1	-	-	-	-	-	-	3	-	-	-	-	5.0	5.0	-	1	4	12	+3
22.20b-28a	6	2	-	-	-	-	-	-	-	-	-	.33	.33	-	-	-	2.0	4.0	6.0	.00	2	5	10	+3
22.28b-24.7a	9	1	-	-	-	-	-	-	-	-	-	5.0	-	3	3.0	-	3.0	9.0	1.0	6	2	9	-	-4
24.7b-15a	8	1	-	-	-	-	-	3	-	-	-	-	-	8	-	-	1.0	8.0	4.0	-	2	5	10	+3
22.16-24.15a	30	5	-	-	.80	-	-	-	-	-	-	4.3	.04	5	7.5	-	.75	4.3	1.9	.40	4	5	8	+1
24.15b-21a	6	1	-	-	-	-	-	-	-	-	-	3	.11	-	-	-	-	6	6.0	.00	4	2	11	-2
24.21b-26	5	1	-	-	-	-	-	-	-	-	-	.33	.11	3	-	-	-	-	5	.00	2	5	10	+3
24.15b-26	11	2	-	-	-	-	-	-	-	-	-	1.3	.11	3	11	-	-	11	11.0	.00	4	4	9	0

Frequencies of the 17 Criteria in Testament of Abraham - Recension A

	No. of times of Greek text	No. of occur. of all	No. of occur. of prepositions/ea. occur. of ἐν — dia (W.gen / W.all / dis)			kata (W.accus / W.all / Dat w.all cases)			Prep w.dative	Hapax w.genitive	No. of occ. of kai for each occ. of de	Percent of repeat articles	Dependent genitives (No. of obj.gen. dep.gen / No. of direct obj. prep. / No. of prep.w.gen.pro.dep.gen)			No. of gen.w. adj.adjec.	No. of times kai adverb.participle	No. of times w.att.for attrib.adjec.	No. of dat.not used w.eis for loc.to the indic.	Tot. no. of transl. Grk. frequencies	No. occ. of crit.where occ.of crit. use too low to be in indic.	Not original Grk. frequencies	Not transl.Grk. frequencies
Translation Frequencies			.06-.01	.18-.01	.49-.01	.18-.01	.19-.01	.27-.01	.024-.01	.07-.01	2.1+	.05-	22+	9-	77-	.35-	10.1+	6+	2-	17	--	--	17
XI.																							
24.27-26.8a	12	1	2.0	2.0	-	-	2.0	-	-	2.0	4.0	.30	2	-	-	5.0	2.0	12	.00	3	8	6	+5
26.8b-17a	9	1	3.0	3.0	-	-	-	-	-	-	4.0	.27	5	3.0	-	3.6	2.3	1.3	.00	3	7	7	+4
24.27-26.17a	21	2	2.5	2.5	-	-	1.0	-	-	1.0	4.0	.28	7	7.0	-	4.0	2.1	3.0	.00	3	9	5	+6
26.17b-23a	6	2	-	-	-	-	-	-	-	-	.67	.22	1	6.0	6.0	2.0	2.0	6	.00	5	5	7	0
26.23b-28.3a	6	1	2.0	3.0	2.0	-	-	-	-	-	2	.27	2	6.0	-	1.0	3.0	2.0	.00	2	9	6	+7
28.3b-13	10	-	1	2	3	-	-	-	-	-	3.0	.12	4	5.0	-	.25	2.0	2.0	-	3	7	7	+4
26.17b-28.13	22	3	1.0	1.7	1.7	-	-	-	-	-	1.8	.19	7	5.5	22.0	.67	2.2	2.8	.33	3	9	5	+6
XII.																							
28.14-19a	6	1	-	-	1.0	-	-	-	-	-	3.0	.14	-	-	-	1.0	1.5	2.0	3.0	1	6	10	+5
XII, XIII, XIV																							
28.19b-30.9a	14	4	.25	.25	-	-	-	-	-	-	.50	.18	7	2.3	14.0	.00	1.4	3.5	.75	4	7	6	+3
30.9b-15a	7	-	-	-	-	-	-	-	-	-	1.5	.40	1	-	-	1.0	3.5	7	-	1	5	11	+4
30.15b-26	11	1	-	-	1.0	-	-	-	-	-	9	.00	2.0	11.0	-	1.0	11.0	11.0	2.0	6	3	8	-3
30.27-32.10a	11	-	-	-	-	-	-	-	-	-	5.0	.14	2	11.0	11.0	.25	2.2	11.0	-	5	3	9	-2
32.10b-16a	6	-	-	1	-	-	-	-	-	-	2	.25	1.0	6.0	-	2.0	1.0	6	-	2	6	9	+4
32.16b-24a	8	1	1.0	2.0	1.0	-	-	-	-	2.0	5.0	.23	3.0	-	-	8	8.0	.00	3	7	7	+4	
32.24b-34.7a	7	2	-	-	-	-	-	-	-	-	.33	.32	2	7.0	-	2.0	3.5	7	.00	4	5	8	+1
34.7b-13a	6	1	1.0	1.0	1.0	-	-	-	-	-	3.0	.19	1.5	6.0	-	3.0	2.0	6	.00	4	7	6	+3
34.13b-18	5	3	-	-	.33	-	-	-	-	-	3.0	.13	1.0	-	-	1.0	5.0	5	.33	3	5	9	+2
34.19-25a	7	1	-	-	3.0	-	-	-	-	-	.50	-	4	2.3	7.0	1.0	7.0	7	.00	4	5	8	+1
28.19b-34.25a	82	13	.24	.38	.54	-	-	-	-	.15	2.1	.19	4.3	5.9	27.3	.82	2.6	13.7	.46	5	8	4	+3
XIV.																							
34.25-36.3a	6	-	-	-	2	-	-	-	-	-	1.5	-	-	-	-	6	6	-	-	1	3	13	+2
36.3b-10a	8	1	1.0	1.0	1.0	-	-	-	-	-	8	-	1	8.0	-	-	4.0	4.0	.00	3	6	8	+3
36.10b-23a	12	-	-	1	-	-	-	-	-	-	2.0	.10	7.0	3.0	-	.50	4.0	12.0	3	2	7	8	+5
36.23b-38.3	3	-	1.0	2.0	-	-	-	-	-	-	3.0	-	2	4.5	-	1.0	9.0	3.0	1.0	3	6	8	+3
34.25b-38.3	35	2	.50	1.5	2.5	-	-	-	-	-	3.3	.04	10.0	5.0	-	.30	5.8	5.8	2.5	3	8	6	+5
XV.																							
38.4-9a	6	-	-	-	1	-	-	-	-	-	2.0	.11	6	1.5	-	6.0	6	-	-	2	6	9	+4
38.9b-19a	10	1	-	-	1.0	-	-	-	-	-	1.5	-	10	1.1	10.0	-	10	2.5	3.0	2	6	9	+4
38.4-19a	16	1	-	-	2.0	-	-	-	-	-	1.6	.04	16	1.2	16.0	1.0	16.0	4.0	3.0	4	6	7	+2
38.19b-28	9	1	-	-	-	-	-	-	-	-	.25	.18	2.0	4.5	-	2	4.5	9	2.0	4	5	8	+1
38.29-40.7a	9	-	1	1	1	-	-	-	-	-	5.0	.10	5	2.3	-	-	4.5	9.0	3	3	7	7	+4
40.7b-15	8	-	-	1	-	-	-	-	-	-	4.0	.22	2	4.0	8.0	2.0	2.7	8	-	4	5	8	+1
38.19b-40.15	26	1	1.0	2.0	1.0	-	-	-	-	-	1.7	.17	9.0	3.3	26.0	1.3	3.7	26.0	6.0	3	9	5	+6
XVI.																							
40.16-20a	4	-	-	-	-	-	-	-	-	-	1	.22	1	-	-	3	1.3	4.0	-	-	6	11	+6
40.20b-42.7a	12	-	-	-	1	-	-	-	-	-	7.0	.20	2.0	2.4	12.0	4.0	2.4	1.7	-	3	6	8	+3
42.7b-12a	6	-	-	-	-	-	-	-	-	-	4	-	3.0	6.0	-	-	3.0	2.0	-	2	3	12	+1
40.16-42.12a	22	-	-	-	1	-	-	-	-	-	12.0	.17	2.5	3.7	22.0	2.3	2.2	2.0	-	3	7	7	+4
42.12b-19a	6	1	-	-	-	-	-	-	-	-	1.0	.11	4.0	3.0	-	1.0	3.0	2.0	2.0	3	6	8	+3
42.19b-26	8	-	-	-	-	-	-	-	-	-	4.0	.25	2.0	-	-	1.0	1.0	2.0	3	1	6	10	+5
42.12b-26	14	1	-	-	-	-	-	-	-	-	2.0	.18	3.0	7.0	-	1.0	1.4	2.0	5.0	2	7	8	+5
XVI. - XVII.																							
42.27-44.5a	7	-	-	-	-	-	-	-	-	-	2	.17	1.5	-	-	2.0	2.3	7	-	1	5	11	+4
44.5b-11	6	1	-	1.0	1.0	-	-	-	-	-	.00	.33	-	-	-	2	3.0	6.0	1.0	2	6	9	+4
44.12-19	8	1	-	-	2.0	-	-	-	-	-	.29	-	6	1.3	-	-	8	8	.00	3	4	10	+1
44.20-25a	6	1	-	-	-	-	1.0	-	-	-	.00	.11	-	-	-	3.0	6	4.0	1	5	11	+4
44.25b-46.5a	7	3	-	-	-	-	-	-	-	-	2.0	.40	7	1.4	7.0	3	2.3	7	2.3	4	6	7	+2
42.27-46.5a	34	6	-	.17	.50	-	.17	-	-	-	.46	.19	8.0	3.1	34.0	2.3	3.4	34.0	2.0	6	6	5	0
XVII.-XVIII.																							
46.5b-11	7	-	-	-	-	-	-	-	-	-	1.0	.09	4.0	3.5	-	1.0	5	7	-	2	5	10	+3
46.12-16a	5	-	-	-	-	-	-	-	-	-	2	.20	.00	-	-	.67	1.0	5	-	-	6	11	+6
46.16b-28a	11	-	-	-	-	-	-	-	-	-	.50	-	12	-	-	.00	.73	11	-	2	3	12	+1
46.28b-48.5	6	-	-	-	1	-	-	-	-	-	3	.33	3	6.0	-	.50	2.0	6	-	3	5	9	+2
48.6-11a	6	-	-	-	-	-	-	-	-	-	3.0	.11	2.0	3.0	-	2	3.0	6.0	-	3	4	10	+1
48.11b-16a	5	-	-	1	-	-	-	-	-	-	1.0	-	2	2.5	5.0	-	3.0	5	-	2	5	10	+3
48.16b-22a	6	1	-	-	-	-	-	-	-	-	5.0	.13	1	-	-	1.0	3.0	6	.00	3	5	9	+2
48.22b-28a	5	-	1	1	1	-	-	-	-	-	2	.17	3	1.7	-	3	1.7	5	-	1	9	7	+8
48.28b-32	5	-	-	-	-	-	-	-	-	-	2	.13	2	-	-	5.0	2.5	-	-	6	11	+6	
46.5b-48.32	56	1	1.0	2.0	2.0	-	-	-	-	-	1.7	.18	9.7	5.6	56.0	.48	1.6	18.7	5.0	3	9	5	+6
XIX - XX.																							
48.33-50.4a	5	2	-	-	-	-	-	-	-	-	1.0	-	3	1.7	-	-	5	2.5	.00	3	4	10	+4
50.4b-9a	5	-	-	-	-	-	-	-	-	-	2	-	-	-	-	2	2.5	5.0	3	-	5	12	+5
50.9b-17a	8	-	-	-	-	2	-	-	-	-	-	.33	2.0	-	-	.25	1.6	8	-	2	4	11	+2
50.17b-22a	5	-	-	1	-	-	-	-	-	-	2	.40	2	-	-	1	5.0	5	-	-	8	9	+8
50.22b-29a	6	-	1	1	1	-	-	-	-	1	.00	.29	7	-	-	2	3.0	3.0	-	-	9	8	+9
50.29b-52.3a	7	2	-	-	-	-	-	-	-	1.5	.00	.43	3	-	-	2	3.5	3.5	1.0	1	7	9	+6
52.3b-11a	8	3	-	-	-	-	-	-	-	-	.00	.38	4	-	-	3	1.6	1.6	1.0	3	5	8	+5
52.11b-21	10	-	-	-	-	-	-	-	3	-	.30	-	5.0	2.0	-	.00	3.3	5.0	3	1	6	10	+5
52.22-54.2a	10	1	-	-	1.0	-	-	-	-	3	.50	-	3	-	-	2	5.0	10.0	5.0	1	6	10	+5
54.2b-9a	7	2	-	-	-	-	-	-	-	-	3.0	1.4	-	-	2	5.0	10.0	5.0	10	1	6	10	+3
54.9b-14a	4	-	-	-	-	-	-	-	-	-	1.0	-	7	-	-	7	7	1.5	4	3	10	-	-1
48.33-54.14a	75	10	.10	.20	.40	-	-	.20	-	.70	1.0	.20	9.8	5.0	-	.64	3.3	4.2	2.4	3	10	4	+7
XX.																							
54.14b-28a	15	5	-	-	.60	-	-	-	-	-	10.0	.18	7.5	2.5	-	1.3	2.1	15.0	.80	4	5	8	+1
54.28b-56.5a	7	1	-	-	1.0	-	-	-	-	-	1.0	.18	7	1.8	-	1.0	5.5	2.3	.00	2	7	8	+6
54.14b-56.5a	22	6	-	-	.67	-	-	-	-	-	5.5	.16	11.0	2.2	-	1.3	2.4	4.5	.67	3	6	8	+3

Appendix 2
Frequencies of the 17 Criteria in Testament of Abraham - Recension B

Translation Frequencies	No. of lines of Greek text	No. of occur. of en	dia	kata	No. of occur. of prepositions/ea. occur. of en			Prep. w. dative	Hopo- w. genitive	Dependent genitives								Tot. no. orig. Grk. frequencies	No. of trans. occ. of crit. w. no equiv. in Grk frequencies	Net original Grk. frequencies	Not translated Grk. frequencies
			W. gen	W. all cases	oti	W. accus.	W. all cases			No. of occ. of kai for each occ. of de	Personal or poss. articles	No. of deps. gen. postpd. ea. prec. dep.	No. of lines/ea. occ. gen. postpd.	Limes/ea. gen. prec. dep.	No. of prep. attr. adj. for each attr. post position	No. of lines/ea. attrib. adjec.	No. of lines/each adverb. participle	No. of dat. not used w. en for ea. occur. of en				
					.06-.01	.18-.01	.49-.01	.18-.01	.19-.01	.27-.01	.024-.01	.07-.01	2.1+.05-	22+	9-	77-	35-	10.1+	6+	2-	17	-	-	17
Entire Rec. B	360	44	.09	.20	.95	.11	.11	.20	.023	.023	4.4	.08	26.4	3.2	22.5	1.1	9.3	4.0	.82	10	7	-	-3
I																							
58.1-6	5	-	-	-	-	-	-	-	-	-	-	.11	7	1.7	-	1.0	5.0	5	-	1	5	11	+4
II																							
58.7-60.3b	8	-	-	-	1	-	-	-	-	-	2.5	-	3	2.7	-	1.0	8.0	1.1	-	2	5	10	+3
60-0c-9a	6	1	-	-	-	-	-	-	1.0	-	4	-	1	6.0	-	1.0	3.0	6.0	4.0	3	5	9	+2
60.9b-18a	8	1	-	-	2.0	-	-	-	-	-	5.0	-	7	1.1	-	-	8	2.7	3.0	2	5	10	+3
60.18b-22b	5	1	-	-	-	-	-	1.0	-	-	-	-	3	2.5	5.0	-	5	5	1.0	3	4	10	+1
60.22c-62.4	6	2	-	-	-	-	-	-	-	-	2.0	-	3.0	3.0	-	-	6	2.0	.50	3	4	10	+1
58.7-62.4	33	5	-	-	.60	-	-	.20	.20	-	4.0	.00	17.0	2.2	33.0	2.0	11.0	2.4	2.2	6	6	5	0
III																							
62.5-11	7	2	-	-	-	-	-	.50	-	-	5	-	2	3.5	-	-	2.0	2.3	.50	3	4	10	+1
62.12-15	4	1	-	-	1.0	-	-	-	-	-	2.0	-	1	4.0	-	-	4	4.0	.00	2	5	10	+3
62.16-64.1a	7	1	-	-	-	-	-	-	-	-	6	-	3	7.0	-	-	7	7	.00	5	2	10	-3
64.1b-8	7	-	-	-	-	-	-	-	-	-	5.0	-	6	1.8	3.5	-	3.5	1.2	-	3	3	11	0
62.5-64.8	25	4	-	-	.25	-	-	.25	-	-	9.0	.00	12	3.1	12.5	.00	8.3	2.5	.25	8	3	6	-5
IV																							
64.9-15a	6	2	-	-	-	-	-	-	-	-	4.0	-	4	1.5	-	-	6	3.0	2.0	4	3	10	-1
64.15b-20	6	-	-	-	2	-	-	-	-	-	4.0	.20	2	6.0	-	-	6	6.0	-	3	4	10	+1
64.21-66.2b	8	-	-	-	-	-	-	-	-	-	1.5	.17	3	2.7	8.0	2.0	4.0	8.0	-	3	5	9	+2
66.2c-8a	6	-	-	-	1	-	-	-	-	-	1.0	.17	5	6.0	-	2.0	3.0	6	-	2	6	9	+4
66.8b-13	5	-	-	-	1	1	-	-	-	-	3	-	4	5.0	-	-	5	5.0	-	2	6	9	+4
64.15b-66.13	25	-	-	-	4	1	-	-	-	-	2.8	.15	14	4.2	25.1	4.0	6.3	8.3	-	4	7	6	-3
V																							
66.14-20a	6	1	-	-	1.0	-	-	-	-	-	5	-	4	2.0	-	-	6	6.0	.00	4	3	10	-1
66.20b-26	6	2	-	-	-	-	-	-	-	-	2.0	.17	6	1.2	6.0	-	6	3.0	.50	4	5	8	+1
66.14-26	12	3	-	-	.33	-	-	-	-	-	7.0	.07	10	1.5	12.0	-	12	4.0	.33	6	3	8	-3
VI																							
66.27-68.3b	8	-	-	-	1	-	-	1	-	-	1.7	-	6	2.7	-	8	1.3	-	1	6	10	+5
68.3c-11a	7	-	-	-	1	-	-	-	3	-	2.0	-	4	1.8	3.5	-	7	2.3	-	2	6	9	+4
66.27-68.11a	15	-	-	-	2	-	-	4	-	-	1.8	.00	10	2.1	7.5	-	15	1.7	-	4	5	8	+1
68.11b-16a	5	1	-	-	-	-	-	-	-	-	-	-	4.0	-	-	-	5	5.0	.00	2	3	12	+1
68.16b-21b	5	1	-	-	1.0	-	-	-	-	-	1.0	.25	2.0	5.0	-	-	5.0	5.0	1.0	2	6	9	+4
68.21c-70.2	6	2	-	-	-	-	-	-	-	-	3	-	2	3.0	-	-	6.0	6	.00	5	2	10	-3
68.11b-70.2	16	4	-	-	.25	-	-	-	-	-	5.0	.09	4.0	5.3	-	-	8.0	8.0	.25	5	3	9	-2
VII																							
70.3-7	5	-	-	-	-	1	1	-	-	-	3.0	.25	4	1.7	5.0	-	5.0	5	3	7	7		+4
70.8-18a	10	1	-	-	-	1.0	1.0	-	-	-	6.0	.00	12	1.3	5.0	.00	3.3	5.0	1.0	3	5	6	-1
70.18b-28b	11	-	-	-	5	-	-	-	-	-	.50	.21	5.0	3.7	-	2.0	5.5	-	-	1	7	9	+6
70.3-28b	26	1	-	5.0	2.0	2.0	-	-	-	-	1.8	.11	21.0	1.9	8.7	.50	4.3	6.3	4.0	3	9	5	+6
70.28c-72.5	6	-	-	-	1	-	-	1	-	-	2.0	.11	5	1.2	-	-	6	6	-	2	6	9	+4
72.6-12	7	1	-	-	-	-	-	1.0	-	-	3	-	2	3.5	-	1.0	7.0	3.5	2.5	3	5	9	+2
VIII																							
72.13-17b	5	2	-	-	-	-	-	.50	-	-	3	-	1	5.0	5.0	-	5	5.0	1.0	4	4	9	0
72.17c-24	7	1	-	-	-	-	-	-	-	-	6.0	.29	4	3.5	7.0	1.0	3.5	3.5	1.0	5	5	7	0
72.25-30a	5	-	-	-	-	-	-	-	-	-	4	.20	-	-	-	-	5	5	-	1	3	13	+2
72.30b-74.6b	7	1	-	-	.30	-	-	-	-	-	2.0	.14	1	7.0	7.0	-	7	7.0	.00	3	5	8	+1
74.6c-13	7	-	-	1	2	-	3	-	-	-	.50	-	1	-	-	-	7.0	1.4	-	0	7	10	+7
72.25-74.13	19	1	1.0	2.0	6.0	-	-	-	-	-	3.0	.10	2	19.0	19.0	-	19.0	3.2	.00	4	7	6	-3
IX																							
74.14-22a	9	-	2	2	3	-	-	-	-	-	5	.50	1	-	-	2.0	3.0	4.5	-	1	8	8	+7
74.22b-27	5	1	-	-	2.0	-	-	-	-	-	3	-	2	-	-	-	5	1.7	.00	2	4	11	+2
IX - XI-																							
74.28-76.4a	5	4	-	-	.25	-	-	-	-	-	.00	.33	4	2.5	-	-	5	2.5	.00	3	5	9	+2
76.4b-8	4	-	-	-	1	-	-	-	-	-	3	-	2	-	-	-	4	-	-	1	4	12	+3
76.9-15b	7	-	-	-	4	-	-	-	-	-	4.0	-	2	7.0	7.0	-	7	7	-	4	3	10	-1
76.15c-20a	6	-	-	1	-	-	-	-	-	-	4	-	2	1.3	-	-	6	5	11	+4			
76.20b-27	8	1	-	-	-	-	-	-	-	-	3.0	.42	4	2.7	-	-	4.0	8.0	.00	5	3	9	-2
78.1-7a	6	-	-	-	-	-	-	-	-	-	3	-	7	3.0	-	1.0	6.0	3.0	-	2	4	11	+2
78.7b-12	5	1	-	-	-	-	-	-	-	-	.50	.20	3	1.7	5.0	-	5	2.5	.00	4	5	8	+1
78.13-21a	8	1	-	-	-	-	-	-	-	-	5	.07	4	-	-	-	8	8	.00	4	3	10	-1
78.21b-80.3b	5	-	-	-	-	-	-	1	1	-	4	-	2	2.0	-	-	6	6.0	-	2	4	11	+2
80.3c-10	7	-	-	-	2	-	-	-	-	-	4	-	1.5	7.0	-	-	7	3.5	-	2	4	11	+2
74.28-80.10	60	7	-	.14	1.1	.14	.14	-	-	-	4.6	.10	11.3	4.0	30.0	.50	20.0	6.0	.00	9	4	4	-5

Frequencies of the 17 Criteria in Testament of Abraham - Recension B

	No. of lines of Greek text	No. of occur. of ἐn	No. of occur. of prepositions/ex. accur. of ἐn							Percent. of prepos. articles	No. of occ. of καί for each occ. of δέ	No. of dep. gen. partit. ex. prop. dep. gen.	Dependent genitives			No. of times/ea. adverb, participle	No. of dep. not used w. att for acc. of ἐn	Tot. no. of transl. Grk. frequencies	Tot. no. of orig. Grk. frequencies	No. of joint. where occ. of other, are less than to be indic.	Not original Grk. Frequencies	Not translat. Grk. frequencies
			διά		κατά								No. of prep. attr. adj. for each attr. adj. past position	No. of times/ea. attrib. adjec.							
			W. gen.	W. all cases	ἐπί	W. accus.	W. all cases	Perf w. all cases	Prep w. dative	Hapax or genitive			No. of times/ea. dep. gen. parts. pronoun									
Translation Frequencies			.06- .01	.18- .01	.49- .01	.18- .01	.19- .01	.27- .01	.024 -.01	.07- .01	2.1+	.05-	22±	9.	77-	.35-	10.1+	6+	2-	17	--	--	17
XII																							
80.11-19b	8	1	-	-	-	-	-	-	-	-	5	-	1	-	-	-	8.0	2.7	1.0	3	3	11	0
80.19c-28b	9	2	-	-	.50	-	-	-	-	-	9	-	-	-	-	1.0	9.0	2.3	.50	2	4	11	-2
80.11-28b	17	3	-	-	.33	-	-	-	-	-	14	-	1	17	-	1.0	8.5	2.4	.67	3	5	9	+2
80.28c-82.1b	6	-	-	-	1	-	-	-	-	-	3	-	2	3.0	-	-	6	6.0	-	3	3	11	0
82.1c-6	5	-	-	-	1	1	1	-	-	-	4.0	.22	2	2.5	-	-	5	5.0	-	2	7	8	+5
XIII																							
82.7-16a	9	2	-	-	-	-	-	-	-	-	5.0	-	6	3.0	9.0	-	9	9	.50	6	2	9	-4
82.16b-28b	12	1	-	1.0	-	-	-	-	-	-	2.5	-	8	4.0	-	1.0	3.0	3.0	1.0	3	5	9	+2
82.28c-84.4b	6	1	-	-	-	-	-	-	-	-	2	-	2	6.0	-	-	6	6.0	.00	4	3	10	-1
84.4c-11b	7	2	-	-	.50	-	-	-	-	-	4.0	-	2	3.5	-	2.0	3.5	7	.50	4	4	9	0
84.11c-16	5	-	-	-	-	-	-	-	-	-	3	.20	-	-	-	1.0	5.0	5	-	1	4	12	+3
84.4c-16	12	2	-	-	.50	-	-	-	-	-	7.0	.11	2	6.0	-	3.0	4.0	12	.50	4	5	8	+1
XIV																							
84.17-25a	8	2	.50	1.5	-	-	-	-	-	.50	2.0	.09	5	4.0	-	-	8	8.0	1.0	3	7	7	+4
84.25b-86.2a	4	1	-	-	1.0	-	-	-	-	-	1.0	-	3	1.5	-	-	4	2.0	.00	2	5	10	+3

Appendix 3

Testament of Abraham
Recension A
Numerical Summaries of Main Units

LINES	DIA		KATA		PERI T	PROS D	HUPO G	KAI	DE	ARTICLE		DEPENDENT GENITIVES				ATTRIBUTIVE ADJECTIVES		ADVERB. PARTICIPLES	DATIVES
	EN	G	T	EIS	A	T						UN-SEP.	SEP.	PREC.	ART. c GS		No ART. c GS		PREC.	POST		
															D S	D P	D S	D P				
2.1-4.10	25	6	-	-	-	-	3	-	-	5	4	26	6	3	5	7	3	-	10	-	3	3
4.11-6.15	37	2	-	-	1	-	-	-	-	7	7	36	9	-	6	4	6	3	7	14	11	5
6:18-8.14	33	2	-	-	2	1	2	-	-	-	12	10	57	1	1	10	11	1	1	3	3	14	8
8.15-28a	13	1	-	-	1	-	-	-	-	-	3	3	13	-	-	2	3	2	1	2	3	1	4
8.28b-10.29	37	7	1	1	2	-	-	2	-	-	15	9	37	8	2	8	9	4	-	7	9	4	3
10.30-12.9a	14	5	-	-	2	1	1	-	-	-	5	4	16	4	-	4	5	-	-	3	-	3	2
12.9b-14.2	25	3	-	1	1	-	-	2	-	-	8	5	24	-	-	2	8	1	2	-	1	14	8
14.3-29	26	6	-	-	-	-	-	-	-	-	5	6	33	4	-	3	6	3	4	1	4	5	5
14.30-16.18a	23	1	-	-	1	-	-	-	-	-	13	6	26	2	-	-	5	-	3	-	4	13	2
16.18b-25	8	1	-	-	-	-	-	-	-	-	2	2	12	5	1	-	3	-	-	4	1	1	-
16.26-18.5	9	-	-	-	-	-	-	-	-	-	4	1	9	1	1	-	2	2	-	-	1	-	2
18.6-20.13	39	4	-	-	2	-	2	2	-	-	10	5	45	8	5	4	9	2	-	2	6	5	10
20.14-22.6a	23	2	1	1	1	-	-	-	-	-	6	2	19	6	1	3	3	2	1	6	-	5	4
22.6b-15	9	1	-	-	1	-	-	-	-	-	5	1	13	2	-	1	2	1	-	1	1	3	1
22.16-24.15a	30	5	-	-	4	-	-	-	-	-	17	4	22	1	-	1	4	-	-	3	4	16	2
24.15b-26	11	2	-	-	-	-	-	-	-	-	4	3	17	2	-	3	-	-	-	-	-	1	-
24.27-26.17a	21	2	5	5	-	-	2	-	-	2	12	3	23	9	-	4	3	-	-	8	2	7	-
26.17b-28.13	22	3	3	5	5	-	-	-	-	-	7	4	30	7	-	3	3	-	1	4	6	8	1
28.14-19a	6	1	-	-	1	-	-	-	-	-	3	1	6	1	-	-	-	-	-	2	2	3	3
28.19b-34.25a	82	13	3	5	7	-	-	-	-	2	35	17	118	27	6	6	11	6	3	14	17	6	6
34.25b-38.3	35	2	1	3	5	-	-	-	-	-	21	6	47	2	1	2	7	1	-	2	4	6	5
38.4-19a	16	1	-	-	2	-	-	-	-	-	8	5	25	1	-	3	12	-	1	1	-	4	3
38.19b-40.15	26	1	1	2	1	-	-	-	-	-	10	6	25	5	1	-	7	1	1	4	3	1	6
40.16-42.12a	22	-	-	-	1	-	-	-	-	-	12	1	25	5	4	3	5	1	1	7	3	11	3
42.12b-26	14	1	-	-	-	-	-	-	-	-	6	3	14	3	2	2	2	2	-	5	5	7	5
42.27-46.5a	34	6	-	1	3	-	1	-	-	-	6	13	38	9	2	5	10	-	1	7	3	1	12
46.5b-48.32	56	1	1	2	2	-	-	-	-	-	15	9	47	10	3	4	9	15	1	11	23	3	5
48.33-54.14a	75	10	1	2	4	-	-	2	-	7	16	16	66	16	4	9	15	15	-	9	14	18	24
54.14b-56.5a	22	6	-	-	4	-	-	-	-	-	11	2	32	6	2	6	10	6	-	5	4	4	4
Total A	793	95	17	28	53	2	6	11	-	11	283	158	901	160	39	99	175	74	24	128	137	178	136

Testament of Abraham
A

LINES	EN	DIA G	T	EIS	KATA A	T	PERI T	PROS D	HYPO G	KAI	DE	Article UN-SEP.	SEP.	PREC.	Dependent Genitives ART. c GS D S | D P	No ART. c GS D S | D P	Attributive Adjectives PREC.	POST	ADVERB. PARTICIPLES	DATIVES
I.2: 1-9a	8	2 -	-	-	-	-	-	-	-	-	-	1	9	1	-	3 | 3	1 | -	4	-	2	2
2.9b-15a	6	- -	-	-	-	-	2	-	-	1	1	6	2	2	- | 2	- | -	4	-	1	-
2.15b-4.5a	5	2 -	-	-	-	-	-	-	-	2	1	7	-	-	2 | 1	2 | -	-	-	-	-
4.5b-10	6	2 -	-	-	-	-	1	-	-	2	1	4	3	1	- | 1	- | -	2	-	-	1
2.1-4.10	25	6 -	-	-	-	-	3	-	-	5	4	26	6	3	5 | 7	3 | -	10	-	3	3
II:4.11-15	5	- -	-	-	-	-	-	-	-	1	1	8	1	-	1 | -	2 | -	-	2	2	1
4.16-23a	7	- -	-	-	-	-	-	-	-	1	2	7	1	-	- | -	3 | -	2	3	5	2
4.23b-29b	6	- -	-	-	-	-	-	-	-	-	1	5	3	-	2 | 1	- | -	1	2	-	-
4.29c-6.1b	5	- -	-	-	-	-	-	-	-	1	1	3	3	-	- | 1	1 | 2	3	1	-	-
6.1c-7a	6	1 -	-	1	-	-	-	-	-	2	2	9	-	-	3 | 1	- | -	-	3	1	-
6.7b-15	8	1 -	-	-	-	-	-	-	-	2	-	4	1	-	- | 1	- | 1	1	3	3	2
4.11-6.15	37	2 -	-	1	-	-	-	-	-	7	7	36	9	-	6 | 4	6 | 3	7	14	11	5
III 6.16-22b	7	- -	-	-	1	2	-	-	-	1	2	12	-	-	1 | 1	1 | -	1	1	2	2
6.22c-27b	5	1 -	-	-	-	-	-	-	-	1	1	12	-	-	2 | 2	- | 1	-	-	2	-
6.27c-33b	6	- -	-	-	-	-	-	-	-	5	-	9	1	-	3 | 5	- | -	1	-	-	5
6.33c-8.3b	4	- -	-	-	-	-	-	-	-	-	1	5	-	1	- | 1	- | -	1	1	1	1
8.3c-7	4	- -	-	1	-	-	-	-	-	2	3	7	-	-	2 | -	- | -	-	-	2	-
8.8-14	7	1 -	-	1	-	-	-	-	-	3	3	12	-	-	2 | 2	- | -	-	1	7	-
6.16-8.14	33	2 -	-	2	1	2	-	-	-	12	10	57	1	1	10 | 11	1 | 1	3	3	14	8
IV. 8.15-22a	7	1 -	-	1	-	-	-	-	-	2	3	6	-	-	1 | 1	2 | 1	-	1	-	3
8.22b-28a	6	- -	-	-	-	-	-	-	-	1	-	7	-	-	1 | 2	- | -	2	2	1	1
8.15-28a	13	1 -	-	1	-	-	-	-	-	3	3	13	-	-	2 | 3	2 | 1	2	3	1	4
8.28b-35b	7	3 -	-	1	-	-	-	-	-	4	3	7	1	-	1 | -	2 | -	2	-	2	1
8.35c-10.6b	6	- -	-	-	-	-	-	-	-	1	-	5	2	-	2 | -	- | -	3	5	-	-
10.6c-14b	8	1 -	-	1	-	-	-	-	-	4	4	12	1	-	3 | 6	- | -	-	1	-	-
10.14c-20b	6	2 -	-	-	-	-	-	-	-	3	1	2	1	-	- | -	1 | -	1	2	1	1
10.20c-29	10	1 1	1	-	-	2	-	-	-	3	1	11	3	2	2 | 3	1 | -	1	1	1	1
8.28b-10.29	37	7 1	1	2	-	2	-	-	-	15	9	37	8	2	8 | 9	4 | -	7	9	4	3

Testament of Abraham
A

LINES	DIA				KATA		PERI T	PROS D	HUPO G	KAI	DE	ARTICLE		DEPENDENT GENITIVES					ATTRIBUTIVE ADJECTIVES		ADVERB. PARTICIPLES	DATIVES
	EN	G	T	LIS	A	T						UN-SEP	SEP	PREC	ART. c GS DS	DP	NoArt. c GS DS	DP	PREC	POST		
V.																						
10,30-12.1a	5	1	-	-	2	1	1	-	-	-	-	3	2	7	1	-	1	1	-	-	-	1	1
12.1b-9a	9	4	-	-	-	-	-	-	-	-	-	2	2	9	3	-	3	4	-	-	3	-	2	1
10.30-12.9a	14	5	-	-	2	1	1	-	-	-	-	5	4	16	4	-	4	5	-	-	3	-	3	2
12.9b-18a	8	2	-	-	1	-	-	1	-	-	-	2	1	12	-	-	2	3	1	-	-	-	3	1
12.18b-25a	8	1	-	-	-	-	-	-	-	-	-	3	3	6	-	-	-	3	-	-	-	1	8	3
12.25b-14.2	9	-	-	1	-	-	-	1	-	-	-	3	1	6	-	-	-	2	-	2	-	-	3	4
12.9b-14.2	25	3	-	1	1	-	-	2	-	-	-	8	5	24	-	-	2	8	1	2	-	1	14	8
VI.																							
14.3-8a	5	-	-	-	-	-	-	-	-	-	-	1	2	9	-	-	2	-	1	1	-	-	1	-
14.8b-17a	9	2	-	-	-	-	-	-	-	-	-	1	2	12	2	-	-	2	1	2	1	3	1	1
14.17b-24	8	3	-	-	-	-	-	-	-	-	-	2	1	9	2	-	1	4	-	-	-	1	2	2
14.25-29	4	1	-	-	-	-	-	-	-	-	-	1	1	3	-	-	-	-	-	1	1	-	1	2
14.3-29	26	6	-	-	-	-	-	-	-	-	-	5	6	33	4	-	3	6	3	4	1	4	5	5
VII.																							
14.30-33	4	1	-	-	-	-	-	-	-	-	-	2	1	4	-	-	-	-	-	1	-	1	1	1
14.34-16.5a	6	-	-	-	-	-	-	-	-	-	-	2	1	7	-	-	-	2	-	1	-	1	8	1
16.5b-11a	6	-	-	-	1	-	-	-	-	-	-	4	1	10	-	-	-	2	-	-	-	1	4	-
16.11b-18a	7	-	-	-	-	-	-	-	-	-	-	5	3	5	2	-	-	1	-	1	-	1	-	-
14.30-16.18a	23	1	-	-	1	-	-	-	-	-	-	13	6	26	2	-	-	5	-	3	-	4	13	2
16.18b-25	8	1	-	-	-	-	-	-	-	v	-	2	2	12	5	1	-	3	-	-	4	1	1	-
16.26-18.5	9	-	-	-	-	-	-	-	-	-	-	4	1	9	1	1	-	2	2	-	-	1	-	2
VIII.																							
18.6-13a	7	-	-	-	2	-	-	-	-	-	-	2	2	9	2	-	1	1	-	-	1	2	2	1
18.13b-23a	10	2	-	-	-	-	-	-	-	-	-	1	1	17	-	-	3	4	2	-	-	1	2	1
18.23b-20.4a	12	2	-	-	-	-	-	-	-	-	-	4	2	11	4	4	-	1	-	-	-	1	-	5
20.4b-13	10	-	-	-	-	-	2	-	-	-	-	3	-	8	2	1	-	3	-	-	1	2	1	3
18.6-20.13	39	4	-	-	2	-	2	-	-	-	-	10	5	45	8	5	4	9	2	-	2	6	5	10

Testament of Abraham
A

	LINES	DIA			KATA		PERI T	PROS D	HUPO G	KAI	DE	Article		Dependent Genitives				Attributive Adjectives		Adverb. Parti- ciples	Datives
		EN	G	T	EIS	A	T						Un- sep.	Sep.	Prec.	Art. c GS D S | D P	No Art. c GS D S | D P		Prec.	Post		
IX. 20.14- 18a	4	-	-	-	1	-	-	-	-	-	1	2	8	1	-	2	-	-	-	-	-	2	-
20.18b- 25	8	-	-	-	-	-	-	-	-	-	1	-	5	3	-	1	2	1	-	4	-	2	2
20.26- 22.6a	11	2	1	1	-	-	-	-	-	-	4	-	6	2	1	-	1	1	1	2	-	1	2
20.14- 22.6a	23	2	1	1	1	-	-	-	-	-	6	2	19	6	1	3	3	2	1	6	-	5	4
22.6b- 15	9	1	-	-	1	-	-	-	-	-	5	1	13	2	-	1	2	1	-	1	1	3	1
X. 22.16- 20a	5	-	-	-	1	-	-	-	-	-	3	-	7	-	-	1	-	-	-	-	1	1	-
22.20b- 28a	8	4	-	-	-	-	-	-	-	-	1	3	2	1	-	-	-	-	-	2	-	12	-
22.28b- 24.7a	9	1	-	-	-	-	-	-	-	-	5	1	9	-	-	-	3	-	-	-	3	1	1
24.7b- 15a	8	-	-	-	3	-	-	-	-	-	8	-	4	-	-	-	1	-	-	1	-	2	1
22.16- 24.15a	30	5	-	-	4	-	-	-	-	-	17	4	22	1	-	1	4	-	-	3	4	16	2
24.15b- 21a	6	1	-	-	-	-	-	-	-	-	3	-	8	1	-	-	-	-	-	-	-	1	-
24.21b- 26	5	1	-	-	-	-	-	-	-	-	1	3	9	1	-	3	-	-	-	-	-	-	-
24.15b- 26	11	2	-	-	-	-	-	-	-	-	4	3	17	2	-	3	-	-	-	-	-	1	-
XI 24.27- 26.8a	12	1	2	2	-	-	2	-	-	2	8	2	12	5	-	2	-	-	-	5	1	-	-
26.8b- 17a	9	1	3	3	-	-	-	-	-	-	4	1	11	4	-	2	3	-	-	3	1	7	-
24.27- 26.17a	21	2	5	5	-	-	2	-	-	2	12	3	23	9	-	4	3	-	-	8	2	7	-
26.17b- 23a	6	2	-	-	-	-	-	-	-	-	2	3	7	2	-	-	-	-	1	2	1	-	-
26.23b- 28.3a	6	1	2	3	2	-	-	-	-	-	2	-	8	3	-	1	1	-	-	1	1	3	-
28.3b- 13	10	-	1	2	3	-	-	-	-	-	3	1	15	2	-	2	2	-	-	1	4	5	1
26.17b- 28.13	22	3	3	5	5	-	-	-	-	-	7	4	30	7	-	3	3	-	1	4	6	8	1
XII. 28.14- 19a	6	1	-	-	1	-	-	-	-	-	3	1	6	1	-	-	-	-	-	2	2	3	3
28.19b- 30.9a	14	4	1	1	-	-	-	-	-	-	3	6	9	2	-	-	5	1	1	-	10	4	3
30.9b- 15a	7	-	-	-	-	-	-	-	-	-	3	2	12	8	-	-	-	1	-	1	1	-	-
30.15b- 26	11	1	-	-	1	-	-	-	-	-	9	-	20	-	1	-	1	1	-	1	-	1	2

Testament of Abraham
A

LINES	DIA		KATA		PERI T	PROS D	HUPO G	KAI	DE	ARTICLE		DEPENDENT GENITIVES				ATTRIBUTIVE ADJECTIVES		ADVERB. PARTI- CIPLES	DATIVES
	EN	G	T	EIS	A	T					UN- SEP.	SEP.	PREC.	ART. c GS D S / D P	NO ART. c GS D S / D P		PREC.	POST		

XIII, XIV.																				
30.27-32.10a	11	-	-	-	-	-	-	-	-	5	1	19	3	-	-	-	1	1	1	4	1	-
32.10b-16a	6	-	-	1	-	-	-	-	-	2	-	3	1	1	-	1	-	-	4	2	-	-
32.16b-24a	8	1	1	2	1	-	-	-	2	5	1	10	3	1	2	-	1	-	-	-	-	-
32.24b-34.7a	7	2	-	-	-	-	-	-	-	1	3	13	6	-	-	1	1	-	2	-	-	-
34.7b-13a	6	1	1	1	1	-	-	-	-	3	1	13	3	2	2	1	-	-	3	-	-	-
34.13b-18	5	3	-	-	1	-	-	-	-	3	1	7	1	1	1	-	-	-	1	-	-	1
34.19-25a	7	1	-	-	3	-	-	-	-	1	2	12	-	-	1	2	-	1	1	-	-	-
28.19b-34.25a	82	13	3	5	7	-	-	-	2	35	17	118	27	6	6	11	6	3	14	17	6	6
34.25b-36.3a	6	-	-	-	2	-	-	-	-	3	2	9	-	-	-	-	-	-	-	-	-	1
36.3b-10a	8	1	1	1	1	-	-	-	-	8	-	12	-	-	-	1	-	-	-	2	2	-
36.10b-23a	12	-	-	1	-	-	-	-	-	4	2	18	2	1	2	4	1	-	1	2	1	3
36.23b-38.3	9	1	-	1	2	-	-	-	-	6	2	8	-	-	-	2	-	-	1	-	3	1
34.25b-38.3	35	2	1	3	5	-	-	-	-	21	6	47	2	1	2	7	1	-	2	4	6	5
XV.																						
38.4-9a	6	-	-	-	1	-	-	-	-	2	1	8	1	-	2	4	-	-	1	-	-	-
38.9b-19a	10	1	-	-	1	-	-	-	-	6	4	17	-	-	1	8	-	1	-	-	4	3
38.4-19a	16	1	-	-	2	-	-	-	-	8	5	25	1	-	3	12	-	1	1	-	4	3
38.19b-28	9	1	-	-	-	-	-	-	-	1	4	9	2	1	-	2	-	-	2	-	-	2
38.29-40.7a	9	-	1	1	1	-	-	-	-	5	1	9	1	-	-	4	1	-	-	2	1	3
40.7b-15	8	-	-	1	-	-	-	-	-	4	1	7	2	-	-	1	-	1	2	1	-	1
38.19b-40.15	26	1	1	2	1	-	-	-	-	10	6	25	5	1	-	7	1	1	4	3	1	6
XVI.																						
40.16-20a	4	-	-	-	-	-	-	-	-	1	-	7	2	-	1	-	-	-	3	-	1	1
40.20b-42.7a	12	-	-	-	1	-	-	-	-	7	1	12	3	3	1	4	-	1	4	1	7	1
42.7b-12a	6	-	-	-	-	-	-	-	-	4	-	6	-	1	1	1	1	-	-	2	3	1
40.16-42.12	22	-	-	-	1	-	-	-	-	12	1	25	5	4	3	5	1	1	7	3	11	3
42.12b-19a	6	1	-	-	-	-	-	-	-	2	2	8	1	1	1	2	1	-	1	1	3	2
42.19b-26	8	-	-	-	-	-	-	-	-	4	1	6	2	1	1	-	1	-	4	4	4	3

111

Testament of Abraham
A

	L I N E S	DIA			KATA		PERI T	PROS D	HUPO G	KAI	DE	ARTICLE		DEPENDENT GENITIVES				ATTRIBUTIVE ADJECTIVES		ADVERB. PARTI- CIPLES	DATIVE
		EN	G	T	EIS	A	T						UN- SEP.	SEP.	PREC.	ART. c GS D S | D P	No ART. c GS D S | D P	PREC.	POST		
42.12b-26	14	1	-	-	-	-	-	-	-	6	3	14	3	2	2	2	2	-	5	5	7	5
42.27-44.5a	7	-	-	-	-	-	-	-	-	2	-	10	2	2	3	-	-	-	2	1	-	-
44.5b-11	6	1	-	1	1	-	-	-	-	-	4	4	2	-	-	-	-	-	2	-	1	1
XVII. 44.12-19	8	1	-	-	2	-	-	-	-	2	7	10	-	-	-	-	6	-	-	-	-	-
44.20-25a	6	1	-	-	-	-	1	-	-	-	1	8	1	-	-	-	-	-	-	2	-	4
44.25b-46.5a	7	3	-	-	-	-	-	-	-	2	1	6	4	-	2	4	-	1	3	-	-	7
42.27-46.5a	34	6	-	1	3	-	1	-	-	-	6	13	38	9	2	5	10	-	1	7	3	1	12
46.5b-11	7	-	-	-	-	-	-	-	-	-	2	2	10	1	1	2	2	-	-	1	2	-	1
46.12-16a	5	-	-	-	-	-	-	-	-	2	-	4	1	1	-	-	-	-	2	3	-	-
46.16b-28a	11	-	-	-	-	-	-	-	-	1	2	1	-	-	-	-	12	-	-	15	-	1
46.28b-48.5	6	-	-	-	1	-	-	-	-	3	-	4	2	-	1	1	1	-	1	2	-	1
XVIII. 48.6-11a	6	-	-	-	-	-	-	-	-	3	1	8	1	1	-	2	-	-	2	-	1	-
48.11b-16a	5	-	-	1	-	-	-	-	-	1	1	4	-	-	-	1	-	1	-	-	-	-
48.16b-22a	6	1	-	-	-	-	-	-	-	1	2	7	1	-	1	-	-	-	1	1	-	-
48.22b-28a	5	-	1	1	1	-	-	-	-	-	1	2	3	-	-	3	-	-	3	-	-	1
48.28b-32	5	-	-	-	-	-	-	-	-	2	-	7	1	-	-	-	2	-	1	-	2	1
46.5b-48.32	56	1	1	2	2	-	-	-	-	15	9	47	10	3	4	9	15	1	11	23	3	5
XIX. 48.33-50.4a	5	2	-	-	-	-	-	-	-	2	2	5	-	-	-	3	-	-	-	-	2	-
50.4b-9a	5	-	-	-	-	-	-	-	-	2	-	7	-	-	-	-	-	-	2	-	1	3
50.9b-17a	8	-	-	-	-	-	2	-	-	-	-	12	6	1	2	-	-	-	1	4	-	1
50.17b-22a	5	-	-	1	2	-	-	-	-	2	-	3	2	-	1	-	1	-	1	-	-	1
50.22b-29a	6	-	1	1	1	-	-	-	1	-	2	5	2	-	2	-	5	-	-	2	2	2
50.29b-52.3a	7	2	-	-	-	-	-	-	3	-	2	4	3	-	2	-	1	-	2	-	2	2
52.3b-11a	8	3	-	-	-	-	-	-	-	-	2	5	3	-	1	-	3	-	1	5	5	3
52.11b-21	10	-	-	-	-	-	-	-	3	1	2	2	-	1	-	-	2	-	-	3	2	3
XX.22-54.2a	10	1	-	-	1	-	-	-	-	5	1	8	-	-	-	-	3	-	2	-	1	5
54.2b-9a	7	2	-	-	-	-	-	-	-	1	2	8	-	2	1	5	-	-	-	-	-	3

Testament of Abraham
A

LINES	DIA			KATA		PERT T	PROS D	HUPO G	KAI	DE	ARTICLE		DEPENDENT GENITIVES				ATTRIBUTIVE ADJECTIVES		ADVERB. PARTI-CIPLES	DATIVES
	EN	G	T	EIS	A	T						UN-SEP.	SEP.	PREC.	ART. c GS D S / D P	NoART. c GS D S / D P		PREC.	POST		
54.9b-14a	4	-	-	-	-	-	-	-	-	3	3	7	-	-	-	7	-	-	-	-	3	1
48.33-54.14a	75	10	1	2	4	-	-	2	-	7	16	16	66	16	4	9	15	15	-	9	14	18	24
54.14b-28a	15	5	-	-	3	-	-	-	-	-	10	1	23	5	2	4	6	5	-	4	3	1	4
54.28b-56.5a	7	1	-	-	1	-	-	-	-	-	1	1	9	1	-	2	4	1	-	1	1	3	-
54.14b-56.5a	22	6	-	-	4	-	-	-	-	-	11	2	32	6	2	6	10	6	-	5	4	4	4
56.5b-10	5	-	-	-	1	-	-	-	-	-	1	-	7	3	2	-	-	-	1	3	1	1	1

113

Appendix 4

Testament of Abraham
Recension B
Numerical Summaries of Main Units

LINES	DIA			KATA		PERI T	PROS D	HUPO G	KAI	DE	ARTICLE			DEPENDENT GENITIVES				ATTRIBUTIVE ADJECTIVES		ADVERB. PARTICIPLES	DATIVES
	EN	G	T	EIS	A	T						UN-SEP.	SEP.	PREC.	ART. c GS D S	D P	NO ART. c GS D S	D P	PREC.	POST		
58.1-6	5	-	-	-	-	-	-	-	-	1	-	8	1	-	4	3	-	-	1	-	-	-
58.7- 62.4	33	5	-	-	3	-	-	1	1	-	16	4	29	-	1	-	14	2	1	2	1	14	11
62.5- 64.8	25	4	-	-	1	-	-	1	-	-	18	2	24	-	-	3	6	1	2	-	3	10	1
64.9-15a	6	2	-	-	-	-	-	-	-	-	4	1	9	-	-	-	4	-	-	-	-	2	1
64.15b- 66.13	25	-	-	-	4	1	1	-	-	-	11	4	23	4	-	6	5	2	1	4	-	3	1
66.14-26	12	3	-	-	1	-	-	-	-	-	7	1	14	1	-	2	7	-	1	-	-	3	1
66.27- 68.11a	15	-	-	-	2	-	-	4	-	-	7	4	20	-	-	2	5	1	2	-	-	9	1
68.11b- 70.2	16	4	-	-	1	-	-	-	-	-	5	1	21	2	2	3	3	2	-	-	2	2	1
70.3-28b	26	1	-	-	5	2	2	-	-	-	11	6	34	4	1	4	11	3	3	2	4	4	4
70.28c- 72.5	6	-	-	-	1	-	-	1	-	-	2	1	8	1	-	-	5	-	-	-	-	-	-
72.6-12	7	1	-	-	-	-	-	1	-	-	3	-	4	-	-	-	2	-	-	1	-	2	2
72.13- 17b	5	2	-	-	-	-	-	1	-	-	5	-	2	-	-	-	-	-	1	-	-	1	2
72.17c- 24	7	1	-	-	-	-	-	-	-	-	6	1	5	2	-	-	1	2	1	1	1	2	16
72.25- 74.13	19	1	1	2	6	-	-	-	-	-	6	2	26	3	-	1	-	-	1	-	1	6	-
74.14- 22a	9	-	2	2	3	-	-	-	-	-	5	-	3	3	-	-	-	1	-	2	1	2	2
74.22b- 27	5	1	-	-	2	-	-	-	-	-	3	-	4	-	-	-	-	2	-	-	-	3	-
74.28- 80.10	60	7	-	1	8	1	1	-	-	-	32	7	79	9	3	13	13	6	2	1	2	10	-
80.11- 28b	17	3	-	-	1	-	-	-	-	-	14	-	18	-	-	-	1	-	-	-	1	1	7	2
80.28c- 82.1b	6	-	-	-	1	-	-	-	-	-	3	-	8	-	-	-	2	-	-	-	-	1	-
82.1c-6	5	-	-	-	1	1	1	-	-	-	4	1	7	2	-	-	2	-	-	-	-	1	1
82.7-16a	9	2	-	-	-	-	-	-	-	-	5	1	12	-	-	3	2	-	1	-	-	-	1
82.16b- 28b	12	1	-	1	-	-	-	-	-	-	5	2	12	-	-	3	3	2	-	2	2	4	1
82.28c- 84.4b	6	1	-	-	-	-	-	-	-	-	2	-	8	-	-	1	1	-	-	-	-	1	-
84.4c-16	12	2	-	-	1	-	-	-	-	-	7	1	8	1	-	-	2	-	-	3	-	-	1
84.17- 25a	8	2	1	3	-	-	-	-	-	1	4	2	10	1	-	2	2	1	-	-	-	1	2
84.25b- 86.2a	4	1	-	-	1	-	-	-	-	-	2	2	10	-	-	-	3	-	-	-	-	2	-
TOTALS	360	44	4	9	42	5	5	9	1	1	188	43	406	34	7	48	96	25	16	20	18	90	36

Recension B
Sub Units

I.58: 1-6 | 5 | - | - | - | - | - | - | - | - | - | 1 | - | 8 | 1 | - | 4 | 3 | - | - | 1 | - | - | - |

II.
58:7- 60:3b	8	-	-	-	1	-	-	-	-	-	5	2	7	-	-	-	3	-	-	1	-	7	2
60:3c-9a	6	1	-	-	-	-	-	1	-	-	4	-	2	-	-	-	1	-	-	1	1	1	4
60:9b- 18a	8	1	-	-	2	-	-	-	-	-	5	1	11	-	-	-	7	-	-	-	-	3	3

Testament of Abraham
Recension B

	LINES	EN	DIA G	T	EIS	KATA Λ	T	PERI T	PROS D	HUPO G	KAI	DE	ARTICLE Un-sep.	Sep.	Prec.	Dependent Genitives Art. cGS D S	n P	NoArt. cGS D S	n P	Attributive Adjectives Prec.	Post	Adverb. Participles	Datives
60:18b-22b	5	1	-	-	-	-	1	-	-	-	-	2	-	-	-	1	1	1	-	-	-	-	1
60:22c-62:4	6	2	-	-	-	-	-	-	-	2	1	7	-	1	-	2	1	-	-	-	-	3	1
	33	5	-	-	3	-	-	1	1	-	16	4	29	-	1	-	14	2	1	2	1	14	11
III. 62:5-11	7	2	-	-	-	-	-	1	-	-	5	-	7	-	-	-	2	-	-	-	1	3	1
62:12-15	4	1	-	-	1	-	-	-	-	-	2	1	4	-	-	-	1	-	-	-	-	1	-
62:16-64:1a	7	1	-	-	-	-	-	-	-	-	6	-	9	-	-	2	1	-	-	-	-	-	-
64:1b-8	7	-	-	-	-	-	-	-	-	-	5	1	4	-	-	1	2	1	2	-	2	6	-
	25	4	-	-	1	-	-	1	-	-	18	2	24	-	-	3	6	1	2	-	3	10	1
IV. 64:9-15a	6	2	-	-	-	-	-	-	-	-	4	1	9	-	-	-	4	-	-	-	-	2	1
64:15b-20	6	-	-	-	2	-	-	-	-	-	4	1	8	2	-	-	1	1	-	-	-	1	-
64:21-66:2b	8	-	-	-	-	-	-	-	-	-	3	2	5	1	-	-	2	-	1	2	-	1	1
66:2c-8a	6	-	-	-	1	-	-	-	-	-	1	1	5	1	-	3	1	1	-	2	-	-	-
66:8b-13	5	-	-	-	1	1	1	-	-	-	3	-	5	-	-	3	1	-	-	-	-	1	-
64:15b-66:13	25	-	-	-	4	1	1	-	-	-	11	4	23	4	-	6	5	2	1	4	-	3	1
V. 66:14-20a	6	1	-	-	1	-	-	-	-	-	5	-	9	-	-	1	3	-	-	-	-	1	-
66:20b-26	6	2	-	-	-	-	-	-	-	-	2	1	5	1	-	1	4	-	1	-	-	2	1
	12	3	-	-	1	-	-	-	-	-	7	1	14	1	-	2	7	-	1	-	-	3	1
VI. 66:27-68:3	8	-	-	-	1	-	-	1	-	-	5	3	10	-	-	2	3	1	-	-	-	6	1
68:3c-11a	7	-	-	-	1	-	-	3	-	-	2	1	10	-	-	-	2	-	2	-	-	3	-
66:27-68:11a	15	-	-	-	2	-	-	4	-	-	7	4	20	-	-	2	5	1	2	-	-	9	1
68:11b-16a	5	1	-	-	-	-	-	-	-	-	1	-	7	-	1	3	-	1	-	-	-	1	-
68:16b-21b	5	1	-	-	1	-	-	-	-	-	1	1	6	2	1	-	1	1	-	-	1	1	1
68:21c-70:2	6	2	-	-	-	-	-	-	-	-	3	-	8	-	-	-	2	-	-	-	1	-	-
68:11b-70:2	16	4	-	-	1	-	-	-	-	-	5	1	21	2	2	3	3	2	-	-	2	2	1

Testament of Abraham
Recension B

	LINES	DIA			KATA		PERI T	PROS D	HUPO G	KAI	DE	ARTICLE		DEPENDENT GENITIVES				ATTRIBUTIVE ADJECTIVES		ADVERB. PARTI- CIPLES	DATIVES
		EN	G	T	EIS	A	T						UN- SEP.	SEP.	PREC.	ART. c GS		No ART. c GS		PREC.	POST		
																D S	D P	D S	D P				
VII.																							
70:3-7	5	-	-	-	-	1	1	-	-	-	3	1	3	1	-	-	2	1	1	-	1	-	3
70:8-18a	10	1	-	-	-	1	1	-	-	-	6	1	20	-	-	3	6	1	2	-	3	2	1
70:18b-28b	11	-	-	-	5	-	-	-	-	-	2	4	11	3	1	1	3	1	-	2	-	2	-
	26	1	-	-	5	2	2	-	-	-	11	6	34	4	1	4	11	3	3	2	4	4	4
70:28c-72:5	6	-	-	-	1	-	-	1	-	-	2	1	8	1	-	-	5	-	-	-	-	-	-
72:6-12	7	1	-	-	-	-	-	1	-	-	3	-	4	-	-	-	2	-	-	1	-	2	2
VIII.																							
72:13-17b	5	2	-	-	-	-	-	1	-	-	5	-	2	-	-	-	-	-	1	-	-	1	2
72:17c-24	7	1	-	-	-	-	-	-	-	-	6	1	5	2	-	-	1	2	1	1	1'	2	1
72:25-30a	5	-	-	-	-	-	-	-	-	-	4	-	4	1	-	-	-	-	-	-	-	-	-
72:30b-74:6c	7	1	-	-	3	-	-	-	-	-	2	1	12	2	-	-	-	-	1	-	-	1	-
74:6c-74:13	7	-	1	2	3	-	-	-	-	-	-	1	10	-	-	1	-	-	-	-	1	5	-
72:25-74:13	19	1	1	2	6	-	-	-	-	-	6	2	26	3	-	1	-	-	1	-	1	6	-
IX.																							
74:14-22a	9	-	2	2	3	-	-	-	-	-	5	-	3	3	-	-	-	1	-	2	1	2	2
74:22b-27	5	1	-	-	2	-	-	-	-	-	3	-	4	-	-	-	-	2	-	-	-	3	-
IX,X																							
74:28-76:4a	5	4	-	-	1	-	-	-	-	-	-	2	4	2	-	-	2	2	-	-	-	2	-
76:4b-8	4	-	-	-	1	-	-	-	-	-	3	-	8	-	-	1	-	-	-	-	-	-	-
76:9-15b	7	-	-	-	4	-	-	-	-	-	4	1	10	-	-	1	-	-	1	-	-	-	-
76:15c-20a	4	-	-	1	-	-	-	-	-	-	2	-	5	-	-	1	3	-	-	-	-	-	-
76:20b-27	8	1	-	-	-	-	-	-	-	-	6	2	7	5	-	-	3	1	-	-	2	1	-
78:1-7a	6	-	-	-	-	-	-	-	-	-	3	-	12	-	-	4	2	1	-	1	-	2	-
78:7b-12	5	1	-	-	-	-	-	-	-	-	1	2	4	1	-	-	2	-	1	-	-	2	-
XI																							
78:13-21a	8	1	-	-	-	-	-	-	-	-	5	-	14	1	-	3	-	1	-	-	-	-	-
78:21b-80:38	6	-	-	-	-	1	1	-	-	-	4	-	9	-	1	2	-	-	-	-	-	1	-
78:3c-10	7	-	-	-	2	-	-	-	-	-	4	-	6	-	2	1	1	1	-	-	-	2	-

Testament of Abraham
Recension B

	LINES	EN	DIA G	DIA T	EIS	KATA A	KATA T	PERI T	PROS D	HUPO G	KAI	DE	ARTICLE UN-SEP.	ARTICLE SEP.	PREC.	Dependent Genitives Art. c GS D S	Art. c GS D P	No Art. c GS D S	No Art. c GS D P	Attributive Adjectives PREC.	Attributive Adjectives POST	Adverb. Parti-ciples	Datives
74:28-80:10	60	7	-	1	8	1	1	-	-	-	32	7	79	9	3	13	13	6	2	1	2	10	-
XII. 80:11-19b	8	1	-	-	-	-	-	-	-	-	5	-	9	-	-	1	-	-	-	-	1	3	1
80:19c-28b	9	2	-	-	1	-	-	-	-	-	9	-	9	-	-	-	-	-	-	1	-	4	1
80:11-28b	17	3	-	-	1	-	-	-	-	-	14	-	18	-	-	1	-	-	-	1	1	7	2
80:28c-82:1b	6	-	-	-	1	-	-	-	-	-	3	-	8	-	-	-	2	-	-	-	-	1	-
82:1c-6	5	-	-	-	1	1	1	-	-	-	4	1	7	2	-	-	2	-	-	-	-	1	1
XIII. 82:7-16a	9	2	-	-	-	-	-	-	-	-	5	1	12	-	-	3	2	-	1	-	-	-	1
82:16b-28b	12	1	-	1	-	-	-	-	-	-	5	2	12	-	-	3	3	2	-	2	2	4	1
82:28c-84:4b	6	1	-	-	-	-	-	-	-	-	2	-	8	-	-	1	1	-	-	-	-	1	-
84:4c-11b	7	2	-	-	1	-	-	-	-	-	4	1	4	-	-	-	2	-	-	2	-	-	1
84:11c-16	5	-	-	-	-	-	-	-	-	-	3	-	4	1	-	-	-	-	-	1	-	-	-
84:4c-84:16	12	2	-	-	1	-	-	-	-	-	7	1	8	1	-	-	2	-	-	3	-	-	1
XIV. 84:17-25a	8	2	1	3	-	-	-	-	-	1	4	2	10	1	-	2	2	1	-	-	-	1	2
84:25b-86.2a	4	1	-	-	1	-	-	-	-	-	2	2	10	-	-	-	3	-	-	-	-	2	-

117

Appendix 5

Syntax Criticism - A Brief Description

In my book Syntactical Evidence of Semitic Sources in Greek Documents (SBL Septuagint and Cognate Studies, 3; Missoula: Scholars Press, 1974) a number of Greek syntactical features were isolated by means of which it may often be determined whether a Greek document, or part of it, is a translation of a Hebrew or Aramaic original. These syntactical features are as follows:[1]

(a) Syntactical features which are less frequent in Greek which is a translation of Hebrew or Aramaic than in original Greek prose writings:

(1) eight prepositional usages: dia with the genitive; dia with all its cases; eis; kata with the accusative; kata with all its cases; peri with all its cases; pros with the dative; hypo with the genitive;

(2) the use of de;

(3) the separation of the article from its substantive;

(4) the placement of a genitive before the word upon which it depends;

(5) the placement of attributive adjectives before the words they qualify;

(6) the use of the adverbial (circumstantial) participle;

(7) the use of the dative case; other than its use as the object of en.

(b) Syntactical features which are more frequent in Greek which is a translation of a Semitic original than in original Greek:

(1) the use of the preposition en;

(2) the use of kai to join main (independent) clauses;

(3) the use of genitive personal pronouns;

---

1. Cf. Martin, Syntactical Evidence, pp. 1-43.

(4) the use of genitive personal pronouns dependent on an anarthrous substantive.

These syntactical features were studied in a variety of Greek documents. For original Greek writers typical of the Koine period the following were selected: Plutarch (<u>Lives</u>); Polybius; Epictetus; Josephus (<u>Contra Apionem</u>, <u>Antiquities</u>); Papyri (300 B.C. to A.D. 100).

For translation Greek the following books were selected as being representative of various levels of Greek in the LXX: Genesis; 1 Samuel; 1 Kings; 2 Kings; Daniel (Hebrew) -- LXX; Daniel (Hebrew) -- Theodotion; Daniel (Aramaic) -- LXX; Daniel (Aramaic) -- Theodotion; Ezra -- Hebrew; Ezra -- Aramaic.

In this study it was found that whenever these syntactical features occur with the following frequencies, the Greek is characteristic of translation Greek rather than original Greek:

1. <u>dia</u> with genitive 6% - 1% as frequent as <u>en</u>;

2. <u>dia</u> with all cases 18% - 1% as frequent as <u>en</u>;

3. <u>eis</u> 49% - 1% as frequent as <u>en</u>;

4. <u>kata</u> with accusative 18% - 1% as frequent as <u>en</u>;

5. <u>kata</u> with all cases 19% - 1% as frequent as <u>en</u>;

6. <u>peri</u> with all cases 27% - 1% as frequent as <u>en</u>;

7. <u>pros</u> with dative 2.4% - 1% as frequent as <u>en</u>;

8. <u>hypo</u> with genitive 7% - 1% as frequent as <u>en</u>;

9. <u>kai</u> (coordinating main clauses) 2.1+ times more frequent than all occurrences of <u>de</u>;

10. 5% or fewer articles separated from their substantives;

11. 22 or more dependent genitives following the word they qualify for each such genitive preceding the word qualified;

12. 9 or fewer lines of Greek text for each dependent genitive personal pronoun;

13. 77 or fewer lines of Greek text for each genitive personal pronoun dependent on an anarthrous substantive;

14. .35 or fewer attributive adjectives preceding the word they qualify for each such adjective following the word qualified;

15. 10.1 or more lines of Greek text for each attributive adjective;

16. 6 or more lines of Greek text for each adverbial

participle;

17. 2 or fewer datives not used as the object of _en_ for each occurrence of _en_.

In the above-mentioned study of these syntactical features two aspects were found to be particularly significant. First of all, these frequencies are most valid for amounts of text more than 50 lines in length. (They are also valid to a modified degree for smaller units of text.)

Further, it was found that the _net_ number of translation Greek or original Greek frequencies was most significant. These _net_ figures are arrived at as follows: Whenever a section has more occurrences of original Greek frequencies than occurrences of translation Greek frequencies, the number of occurrences of translation Greek frequencies was subtracted from the number of occurrences of original Greek frequencies, and the resulting number is the _net occurrences of original Greek frequencies_.

Conversely, whenever a section has more occurrences of translation Greek frequencies, the number of occurrences of original Greek frequencies was subtracted from the number of occurrences of translation Greek frequencies, and the resulting number is the _net occurrences of translation Greek frequencies_.

For convenience of representation, _net_ original Greek frequencies in the charts are expressed as positive numbers and _net_ translation Greek frequencies are expressed as negative numbers.

Using these net original Greek and net translation Greek frequencies, a range of 35 spaces extending from +17 to -17 can be established.

In the above-mentioned study it was found that the Greek documents originally written in Greek and consisting of 138 to 630 lines fell within a limited area at one end of the range (in the area occupied by +17 to +15 net original Greek frequencies) whereas the Greek documents known to be translations of Semitic originals, consisting of 58 to 634 lines, fell in a limited area at the opposite end of the range (in the area occupied by -4 to -14 net translation Greek frequencies), separated from the area occupied by original Greek documents by 18 spaces (+14 to -3). Similar ranges were established for smaller units of Greek text.

REASSESSING THE "RECENSIONAL PROBLEM" IN TESTAMENT OF ABRAHAM
Robert A. Kraft

Study of the Testament of Abraham (T Abr) has proved especially difficult because of the complicated problems involved in assessing the relationship between the two radically different Greek forms ("recensions") in which it has been preserved. Briefly, the relevant data currently available may be outlined as follows:[1]

(1) Shorter Form ("Recension B").--Schmidt identifies three sub-groupings of Greek MSS, two of which (E-Slav and ADC) go back at least to the 11th century (the date of their oldest extant representative) and the third to the 14th century (MSS BFG). Another sub-group is not known from Greek MSS but is preserved in the closely interrelated Coptic-Arabic-Ethiopic versions, and seems to be represented already by a fragmentary fifth century Sahidic MS.[2] There is also a Roumanian version containing an "abridged" short form, the oldest MS of which is from the 16th century.

(2) Longer Form ("Recension A").--Schmidt lists 18 Greek MSS of the longer form, the oldest of which is from the 13th century (MS E). There is, in addition, a Roumanian version of the longer form (its oldest MS is 18th century) which agrees closely with Greek MSS DLM (14th to 16th centuries). Some of the "longer form" MSS have relatively shorter texts (although there does not seem to be a family relationship among them) than others--e.g. K (16th century), N (17th century), O (18th century). Schmidt also notes the existence of 12 other Greek MSS (mostly 15th through 18th centuries) which had not yet been classified with precision in 1971.

Thus the oldest preserved attestation is for the Coptic-Arabic-Ethiopic shorter form, which seems to have been in circulation already in fifth century Egypt. Extant evidence for other shorter form

---

[1] A new edition of the material is in preparation, by J.Smit Sibinga and F.Schmidt. Most of the following information comes from Schmidt's 1971 dissertation. For precise bibliographical information, see above, p. 12.

[2] M. Weber of the Institut für Altertumskunde at the University of Cologne plans to publish this material; see M.Philonenko, Le Testament de Job = Semitica 18 (1968) 61 n.1.

sub-groupings and for the longer form dates from much more recent times. Analysis of possible references to T Abr in ancient and medieval/byzantine lists and writings have not proved particularly helpful in establishing clear evidence for the earlier existence of T Abr in any of its known forms.[3] The writing was relatively popular in byzantine Christian circles as material used in commemoration of the lives and/or deaths of the "holy fathers" (particularly Abraham, Isaac, Jacob) on the liturgical calendar.

"Recension" Problems in Other Literature.--There is nothing particularly unique about the existence of differing "recensions" of the same material in the literature preserved by Christians throughout the byzantine/medieval period. A wide range of phenomena, from relatively simple textual variation within a rather closely related group of MSS (similar to that within NT MSS, including the "western text" problem in Luke-Acts!) to extremely divergent and complex situations (like the "synoptic problem" in NT), is well attested. With particular reference to writings with a strongly "Jewish" flavor, including Greek Jewish scriptures, the following examples may help to illustrate the extent of the problem:

(1) largely "quantitative" differences, with longer or shorter versions of what seems to be virtually the same base text.-- e.g. Job or Jeremiah in the Old Greek forms compared with Hexaplaric forms "corrected" towards the known Hebrew text; the two Greek forms of Tobit; the form of T Job in MS V compared with that in S or P; the longer and shorter forms of Paraleipomena Jeremiou, and probably of Joseph and Asenath; various forms of the Lives of the Prophets. On the whole, the difficult situation regarding Greek forms of T Solomon also seems to fit here, at least according to its editor, McCown,[4] and perhaps "Apocalypse of Moses"/Life of Adam and Eve as well.

On the strictly Christian side of things, the longer and shorter versions of the Ignatian Corpus provide an excellent example of this phenomenon worked out in a relatively mechanical manner.

---

[3] Most of the evidence was discussed by James, 7-34. His desire to find that the extant T Abr was referred to by Origen was rejected immediately by reviewers such as Schürer and Weyman (see below, n.12).

[4] C.C.McCown, The Testament of Solomon (Leipzig: Hinrichs, 1922), 32-38.

(2) largely "qualitative" differences, with alternative ways of stating the same things and no clear reflection of a single Greek vorlage behind the differing forms.--E.g. in material that is translated from Semitic such as the Old Greek vs. Theodotion-Aquila-Symmachus (etc.) in general (and especially in Daniel) or the Old Greek vs. the Barberini version of Habakkuk 3 in Greek Jewish scriptures. Perhaps the relationship of Old Greek Ezra-Nehemiah to "1 Esdras" also fits best under this heading.

(3) a combination of (1) and (2) with large scale quantitative differences in versions of the same material which do not seem to share a common Greek base.--Perhaps the two Greek forms of Esther illustrate this phenomenon (if indeed they represent different Greek base texts); at least in some passages, the Testaments of the 12 Patriarchs also seem to fit into this category.

Theories about the Relation of the Recensions in T Abr.--T Abr is an excellent example of the third category. Although they tell basically the same story, the longer and shorter versions of T Abr have very little in common with regard to their vocabulary and syntax. And while the "longer" form frequently supplies materials not present in the "shorter," the opposite sometimes occurs. This complex situation received much attention from M.R.James in his early edition of the text, and has been reexamined from various perspectives thereafter.[5]

James was ambivalent about the relationship of the different forms. "[Recension] A presents us with what is on the whole the fullest, clearest and most consistent narrative. Its language, however, has been to some extent medievalized. B is an abridgement whose language is on the whole more simple and original than that of A..., [but] it is not an abridgement made from A. [The Arabic (James did not have access to the Coptic and Ethiopic) represents] an independent abridgement, not made from either A or B, though as a rule more nearly related to B than to A. ...It inserts matter not found in A or B, and is shorter than either" (p.49). "B preserves the greatest proportion of the original language, A the greatest

---

[5] For other surveys of the literature, see Schmidt's dissertation, I.115-124, and Delcor, 24-28 and 77f.

proportion of the original story" (p.51). James concludes that T
Abr, as he tries to reconstruct it from the preserved witnesses, is
"a very much mangled réchauffé" of an earlier, now lost (in 1892)
Apocalypse of Abraham[6], preserving "all the main features of the old
book"--T Abr is a "popular" Christian work composed in second century
Egypt (incorporating some earlier legends) by a "Jewish Christian"
(at least for the apocalyptic portion; p. 23) and received its
present preserved form(s) "perhaps in the 9th or 10th century"
(p.29).[7]

There were immediate reactions and disagreements. Kohler and
Ginzberg (see also Ehrhard)[8] argued that T Abr was of Jewish Origin,
and Ginzberg implied that the differing Greek recensions were separate (and not very faithful) translations of a Hebrew original.
Riessler also posited a Semitic original and preferred the shorter
form (B) to the "christlich überarbeitet" longer form.[9] Box continued the same general line of argument, speaking of a first century
Palestinian Hebrew original that was freely adapted into Greek in
Egypt (Alexandria?) and must be reconstructed from both the longer
and the shorter Greek forms (following James).[10] A modification of

---

[6]The publication by N.Bonwetsch of an old Church Slavic version
of an Apocalypse of Abraham in 1897 doubtless caused James to have
second thoughts; see his relatively vague statements in The Lost
Apocrypha of the OT (London: SPCK, 1920), 17.

[7]The position of James is followed, on the whole, by W.A.Cragie
in his introduction to the first English translation of
T Abr in the supplementary volume to the "Ante-Nicene Library" series (American
ed. = "Ante-Nicene Fathers," vol. 10) in 1897, and also by J.-B.Frey
in his article for the Dictionnaire de la Bible, suppl. I (1928)
33-38.

[8]K.Kohler, "The pre-Talmudic Haggada II.C.--The Apocalypse of
Abraham and its Kindred," JQR 7 (1895) 581-606; L.Ginzberg, art. in
Jewish Encyclopedia 1 (1901) 93-96; A.Ehrhard, Die altchristliche
Litteratur und ihre Erforschung von 1884-1900: vol. I, Erste
Abteilung, Die vornicänische Litteratur (Freiburg im Br.: Herder,
1900) 184-185. See also J.Kaufmann (ed. M.Soloweitschick) in Encyc.
Judaica 1 (1928) 564, and the unsigned article in the Universal
Jewish Encyclopedia 1 (1939) 40.

[9]Altjüdisches Schrifttum (1928), 1333. See also his longer
article on "Das Testament Abrahams, ein jüdisches Apokryphon,"
Theol. Quartalschrift 106 (1925) 3-22.

[10]G.H.Box, The Testament of Abraham (London: SPCK, 1927),
vii-xv and xxviiif.

this approach is implied by Kohler's 1923 description of T Abr as a Jewish "Alexandrian product of the first Christian century"--see most recently D. Flusser's claim that T Abr was "composed by a Jew, writing in Greek, and was possibly based on a Hebrew (or Aramaic) original."[11]

On the other side of the coin, some critics viewed T Abr as clearly a Christian composition (not "Jewish Christian" with James), and even dated it later than did James. Schürer pointed out that such legends and apocalyptic materials were composed by Christians for a long time, Weyman compared T Abr to post-Constantinian "Christian" writings from Asia Minor, and Weinel thought T Abr was "probably a very late Christian book."[12] These critics also agree that T Abr cannot be identified with the story told by Origen about the death of Abraham, as James attempted to do.

In more recent discussions, Turner has subjected the language and content of the two Greek forms of T Abr to close scrutiny and presents a suitably complex picture of the origins and relations of the two.[13] He finds that B contains Greek material of very early date--perhaps as early as parts of Jewish Greek scriptures and the Testaments of the twelve Patriarchs (p.203)--but that the preserved form of B dates from the late second or the third century, "from the same period, if not the same hand or school, as the original edition of the Testament of Solomon" (p.190). Since the A form does not seem to be derived directly from B, and yet seems secondary to B, Turner suggests that

---

[11]Kohler, Heaven and Hell in Comparative Religion (New York: Macmillan, 1923), 77 and 80 (he does not specify what he thinks the original language was); Flusser in Encyclopaedia Judaica 1 (1971), 129--Flusser considers the longer "version" more original than the shorter, but declines to propose a specific date of composition for the work.

[12]E. Schürer, review of James in TLZ 18 (1893) 279-281, (see also his Geschichte des jüdischen Volkes im Zeitalter Jesu Christi, vol. 3 (Leipzig: Hinrichs, 1909⁴) 338f); C.Weyman, review of James in Byzantinische Zeitschrift 2 (1893) 642f; H. Weinel, "Die spätere christliche Apoklyptik" in Eucharisterion 2 (Festschrift Gunkel, ed. H.Schmidt; Göttingen: Vandenhoeck und Ruprecht, 1923), 170-172.

[13]N. Turner, The Testament of Abraham: a Study of the Original Language, Place of Origin, Authorship, and Relevance (unpublished Univ. London Thesis, 1953). Some of his conclusions were summarized in his article "The Testament of Abraham': Problems in Biblical Greek," NTS 1 (1954/55) 219-223. The following discussion and quotations are drawn from a revised, shortened form of his dissertation which he kindly supplied to the author in 1973.

> Recension B...is a shortened form of an older text [of Egyptian, Jewish origin--see his ch. 5], and Recension A is dependent on this rather than on our present text [of B]. This is supported by the fact that occasionally the one recension is found to supplement the other, and that they make better sense when taken together. (p.207)
>
> ...Recension B is earlier and closer in form to any original Hebrew work [that may underlie the preserved materials]. Recension A was a later translation made either directly from the Hebrew, or else it is a recension of such a translation [i.e. of the older form of B? see above and p. 203]; it is not based on Recension B, as the language in parallel passages does not overlap. (p. 211)

Turner would date the A version "in its present form...after the fifth or sixth centuries. I do not think it is a Christian redaction" (p.217f). Indeed, it may rest on a third century edition of the longer form; any "Christian influence came after the separation of the recensions" (p.213).

In his 1971 dissertation, Schmidt speaks with less hesitation about the relationship of the "recensions." For him, T Abr is a product of "popular Essenism" (see Kohler in 1895), written ("probably") in Hebrew in Palestine during the first half of the first century CE, then translated into the short Greek form before the beginning of the second century. The long form is a revision of the (Palestinian) short form, made in the Jewish diaspora of lower Egypt in the opening years of the second century (pp.118-121). Schmidt has modified his conclusions slightly with regard to relative dating in the article included in this volume: The shorter form of T Abr is now dated to the second half of the first century (with the question of its original language left more open), and the longer form to the second or perhaps the beginning of the third century, with possibly an "intermediate form" (represented by the preserved Coptic) developing sometime inbetween (see above, pp. 76-80).

Nickelsburg's 1972 study of one aspect of the T Abr material led him to radically different conclusions regarding the relation of the longer and shorter forms. He concluded that "Recension A is prior to Recension B" with respect to the judgment scene and the "one soul" material, and thus called for a reassessment of the relation of the two forms (above, p. 58). In his new contribution to the problem, prepared for this revised volume, Nickelsburg reaffirms his earlier position in words reflecting M.R.James' conclusions cited above:

> The structure of Recension A is more primitive than that of Recension B, although the latter may contain some primitive elements and wording which were revised in Recension A. (above, p. 92)

Delcor also discusses the "recensional" problem but comes to no firm conclusions. He sees both A and B as developments from a common "Greek original" (p.6, see also p.34) of Jewish Therapeutic origin (p.73) composed around the turn of the era (pp.76f), and traces both to an Egyptian setting (p.78), although the respective forms differ widely from each other in outlook (p.14).

The Main Issues and Types of Argument.--This is not the place to enter into a detailed evaluation of the various detailed arguments advanced over the years. It is helpful, however, to attempt to identify the sorts of arguments and issues on which the discussions have been based:

(1) Language. On the whole, the commentators seem to agree that the Greek of the shorter form often has a more "primitive" flavor than that of the longer form, in relation to other preserved examples of Jewish and early Christian Greek. The language of form B also has more of a "Semitic" cast, although A is not lacking in Semiticistic passages or constructions. On the other hand, a relative preponderance of "later" words and constructions appear in A by comparison with B (see esp. Turner).

(2) Coherence in Form and in Content. According to some commentators (e.g. James and Nickelsburg), the preserved form(s) of A sometimes present a relatively coherent sequence and structure in sections that are more problematic in B. Occasionally a detail in B can best be explained in terms of what is found in A, which is taken as an indication that B is an abridgment of A.

(3) Thought World. Schmidt attempts to argue that only the longer form contains characteristically "Egyptian" expressions and ideas, while both forms reflect "Palestinian-Essenic (-Iranian)" themes. Thus B is thought to represent an earlier development which came to be "Egyptianized" in the A form.

"Recensions" and the "Original": What Model to Use?.--Unfortunately, much of the discussion about the "recensional" problem in T Abr has not been sufficiently selfconscious about what is thought to constitute the "original" of T Abr and how the preserved materials are thought to relate to such an "original." The possibilities are manifold, and any attempt to describe them in detail would be extremely complex. Questions about the interrelation of MSS exhibiting virtually the same narrow textual base (textual criticism proper)

often overlap and blend with questions about the relation between
two or more larger textual units which have similar content but fairly
divergent basic texts (often called different "recensions" or versions
or forms of a writing). Questions about originally independent
smaller units of written or oral materials which may be added to a
"recension" by its editor are closely related to problems regarding
the use of such materials in the "original" composition of a writing
that contains traditions of various sorts (e.g. legend, apocalypse,
paraenesis). Supportive evidence from the literatures of hellenistic-
Roman and byzantine/medieval times is available for a great number of
possible models. An attempt is made below to outline some of the
more obvious possibilities as they relate to previous discussions of
T Abr. As will become apparent, individual aspects of some of the
models are interchangeable.

(1) Preserved Greek Original → Preserved Greek Recension

(2) (Lost Gk Orig) → Preserved Gk Rec #1 → Preserved Gk Rec #2

(3) (Lost Gk Orig) ⟨ Preserved Gk Rec #1
                    Preserved Gk Rec #2

(4) (Lost Semitic Orig) → Preserved Gk Translation → Preserved Gk Rec

(5) (Lost Semit Orig) → (Lost Gk Tr) → (then patterns ##2 or 3 above)

(6) (Lost Semit Orig) ⟨ Preserved Gk Tr #1
                       Preserved Gk Tr #2

(7) (Lost Semit Orig) ⟨ (Lost Gk Tr #1) → Preserved Gk Rec #1
                       (Lost Gk Tr #2) → Preserved Gk Rec #2

(8) (Lost Semit Orig) ⟨ (Lost Semit Rec #1) → Preserved Gk Tr #1
                       (Lost Semit Rec #2) → Preserved Gk Tr #2

(9) (Lost   ) (Lost Semit Rec #1) → (Lost Gk Tr #1) → Preserved Gk Rec #1
    (Semit)⟨
    (Orig)   (Lost Semit Rec #2) → (Lost Gk Tr #2) → Preserved Gk Rec #2

(10) (Various Individual Traditions) ⟨ Preserved Gk Orig #1
     (in Gk and/or in Semit   )   Preserved Gk Orig #2

(11) (Various Individual) ⟨ (Lost Semit Orig #1) → Preserved Gk Tr #1
     (Semit Traditions)   (Lost Semit Orig #2) → Preserved Gk Tr #2

(12) (as in #11 but with   → (Lost Gk Tr #1) → Preserved Gk Rec #1
     both Gk Tr Lost, thus:) → (Lost Gk Tr #2) → Preserved Gk Rec #2

Variations on these models, or other similar models are not difficult
to construct. Additional complicating factors that deserve at least
passing mention include the possible existence and interpenetration
of more than two "recensions" in Semitic forms, or in Greek forms;
possible complications arising from material being translated from
one language/dialect to another, then later being retranslated to
the former (e.g. Hebrew → Aramaic → Hebrew #2, or Greek → Coptic →
Greek #2); possible periods of primarily oral transmission based on

an earlier written text and resulting in a later written text (e.g. Greek text #1 → oral transmission → Greek text #2). And when the demonstrable realities of cross-fertilization between textual/recensional streams during centuries of transmission are recognized, the possible developments and relationships become almost infinitely complex! Without any recognition of the many possibilities, not to mention serious discussion of which possibilities are more or less likely with reference to T Abr, confident solutions to the "recensional problem" in T. Abr seem quite unwarranted.

The relevance of such considerations for discussions of the relationship between the shorter (B) and longer (A) forms of T Abr should be obvious. The argument that one of the extant forms essentially derives (by expansion or abridgment or adaption) from the other assumes a model like #1 (= #4) or #2 (= #5a). It is really more concerned with reconstructing the "original" of T Abr than with exploring strictly "recensional" problems, and would be largely irrelevant in models ##10-12, where no single "original" is envisioned.

General Critique of Earlier Arguments.--Indeed, a host of relatively unexplored assumptions undergird the aforementioned arguments from language, coherence and thought world concerning the relationship of the preserved "recensions" and their respective origins. Can we assume, for example, that the sought for "original" of T Abr was composed (compiled?) by an author/editor who was self-conscious about consistency or coherence? (i.e. "recension" in its strictest sense). It is neither impossible nor improbable that the author/editor of the "original" simply gathered materials at hand and juxtaposed them in whatever way proved most convenient at the time. We cannot simply take for granted that such a person would be concerned with (or even aware of) the fact that some of the materials might be structurally or actually incompatible or incomplete (e.g. an episode or two derived from what was once a more coherent apocalypse; a vignette about Sarah or Isaac no longer moored to similar materials with which it once circulated). To use "coherence" as a criterion for determining relative chronological priority and/or "originality" of a writing is to predetermine arbitrarily how the "original" must have been. Supporting evidence for such an assumption is not easy to find, especially in the sort of materials represented in T Abr.

The argument that both forms of T Abr preserve evidence of a common outlook (Iranian-Palestinian-Jewish according to Schmidt), but that a characteristically different perspective ("Egyptian/Alexandrian") has been superimposed upon it in only one of the two preserved forms has similar weaknesses. Is there any reason to believe that characteristically "Palestinian" (if such terminology is appropriate !) Jewish traditions were unknown among Jews in Egypt (or anywhere else, for that matter !), or that characteristically "Egyptian" (?) Jewish traditions were unknown in Palestine (etc.) at any time during the hellenistic-Roman period (or even later)? Schmidt appeals to Turner's linguistic arguments for positing a Hebrew original of T Abr and argues that it is "natural" for such a Hebrew writing to be of Palestinian provenance. Interestingly, however, Turner himself argued strongly for an Egyptian/Alexandrian origin of even the proposed Hebrew original! More data is needed in this discussion! The cultural-geographical labels are perhaps convenient, but are also potentially misleading. Nevertheless, Schmidt's argument that one form of T Abr superimposes a different perspective on an outlook common to both forms is significant for the recensional question if we can assume that there is some sort of direct literary relationship between the two preserved Greek forms. But that assumption also remains to be demonstrated, or even argued with precision. And if we appeal to models like ## 10-12 above, the problem of relative priority and "originality" of the preserved forms loses much of its significance. The "Egyptianized" form could be just as "original" as the other, if they both used traditional, non-Egyptianized Jewish materials. At the present stage of developments in the study of T Abr, however, this seems to be a relatively unrewarding line of discussion. Until the "recensional problem" is examined with greater care, firm conclusions regarding the "original" or T Abr are premature.

Unexamined assumptions also plague the use of potentially more controllable evidence such as vocabulary and style in the preserved Greek forms of T Abr. The presence or absence of "Semitic" Greek in a particular section of T Abr may not tell us anything directly about the composition or recension of T Abr, but only about the background of one of the sources used by the compiler--or added by a redactor! The presence of "late" words/constructions is perhaps potentially more telling, if it can be assumed that some direct and significant relationship obtains between the date of the preserved MSS and the date of the textual archetype they represent (whether that archetype is the "original" composition, or a recension thereof). Presence or absence of "Septuagintal" terminology is also potentially relevant, if only we could trace with some precision the history of Jewish Greek scriptural texts in Jewish and Christian hands in the relevant times and places. But hard data in these matters is difficult to obtain, and we often remain happily unaware of the precariousness of the foundations/assumptions on which our discussions rest.

In short, the view one takes of the "recensional problem" is closely intertwined with one's view of the origin of T Abr and of the Jewish and/or early Christian world(s) in which it is thought to have originated. If one assumes that an actual Hebrew or Aramaic original text of T Abr once existed (not simply Semitic "sources" and traditions, whether written or oral), one can appeal to translation differences to account for some of the fundamental diversity in vocabulary and syntax between the preserved longer and shorter forms. If one thinks that there once was a single Greek original of T Abr (whether that was a translation or not) from which all other extant forms derive, one's options for discussing the "recensional problem" are more limited. It is doubtful that any satisfactory solution to either the "recensional problem" or to the problem of the origins of T Abr will emerge until such possibilities are discussed in detail and assessed carefully in the light of available evidence (including analogies from how other similar writings developed). There is a great deal of available relevant evidence that can be drawn from various sources. Unfortunately, in our impatience and enthusiasm to discover and interpret new data of possible significance for our field(s) of primary interest (e.g. Jewish pre-Rabbinic literature and thought), we are too often prone to neglect the basic task foundational to all controlled historical investigation of working carefully and consistently from what is securely known or relatively sure to what is unknown or only suspected.

Working Backwards towards the Origin of T Abr.--This much is clear: A short form of T Abr was available in Sahidic in fifth century Egypt, and from at least the eleventh century onward, T Abr in various forms and languages had become very popular among eastern Christian copyists and compilers who transmitted hagiographical material for use in connection with the liturgical calendar for remembering the lives and/or deaths of revered persons. The same can be said of a large body of writings, including several for which Jewish origin has sometimes been claimed--e.g. Lives of Adam and Eve, Lives of the Prophets, Paraleipomena Jeremiou, Testament of Job.[14] Whatever the ultimate origins and

---

[14] For a convenient and indispensible handbook to such materials, consult F.Halkin, Bibliotheca Hagiographica Graeca (3 vols.; Brussels: Société des Bollandistes, 1957³), and the Analecta Bollandiana series in general.

literary history of these materials, their place in Christian usage
(and piety) is well attested simply on the basis of the preserved MSS.
And it is here that our quest for solutions about earlier phases of
development must begin if we are to pursue a systematic and rigorously
controlled approach to the problem.

When we start with the preserved Greek materials, two obvious
lines of investigation are open once the basic, textcritical relationships within the families of MSS are established: (1) Analysis of
primarily linguistic features (vocabulary and syntax) found in each
identifiable textual stream, and (2) careful attention to determining
for what reasons the texts were transmitted and the uses to which they
were put by the preservers. Ideally, the data from such investigations
would converge to produce at least a rough picture of the circumstances
(date, place, occasion) that gave rise to the available textual streams.
If, as would often be the case, there remained questions as to whether
the text had an earlier history, used older sources, etc., such questions could then be discussed with more precision by using similar
approaches. Since we already know (from the Sahidic version) that the
shorter form (B) was in circulation half a millennium earlier than its
oldest available Greek attestation, studies on that material could
move more quickly and surely towards the earlier periods, in compariwon to studies of the longer form (A).

There is, of course, nothing new to this type of analysis. Unfortunately, we often lose sight of the intermediate steps in our impatience to move from the known MSS to the "original." Studies of
T Abr and its "recensional problem" have tended to be deficient in
these regards. For example, although M. R. James had already noted,
almost in passing, certain "late" or "medieval" syntactical features
found especially in T Abr's longer form (A), this matter has not been
examined in any detail by subsequent commentators. Turner does focus
attention on what he considers to be "Christianization" of some words
and passages in T Abr (based on James, pp. 50f), but fails to offer
a systematic study of all the data--Turner treats syntax only in connection with his claim that T Abr often contains Semiticized Greek.
It is entirely possible, however, that close attention to syntactical
features in this and related materials could provide clues to identifying with more precision the most recent recognizable stages of
development, perhaps even kinds of "school activity" that took place
among Christians in editing and circulating primarily "Jewish" texts.

Unfortunately, appropriate information about pertinent aspects of "scribal" practice in the byzantine period, including the conditions under which new copies and editions of older materials were produced, is not conveniently accessible.[15] Some information can be distilled from detailed acquaintance with codicological, textcritical and philological data from the period, but that is a demanding and time consuming path. Nor is there much information conveniently available regarding Christian (and Jewish ?) motivation for preserving and consulting the various writings of "Jewish" cast that have survived through the byzantine period. Consequently, few students of Judaism and Christianity in the hellenistic-Roman period are in a position even to begin the sorts of investigations suggested above. And insufficient awareness of or focus upon these aspects of the investigation of T Abr have contributed heavily to the methodological inadequacy of some of the arguments offered in discussions of the "recensions," and ultimately of the "original text" of T Abr.

Towards a more Satisfactory Linguistic Analysis.--The brief comments of James and Turner regarding syntactical features in T Abr have been alluded to above, and Martin's detailed syntactical analysis appears elsewhere in this volume. While this is not the place to attempt a new and systematic examination of the data, it is perhaps fitting to provide a few guidelines regarding what needs to be done if the methodology outlined above is to be pursued with rigor. It would be extremely helpful if we could identify with some precision the characteristic linguistic features that might be expected in materials that are produced, reworked or updated by Christian editors for byzantine Christian usage. Awareness of certain obvious changes that appear as hellenistic Greek develops towards modernity is indispensible at this point. To the extent that the origin and popularity of some changes could be pinpointed with reference to time and place, precision in analysis would proceed apace. A detailed handbook of updated data from the byzantine period would be extremely valuable to the student of these materials.[16]

---

[15]Some helpful material is available in works such as R. Devreesse, Introduction a l'etude des manuscrits grec (Paris: Klincksieck, 1954).

[16]For an introductory survey of the developments in post-classical Greek (with extensive bibliography) see R. Browning, Medieval and Modern Greek (London: Hutchinson University Library, 1969). More extensive, but also somewhat outdated material is available in A. N. Jannaris, An Historical Greek Grammar...from Classical Antiquity down to the Present Time (London: MacMillan, 1897).

James gives two examples of "late forms and constructions" in the longer "recension" of T Abr--εἰπεῖν τινά (rather than τινί or πρὸς τινά), and ἀπό plus accusative (rather than genitive). He adds that "the neo-Greek particle ἅς" (contraction of ἄφες--"permit that," "in order that") appears in the 14th century MS B of the shorter form at 5.4. Lampe's <u>Patristic Lexicon</u> lists only one example of ἅς, from the seventh century; it also occurs in chs. 26-27 of the Apocalype of the Holy God-Bearer (Mary) which M. R. James edited from an eleventh century MS (<u>Apocrypha Anecdota</u> 1, 1893). Liddell-Scott[9] includes ἀπό + accusative as a construction found "in later Greek" and refers to a fourth/fifth century papyrus; Lampe also lists two sixth century church fathers as examples of this phenomenon (assuming that the extant MSS accurately preserve sixth century usage). The εἶπεν τινά ("he told him") construction is not normal in T Abr (πρὸς τινά is most frequent) but does appear in chs. 1, 4, 15. It is frequent in the "Apocalypse of Sedrach" (ed. James in <u>Apocrypha Anecdota</u> 1, from a 15th century MS) and occurs at least once (2.24) in the closely related Greek Apocalypse of Esdras (ed. Tischendorf, <u>Apocalypses apocryphae</u> [1866], p. 26 n. 30, from a 15th century MS).[17] Careful attention to these and other similar phenomena would perhaps provide desired clues to the more recent history of some of the writings under consideration.

It is in this connection that R. Martin's attempt to isolate syntactical criteria for identifying translation Greek suggests new possibilities of analysis while at the same time failing to be sufficiently controlled for immediate application to material such as T Abr. Martin's primary focus in developing his technique was New Testament literature--could it be demonstrated that portions of Acts, the gospels, etc., were translated from Semitic sources? His control data was drawn from non-translated literature of relatively known date (hellenistic and early Roman periods) and from known translation literature of approximately the same period. But it is clear that the Greek language (and its various dialects) underwent various changes in the centuries

---

[17]Turner also mentions "εἶπε with accusative of indirect object" in "Recension A" as possible but relatively "more doubtful" evidence of Semitic/Hebraic influence on T Abr; he notes that in Greek, "verbs of saying...often govern a direct object" (p.68), but that is not particularly relevant for the question of what construction is used to designate the addressee. On the broader issue of the declining use of the dative, see J. Humbert, <u>La disparition du datif en grec</u> (du Ier au X^{er} siècle) (Paris: Champion, 1930), esp. 37f, 162ff, 185-89; also Browning, <u>Greek</u>, pp. 17, 43, 64.

from New Testament times to the present. Insofar as the influence of Christianity came to be very strong in Greek speaking areas (primarily the eastern Roman, or byzantine world), it is not impossible that in some respects Christian Greek came to assimilate some syntactic features that originated in or corresponded to the world of earlier "translation Greek." In order to apply "syntax criticism" convincingly to materials of unknown date and origin, a wider spectrum of control data would be needed, including examples from various sorts of Christian writings from the second or third century onward. Such a spectrum of characteristic syntactical features needs to be constructed, with close attention to date, location and even (if possible) education/training of the author, not to mention type of literature (e.g. poetry vs narrative or discourse; homiletic vs polemic or theological/philosophical treatise). It might then become possible to measure texts like the longer or shorter forms of T Abr against that spectrum and arrive at more convincing results. For the moment, however, unless we assume that both forms of T Abr are datable to around the turn of the era, or assume that Greek syntax did not change significantly during the first millenium of the common era, at least for the criteria used by Martin, his attempt at applying his analytic techniques to T Abr must remain unconvincing--along with being potentially promising![18]

The Thought Worlds of the Copyists and Compilers.--In addition to applying linguistic criteria in an attempt to determine more precisely the most recent history of the document(s) under examination, content and (if possible) intent need to be analyzed within the framework of the identifiable transmitters of the material. What needs were met by Christians copying and recopying T Abr? Did the different forms of T Abr have different functions for their users? Were the motives at work in the transmission and preservation of such materials sufficient to cause the actual composition and/or construction of some of the materials themselves? It should not be assumed that a document composed or compiled by a Christian will necessarily contain characteristically "Christian" contents. Little systematic information is available

---

[18] In another connection, I hastily applied Martin's criteria 1-9 to some fourth century Christian homiletic material (preserved in MSS of later date) that almost certainly did not originate as translated Greek. Nevertheless, some of the results fell within Martin's ranges for translation Greek, possibly partly because of the influence of Semiticizing Greek (via Old Greek scriptures, etc.) on the homilist and his tradition, and perhaps also because of the homiletic nature of the materials.

on such issues as the above, although the tireless work of the Bollandist fathers in Belgium has created tools and studies that can be used with great profit in this aspect of the investigation (see above, n.14).

In very general terms, it is obvious that Christians came to view and use their Jewish heritage in a variety of ways.[19] Overtly Christian interests in themes that are thought to point concretely to the coming and activity and significance of Joshua/Jesus the Messiah/Christ abound, and have received wide notice. But Christian interest was not limited to "christologically oriented" materials from Judaism that were applied specifically to Jesus and his appearance in history. Many Christians still looked for a future eschatological/apocalyptic consummation, and thus helped maintain a continuity with similar pre- and non-Christian Jewish interests. This applies not only to the preservation of large bodies of Jewish materials relating to the end times, but also to the reworking of such materials in forms that range from covertly Christian (e.g. Greek Apocalypse of Esdras or of Sedrach) to obviously Christian (e.g. Apocalypses of various Apostles and of Mary). Christians who produced ethical treatises often treated their Jewish ethical heritage similarly--preserving, reworking, initiating. But to the degree that the nature of the material requires fewer explicit references to characteristically Christian persons and views, to that degree it is difficult to distinguish what "originated" from Christian as opposed to Jewish pens or minds. To a large extent, many Jews and Christians had similar attitudes towards such things as praise of God (prayers, psalms), ideals of personal and community morality (what constitutes "righteous" living), and expectations regarding future rewards and judgment (personal and cosmic). As had already been true in pre-Christian Jewish contexts, the ancient heroes of Jewish scripture and tradition were used widely as examples in homiletic exhortation and community commemoration. The author of Hebrews helps set the stage for what later explodes into the rich Christian hagiographical tradition preserved for us. And Christian monasticism provided an eager vehicle for heightening the focus on "righteous persons" of every sort who could serve as moral examples for the spiritual athletes struggling towards the goal of perfection.

Is it possible to trace more specifically the course of such

---

[19] See R. A. Kraft, "The Multiform Jewish Heritage of Early Christianity" in vol. 3 of Christianity, Judaism and Other Greco-Roman Cults, ed. J. Neusner (M. Smith Festschrift; Leiden: Brill, 1975), 174-199.

developments in Christian circles? How does the ideal of the righteous
person change over a period of centuries, or vary from place to place?
How are the eschatological/apocalyptic expectations affected as new
situations arise? In what terms do authors throughout the centuries
view impending death? What can we learn from a close examination of the
rampant angelology/demonology of some (especially monastic) Christian
materials? What contacts did Christians maintain with Jewish and
Jewish Christian communities and traditions throughout the relevant
period? Are there helpful clues in the multifaceted history of
Christianity during its first millennium of existence that can help us
understand better the ways in which Jewish traditions were preserved,
adopted, adapted, expanded, abridged, and recast through the centuries?
Very little systematic information is available, although the recent
Nag Hammadi discoveries have led the way in encouraging a reassessment
of older pictures of early Christian developments. Hopefully, continued
efforts will be made to expose the variety of interests and activities
that obtained especially among those Christians most responsible for
producing and preserving the literary heritage on which we so heavily
depend. Study of writings such as T Abr will both contribute data to
such an investigation and will receive new impetus from it. In any
event, this seems to me to be the only available controlled route back
towards solving the problems of the recensions, and ultimately the
origins of T Abr. In this light, many aspects of the current discussions are simply premature, whether or not they ultimately may prove
to have been accurate.

THE GENRE TESTAMENT AND THE TESTAMENT OF ABRAHAM

Anitra Bingham Kolenkow

Although the Testament of Abraham (hereafter TA) is by title a testament and has the customary death-bed locale, the work itself does not show Abraham giving a testament. To decide whether TA belongs to the testament genre, one must ask questions both about Abrahamic traditions and about the testament genre. Is there anything in the Abrahamic tradition that would justify TA in saying that Abraham did not write a testament? What type of testament would TA be? What are the paraenetic or theological aims of the author, and how does the author support these aims in TA? Further, since Abraham confesses a sin even though he is a model of the righteous man, what is the locus or venue of works about the sin of the righteous?

A. The Story of TA

The story of TA is one of a crochety, righteous old man who barely recognizes angels and who wants to avoid death. Abraham will not set his house in order (make a testament), even though he is past the normal age of death and an angel has told him to make a testament because he is to die today (15). Abraham attempts to delay death by seeking trips over the earth and asking Death about death's forms. However, during the trip over the earth, Abraham turns into a sinner;[1] Abraham sees the unrighteous and wishes to kill them. God speaks against Abraham's wish--and says that the divine will is not to condemn but to change the sinner. Abraham is sent to heaven so that he (and the reader) may learn that heaven's will is not to condemn men. Then, in Abraham's discussion with Death, Death pictures himself killing men mainly by untimely death. Before his death, Abraham repents of his sin and persuades both Michael and Death to pray for the untimely dead. Finally Abraham dies--still not having set his house in order--and is welcomed in heaven.

B. The Lack of a Testament in the Tradition about Abraham

As noted above, TA is entitled a testament and ends with the death of Abraham. Yet Abraham never gives a testament in TA.[2] In fact, the constant question (and leitmotif) of the work is "How can God persuade Abraham that it is time for him to die--and therefore time to 'set his house in order' (that is, make a testament)?"[3] Why does TA's author make this emphasis? Is there a tradition that Abraham never gave a testament? Such a tradition would explain the lack of a testament while allowing the writer to play with testamentary characteristics.

Gen 25:5-6 seems to be the focal point of the tradition that Abraham did not give a testament. In contrast to the stories of Isaac (Gen 27:27ff.) and Jacob (Gen 48:9ff.), the Genesis texts do not show Abraham giving a testament of any kind. In Gen 25:5-6, Abraham is said to give all he had to Isaac and to give gifts to his other children. Since these gifts are given before Abraham's death, the question for the third generation Tannaim is "What could Abraham have given before his death?"[4] Later rabbis who are adduced in the discussion say that Abraham did not give the blessing to Isaac because such a gift would mean that others would not receive the blessing (Gen R. 61:6). The Palestine Targum Jonathan of Gen 25 says, "And because Abraham had not designed to bless Ishmael, therefore he blessed not Izhak; for had he blessed Izhak and not Ishmael, it would have kept them in enmity." (Etheridge)

An even earlier account, Jub 20-22, notices and fills in the lack of testament. Jub 20 has Abraham give gifts to his sons. Then, Jub 21 says that five years later Abraham gave testamentary commands (21:1) and blessings (21:25) to Isaac. At that point, Abraham is said not to know when he is going to die (21:1). This passage thus explains why Abraham had not given a testament earlier and yet shows his attempt to do so (even though he does not know when he is going to die). Then, Jub 22 has Abraham engage in the typical pre-testament motifs (receiving a meal that he may give blessing, etc.; cf. Gen 27:4, 2 En 56:1-2)[5] and give blessing and commandments (22:25) just before his death--although even his grandson Jacob is not aware when Abraham is to die. Jubilees would seem to have apologetic motifs--making clear what it thinks ought to have been in scripture by what it adds. However, Jubilee protests too much about "no one knowing when Abraham was going to die." Further, the insertion of two testaments shows that even in the time of Jubilees there was discussion of what testaments Abraham had neglected.

TA seems to know of and rely on the biblical lack of an Abrahamic testament. It uses an "urging to set affairs in order," dispose of possessions and/or bless his son as the leitmotif in the story (1, 4, 8, 15). Knowing heaven's desire that he prepare to die, Abraham effectively bribes both Michael and Death--both think they will get Abraham to arrange his affairs and die if they humor his requests to see the earth and to know Death's forms. Yet, even in the end, Abraham has not given his testament or blessing. Abraham is pulled intestate from the land of the living. The lack of a testament is thus a "given" for the author. It enables him to introduce unknown information about sin, heaven, and Death (about which Abraham should have given a testament) and still conform TA to the biblical image of a testamentless Abraham.

C. The Types of Testament and the Presentation in TA

If TA is a testament, to what type of testament would its material correspond? Jewish Hellenistic death-bed testaments may be divided into two major types:
> ethical commandments--described by K. Baltzer and typified in the Testaments of the XII Patriarchs whose aim is to give men examples of good and evil deeds and their rewards and ask that men follow the path of good;
> blessings--which give a forecast of the future (in the Hellenistic period, after a trip to heaven)--1 Enoch, Life of Adam and Eve (VAE) 30-34.[6]

Both types have biblical models. R. H. Charles[7] argues that the general (ethical) testament uses the verb צוה both by itself in T Reub 1:1 (cf. T Benj 1:1; T Levi 1:1; T Zeb 1:1) and Jub 22:25 as well as in the "setting a house in order" motif of 2 Sam 17:23; Is 38:1; 2 Kgs 20:1 (cf. 4 Ezra 14:13). One should also compare this to the use of "commandments of the Lord" in Deut 30. The term "blessing," used in relation to a forecast of the future, is in Gen 27:27; 48:20; Deut 33:1; 1 En 1:1; 2 En 64:4; VAE 30:1 and Jub 22:25.[8]

The Jewish blessing testament, as noted above, used trips to heaven before death as bases for forecast of the future; the man was given such knowledge at the hour of his death.[9] The

model for such trips seems to have been the Hellenistic nekyia.
> The basic nekyia is the story of a trip to the otherworld to give the traveler acquaintance with those who sinned on earth--so that the traveler may repent (cf. Plato's myth of Er, Plutarch's On Divine Vengeance 7:563ff.). The nekyia is also used to give knowledge of of the future (cf. Vergil's Aen 6:426ff. and the Sibyl's forecast in Plutarch, On Divine Vengeance 7:566).

Because TA's account of a trip to heaven is like that of many Jewish blessing testaments, TA might at first sight seem to be an apocalyptic blessing testament given by the righteous. However, TA has no forecast of the future (from the time of the patriarch to the present and into the future), as is common in apocalyptic forecasts.
> This is unlike the common pictures of Abraham receiving prophetic visions among the portions (Targum Neofiti Gen 15:12; 2 Bar 4:5; 4 Ezra 3:14; LAB 18:5; Apoc Ab 9-32).

Further when one looks again at the structure of nekyias, one realizes where the true parallels lie in TA. The nekyia's most common usage is to make a man realize how dire is his sin and make him repent of the sin because the man sees its punishment on his nekyia. This insight into nekyia enables the critic to recognize the importance of TA's motif, "recognition of a sin during a trip to heaven." In TA, Abraham (before his death) becomes a sinner and then recognizes and confesses his fault during his trip to heaven. The view of heaven serves to make clear the paraenesis. Abraham's story then would be like those of the patriarchs in the Testaments of the XII Patriarchs who tell the story of their sin and confess their fault. Abraham confesses the sin of "wanting to destroy evildoers" (14)--a rather "new" sin.[10] Since the "lack of a testament" is explained by common haggadah and emphasized by the story, the testamental characteristics (the death-bed location, the emphasis on testament and the account of the recognition of sin in heaven with repentance) qualify the work as a paraenetic testament in purpose.

In spite of its similarity to the nekyia genre, however, TA differs from those nekyias and testaments which speak about the ordinary sinner. Abraham has no sin in his life and for that reason is a good image of the righteous man--the man who is vulnerable to the sin emphasized in TA. Abraham's trip over the earth gives an occasion for sin. The trip to heaven gives a chance to understand the divine will and then for Abraham's repentance. This nekyia, however, unlike most nekyias, does not emphasize sin's punishment in order to get the sinner to repent from fear of punishment. Rather, the author of TA has used the trip to show the compassionate aims of heaven and the terrifying splendor and threat of judgment so that Abraham may be moved to act compassionately-- to intercede for man. Thus both heaven and Abraham become models for men. TA emphasizes not only the sin of "wanting to destroy sinners" but also the virtue of intercession and care for man.

D. How to Establish the Validity of a "New" Sin--The Uses of a "Non-Testament" Testament

If a work would teach a doctrine "de novo," with no history of tradition or tradent, the work must account for the reason why the doctrine and the work had been unknown before this time. The author must give both doctrine and work an inner validity--causing the reader to say, "Yes, the teaching is self validating."

The New Sin and the Lack of Testament   The occurrence of Abraham's sin just before the time of death and the lack of an Abrahamic testament provide rationales for a previously unknown story. Since Abraham sinned just before death, received revelation in heaven and did not give a testament, who on earth could have known? Thus the lack of a testament not only provides an impetus to the story; the lack of testament also explains certain "unknowns" to the reader.

Validation of Story and Doctrine by Biblical Allusion
The author must still produce a work which testifies to the validity of a "new" doctrine or sin. How does the author do this? The work begins and ends with the common picture of the hospitable Abraham. The work then has Abraham told he should set his house in order because he is going to die (as Hezekiah has been told by Isaiah, Is 38:1-3) and tells of Abraham's reluctance to die. Abraham as everyman seeks to put off the hour of death. As Hezekiah weeps, so TA says there is grief in Abraham. The work gains further validity by showing Abraham doing what prophets commonly do--call down fire or wild beasts on sinners (cf. 1 Kgs 18:38; 20:36; 2 Kgs 1:10-11). This is what the righteous often would like to do. The work then has God reply (15), as in Ezek 18:23, 32; 33:11) that God does not desire the death of the wicked but that the wicked may repent

and live.[11] This is the fundamental saying of TA--which throws the reader back on his heels. The Ezekiel saying makes the reader realize that God opposes what the reader takes for granted--that the righteous rightly may seek to destroy the wicked.

At this point in the story, God orders Abraham taken to heaven so that Abraham may see the judgments there and repent of his sin. The author presents the terror and splendor of heavenly judgment-- and yet the latent will and possibility of a heaven where God cares for man, Adam is concerned for man, and man judges man.[12] The knowledge of God's will and the pictures of heavenly figures prepare both the reader and Abraham for response to the picture of a heavenly judgment of a soul--a soul with an equal weight of good and bad deeds. Abraham takes up his biblical role as intercessor (as for Sodom) and intercedes for the soul. The soul is saved--and the reader has a recognizable model for a virtue opposite to the sin (intercession as opposed to "seeking to destroy").[13] Abraham recognizes his sin and confesses that his action, in seeking the death of sinners, was wrong. A voice comes again informing Abraham that Abraham is forgiven (and thus confirming Abraham's sin). More importantly for the continuing story, God tells not only that He had brought back to life those whom Abraham thought he had killed, but God also gives a general "theological" basis for this action, "I do not requite in death those whom I destroy living on the earth." Like the previous divine statement that God does not desire the death of the wicked, this statement would be a known piece of theology (cf. 1 En 22:12, where one has a division for sinners who are slain in the days of sinners but whose spirits will not be slain on the day of judgment; cf. also 1 En 103:6).[14] Again the reader would be shocked and yet agree--recognizing that the common desire to catch a sinner in his sins (so that the sinner would immediately go to judgment) might mean that one would save sinners from dire punishment in the judgment. God has arranged his salvation so that those who destroy sinners are really saving them. Putting such a teaching in the time of Abraham means that this is ancient teaching--antedating even Moses' laws.

<u>The Reexamination of Ezekiel's Teaching in TA</u>. By having God use the words of Ezek 18 and 33 in a nekyia context, TA translates Ezek 18's verdict into the terms of a society which thought of everlasting punishment after death. TA is a new

Ezekiel for a world which believed in such punishment. In Ezek
18, the unrighteous are punished by death (an untimely death,
since it is a punishment and not the normal end of life).
As Ezek 18 emphasizes ethical reward in life and no excess
punishment beyond the life of a man (for his son), so TA says
there is no punishment beyond untimely death. Such death is
its own punishment. "Do not worry if you are a sinner and get
caught by untimely death. There will be no other judgment or
punishment beyond death. All justice is oriented so that the
reasonably just man (even one who has half sins and half good
deeds) will not suffer." [15]

> It is not made clear what happens to the righteous who
> die untimely, but one would assume a positive judgment
> and life in heaven in line with the positive judgment
> given the half-good soul.

Death as the Image of the New Sin   TA's story of Death
and Abraham is the final component of the author's attempt to
convince the righteous that it is evil to seek immediate death
for sinners. Where before God feared Abraham would destroy the
whole creation and a voice said that God wishes to destroy no
one, now Death boasts that he (Death) is the destroyer of the
world (17--a typical motif in Jewish literature). He is "all
destroying death," the one who devastates the world for seven
ages and leads all men to Hades. Thus Death is portrayed as
the model and extreme case of what Abraham had sought to do.
By this time, however, Abraham has changed. Abraham again
prays (and persuades Death to pray) for the servants who have
died untimely. When Abraham uses his "not wanting to die until"
motif for the last time, Abraham hears Death's account of the
deaths Death brings. And.... Abraham is able to ask the
question which shows that most of Death's supposed power
actually serves God's merciful purposes. When Abraham asks
Death to tell of Death's many faces, Death lists all the types
of death[16] and boasts of sudden deaths. Abraham then asks
(almost by-the-by unless one remembers the statements of God to
Abraham earlier in the story), "Is there an untimely death?"
Death replies that there are seventy-two kinds of death--and
only one is just. Death has proclaimed his own invalidity as
world destroyer--for God has said earlier that all who die untimely will not be subject to punishment in the judgment.
Death may think that he is bringing harm to all who are
sinners, but he is saving them from punishment. The ironic

import of Abraham's question and Death's answer puts the capstone on this testament about the sin of the righteous in wishing untimely death upon the unrighteous. Death's picture of himself puts on a major scale what might seem a minor sin of the righteous--and shows divine reaction to it. Abraham has brought death by fire and wild beasts--so does Death. However, through divine decree such deaths are said to circumvent the common picture of the fate of sinners.

Thus TA establishes the validity of its story and of its teaching by using common biblical motifs to describe the events of the story. In TA's presentation of heaven's will, the author refurbishes and plays upon the theology of Ezek 18 and 33-- where the prophet says that God seeks repentance and life and does not punish beyond the life of man. Ezekiel's words become the basis of TA's address to a world which believed in punishment after death. TA's picture of Death the destroyer of the world (largely through untimely death) shows Death as the antithesis of the will of heaven. These are the ways of life and death. Finally, TA shows that God has made heavenly decisions to nullify the way of death. This theology serves as a mythical model for TA's ethics-- an ethics which condemns Abraham's desire to destroy sinners and affirms Abraham's intercession for man. However, one may also ask if the human model does not also serve as a model for the human understanding of what heaven wills.

> It has been noted in this section that the vision of heaven reinforces paraenesis. Is TA also an anti-apocalyptic work? TA has ideas which differ from those common in apocalyptic circles. Why would God hurry the end (cf. 2 Bar 20:1; 83:1)? Death says he has seven ages to work (19) and the righteous will stay in paradise with Abraham after they die. Each individual soul is judged or put away (after untimely death). There is even the possibility of intercession after death (as shown in Abraham's intercession for the soul with balanced good and evil deeds--an intercession which 4 Ezra 7 would say was impossible). Violence is not the forerunner of the endtime (as in much apocalyptic) but is merely the product of death-out-of-hand which serves God's purposes in eliminating judgment for most men. The judgment material of TA is not part of an apocalypse seeking the overthrow of the now powerful wicked and the coming of a time when the downtrodden or persecuted righteous will receive power and bliss. The judgment material of TA may be called ethical placebo rather than political apocalypse. Rather like Plato's Er myth,[17] TA's objects are both to get individual men to turn from evil ways and to assure most men that they

will have an even chance in heaven. As the myth of Er shows that all men may find usable future lives if they choose carefully, so TA says that most men need fear no punishment after death.

These positions, however, are not anti-apocalyptic; they only present the opposite of what most apocalyptic works argue. What makes TA anti-apocalyptic is the change of meaning which TA gives the picture of the two gates. Most apocalypses see the gates as the end; punishment is the automatic fate of those who go through the wide gate. TA says a balanced judgment occurs there, with the possibility of concern and mercy. Further, God has willed that those like Death and Abraham, who seek to kill men untimely, are actually saving men from punishment. Untimely death is the fate of most men and God has willed that untimely death means that a man will undergo no further punishment. Thus the picture of terrible judgment may be valid, but it is not relevant for most of mankind. TA's reorientation of the common understandings of judgment and punishment show that TA is reacting against an apocalyptic world view.

E. Works Which Use the Failings of the Righteous to Teach

If TA is a work about a righteous man (Abraham) and yet TA emphasizes the righteous man's sin, what is the intended effect and psychological method of a type of literature which uses the failings of the righteous to teach the faithful? This literary category includes the stories of Jonah (who wished that foreigners would die rather than repent) and of Job and Ezra (who questioned God about his ways).[18]

The problem which such stories solve is, "How does one work with overconfidence and self-righteousness when one is talking to the righteous? These stories become parables which the reader can apply to himself without hurting his ego too much--because the stories are about great men whom otherwise he admires. The testament or the direct account of the man (with his confession that he was wrong) also means that the reader cannot justify himself in the same sin, saying, "It is all right for me; see, great men do it." Rather the confession says to the reader, "Even the righteous fail--Abraham does not recognize angels, does not do what God wants, and acts like Death in seeking to kill people. A great man will recognize his sin and repent." In such stories it is emphasized that the great man is righteous (Job gives to the poor, Abraham welcomes guests, Ezra is one of the few righteous).[19] This reinforces identification with or admiration of the figure. Then the figure does wrong or becomes the exemplar of what the author considers wrong. God speaks against the wrong and the figure then confesses that he is wrong. TA makes clear where God and Abraham differ. In this genre, God's speech defining what He wills is an important counterbalance to the sin of man (cf. Jonah 4:10-11). Abraham sins (in wishing to destroy sinners), heaven speaks against this--and Abraham's confession (as Job's and Ezra's) puts Abraham on the side of God. Abraham's intercession and concern for man show that he has returned to his role of the righteous man seeking to save men. The account of the conversation between Death and Abraham not only enables Abraham (and the reader) to be told about Death, but the account also shows Abraham again returning to his normative function of praying for others. Thus at death Abraham's righteousness is uncontested and it is affirmed that Abraham goes to the paradise of the blessed.

> It may be asked whether TA is only of the genre "works which use the failings of the righteous to teach"? In fact, testaments which use the failings of the righteous are a sub-category of the more general "works about the failings of the righteous." One needs the conjunction of categories to properly delineate the work. Not all testaments are works about failings; nor are all works about failings testaments. The critic needs both categories to define the work or he will not understand what the author is doing.

Thus the author of TA uses Abraham's biblical lack of a testament to provide the means for recognition of a generally unrecognized sin--the desire of the righteous to destroy sinners. Abraham becomes an example of one who commits the sin. The audience hears the will of God (in the words of Ezekiel) and Abraham is taken to heaven to learn to repent. The repentant Abraham hears more of the divine will-- and Abraham's later history becomes the means of the reader's obtaining further knowledge about Death. What Death does is, on a large scale, what had been Abraham's sin. God's previous revelation shows the ultimate invalidity of what Death claims to do. Thus the story of the sin of the righteous becomes a vehicle both to condemn the sin and to show that what many fear about death and judgment is unwarranted. In studying TA, the critic may see TA's support of its argument by biblical precedent and TA's use of the genre, "the story which uses the sins of the righteous to teach." TA thus builds a testament for Abraham.

[1] Fear that Abraham may fall into sin may already be in the back of the reader's mind. Abraham is, as an old man will, losing his old virtues and having his idiosyncrasies -- and now refusing to obey God's will.

This paper sees the A (long) version as reflecting more of the original story than the B (short) version and therefore will discuss the A story. The B version has the same emphasis on the three main testamental themes in TA -- setting one's house in order, hospitality and the contrast between Abraham (who needs to be turned around before he destroys the whole world), and a God who wills that all repent and live. The B version also has certain motifs (not in the A version) which further emphasize the outline of the A story. The B version prepares for the problem of Abraham's desire to have men killed by having God tell the angel to do what Abraham commands (8). However, the B version is bowdlerized into merely a view of heaven --with no condemnation. Abraham (and those like him -- a phrase typical of 2 Baruch and 4 Ezra) is told that he will go through the narrow gate. B also contains further motifs relevant to the story of A which are not in A, but B omits their relevance to Abraham and does not contain the material (now found in A) to which they point. B says Death leads men to the place of judgment, but does not have Death take Abraham (as A). B asks, "How should a judge have mercy on those who have no mercy?" (a direct slap at Abraham). In B, Enoch also says that he himself does not desire to condemn souls because he has not died himself (another implied slap at Abraham). These motifs would naturally lead into A's material of Death taking Abraham and Abraham sinning and confessing his sin. However, no such material occurs in B, thus suggesting that B knew A's material but omitted it. B also adds motifs so that where the A version first has Abraham shown only the earth (where he sins) and then shown heaven to get him to repent, B has Abraham ask for one joint trip over earth and to heaven. God then takes Abraham's soul (and not Death, as in A). If one did not have the "Death as taker" and anti-judgment motifs (listed above) in B, one might say that TA was originally a pre-death apocalypse and that B was closer to the original. However, these arguments and elements suggest that A is closer.

It may not mean, however, that A was B's model because B bowdlerizes. The "not seeking to hurt" motif in B (and not in A) would seem to speak against this. Both B and A use an original which is neither B nor A. This point would also be fostered by the use together in VAE 30-34 of motifs which are found in A or B (number of blows of death, ascent to heaven by angels at an appointed hour). The motifs in B (of not harming) only argue that A's motif of Abraham as sinner and the theme of opposition to killing are original -- and that TA's original form was not that of an apocalypse.

S. E. Loewenstamm (below, 219-25) suggests the dependence of TA upon the story of Deut R. 11. This is a useful question to raise since both works use the motif of a patriarch avoiding death, outfacing an angel and then confronting Death. However, because Deut R. 11 is more like B (God takes Moses' soul) and A contains the structure closest to TA's earliest form, it would be argued that Deut R. 11 takes its content from B and is not the source of A.

Deut R. 11 goes even beyond B. Deut R. has Moses rather than Death give a revelation of his power. Such emphasis on the power of Moses seems a haggadic elevation of the figure of

Moses, giving Moses powers that are denied Abraham in a similar story (of a patriarch who refused death, demanded to see the earth and had to be forced to die because ordinary angels could not persuade him to go peaceably). Deut R. 11 would show the power of Moses rather than Death. Deut R. 11 is also generally allusive and not specific in its revelation. It does not tell what Moses saw when he went to heaven, nor does it give revelation about death. One should also note Delcor's argument (discussed in the article on TA's angelology, below, pp. 154f.) that TA does not use the motif found in Deut R. that Michael and Death fought over Moses' soul. Deut R.'s use of this motif would again seem haggadic elaboration of TA's motif .

[2] The major studies on TA used in this article are:
M. R. James, The Testament of Abraham (Cambridge, Eng.:University Press, 1892)
G. H. Box, The Testament of Abraham (London: SPCK, 1927);
F. Schmidt, Le Testament d'Abraham (Thesis: Strasbourg, 1971);
M. Delcor, Le Testament d'Abraham (Leiden: E. J. Brill, 1973); as well as the volume of which the present work is a revision. The problem of whether TA is a testament is often solved by saying that the work is a prelude to a work now lost or that the work contains the information necessary to a testament. Cf. discussion in A. B. Kolenkow, "What is the Role of Testament in the Testament of Abraham," HTR 67 (1974) 182.

[3] This leitmotif and its use in testaments will be discussed below.

[4] Cf. Kolenkow, "Role.," where it is further noted that the Testament of Isaac uses the point of Abraham's not having made a testament to portray him as one who has special interest in those who do not make testaments.

[5] Jubilees knows that Abraham ought to do what Enoch does in 2 En. 55:1ff. and would seem to build its story on some such group of motifs. For the rabbis and Jubilees, a testament must be given on a death-bed to be valid.

[6] K. Baltzer, The Covenant Formulary (Philadelphia: Fortress, 1971) 144-161. A. B. Kolenkow, "The Genre Testament and Forecasts of the Future in the Hellenistic Jewish Milieu," JSJ 6 (1975) 57-71.

[7] R. H. Charles APOT II 47.

[8] There are also works which combine the forms; cf. Jub 22:25 (commandments and blessing); Deut 30 -- commandments, Deut 33 -- blessing; T Levi -- things that are ordained....and what should befall them until the day of judgment; 2 En 55ff. The wording often occurs somewhat before the presentation and the patriarch declares what he intends.

[9] The man at the hour of his death was supposed to have such knowledge. Socrates says, "In the hour of death men are gifted with prophetic power." (Apol 39, cf. Phaedo 85). Philo agrees in his description of Moses that the time of Moses' death was a time when Moses no longer uttered "general truths" but prophesied the future (VM 2:228f.).

[10] The Psalms, for example, cry that sinners and Yahweh's enemies be destroyed. TA portrays such desire as sin. Such "sin" is not emphasized by Schmidt (Testament, 43) who sees the work as one about the virtue of hospitality or Delcor who emphasizes apocalyptic and says paraenesis is absent (Testament, 43). However, see Nickelsburg (in this volume above, p. 26) who says the judgment scene is not eschatological but has a didactic function. The role of Abraham's hospitality, mentioned at the beginning and end of the work, seems used to foster the picture of Abraham's essential righteousness.

[11] On word usage, cf. Delcor, Testament 130. TA would also say that God could bring death when he willed, cf. "If I permit death to come to you, then one may see whether you come or not." God is in final control of Death.

[12] Cf. the targums on Gen 9:6; 1 Cor 6:2 on man as judge; VAE 48:2 on Adam's sorrow and joy. Cf. 1 En 22:7, where Abel seeks vengeance in heaven on his brother. Delcor discusses the Cain-Abel motif at length (Testament, 143-5).

[13] Intercession is a common virtue, cf. Ps 106:23; Num 11:2; 14:13-20 (Moses); Gen 18:23 (Abraham, and see list in 4 Ezra 7:107-11); 2 Mac 15:12-16; As Moses 12:6; 2 Bar 85:12.

[14] There are many citations suggesting that judgment in this world means no judgment in the next; cf. Palestine Targum Gen 38; Rom 12:20; 2 Mac 6:13; 2 Bar 78:6; M Sanhedrin 6:2.

[15] татьяна TA's picture of Abraham sinning before his death may also pick up Ezek 33:13's motif of the "importance of sin even though one had been righteous before." Abraham had sinned and the interplay with Ezekiel in TA would set the "Ezekiel knowing reader" on the edge of possibility that even Abraham might have died a sinner (and, according to Ezekiel, that would be that). The reader would want a change in the stricture of Ezekiel so that Abraham's other righteous deeds will enable Abraham to go to heaven and not just lie in the earth. Thus the reader applauds TA's presentation of the heavenly weighing of souls -- so that good deeds may overbalance bad. Thus TA would use Ezekiel's doctrine not only to justify TA's "new" doctrine, but also to move the heart of the reader with the intent of the story -- knowing how close Abraham had come to dying a sinner.

[16] The picture of Death having several faces or disguising himself is common in the literature of the period; Sir 39:27-31; VAE 9:1; AM 17:1; 2 Cor 11:14; Apoc Elijah 13:14. The Apocalypse of Elijah has many of the same motifs as TA including death as a destroyer (1:4-5), death changing garb and emphasis on the intercession of the just (3:68, 7:82). The Apocalypse of Paul has fiery angels sent to sinners and beautiful angels sent to the righteous (11).

[17] Cf. G. H. McCurdy, "Platonic Orphism in the Testament of Abraham," JBL 61 (1942) 213-26.

[18] Even the wicked among Joseph's brethren in the Testaments of the XII Patriarchs are only "has been" wicked. They give testaments as righteous men, repent and tell about

their past to warn their heirs against their sin and show the heirs the path of virtue.

[19] Jonah is a prophet -- which would set him up as called by God, but he is never shown as really repenting of his ways. He begins by avoiding the task although he does know the will of God. There is a statement of God's will at the end also (but there is no confirming statement by Jonah). Thus the story varies from other examples of the category, perhaps being influenced by the apologetic motif of the prophet forced against his will to prophesy -- which the work plays with for its own purposes.

THE ANGELOLOGY OF THE TESTAMENT OF ABRAHAM

Anitra Bingham Kolenkow

The angelology of the Testament of Abraham (hereafter TA) is similar to that of other works of Hellenistic Jewish literature in its elaboration of biblical angelic characteristics. TA especially uses angelic characteristics to show both heaven's present concern for men and a correlate concerned judgment after death. This paper will emphasize both the "history of religions" background of TA's angelology and TA's use of such angelology for its own theological purposes.[1]

A. Earlier Studies of the Angelology of TA

Earlier studies of TA[2] do not stress or correlate these aspects of TA's angelology. M. R. James' introduction to his edition of TA briefly cited parallel examples of angelology found in Enoch, the Assumption of Moses, 4 Ezra, Gen 18 and Tobit. James was not interested in the picture of the angel Michael (nor in TA's general presentation of angels). James was interested in TA's presentation of Death--discussing parallels in Egyptian-Christian texts and noting that Death was originally not an angel because Death had to disguise himself as an angel. James, however, barely mentions TA's theological interests except as they enable him to distinguish between recensions (cf. his discussion of intercession).

G. H. Box almost seems an epitomizer of James. However, Box adds a list of typical characteristics of angels (taking men's souls, driving the wicked to destruction, interceding). Box does not emphasize how TA's angelology differs from, or is similar to comparable doctrines found in other literature. Further, he does not suggest how TA's angelic characterizations may reflect the theology of TA's author.

The recent thesis of F. Schmidt gives a much more coherent presentation of TA's angelology than either James or Box. Schmidt cites works which show angelic characteristics similar to those in TA (Michael bowing before God at sundown, angelic hierarchy, the carrying of souls to heaven and subaltern functions at judgment). Schmidt also stresses that Death is an angelic servant of God. Schmidt enumerates the functions of angels between men and God (transmitters of decisions and requests, interpreters of dreams and intercessors). Schmidt also notes angelic characteristics (departure at sunset, not mounting an ass) and supernatural events induced by the presence of angels (tears becoming pearls, the talking tree). Schmidt, however, sometimes relates one characteristic to another where the connection is doubtful. Schmidt thus says that the speech of Michael identifies Michael as an angel (a point not clear from the text) and relates this to the language of creation taught Abraham by an angel in Jub 12:25-27. Schmidt, comparing stories in the Acts of Thomas and Philo, suggests that Michael refused to mount a horse because angels do not participate in the corporeal. This Schmidt ties to the well documented donnée that angels do not eat and drink.

Schmidt's study of angelology is used to suggest a place of origin for the two recensions of TA. Again, the problem with his theories (although certain of his conclusions would seem valid) is his support of valid points with other points that are not as valid. He would like (in spite of an admitted lack of evidence) to see the angelic flight to heaven as proving an Essene background for TA (although the documents where similar doctrines are found are not Essene). Schmidt rightly uses differences in angelic motifs in the two recensions to differentiate between the recensions--the short recension showing the superiority of Abraham to angels, the long recension abasing men and stressing the titles of Michael. Schmidt, however, uses dubious arguments again when he tries to associate angelic characteristics with country of origin. Schmidt sets the short recension's picture of Death's two heads in the context of biblical presentations (Amos 9:3-4, Job 20:15 LXX, etc.). Schmidt then relates the long recension's emphasis on the many visages of Death to Egyptian pictures of Tithoès (although he notes that such pictures are found all over, early and late, in texts which could have influenced Judaism such as those from Ugarit).

M. Delcor presents his studies of Michael and Death as part of his examination of TA's eschatology. The most useful function of his presentation is that Delcor notices the differences between TA's angelology and what is common in the angelology of other works. Delcor notes, for example, that although one might expect a war between Michael and Satan over the soul of Abraham as happens in the similar tale about Moses in midrash on Deut 31:14 (cf. Jude 9), there is none. Delcor also notes that there is no reference to Michael's trumpeting to the dead at resurrection (in fact there is no reference to resurrection). Such differentiations are important for a study of TA's background and interests.[3]

These studies show the continuing need to delineate the angelology of TA's period and to discuss how both recensions of TA use such angelology to develop their story of Abraham.

B. Angels in the Hebrew Bible and Later Literature

The biblical presentations of angels may be divided into two major categories--one, describing what God does on earth; the other, describing an entity separate from God. The second would seem basic to the presentation of angels in TA and is employed in the angelology of Hellenistic Judaism.

1. The Angel as One Who Appears to Give Revelation to Men and Returns to Heaven--the Mediator.

Judg 6 and 13 (cf. Gen 18) show in outline the expected biblical behavior of mediating angels. In these passages, the angel appears (either as one who is with persons, but unrecognized, or one who suddenly appears). The angel gives his message and is offered a meal (which he may refuse--on the basis of the common belief that angels do not eat earthly food). In Judges, the meal is turned into an offering closely associated with the departure of the angel (6:19-21; 13:19-20), and the departure is accompanied by the confession of witnesses as to who the angel is and what he has done (6:22; 13:21-22). This type of angelic appearance is used for commissioning.

The book of Tobit shows an author's modification of such a common presentation[4] so that the angel may reveal the healing secrets (to a group of healers?).[5] Tobit contains what must be a common angelology of the period--divine sending (3:16), angelic epiphany (5:4), note that the angel does not eat earthly food (12:19, cf. 2 Enoch 56:2), ascension with confession of witnesses (12:20-22). What is new is to show the meal becoming the basis of a means of healing--the angel telling his practitioner, Tobias, about the parts of the meal which are useful for healing and then instructing Tobias in healing.

1 Enoch shows the angel Uriel giving revelation about the endtime and heavenly rewards and punishments. Uriel informs Noah about the endtime (10:1) and also serves as a guide to heaven for Enoch (18:14; 19:1; 21:5ff.; 27:1ff.).[6] Both Raphael (22:3; 32:6) and Michael (24:6-25:6) answer human queries. Thus angels are revealers not only on earth but in heaven.

Dan 7, 8 and 9 (and the works modelled on these chapters) show the angel as interpreter of visions about history and the endtime. In Dan 7, Daniel approaches one (an angel) who stands. In Dan 8, God has Gabriel tell Daniel the meaning of visions. In Dan 9, the angel Gabriel comes while Daniel is at prayer. Daniel has been meditating on scripture and Gabriel interprets it for him. 4 Ezra and 2 Baruch use Danielic angelology.

2. Dialogue Between God and Angels

In the preceding section it was noted that in Tobit God asks Raphael to go to Tobit. The dialogue between God and an angel is a common feature of later biblical literature. Job presents a dialogue between God and Satan. Job also speaks of angelic intercession (33:23-24). In Zechariah, the angel of the Lord interceded with God for Jerusalem (1:12) and talks to Satan (3:1). In Dan 8:16, a voice tells Gabriel what to tell Daniel. One should also note the earlier presentation of Isa 6 where God speaks and Isaiah is the one who answers in the heavenly court.[7]

3. Other Functions of Angels

The Bible also shows angels used for purposes other than revelation, especially for leading in battle or leading persons toward destruction. In Exod 23:20, God says he will send an angel before the Israelites (cf. also Gen 24:7,40, where an angel is sent with Isaac--and in Tobit where an angel is sent with Tobias). Ps 35:5-6 speaks of an angel of the Lord driving and pursuing evildoers. Isa 37:36-37 and 2 Sam 24:16 speak of angels as destroyers. Gen 19 speaks of an angelic visitation and testing. 2 Sam 14:16 speaks of angelic discernment between good and evil. Such functions multiply in later periods.[8]

C. TA's Parallels in Hellenistic Jewish Angelology

Although TA alludes to the angelic epiphany of Gen 18, has destroying angels, typical biblical chariot transportation, and uses the kind of angelic motifs already found in Tobit, what is remarkable about TA's presentation is the number of parallels between the angelic motifs of TA and those of second century CE (or later) texts--2 Enoch, the Life of Adam and Eve (VAE), and the Apocalypse of Moses (AM). These parallels may suggest the time and circle of TA's author.[9]

2 Enoch, VAE and AM contain a large number of the incidental and important angelic motifs found in TA.[10] 2 Enoch 1 has angels come and take Enoch to heaven, telling those in his household what to do without him. 2 Enoch speaks of a chief captain of angels (22:6; 33:10; cf. 19:3; 20:1 and Rev 12:7; Dan 8:11 LXX). 2 Enoch emphasizes the angelic recording of the deeds of men (19:5).[11] The singing of angels is noted in 2 Enoch and AM (2 Enoch 17:1; 19:3; 23:1, AM 17:21; 22:3), especially their singing of the Trisagion (2 Enoch 21:1). All three works emphasize the angelic function of raising up, caring for and anointing dead men (2 Enoch 22:8; AM 43:1; cf. VAE 41:1-3; AM 40:1). In AM and VAE as well as TA, angels are especially merciful (concerned with the hero--and the Devil even pretends he is an angel by weeping in VAE 9:1). Angels join in prayers for the dead (AM 35:2; 37:2; VAE 21:2; 9:3).[12] The Devil (Death) is an angelic figure who changes his features (VAE 9:1; AM 17:1) and pursues man (VAE 11:2-5). However, Delcor rightly makes the point that the differences in angelology are important. For example, although VAE, AM and TA agree on many points, VAE and AM argue for resurrection in their angelic motif material; TA does not. The similarities may show the time and circle in which TA was written; the differences show at least that TA did not use (or necessarily agree with) all the theological views of such parallel works. However, one may argue that the parallels in 2 Enoch, VAE and AM are with both recensions of TA--and thus argue that it is difficult to

158

separate the recensions on the basis of country of origin.

D. TA's Use of Angelology to Advance the Story

TA uses such angelology[13] to present its story and introduce its theological points. In order to persuade Abraham to prepare for death, Isaac is given a dream and Michael takes the common angelic role of interpreter. Michael then explains the views of heaven which Abraham sees on his trip. By such explanations, the angel serves as a vehicle for the author's theology. Thus the author's views are reflected in those of Michael, who speaks of the concerns for men on the part of various heavenly figures: Adam who cries for men; an angel who balances good and evil deeds (thus giving man a fair chance); Abel who is a man judging man;[14] and Enoch (or angels) who faithfully record men's deeds.[15] Even Abraham's lack of a testament is explained in the story by the common motif of angelic concern for, and knowledge of the righteous, which make Michael hesitant to be precipitant with Abraham. In the long recension, the motif of angelic intercession for man is used to show further possibilities of compassion in heaven since Abraham and Michael are able to pray for and save souls whose good and evil deeds are in balance.

E. TA's Use of A Common Picture of Death--and the Long Recension's New Theology

The angelic commonplace that Death has many faces is used to explain why Death gets Abraham and, in the long recension, to give further reasons why men should not fear judgment--especially after untimely death.

The picture of Death as a deceiver, changing his features, enables the author to suggest both why Abraham was able to ask Death questions and how Abraham ultimately is taken away. Death's normal face is so horrifying that men (even Abraham) faint when he appears. However, as Death first approaches Abraham, Death puts on a garb of beauty (and the author uses a motif found in Sirach and elsewhere).[16] Abraham is thus able to ask him questions. The presentation in TA suggests that TA's author argues that the beautiful face of death is only a mask and that Death is basically dreadful. TA's author also uses the dishonesty of Death to have Death grab Abraham when an honest angel would not do so. Thus Death finally takes Abraham away from earth (as angels would not).

TA's long recension uses Death's many faces as a commonplace to present the recension's own theology of untimely death.

> In his discussion of untimely death, Schmidt recognizes the importance of untimely death for both recensions and cites parallels from Egyptian literature, Augustine, and various astrological works. However, for Schmidt untimely death is merely the lot of the impious; Schmidt does not note the argument made in the long recension of TA.

In both recensions of TA, God is presented as invalidating untimely death by raising up the servants (of Abraham) whom Death has killed. Further, God says He does not want Abraham to bring destruction on the world because God wants sinners to repent and live. Thus in both recensions, God does not seek men's death. Untimely death is brought about by figures other than God. The long recension adds that anyone who dies untimely has already received punishment.[17]

The author of the long recension continues his theological emphasis in the story of the conversation between Death and Abraham. Abraham tries to delay Death by asking about Death's many faces. Death says he sends many to Hell--and lists the types of death. Abraham finally and very quietly inquires whether there is an untimely death. Death replies that there are seventy-two deaths, one of which is the just death occurring at its alloted time; the rest are those who go to death within one hour (i.e. suddenly). The irony is all there. According to the earlier saying of God, all those whom death has taken violently (i.e. seventy-one of seventy-two deaths) will receive no further punishment. Death may see himself marching sinners off to Hell, but he actually saves them from further punishment. The commonplaces that the angel of death has many faces and brings violent death is turned to the author's theological point of the mercy of heaven.[18]

Thus TA uses an angelology typical of his period to present his theology. The story of TA is developed through the donne\'es of such angelology. The angelology also is used to promote the theology of the author--to show what is invalid (killing untimely) and what is valid (to intercede for men). These are arguments for TA's dogma that God does not judge further those who die untimely. The power of myth is that it uses characteristics of gods, men or angels (well known to its audience) to establish the validity of its argument. Mythical commonplaces and known possibilities validate the story.[19]

[1] This is a revision of a paper which first appeared in Septuagint and Cognate Studies 2 (1972)228-45. Part of the earlier paper appears in the present volume in the immediately preceding paper.

[2] See above, p 150, n. 2.

[3] On the significance of these motifs, see above, p. 149, n. 1. I assume a different author for the long and short recensions of TA.

[4] F. Zimmermann (The Book of Tobit [New York: Harper, 1958] 112) recognized the relationship of Judges and Tobit.

[5] Angels know methods of healing, cf. 1 Enoch 40:9.

[6] The use of an angelic guide to the otherworld seems to reflect an adaptation of the guides to the underworld used by Homer, Vergil, etc. As discussed by T.F. Glasson (Greek Influence on Jewish Eschatology [London: SPCK, 1961] 8-11, the guided trip to the underworld (nekyia) is a typical feature of Homeric epics and is a more likely source for Jewish literature in this period than the Gilgamesh epic (although the Gilgamesh epic may have been a source for Homeric literature).

[7] Zechariah also shows a prophet conversing with an angel. The conversations are the basis for a call to prophesy (Zech 1:7ff.; cf. 2-8; 1 Kgs 22; 1 Enoch 15:2; Isa 6).

[8] 1 Enoch 41:1 notes angelic weighing of the works of men; cf. other weighing (43:2; 60:12; 61:8).

[9] TA also uses an angelic attempt to get a man to set his house in order before he dies. Although this was a prophetic function in Isa 38, the Isaiah call and task reflect what must have been common angelic motifs, now picked up in TA.

[10] The relationship of the Apocalypse of Paul to TA is not clear. James suggests that the short recension of TA added material to the basic form of TA from the Apocalypse of Paul (AP). AP uses parallel material to that of TA: angels worshiping God at sunset (which is compared to man's worship, 7); a soul which says it has not sinned but has slain one person and committed adultery, etc. Cf. above, p. 151, n. 16, for further parallels not only with AP but with the Apocalypse of Elijah.

[11] This is parallel to the long recension where angels record the good and evil deeds of men (but cf. short rec., ch. 10). 2 Enoch makes Enoch a recorder. In 2 Enoch 22:12, the angel brings books and writing utensils to Enoch (cf. the short "recension.)" The angel is no longer the only recorder, but tells secrets to Enoch so that Enoch can become recorder (23: 2-4). Enoch is also told secrets of creation unknown to angels.

[12] Cf. above, p. 151, n. 16.

[13] This author is still not convinced by Schmidt's argument that TA is influenced by Persian works. There seem to be too many other Jewish parallels.

[14] Cf. above, p. 151, n. 12.

[15] The point that no deed is forgotten is shown by reference to the books of the cherubim.

[16] Cf. above, p. 151, n. 16.

[17] Thus one might argue that the long recension has moved from the original structure of the story. The short recension, however, does not seem original either (cf. above, p. 149, n.1).

[18] The type of solution to the problem in TA (especially in the long recension) should be contrasted both with dualism and with a complete subservience of death to God. It also should be contrasted with a doctrine of disobedient angels and their punishments found in 1 Enoch. God turns the judgment of man and the actions of death (in causing untimely death) into life for the persons involved.

[19] Apuleius' *The God of Socrates* shows the Hellenistic use of a man's guardian demon who seizes the man to take him to judgment immediately after death. Apuleius reflects Plato's Phaedo, and Apuleius' thought should be considered representative of one current in a Hellenistic world which was the context for TA.

PART TWO

ON PARALLEL TRADITIONS

ABRAHAM TRADITIONS IN THE TESTAMENT OF ABRAHAM AND IN
THE "REWRITTEN BIBLE" OF THE INTERTESTAMENTAL PERIOD

Daniel J. Harrington

This report presents information concerning the Abraham traditions in the *Testament of Abraham* (hereafter TAbr) and in pieces of intertestamental Jewish literature sometimes described as rewritings of the Bible--*Jubilees*, the Qumran *Genesis Apocryphon*, Pseudo-Philo's *Biblical Antiquities*, Philo's *De Abrahamo*, and Josephus' *Antiquities*. A "tradition" is not a direct quotation or mere paraphrase of the biblical text; rather, it is an imaginative development stemming from reflection upon the figure of Abraham. After the major Abraham traditions in both Greek recensions of TAbr have been isolated, the Abraham traditions in each of the other works listed above are examined and their points of contact or contradiction with TAbr are discussed. Such a procedure allows us to recognize that there are different "readings" of the Abraham material from Genesis and to see how these agree and differ with the reading in TAbr. Omissions of biblical incidents (e.g. *Jubilees* omits mention of Abraham's deceptions in passing Sarah off as his sister) are not considered, because these necessarily involve an argument from silence. Also, motifs attributed to figures other than Abraham in the Jewish tradition but to Abraham in TAbr are not taken into account, because this paper is intended as a sounding, not as a comprehensive presentation of all the possible evidence.

The major motifs connected with Abraham in the long Greek recension of TAbr are these: Abraham the friend of God lived 995 years and was extraordinarily hospitable to all kinds of people. Michael was sent to him to announce his death (1). He met Michael while he sat beside his implements for plowing and was greeted as the elect soul (2). Abraham heard the tree praising God in a human voice and saw the angel's tears turning into precious stones (3). Michael is given instructions by God about how Abraham's death will be announced by Isaac's dream and how he can share in the meal set before him by Abraham (4). Isaac is frightened by his dream about Abraham's death (5). Sarah identifies Michael as one of the three visitors of Genesis

18 and tells how the unblemished calf apparently eaten by those visitors was restored to life (6). Michael interprets Isaac's dream of the sun and the moon being taken away as referring to Abraham and Sarah respectively, and then reveals himself as the angel sent to announce Abraham's death (7). When God's command is transmitted by Michael, Abraham submits obediently and requests the opportunity of seeing the whole inhabited world and everything created by God's word (8-9). Taken in the cherubic chariot to view the whole world, Abraham calls forth destruction on those caught in sinful acts; his pitilessness is contrasted with the patient mercy of God who waits for a person to die before he is judged (10). At the first gate of heaven he sees the glorious Adam watching many lost souls being led through the wide gate and the few saved souls being conducted through the narrow gate (11). He is then shown the wondrous man "like a son of God" judging and presiding over the weighing of souls (12). The wondrous judge is identified as Abel, and his two angelic assistants as Dokiel and Puruel respectively (13). Through the intercession of the prayer of Abraham and Michael, the soul whose good and evil works balanced out was saved (14). Even though he refuses to accept death, he is spared by God because his goodness even surpasses that of his contemporary Job (15). Death is sent to Abraham and appears in various frightening forms (16-17). Abraham intercedes for his dead servants, and they are revivified (18). Abraham enters into dialogue with Death, and finally accedes to God's will. Abraham's bosom is described as the resting place of the just (19-20).

Additional motifs are found in the short Greek recension: Abraham was holding Isaac in his arms when Michael arrived (2). Abraham's soul will be taken up to heaven, but his body is to remain on earth for 7,000 years until the resurrection of the dead (7). Abraham is taken to the River Oceanus to see the two gates (8). He is too big to enter through the gate (9). His prayer restores his servants to life (14). The discussion that follows is keyed to the long Greek version mainly because it has more haggadic features, though most of the traditions are found in both recensions; for a synoptic outline of the content of the two recensions, see M. Delcor's *Le Testament d'Abraham* (Studia in Veteris Testamenti Pseudepigrapha II; Leiden: Brill, 1973), pp. 6-11. The method of presentation in this paper does not imply a firm decision about the priority of the long version.

The most significant Abraham traditions in *Jubilees* are these: Abram was named after his maternal grandfather (11:15). His ancestors were idolators, though he was not (11:16). He devised a way of keeping the ravens away from the seed and invented a method of plowing (11:18-24). Rising by night, he burns the house of idols at Ur (12:12). Abraham observes the stars (12:16) and learns Hebrew (12:26-27). He is told by Terah to come back for him (12:31). Abraham celebrates his covenant with God on the 15th of Siwan (14:20), and Isaac is born on the same date (16:13). He is the first to celebrate Tabernacles (16:21). Mastema instigates the sacrifice of Isaac (17:16). Because of his patience in the ten trials, Abraham is recorded on the heavenly tablets as the friend of God (19:8-9). He foresees that his seed will continue through Jacob rather than through Esau (19:15-31) and gives farewell speeches to all his sons (20), to Isaac alone (21), and to Jacob (22). He dies with Jacob lying in his bosom (23:2), at the age of 175 years (23:9). There are some interesting parallels with TAbr. In Jub 11:23-24 Abraham is described as the inventor of plowing, and in TAbr 2 Michael meets him near his plowing equipment. The large amount of space devoted to Abraham's speeches before his death in Jubilees 20--23 stands in contrast to the surprising lack of a farewell speech in TAbr. The notion that Jacob is resting in Abraham's bosom when he dies (Jub 23:2) may have something to do with the tradition that Abraham's bosom is the resting place of the just (TAbr 20).

Among the Abraham traditions in the Qumran *Genesis Apocryphon* are these: The dream of the cedar (Abraham) and the date-palm (Sarah) is described and interpreted (19:14-21). Sarah's beauty is recognized and described at length (19:22--20:8). Pharaoh is punished in answer to Abraham's prayer (20:16); but when Hirqanos learns Abraham's true identity from Lot, Pharaoh is healed through Abraham's prayer and the laying on of his hands (20:28-29). Abraham makes a grand tour of the promised land (21:8-19). Ten years elapse between his departure from Haran and the promise of Gen 15:4 (21:27-28). There may be some contacts between the *Genesis Apocryphon* and TAbr. The tour over the land that is based on Gen 13:17 in *1QapGen* 21:8-19 and the world-tour in TAbr 10 are somewhat similar.

The cedar/date-palm vision in *1QapGen* 19:14-21 bears some resemblance to the sun/moon vision of TAbr 7, and the power of Abraham's prayer is emphasized in both *1QapGen* 20:16,28-29 and TAbr 14,18.

The following are the major traditions connected with Abraham in Pseudo-Philo's *Biblical Antiquities*: Abraham's ancestors were not idolators (4:16). He refused to participate in building the tower of Babel and was rescued from the fiery furnace (6:3-18; 23:5; 32:1). The place where this happened is called "by the name of Abram and in the language of the Chaldeans 'Deli,' which means 'God' (6:18)." Isaac offers himself willingly to be sacrificed (18:5; 32:2-4). Abraham is raised above the heavens and shown the stars (18:5). He is also shown the place where iniquities are expiated and where torches illumine the just (23:6). Isaac was born in the seventh month of his mother's pregnancy (23:8). The angels envied Abraham and were jealous of him (32:1). The closest points of contact between Ps-Philo and TAbr involve Abraham's world tour in the heavenly chariot (10) and his vision of the judgment process (11-14). In Ps-Philo 18:5 Abraham is raised above the firmament and shown the arrangements of all the stars: "quando levavi eum super firmamentum et ostendi ei omnium astrorum dispositiones." But whereas in Ps-Philo Abraham sees the arrangements of the stars, in TAbr he sees the various kinds of evil being done on earth. In Ps-Philo 23:6 Abraham sees "the place of fire where the deeds of those doing wickedness against Me will be expiated...and the torches of fire by which the just who have believed in Me will be enlightened." But whereas in Ps-Philo Abraham sees the places of judgment, in TAbr he is granted a vision of the process itself. Also, there are contradictions on two minor points. In TAbr 15 Job is Abraham's contemporary, but in Ps-Philo 8:8 Job marries Dinah. In TAbr Michael admires Abraham, but in Ps-Philo 32:1 the angels are jealous of him. Finally, the two most significant motifs regarding Abraham in Ps-Philo--the escape from the fiery furnace and the binding of Isaac--are totally absent from TAbr.

The major Abraham traditions in Philo's *De Abrahamo* are these: Abraham is a symbol of virtue acquired by teaching (52), departs from his homeland with great speed (62-67), rejects the Chaldean astrology in which he was reared (70-71), has a name meaning "elect father of sound" (82), and wanders in the wilderness of mystic solitude (85). Sarah recognized the angelic visitors as spiritual beings (113). Abraham's hospitality is a by-product of his piety (114), and the angels only appear to eat and drink (118). Abraham's willingness to sacrifice Isaac (178-199), his settlement with Lot out of his desire for tranquillity (216), Sarah as the perfect wife (245-246), Abraham's equanimity at Sarah's death (255-261), his role as a model of faith (268) and as *nomos kai thesmos agraphos* (276) are discussed. What do *De Abrahamo* and TAbr have in common? In both DeAbr 118 and TAbr 4 the angels only appear to eat, and in DeAbr 114 and TAbr 1 Abraham's hospitality is extolled. Most important of all is the notion that just as Sarah recognized the three visitors as spiritual beings (DeAbr 113), so she is the one who recognizes Michael as an angel (TAbr 6).

Among the Abraham traditions in Josephus' *Antiquities* these seem most important for our purposes: Sarah was Abraham's niece (1:151,211). Abraham was the first monotheist (1:154-157), was king of Damascus (1:159), went to convert the Egyptians (1:161), and taught them arithmetic and astronomy (1:167). The angelic visitors only seemed to eat (1:197), and Abraham was the model of liberality and hospitality (1:200). Isaac offers himself willingly to be sacrificed (1:232). The major point of contact with TAbr is the tradition that the angelic visitors only seemed to eat (Ant. 1:197) and Michael's food being eaten not by him but by a devouring spirit (TAbr 4). Both Ant. 1:200 and TAbr 1 call attention to Abraham's hospitality.

Conclusions: The results of this investigation of parallels between TAbr and the five examples of the "rewritten Bible" are modest. Only in Jubilees 20--23 is much emphasis placed on the events preceding Abraham's death, and there we have farewell speeches in the testament form rather than the events narrated in TAbr. The most significant parallels are these: (1) Abraham's extraordinary hospitality is praised in TAbr 1, Philo's *De Abrahamo* 114, and Josephus' *Antiquities* 1:200, but all three texts clearly have Genesis 18 as a common starting point. *De Abrahamo* 114: "We have described Abraham's hospitality which was but a by-product of a greater virtue. That virtue is piety, of which we have spoken before, and it is quite clearly seen in this story even if we think of the strangers as men" (trans. Colson). *Antiquities* 1:200: "...and Lot invited them to be his guests, for he was very kindly to strangers and had learnt the lesson of Abraham's liberality" (Thackeray). (2) In both TAbr 2 and Jub 11:18-24 Abraham is involved in agriculture. Jubilees 11:23-24: "And in the first year of the fifth week Abram taught those who made implements for oxen, the artificers in wood, and they made a vessel above the ground, facing the frame of the plough, in order to put the seed thereon, and the seed fell down therefrom upon the share of the plough, and was hidden in the earth, and they no longer feared the ravens. And after this manner they made (vessels) above the ground on all the frames of the ploughs, and they sowed and tilled all the land, according as Abram commanded them, and they no longer feared the birds" (Charles). (3) The tradition in *De Abrahamo* 118 and Josephus' *Antiquities* 1:197 that the angelic visitors of Genesis 18 only seemed to eat is a good parallel to Michael's hesitancy to partake of the food set before him in TAbr 4. *De Abrahamo* 118: "It is a marvel indeed that though they neither ate nor drank they gave the appearance of both eating and drinking" (Colson). *Antiquities* 1:197: "On their assenting, he ordered loaves of fine flour to be made forthwith and killed a calf and cooked it and brought it to them as they reclined under the oak; and they gave him to believe that they did eat" (Thackeray). (4) It is Sarah who recognized the angelic visitors according to *De Abrahamo* 113 and who recognized Michael according to TAbr 6. *De Abrahamo* 113: "It was then, I think, that she first saw in the strangers before her a different and grander aspect, that of prophets or angels, transformed from their spiritual and soul-like nature into human shape" (Colson). (5) The parallel between Isaac's dream of Abraham and Sarah as the sun and the moon respectively (TAbr 7) and Abraham's dream of the cedar and the date-palm (*1QapGen* 19) is purely formal. *Genesis Apocryphon* 19: "And on the night of our entry into Egypt, I, Abram, dreamt a dream; (and behold), I saw in my dream a cedar tree and a palm tree...men came and they sought to cut down the cedar tree and to pull up its roots, leaving the palm tree (standing) alone. But the palm tree cried out saying: 'Do not cut down this cedar tree, for cursed be he who shall fell (it).' And the cedar tree was spared because of the palm tree and (was) not felled" (Vermes). (6) Abraham's world tour in TAbr 10 is loosely paralleled by his extensive tour of the land in *1QapGen* 21 and more closely connected with his tour of the heavens in Ps-Philo 18:5. *Genesis Apocryphon* 21: "And I, Abram, departed to travel about and see the land. I began my journey at the river Gihon and travelled along the coast of the sea..." (Vermes). *Ps-Philo* 18:5: "And God said to him: Was it not concerning this people that I spake unto Abraham in a vision saying: *Thy seed shall be as the stars of the heaven*, when I raised him up above the firmament and showed him all the orderings of the stars, and required of him his son for a burnt offering?" (James). (7) TAbr 11-14 and Ps-Philo 23:6 suggest a relation between Abraham and the judgment of sinners, but the parallel is not exact. *Ps-Philo* 23:6: "And I sent a sleep upon him and compassed him about with fear, and I set before him the place of fire wherein the works of them that commit iniquity against me shall be avenged, and I showed him the torches of fire whereby the righteous which have believed in me shall be enlightened" (James). (8) The power of Abraham's intercessory prayer is stressed in both TAbr 14,18 and *1QapGen* 20:16,28-29, but this is a commonplace attached to many religious figures. *Genesis Apocryphon* 20: "I prayed that night and I begged and implored....So I prayed (for him)...and I laid my hands on his (head); and the scourge departed from him and the evil (spirit) was expelled (from him), and he lived" (Vermes). (9) The parallel between Abraham's bosom as the abode of the just in TAbr 20 and as Jacob's resting place in Jub 23:2 (cf. 23:26) is purely verbal. *Jubilees* 23:2: "And notwithstanding all this Jacob was lying in his bosom, and knew not that Abraham, his father's father, was dead" (Charles).

ABRAHAM TRADITIONS IN EARLY CHRISTIANITY

Roy Bowen Ward

For the benefit of the members of the Pseudepigrapha Seminar, this paper aims to lay out the references to Abraham which are to be found in the earliest literature of early Christianity. In some cases references are merely conventional, e.g. in the references to the "God of Abraham, Isaac and Jacob;" in some cases the Abrahamic material appears to be derived immediately from the text of Scripture; in some cases the material is mediated through traditions about Abraham current in Jewish lore. Since the Seminar has as its focus the Testament of Abraham, the early Christian references to Abraham have been examined especially for possible parallels to the Testament of Abraham.[1]

1. Paul

Abraham is mentioned expressly in three letters of the Pauline corpus: Galatians, 2 Corinthians and Romans.

1.1 Galatians (3:6, 7, 8, 9, 14, 16, 18, 29; 4:22)

In Galatians Paul introduces Abraham in 3:6 with the quotation of Gen 15:6. What concerns Paul primarily is the question, who are the sons (υἱοί) or offspring (σπέρμα) of Abraham; and this theme is a thread which runs through discussion from 3:7 to the end of ch. 4. Based on Gen 15:6 (ἐπίστευσεν τῷ θεῷ) Abraham is the father of οἱ ἐκ πίστεως. By associating Gen 15:6 with Gen 18:18 (ἐνευλογηθήσονται ἐν σοὶ πάντα τὰ ἔθνη), Paul can argue that God justifies the Gentiles ἐκ πίστεως (3:8). To this Paul adds in 3:16 reference to τὸ σπέρμα (Gen 12:7; 22:17, 18), which here he understands

---

[1] The text of the Greek recensions used in this paper is that edited by M. R. James, "The Testament of Abraham," Texts and Studies, vol. 2, no. 2 (1892). The English translation used is that by Michael E. Stone, The Testament of Abraham (Texts and Translations 2, Pseudepigrapha Series 2, Society of Biblical Literature, 1972). Primary attention has been given to the longer recension (A).

as referring to Christ. Thus, if Gentiles are in Christ (3:27), they are Abraham's σπέρμα and heirs according to the promise (3:29).

This argument directed against the judaizing program in the Galatian churches is primarily exegetical rather than traditional. Furthermore, the argument is novel. For example, in Jewish tradition the σπέρμα of Abraham is usually synonymous with the Jewish people (TAbr (A) III, VIII; TLevi 8:15; Psa Sol 9:17; 18:4; IV Macc 18:1).[2] Although his hermeneutical method of interpreting σπέρμα may be traditional,[3] his result, viz. identifying it with Christ, is not.[4] It may well be that Paul's concern with the question of the sons/σπέρμα of Abraham was occasioned by the concern of the judaizers who understood σπέρμα of Abraham as referring to Jews, that is, individuals who have been circumcised.

1.2 2 Corinthians (11:22)

The single reference to Abraham in 2 Corinthians occurs in Paul's polemic against the super-apostles who have come into the Corinthian church. "Are they σπέρμα of Abraham? So am I" (11:22). The designation, σπέρμα of Abraham, is apparently the self-designation of Paul's opponents.[5]

1.3 Romans (4; 1, 2, 3, 9, 12, 13, 16 (and passim); 9:7; 11:1)

In Romans Paul twice refers to σπέρμα of Abraham in the traditional meaning of Jews (9:7, 11:1), although he argues that "not all are children (τέκνα) of Abraham because they are his descendants (σπέρμα) (9:7).

In ch. 4 Paul focuses on Abraham. As in Galatians, this passage is largely exegetical, beginning with the quotation of Gen 15:6 (4:3). The reference to "one who . . . trusts him who justifies the ungodly" (4:5) is similar to the figure of Abraham in TAbr (A) XIV where he intercedes to God for

---

[2] "Philo's Place in Judaism: A Study of Conceptions of Abraham in Jewish Literature II," HUAC 26 (1955), 158.

[3] E. E. Ellis, Paul's Use of the Old Testament (1957), pp. 70-73.

[4] In other passages Paul uses σπέρμα Abraham with its conventional meaning: 2 Cor 11:22; Rom 9:7; 11:1.

[5] See D. Georgi, Die Gegner des Paulus im 2. Korintherbrief (WMANT 11, 1964), pp. 63-82.

sinners.[6] Going beyond his argument in Gal., Paul notes that the reckoning of Abraham as righteous (Gen 15:6) occurred before he was circumcised (Gen 17:10). Thus, he can be considered "the father of all who believe without being circumcised" (4:11).[7] The argument in 4:13-17 follows generally the line taken in Gal. -- that the promise is ἐκ πίστεως, for those who share the faith of Abraham, the father of us all (4:16). At this point the argument moves in a different direction than it does in Gal., pointing to the hopeful trust of Abraham. With reference to the apparent failure of God to fulfill the promise through Abraham's descendants when, in fact, he had no descendants, Abraham believed. He was "fully convinced that God was able to do what he had promised" (4:21), that is, he was convinced that God would provide descendants despite his old age and Sarah's barrenness. It is at this point that Abraham serves as an especially relevant model for the problem with which Paul is concerned in Romans.[8] TAbr (A) VII mentions the miraculous birth to "the sterile Sarah," but the point is different. In TAbr God tells Abraham through Michael that he has granted Abraham everything for which he has asked, but death is inevitable. Paul, on the other hand, uses the example of Abraham's hopeful trust as a model for Christians' trust in resurrection, which for Paul is the overcoming of death (cf. I Cor 15:20-26).

4. In summary, we see that Paul's use of Abraham stands almost by itself, determined by his exegesis of scripture for particular purposes. The portrait of Abraham in Paul owes little if anything to traditions about Abraham in post-biblical Judaism in general and in the TAbr in particular.

---

[6] Cf. Anitra Kolenkow, "The Ascription of Romans 4:5," HTR 60 (1967), 228-230.

[7] The argument appearing in Rom 4:10-12 concerning circumcision would have been ideally suited for Paul's polemic against the judaizers in Galatia where circumcision was expressly an issue. Perhaps this is a further indication that Paul's use of Abraham is primarily derived exegetically -- in this case, from his scripture study accomplished in the interval between writing Galatians and Romans.

[8] See J. Munck, Paul and the Salvation of Mankind (ET 1959), p. 133.

2. Gospel Tradition

2.1 Synoptic Tradition
(Mt 1:1, 2, 17; 3:9, 9; 8:11; 22:32
Mk 12:26
Lk 1:55, 73; 3:8, 8, 34; 13:16, 28; 16:22, 23, 24, 25, 29, 30; 19:9; 20:37.)

Abraham is mentioned only once in Mark; Mk 12:26 (followed by Mt 22:32 and Lk 20:37). Here the reference comes from Ex 3:6, "I am the God of Abraham, and the God of Isaac, and the God of Jacob." (Compare also Acts 7:32 where Ex 3:6 is again cited.)

Reference to Abraham in Q material is also rare. In the pericope, "John's Preaching of Repentence," John warns those coming to be baptized not to say, "'We have Abraham as our father'; for I tell you, God is able from these stones to raise up children to Abraham." (Lk 3:8 = Mt 3:9).

The minatory saying about Abraham, Isaac and Jacob in the kingdom (Mt 8:11 and Lk 13:28) appears in Mt and Lk in different contexts and in slightly different versions.[9] In Mt this saying is added to the pericope about the centurion's servant, while in Lk it occurs within a collection of teachings on exclusion from the kingdom. In both versions Abraham, Isaac and Jacob will be in the kingdom while the sons of the kingdom (Lk = you) will be thrown out. In both versions the heirs of the kingdom will "sit at table" (in Mt with Abraham et al.). The motif of eating with Abraham appears in a somewhat different way in TAbr (A) IV, V, where Abraham's hospitality is extended to the angel Michael in terms of eating together.

That Abraham, Isaac and Jacob will be found together with the righteous is common to Jewish tradition. For example, the martyrs in IV Macc say, "After this our passion, Abraham, Isaac and Jacob shall receive us into their bosoms, and all our forefathers will praise us" (13:17). In TLevi 18:14 Abraham, Isaac and Jacob exult after the opening of the gates of Paradise, etc. In TJud 25:1 Abraham, Isaac and Jacob arise to life after the sceptre of Judah's kingdom shines forth. In TBen 10:6 Abraham, Isaac and Jacob will rise on the right hand in

---

[9] Cf. R. Bultmann, The History of the Synoptic Tradition (ET 1963), pp. 61, 116.

gladness when the Lord reveals his salvation to the nations."[10]

The remaining references to Abraham in the synoptics come from special sources. Abraham occurs in the genealogies of both Mt (1:1, 2, 17) and Lk (3:34). In the <u>magnificat</u> of Mary the merciful acts of God are described as being in accordance with the promise to Abraham and his σπέρμα forever (Lk 1:55). In the hymn of Zechariah a similar theme appears in a promise-fulfillment context: God has remembered his holy covenant, "the oath which he swore to our father Abraham" (Lk 1:73). In Lk 13:16 an infirm woman is identified as "a daughter of Abraham," and in Lk 19:9 Zacchaeus is identified as a "son of Abraham."

The remaining passage where Abraham is mentioned is in the story about the rich man and Lazarus in Lk 16:19-31. The story itself is probably, as Gressmann proposed, dependent on an Egyptian tale, whose closest descendent is the Demotic tale of Satme.[11] The role of Osiris in the Egyptian tradition has been replaced in the Lukan story by Abraham. Of particular interest is the description of Lazarus after death in the bosom of Abraham (16:23). In TAbr (A) XX the voice of God spoke: "Take, therefore, my friend Abraham to the garden (paradise), where the tabernacles of my righteous ones and the abodes of my holy ones Isaac and Jacob are in his bosom, where there is no toil, no sadness, no sighing, but peace and joy and endless life." (Cf. IV Macc 13:16; b. Talmud, Kidd., 72b.).

Further, it is said in Lk 16:22 that Lazarus "was carried by the angels" to Abraham's bosom. So also in TAbr (A) II Abraham's soul was escorted to heaven by angels. However, as K. Grobel has noted, in the Lukan story it is not evident that Abraham and Lazarus are "up" in heaven. The narrative follows more closely the Egyptian tradition about

---

[10]This tradition is continued in Christianity, for example, in the <u>Acts of Paul</u> 27: "I saw Abraham, Isaac, and Jacob, Lot and Job and other saints . . . All those who have given hospitality to strangers, when they come forth from the world, first worship the Lord God and are handed over to Michael and by this route are led into the city, and all the righteous greet them as sons and brothers and say to them, 'Because you have kept humanity and hospitality for strangers, come, receive an inheritance in the city of our God.'"

[11]See K. Grobel, ". . . whose Name was Neves," <u>NTS</u> 10 (1963/64), 373-382.

Amnte[12] than the model provided in TAbr.

2.2 John (8:33, 37, 39, 39, 39, 40, 52, 53, 56, 57, 58)

All of the references to Abraham in the Gospel according to John occur in Jn 8 where the Jews appeal to the fact that they are σπέρμα Abraham (8:33, 37) (cf. τέκνα of Abraham (8:39).). Accordingly, they claim never to have been in bondage to anyone (cf. Josephus Bell. VII, 336: "we preferred death to slavery"). When the Jews claim Abraham as "our father," the Johannine Jesus says, "you would do what Abraham did, but now you seek to kill me, a man who has told you the truth which I heard from God; this is not what Abraham did" (8:39, 40). If this passage means that Abraham would not kill a divine messenger, then it may refer to a scene like that of Gen 18[13] where he welcomed three men who speak for Yahweh (18: 10, 13) and who apparently are angels (cf. 19:1). This story serves as a basis in the tradition to portray Abraham as one who offers hospitality to strangers. In TAbr (A) II Abraham goes out to greet Michael, "as he usually met and welcomed all strangers."

When the Johannine Jesus states that the one who keeps his word will never see death, the Jews ask if he is greater than Abraham who died? (8:53). It is not self-evident why the fact that Abraham died would suggest that Jesus was greater than Abraham, unless the meaning is that although Abraham could not ward off death, Jesus can for the one who keeps his word. This is reminiscent of the attempts of Abraham in TAbr to ward off death, at first, refusing to follow Michael (TAbr (A) VII, XV.). Finally, Abraham sees Death and also refuses to follow him (TAbr (A) XVI). Abraham invites Death to beseech God to raise up those who have died untimely, and it is done for these (TAbr (A) XVIII). Again Abraham resists Death (TAbr (A) XIX), but Death deceived Abraham by getting Abraham to embrace his hand; Death could be warded off no longer (TAbr (A) XX).[14]

---

[12] Grobel, art. cit., pp. 378f.

[13] As suggested by R. E. Brown, The Gospel According to John I-XII (Anchor Bible 29, 1966), p. 357.

[14] M. R. James understands this theme in TAbr in terms of Abraham's "fear of death;" op. cit., pp. 64ff. However, it is not obvious that fear is the central motiff.

If we could presume this tradition as a background, the Johannine discourse would present the difference between Jesus and Abraham in even sharper terms. Thus, e.g., we could read 8:53: Are you greater than our father Abraham who resisted Death but who, nevertheless died?[15]

The Johannine Jesus continues, "Your father Abraham rejoiced that he was to see my day; he saw it and was glad" (8:56). There has been considerable debate concerning when Abraham was supposed to have seen "my day."[16] One possibility is that this refers to a revelation given to Abraham during his lifetime, based mainly on Gen 15:7-21.[17] This revelation is attested, e.g., in IV Ezra 3:14: ". . . thou didst choose thee one from among them whose name was Abraham: him thou didst love, and unto him only didst thou reveal the end of the times secretly by night." (Cf. Syr. Baruch 4:4; Apoc. Abr. 9-32). This tradition is also attested in rabbinic tradition, e.g., in Gen R 44:25 where R. Akiba claims that the age to come had been revealed to Abraham. So also in TAbr Abraham is taken up in a chariot to see all the world and the scene of judgment at the first gate of heaven (TAbr VIII-XIV.). If the Johannine statement refers to such a revelation, it refers only to the fact of the revelation, not the contents of the revelation in TAbr. Abraham in TAbr was not "glad" in what he saw.

3. Acts of the Apostles (3:13, 25; 7:2, 16, 17, 32; 13:26)

All of the references to Abraham in Acts are to be found in speeches.

In the speech of Peter on Solomon's portico God is identified as "The God of Abraham and of Isaac and of Jacob . . ." (3:13). Gen 22:18 is quoted in announcing that the blessings of the days or promise are now available to the sons of the prophets and of the covenant.

---

[15] R. Bultmann quotes Schlatter: "The fact that Abraham died is the most conclusive proof of the inevitability of death;" The Gospel of John (ET 1971), p. 325, n. 4. But the TAbr tradition adds the element of Abraham's active resistance to death.

[16] Brown, op. cit., pp. 359f.

[17] See N. A. Dahl, "The Johannine Church and History," Current Issues in New Testament Interpretation (ed. by W. Klassen and G. F. Synder, 1962), p. 134.

The speech of Stephen begins with the call of Abraham (7:2)[18] and relates the Abrahamic history (7:2-8), including the promise of an inheritance to his σπέρμα (7:5). Reference is made to the tomb which Abraham bought (7:16) and to the promise granted to Abraham (7:17). Ex 3:6 (God of Abraham . . .) is quoted in reference to Moses and the burning bush.

In the speech of Paul in Antioch of Pisidia he addresses the Jews, "Brethren, sons of the family of Abraham" (13:26).

In these passages Abraham is primarily a historical figure whose importance lies primarily in the promise given him. In his study on Abraham in Luke-Acts N. A. Dahl concludes,

> Luke, if I am correct, keeps closer to the Old Testament narratives and references to Abraham than does any other Christian or Jewish writer of his time. He gives very little room to legendary accretions and refrains from daring theological interpretations.[19]

This assessment is more accurate for the Acts material than for the Abraham material in Luke (above on Lk 16). In any case, there is no particular relationship to Abraham traditions such as are to be found in TAbr.

4. James (2:21, 23)

In the Epistle of James Abraham appears along with Rahab as historical examples within the diatribe, 2:14-26.

> Was not Abraham our father justified by works, when he offered his son Isaac upon the altar? You see that faith was active along with his works, and the scripture was fulfilled which says, 'Abraham believed God, and it was reckoned to him as righteousness'; and he was called the friend of God. (2:21-23).

This example has an obvious relationship to Gen 22 (the offering of Isaac) and Gen 15:6 (quoted in 2:23). But the reference to πίστις and ἔργα are less obvious.

The πίστις of Abraham is presupposed without explicit

---

[18] On the differences between the Lukan account and Gen, see E. Haenchen, The Acts of the Apostles (ET 1971), p. 278.

[19] N. A. Dahl, "The Story of Abraham in Luke-Acts," Studies in Luke-Acts (ed. by L. E. Keck and J. L. Martyn, 1966), p. 153.

reference,[20] and we have argued that this is also the case for Abraham's ἔργα[21] -- that is, Abraham is used as a well-known example of hospitality, but without referring explicitly to the famous story of his reception of the three men (Gen 18) or to the traditions based on the incident. Included in these traditions is the portrait of Abraham in the TAbr where he appears at the crossroads of the oak of Mamre as the paradigm of the hospitable man. In TAbr (A) I Abraham is introduced as exceedingly hospitable (πάνυ φιλόξενος), one who welcomed all, and who is addressed by God as "my beloved friend" (ὁ ἠγαπημένος μου φίλος). In TAbr (A) XVII Death explains to Abraham that he has come to him in a beautiful appearance because of "your righteous deeds and the boundless sea of your hospitality and the greatness of your love of God."[22]

This understanding of Abraham's ἔργα in James would be parallel to that of Rahab whose ἔργα are explicitly described as hospitality: ὑποδεξαμένη τοὺς ἀγγέλους καὶ ἑτέρᾳ ὁδῷ ἐκβαλοῦσα (2:25).

The reference to the ἔργα of Abraham does not come to the reader completely without preparation. In Gen 18 Abraham sees the three men, he receives them, he washes their feet, he provides rest and food (Gen 18:4-8), and then he sends them on their way (Gen 18:16). The little parable in James 2:15, 16 is similar to this account of Abraham's hospitality in one important respect: the scene depicted is that of the opportunity to care for someone in need and then send him on his way (ὑπάγετε ἐν εἰρήνῃ, 2:16). This is precisely what Abraham did and that for which he was famous in later tradition.[23]

Although the name of Abraham does not appear elsewhere in James, the exhortation on prayer in 5:14-16 is reminiscent of the righteous Abraham and his powerful prayers in TAbr.

---

[20]Cf. M. Dibelius and H. Greeven, James (Hermeneia, trans. M. A. Williams, ed. H. Koester, 1976), ad loc.

[21]R. B. Ward, "The Works of Abraham," HTR 61 (1968), 283-290.

[22]See also rabbinic literature: ARN I. ch. 7; Gen R 49, 4; 56, 5 and Ward, art. cit., pp. 286f.

[23]See Midr. Psa on 37:1; Yashar, wa-yera 42b; Ward, art. cit., p. 288.

In TAbr (A) XIV Abraham prayed for sinners, and in TAbr (A) XVIII he prays for those who died untimely and they were raised. In Jas 5:15 it is said that "the prayer of faith will save the sick man, and the Lord will raise him up; and if he has committed sins, he will be forgiven." Further, in Jas 5:16 it is said, "The prayer of a righteous man has great power in its effects" -- a statement which fits well the prayers of the righteous man Abraham in TAbr.

5. I Peter (3:6)

In I Pet 3:6 Sarah's obedience to Abraham (Gen 18:12) is used to support the exhortation for wives to be submissive to their husbands. Specifically, the Petrine passage says that Sarah called Abraham "Lord." This title is regularly used in the TAbr by Sarah in addressing Abraham: TAbr (A) V, VI, XV.

6. Hebrews 2:16; 6:13; 7:1, 2, 4, 5, 6, 9; 11:8, 17 and passim)

In the Epistle to the Hebrews it is said that Jesus is concerned for his "brethren" (from Psa 22:22, quoted in Heb 2:12) -- not angels, but the σπέρμα of Abraham (2:16). Here σπέρμα of Abraham appears not to refer to the Jewish people, but the (new) people of God.

In Heb 6:13 reference is made to the promise to Abraham (Gen 22:16-17) given with an oath and to Abraham's patient endurance. The argument runs in a strange way. In 6:14 the quotation is changed so that it is Abraham, not his seed, to whom the blessing comes. The argument is in the tradition of Jewish-Christian exegesis (also behind Philo).[24]

In Heb 7 Abraham is mentioned as one who offered tithes to Melchizedek (Gen 14), thus showing Abraham to be inferior to Melchizedek (7:7), of whose priesthood (Psa 110) Jesus became a high priest forever. (Cf. Jub 13:25-27; Josephus Ant I. 179-182; Gen R 43.)

In Heb 11 Abraham figures prominently as an example of faith -- that is, trust, based only on the word and related to the future. Thus by faith Abraham obeyed the call to do out to a place which he was to receive as an inheritance (11:8);

---

[24]See H. Koester, "Die Auslegung der Abraham-Verheissung in Hebräer 6," Studien zur Theologie der alttestamentlichen Überlieferungen (ed. R. Rendtorff and K. Koch, 1961), pp. 95-109.

and Aaron. This startling reinterpretation apparently originated from the same circles of priests which attached Aaron to the early tradition and also identified Moses' rod with that of Aaron which was kept by the "tablets of Testimony" (Num 17:25; Eng., v. 10). Even in the reshaped form of the story, Aaron's part in the plot remained a modest one. He merely did not react upon God's command to bring the water forth solely by the spoken word, and it was only Moses who actively defied the Lord's order. At first he uttered rash words of incredulity and addressed the people:

> Hear now, ye rebels, are we to bring forth water for you out of this rock? (Num 20:10)

Even after he had mustered some strength, he did not perform God's command, but rather struck the rock repeatedly, as if to underline the need of a forceful physical action.

This involved narrative reflects theological criticism, applied to an early tradition. A warrior deity, who rules after defeating mighty forces, uses a weapon, as it is appropriate for him. Likewise, it is befitting that his servant use this instrument at the deity's bidding. However, this does not befit God, who created the world purely by His word. His messenger should work wonders by the power of the word which God has put into his mouth. If this messenger does not believe in the omnipotence of God's word, and because of the weakness of his faith, requires a material instrument, he is considered as though he had refused to sanctify God's name in public. The story, therefore, indicates a crisis in religious thinking. An ancient tradition related that Moses caused the waters to come forth with a blow, whereas the late religious consciousness urgently postulated the flowing by means of the word. The present version reflects both the early narrative and its censure in later theology. It acknowledges as a fact that Moses was ordered to take the rod, and that he struck the rock with it and caused the waters to flow, but it reinterprets this act as a transgression.

The nature of this transgression has been already defined by Rashi in his commentary upon Num 20:12:

by faith he looked forward to the city of God (11:10). So also Sarah believed the promise of God that she would have descendants (11:11, 12). And Abraham, when he was tested, offered Isaac, despite the fact that Isaac was the child of promise (11:17-19).

7. I Clement (10:1, 6, 6, and passim; 17:2; 31:2)

In I Clem 10 Abraham "the Friend" appears as an example of those who were faithful in their obedience. Cited are the call of Abraham (Gen 12:1-3), his separation from Lot (Gen 13:14-16) and his offering of Isaac (Gen 22). In 10:7 it is said that a son was given to Abraham because of his faith and hospitality. Hospitality is also noted in the examples which follow, viz. of Lot and Rahab (I Clem 11, 12).[25] Although the bulk of this section is composed from Genesis quotations, Abraham's title, "the Friend," and the emphasis on hospitality belong to the Abrahamic traditions, including TAbr.

In I Clem 17:2 Abraham, "the Friend of God," appears as an example of humility, along with Job and Moses.[26]

In I Clem 31:2 Abraham, "our father," appears as an example of one blessed by God. He received the blessing because he worked righteousness and truth through faith.

8. Ignatius (ad Philad, 9:1)

In Ignatius' letter to the Philadelphians the High Priest is said to be the door of the Father, through which enter Abraham and Isaac and Jacob and the Prophets and the Apostles and the church. This is in line with the rather general opinion that these patriarchs will share in God's salvation.

9. Barnabas (6:8; 8:4; 9:7, 8; 13:7, 7, 7.)

In the Epistle of Barnabas reference is made to the good land promised to Abraham, Isaac and Jacob (6:8), understood eschatologically as the new creation. The same triad (who are "great before God") appears in 8:4 as an explanation why there are only three children who sprinkle in the red heifer ritual.

---

[25] See H. Chadwick, "Justification by Faith and Hospitality," Studia Patristica 4 (T.U. 79, 1961), 281-285.

[26] Cf. ARN 42; Lev R 11; and Sandmel, art. cit., p. 203.

In Barn 9:6-8 the author offers a gnosis on Abraham's circumcision (Gen 17). Abraham is said to have received the teachings of the three letters, which the author interprets on the basis of Gen 14:14 -- 318 = IHT, representing IHσους and T (i.e. the cross.)[27]

In Barn 13:7 the author paraphrases Gen 15:6 and proceeds to state: "Behold I have established you, Abraham, as the father of nations which believe in God while uncircumcized" -- a statement which belongs to a tradition similar to that in Paul, Rom 4:11.[28]

10. Summary

It is apparent that early Christians employed Abraham in an eclectic manner, according to their needs. Of special prominence was the promise to Abraham and the identification of Abraham's σπέρμα. For the most part, this use of Abraham depended on exegesis of scriptural texts, not Jewish lore (although the exegetical method employed was related to traditional methods).

Closer to Jewish lore about Abraham were such passages as the story of the Rich Man and Lazarus (Lk 16), the Johannine discussion about Abraham (Jn 8) and the use of Abraham as an example in parenetic traditions (Jas 2; 1 Pet 3; Heb 11; 1 Clem 10; 17; 31). It is not obvious that TAbr is in any case a direct source for this material, but at several points there are parallels which may suggest at the least common traditions.

---

[27] Cf. R. A. Kraft, "Barnabas and the Didache," The Apostolic Fathers, vol. 3 (1965), pp. 108f.

[28] Cf. R. A. Kraft, op. cit., p. 123.

THE DEATH OF MOSES*

Samuel E. Loewenstamm

[p. 142] The death of Moses occupied the mind of apocryphal and midrashic writers unceasingly. They never tired of seeking new and innovative ways to understand it. The origins of this lengthy and complicated dialectical process are inherent in the Bible itself. The biblical description of Moses' death is shrouded with the grandeur of mystery. Moreover, we encounter passages in the Bible that ascribe Moses' passing to a special decree of God. Therefore, it is evident that already in biblical times Moses' death had become a theological problem and that it is with this problem that the transmittors of later tradition continued to wrestle unceasingly.

One cannot approach this complex of highly variegated lore without asking the fundamental question: Why did Moses' death become a vexing problem even though the man passed away in ripe old age.[1]

It seems that there were two problems that called for solution. The first is explicit already in the Torah. It was hard to grasp why Moses was doomed to die in the wilderness of Moab and was not permitted to enter and see the land for which he had yearned (Deut 3:25). Who could be more worthy of this privilege than he, since he had brought the children of Israel out of Egypt at the command of God, given them God's Torah, and led them for forty years in the wilderness?

To these questions about God's justice and the way of His special providence for His servant Moses was added another, much more profound question: How could it even be imagined that the man of God was mortal--the very man to whom God spoke face to face, as a man would to his neighbor, at whose disposal God

---

*This paper is the revised version of an article, dedicated to my teacher and master, Prof. Gershom Scholem, which appeared in Hebrew in *Tarbiz* 27 (1958) 142-57. Page numbers of the original edition are in square brackets. The translation is by Kenneth S. Cohen, Temple University and Reconstructionist Rabbinical College.

placed His glorious arm in order to split before him sea and stone, and to whom God gave the tablets written by the finger of God? Is it conceivable that he was subject to death like all flesh and blood? This problem is not formulated until the period of post-biblical literature. However, we shall attempt to establish the hypothesis that questions of this kind were not foreign to the religious thought in biblical times and that they provide the key for the explanation of the mystery surrounding Moses' death in the biblical account.

From these two basic questions developed the traditions with which we will attempt to deal below. In our treatment we shall distinguish between the answers given to each of these questions, although in the tradition itself one recognizes here and there a certain dovetailing of the two spheres. In addition, we will include in our survey a treatment of an extraordinary apocryphal text that transforms the theme of Moses' death into a dispute over the theological doctrine of dualism.

A. Explanations for Moses' Death Outside the Land

The Torah attributes Moses' death outside the land of Israel to God's explicit decree regarding His servant and the greatest of His prophets. One reason is set forth at length in the story of Meribat Kadesh (Num 20:1-13) and referred to in Num 27:14; Deut 32:51 (cf. also Num 20:24). [p. 143] An alternative reason is hinted at with extreme brevity in the Deuteronomic version of the story of the spies (Deut 1:37). There Moses recounts God's reaction to the sin of the people:

> And the Lord heard the voice of your words, and was wroth, and sware, saying, "Surely not one of these men of this evil generation shall see the good Land, which I sware to give unto your fathers, save Caleb the son of Jephunneh; he shall see it, and to him I will give the land that he hath trodden upon and to his children, because he hath wholly followed the Lord. Also the Lord was angry with me for your sakes, saying, thou shalt not go in thither; Joshua the son of Nun, which standeth before thee, he shall go in thither" (Deut 1:34-38).

Here the decree that the people had to die in the wilderness immediately brings with it the additional decision that

Moses, *too*, shall not enter the Land. That is to say, Moses has been included among those who are doomed to death in the wilderness. Even this relatively early motivation for Moses' death in the wilderness is of secondary character. As scholars have already shown, the basis of the incident of the spies rests upon a Calebite tradition which glorifies Caleb and the land of his inheritance.[2] The following passage pertains particularly to this Calebite tradition:

> But My servant Caleb, because he had a different spirit in him and hath followed Me fully, him will I bring into the land wherein he went; and his seed shall possess it (Num 14:24; cf. Deut 1:35,36).

This indicates that only Caleb and his descendants would inherit the land of Hebron, while the rest of the children of Israel would never come to it. The interweaving of this particularistic tradition into the framework of general Israelite tradition required that it be reinterpreted. The notion of what the Land was broadened, and soon it was impossible to state that the descendants of the children of Israel would not reach it. Only the generation of sinners would not enter the Land, but their descendants would possess it (Num 14:31), and likewise, Deuteronomy restricted the punishment to "this evil generation" (Deut 1:35).

With this new outlook, an explanation was required as to why Joshua entered the Land and was not counted among those who were to die in the wilderness. Accordingly, Deuteronomy juxtaposes with the story of the spies (in which Joshua takes no part whatever) the verses in which it relates that Moses appointed Joshua to be the leader of the people and the conqueror of the Land, because [p. 144] God had decreed that Moses would die outside of Israel. This formulation answered in one stroke two questions: 1) Why did Joshua enter the Land, even though he did not have the right that the good spy Caleb had?; 2) Why was Moses prevented from entering? However, it is clear that these forced answers were not satisfactory, for Joshua was rewarded without deserving it, and Moses was punished without sinning.

These queries were eliminated by two suppositions: 1) Joshua also was a good spy. This conclusion was drawn into the final redaction of the chapters concerning the spies in Numbers.

2) Moses sinned. This idea took shape in a reinterpretation of the tradition about the sin of the people by the waters of Meribah (Num 20:1-13). The story represents a late stage in the development of the motif that God let gush forth streams of water, shaking or hitting and splitting rocks. It may be tentatively suggested that the original pattern for this Divine action was God's mighty deed which demonstrated His rule over the forces of nature. It is in this (cosmic) sense that traditional Jewish exegesis interprets Job 28:9-10:

> He putteth forth His hand upon the flint (חלמיש).
> He overturneth (הפך) the mountains by the roots.
> He maketh rivers flow, splitting the rock (בצורות יארים בקע).[3]

True, many modern scholars hold the view that this verse speaks of the mighty deeds of men and interprets יארים ad hoc in the sense of mine-shafts or drainage channels.[4] But even if the verse should deal with human actions, its formulation draws heavily upon the traditional style in which Divine attainments were glorified.[5] This statement is borne out by the close affinity of Job 28:9,10 to passages describing Divine deeds of this kind as acts of salvation within a historical framework. The transition from the cosmic aspect to the historical one is easily recognized in Ps 114:7,8:

> Tremble, thou earth, at the presence of the Lord, at the presence of the God of Jacob; Who turneth (החפכי) the rock (צור) into a pool of water, the flint (חלמיש) into a fountain of waters.

In the majority of passages, the cosmic aspect disappears completely and nothing remains but an act of salvation performed by miraculous means, as in Isa 48:21:

> And they thirsted not when He led them through the deserts. He caused the water to flow out of the rock for them; He clave the rock (יבקע צור) and the waters gushed out.

Likewise Ps 78:15-16:

> He clave rocks (יבקע צרים) in the wilderness, and gave them drink abundantly as out of the depths. He brought streams (!) out of the rock. And caused water to run down like rivers (!) (vv. 15,16).

Cf. also Deut 8:15; Ps 105:41.

In more sophisticated versions of this motif, the wonder is the climax of an episode in which God tests the people, or the people test God.

The first version stems from the question: Why does misfortune befall the people at all since God can prevent misfortune in the first place? This question was renewed constantly when people were in distress. The answer was that God brought calamities upon His people only in order to test them and to make them prosper in the end. This notion is clearly implied in Ps 81:8:

> Thou didst call in trouble, and I rescued thee; I answered thee in the secret place of thunder; I proved thee at the waters of Meribah.

The intention of this historical allusion is sufficiently clear. The psalm was composed at a time when enemies oppressed the people (v. 15) to such a degree that part of them abandoned hope of being rescued by God and turned to other gods (v. 10). Hence it is understandable why this motif sometimes assumed the alternative form of a trial in which the people put their God to test. The time of calamity is also the time of a crisis of belief. Here we may mention, first of all, Psalm 95, which attributes the punishment of those who had to die in the wilderness to the incident of Massah and Meribah. A similar tradition is further alluded to in the blessing of Levi (Deut 33:8), which can be explained on the basis of partially parallel passages in Exod 32:26ff. The people tested and quarrelled with their God at Massah and Meribah and appear to have turned to other gods. God displayed His might to the people and gave them what they wished, but along with this, He commanded the Levites to punish the sinners severely. Because the Levites stood this test, they were rewarded with the priesthood.[6]

It is against this background that the stories of Massah and Meribah (Exod 17:1-7) and Meribat Kadesh (Num 20:1-13) should be interpreted. In these texts an act of Moses replaces direct Divine action. [p. 145] Even so, the first of these stories greatly emphasizes the unity between God and Moses. Moses reproves the rebellious people with the double question:

"Why strive you with me? Wherefore do you try the Lord?" (Exod 17:2).

Thus he impresses the idea that the strife with him and the trial of God are just two aspects of the same dispute. At the climax of the story, it is not only by God's command that Moses takes the rod and strikes the rock, but this action is performed in the very presence of the Lord who stands before His servant.[7] The punishment mentioned in Psalm 95 is omitted in this version.

The same motif underlies the story of the waters of Meribah. There also the people suffer from thirst in the wilderness. The theme of the trial is even couched in the most outspoken terms:

> These are the waters of Meribah where the children of Israel *strove* with God and He sanctified Himself in them (Num 20:13).

The aetiological explanation of the name Meribat Kadesh thus does not refrain from the open statement of a striving with God, an unusually blunt formulation.[8] Therefore, it is more than probable that in the pre-biblical version, the people were punished severely, presumably with death in the wilderness. This hypothesis is suggested by Ps 95:8-11, which states that the people were doomed to death in the wilderness because of their sin at Massah and Meribah.

It is generally admitted that traditions about Meribat Kadesh and Massah and Meribah are variations of one and the same motif. We may even go a step further and conjecture that in the old narrative about Meribat Kadesh, Moses also had been included in the punishment of the people, as in Deut 1:37. In any event, it is obvious that in the present version, the punishment of the people has been omitted and that the penalty inflicted upon Moses and Aaron bears a strictly personal character. Their sin results from a complicated reinterpretation of the ancient narrative. The present text maintains the ancient tradition that Moses took the rod upon God's command, struck the rock with it, and that it was then that the waters gushed forth. The act of striking, however, is in this version no longer the fulfillment of a divine command, but a transgression of God's order to speak to the rock, given to Moses

> For had you spoken to the rock and it had brought
> forth water, I would have been sanctified before
> the whole congregation, for they would have said,
> "If this rock, which cannot speak [p. 146] or hear
> and needs no maintenance, fulfills the command of
> the Almighty God, how much more should we."

The story in its present form can be adequately interpreted, therefore, as the outcome of a theological criticism leveled at an ancient tradition, and there is no justification for the attempts of scholars to construct by way of its analysis two complete stories combined by the hand of a redactor.[9]

However, although the final revision laid the stress upon the sin of Moses, this was not sufficient to uproot the early idea that it was the sin of the people which was the decisive factor. This is evidenced by the post-exilic Psalm 106, which adduces mitigating circumstances for Moses' sin:

> They angered him also at the waters of Meribah, and
> it went ill with Moses because of them; for they embittered his spirit, and he spoke rashly with his
> lips (vv. 32-33).

It may well be that these verses result from an exegesis which related Deut 1:37 to God's anger with Moses by the waters of Meribah. In any event, they are far from an outright condemnation of Moses' behavior at this incident.

Therefore, it is not surprising that the secondary explanation of the punishment meted out to Moses did not satisfy our Sages, who continued to ask the age-old question: Why was Moses not worthy to enter the land of promise? In the responses of the midrash to this question one can distinguish three tendencies.

1) The midrash accepts the reason that Moses sinned at the waters of Meribah, but scrutinizes all of Moses' actions in order to uncover within them additional sins. Thus, for instance, we learn in the *Mekhilta de Rabbi Shim'on ben Yoḥay*:[10]

> Thus God held Moses fast for six days, but on the
> seventh Moses said, "Send, I pray Thee, by the hand
> of him whom Thou wilt send." God swore to him that
> he would not enter the land of Israel, as it is
> written, "therefore ye shall not bring, etc." (Num
> 20:12). (*Shemot* 3:8).

In Midrash *Tanḥuma*,[11] six sins of Moses are enumerated:

> The Holy One, blessed be He, said to him, "Moses,
> you have committed six transgressions and I have not

exposed one of them. First you said: 'Send, I pray, Thee, by the hand of him whom Thou wilt send' (Exod 4:13) and 'For since I came to Pharaoh to speak in Thy name' (Exod 5:23), 'it was not the Lord who sent me' (Num 16:29), 'But if the Lord make a new thing' (Num 16:30), 'Hear now, ye rebels' (Num 20:10), 'And behold, ye are risen up in your fathers' stead, a brood of evil men' (Num 32:14), and Abraham, Isaac, and Jacob were sinners, for you said as much to their descendants?" (*Wa-ethannan* 6).

2) With this there is in the later midrash a return of the old idea that the judgment of Moses was like the judgment of those who had to die in the wilderness. This notion is expressed with exemplary clarity in Midrash *Numbers Rabbah*:[12]

> The Holy One, blessed be He, said to Moses, "By what right do you request to enter the land?" This may be illustrated by a parable. It is like the case of a shepherd who went out to feed the flock of the king. The flock was carried off as booty. When the shepherd tried to enter the royal palace, the king said to him, "If you come in now, what will the people say? That it was your fault that the flock was carried off!" So in the present case as well, the Lord said to Moses, "Your glory is that you have taken out of slavery sixty myriads of people. But you have buried them in the wilderness and will bring into the land a different generation! This being so, people will think that the generation of the wilderness have no share in the World to Come! No, better be beside them" (*Huqqat* 13).

However, in the *Tanhuma* version,[13] this midrash appears as God's reply to Moses' request that it be written in the Torah why he was punished, lest men think [p. 147] that he died for the same sin as the wilderness generation (*Huqqat* 32).

3) More surprisingly, we find in *Aboth de Rabbi Nathan*[14] that God said to Moses:

> You yourself have not transgressed. You are to die only because of the decree against Adam (as it is written) "your first father sinned" (Isa 43:27) (ch. 25, version B).

Yet we must point out that this midrash does not deal with the question of why Moses was prevented from entering the promised land, except in an incidental manner, and the matter that chiefly concerns the midrash is the fate of Moses' soul, rather than the ethical providential question: What is the reason for his death outside the promised land?

B. Biblical and Midrashic Accounts of Moses' Death

The introduction to the narrative about Moses' death (Deut 32:48-52) begins with God's words to him:

> And die in the mountain whither thou goest up, and be gathered unto thy people, as Aaron thy brother died in Mount Hor and was gathered unto his people, because you trespassed against Me in the midst of the children of Israel at the waters of Meribah at Kadesh in the wilderness of Zin, and because ye sanctified Me not in the midst of the children of Israel (vv. 50-51).

These passages seemingly suggest that the report of Moses' death has been modeled on that of Aaron's (Num 20:22-29). However, from a traditio-critical point of view, the opposite seems more probable for three reasons: 1) the ascent of Moses to the mountain is clearly motivated. Though not found worthy of entering the Land, Moses was at least privileged to see it in its entirety[15] from a high mountain (Deut 34:1-4; cf. 3:23-28). No reason is stated for Aaron's death on a mountain. 2) Moses climbs the mountain alone. Nobody else is involved in this event. In the account of Aaron's death, God turns to Moses and Aaron, instructing Moses to take with him Aaron and Eleazar. The reason for this becomes evident in the statement that Moses stripped Aaron of his garments before his death, and he put them on Eleazar his son, thus appointing him as his father's successor. This appointment is obviously the main point of the story. The ascent to the mountain serves the sole purpose of enhancing the solemnity of this act. 3) Moses' burial is mentioned; Aaron's is not. This omission confirms the conjecture that the interest of the story is concentrated upon Eleazar.

The narrative about Moses' death reveals his close relation to God throughout. The very report that a man has been told by God when he is to die, and at which place, is exceptional, though echoed in the account about Aaron. In its continuation, the text does not content itself with the simple statement that Moses saw the land from the mountain, but rather stresses twice that it was God who showed it to him (Deut 34:1, 4). The same motif is strongly emphasized in verse 5:

So Moses *the servant of the Lord* died in the land
of Moab *according to the word of the Lord*.

This statement is followed by an astonishing description
of his burial:

And He[16] buried him in the valley in the land of
Moab over against Beth-Peor, and no man knoweth his
sepulchre unto this day (v. 6).

The passage adumbrates that God in His glory--and He
alone--attended to Moses' burial, and for this reason, his
gravesite has remained forever a secret to men.

The mystery that surrounds the story of Moses' burial requires an extensive analysis of all the Jewish sources that struggle with this enigma; and it is only through analysis of these sources that we can come to understand it. Before we turn to this study, however, let us briefly note that in modern times, the story of Moses' death encouraged the propensity to guesswork on the part of scholars whose hearts beat with strong desire to rebel against religious tradition. These scholars approached the problem with the intention of laying bare the factual kernel of the events, piously glossed over, is it were, in the report of the Torah. Small wonder, then, that this kernel seems so pathetic.

This line of speculation gave rise to the article by Goethe,[17] which confidently established that Joshua and Caleb murdered Moses. This action seemed to Goethe to be necessitated by the demands of the historical situation. According to him, the man Moses was never [p. 148] gifted with the talent required to lead the people. His lack of practical sense, recognizable in all his actions, was revealed in its most frightening form before his death, when the children of Israel were encamped in the wilderness of Moab. Time was urgent and desperately required a quick and effective plan for the conquest of the land. And here, at the same crucial moment, pregnant with dangers, Moses wasted precious time by delivering to the people all the long and unnecessary sermons preserved in the book of Deuteronomy. Thus Joshua and Caleb, men of action, came to the clear recognition that the only way to deliver Israel was through the death of Moses. They murdered the old leader, who was going to bring disaster upon the people, hid his body, and for this simple reason no one knew where he was buried.

A generation ago, Sellin[18] expressed a similar idea. But since he was a professional biblical scholar, he felt a necessity to seek substantiation for his claim in the Bible. He searched and found it in the account of Phinehas (Num 25:1-9). According to Sellin's critical analysis of this story, Moses sought to hang the leaders of the people as punishment for their fornication with the alien women, but the priests violently opposed him. Moreover, in their argument against him, they used his marriage to the Cushite woman. The matter reached such proportions that Phinehas, son of Eleazar, stabbed Moses. Sellin reveals further evidence for his hypothesis in several obscure verses in the book of Hosea, which, according to him, require emendation. His corrected version clearly testifies to the murder of Moses.

Yet Sellin's was not the final word on this matter. Freud[19] added to Sellin's biblical research a broad psychoanalytical explanation that won for Sellin's point of view followers from the general public. We must content ourselves with the brief remark on these same imaginative musings: it is abundantly clear that they have no value in the study of the tradition of Israel.[20]

More serious consideration is due to the suggestion by Noth,[21] who deals with the problem of Moses' burial from the standpoint of historical topography. Noth relies on the explicit verse, that Moses died in the land of Moab, and he attempts to prove that the vicinity of Beth-peor remained in the hands of Moab some time after the death of Moses. Because of this, the location of Moses' grave was forgotten among the people of Israel, and nothing was retained save the general knowledge that he was buried in the valley opposite Beth-peor. This hypothesis merits attention from a historical point of view, but it fails to explain fully the intent of the text. The statement that Moses' gravesite remained unknown is immediately preceded by the report of his burial by God and calls for interpretation in the light of this context.

Having introduced this religious problem to our study, we must now note, first of all, that even the very fact of Moses' death was disputed by our Sages. We learn in *b Sotah* 13b:

> Others declare that Moses never died; it is written here, "so Moses died there," and elsewhere it is written, "and he was there with the Lord" (Exod 34: 28). As here (i.e., in the later passage) it means standing and ministering, so also there (i.e., the former passage), it means standing and ministering.

This same midrash recurs with minor changes in a number of texts, among them *Sifre, Ha'azinu*, ch. 357. [p. 149] The vacillations of Hebrew tradition may also be discerned in the descriptions of Moses' death given by Josephus and Marqah.

The first relates:

> And, while he bade farewell to Eleazar and Joshua and was yet communicating with them, a cloud suddenly descended upon him and he disappeared in a ravine. But he has written of himself in the sacred books that he died, for fear lest they should venture to say that by reason of his surpassing virtue he had gone back to the Deity (*Ant.* 4.8, 48, §326).[22]

Josephus considers Moses' ascent to the mountain and his disappearance in a cloud to be facts, attested by Eleazar and Joshua, this in contrast to Moses' death, which was attested only by Moses' own testimony in the Torah. Moses considered it necessary to make this point clear because he feared that people would conclude from the testimony about his concealment in a cloud that he returned to God.

A similar report is extant in *Memar Marqah*,[23] the work of the Samaritan writer, Marqah, who wrote his book seemingly in the second half of the fourth century C.E. Marqah relates that

> ...the great prophet Moses ascended Mt. Nebo with great majesty crowned with light....Bitter was the hour when the great prophet Moses entered into a cloud and was lifted up as a light.[24] When the great prophet Moses was hidden from the sight of the congregation, everyone was in distress and tears.

In spite of Moses' mysterious concealment, Marqah asserts that he died. After his disappearance, the glory embraced him and conducted him into a cave on the mountain and there he deceased (V:3).[25] This depiction conforms to the main thesis of

Josephus that: a) Moses disappeared in a cloud without being seen again; and b) he nevertheless died.

A variant of this tradition has been preserved in a Catena, preserved by Fabricius (*Codex Pseudoepigraphicus Veteris Testamenti* II):[26]

> There exists a passage in an apocryphal and mystical codex where the created things are treated in a subtle manner (stating) that at the time when Moses was about to die a luminous cloud surrounded the place of his sepulchre and blinded the eyes of the bystanders. Therefore, nobody could see either the dying lawgiver or the place where his body was buried.

The general tenor of the Catena agrees with Josephus and Marqah. But the text has also features of its own: the luminous character of the cloud which blinded the eyes of the bystanders and the identification of Moses' burial with the place of his concealment.

A combination of the midrashim which deny Moses' death with the reports on his disappearance in a cloud and his subsequent death leads to the reconstruction of a tradition in which Moses approached God ascending a mountain and was exalted from there to heaven by the cloud of Divine Glory.[27]

We venture to surmise that the text of the Torah should be interpreted on the same lines as the post-biblical texts describing Moses' mysterious disappearance, i.e., as a toning down of a tradition relating Moses' ascent to heaven. The Torah admits that Moses vanished on a high mountain and that no one knows where he is buried, but it adds that one may not interpret this as an assumption to God. Moses went up to the mountain only so that God might show him from there the land of Israel for which he yearned. He died there, yet he was not buried on the mountain close to God, but rather in the valley, as is the lot of a common man. However, at the same time, the Torah makes it clear that this entails no belittling of Moses, for the man of God died at the command of the Lord, and God Himself undertook his burial. This carefully balanced report can adequately be interpreted as a cautious rejection of a myth predicating Moses' assumption. The story of Elijah's ascension (2 Kgs 2:11) clearly proves that this motif is not foreign to biblical thought. It is difficult to assume that the image of Moses, the man of God par excellence, underwent a lesser degree of mythologization than that of Elijah.[28] It seems, therefore, that the Torah reaches a certain compromise between mythological thought, which does not recognize an absolute barrier between the divine and human spheres, and rationalistic theology, which sets between the two spheres a distance like the distance between heaven and earth. The antagonism between these approaches, bridged over in the Torah, becomes manifest again in the midrash.

On the one hand we learn,

> R. Jose said, "The Shekhina never descended to earth, nor did Moses and Elijah ascend [p. 150] to heaven, as it is said, 'The heavens are the heavens of the Lord, but the earth hath He given to the children of men.'" (b Sukkah 5a)

However, against that, we note in Midrash *Deuteronomy Rabbah*[29] the outspoken mythological slogan:

> The heavens are the heavens of the Lord, but the earth hath He given to the children of men" (Ps 115:16). Moses, however, came and changed the earthly things into heavenly things and the heavenly things into earthly things, as it is written, "And Moses went up unto God" (Exod 19:3); "And the Lord came down upon Mt. Sinai" (Exod 19:20) (*Ha'azinu* 2).[30]

In an intricate way, the Torah reduced the contrast between the thesis that Moses underwent the death of an ordinary man and its antithesis that he ascended to God. But in the post-biblical period, even this carefully mitigated admission called for further softening by the idea of the resurrection of the dead. This solution is adumbrated in *Sifre*[31] on the passage, "And the Lord showed to him all the land...unto the hinder (i.e., western) sea" (Deut 34:2):

> Do not read עד הים האחרון "unto the hinder sea," but עד היום האחרון "unto the last day." This means that He showed to him all the world from the day it was created until the day when the dead will become alive" (§357).

This is to say that God did not content Himself to show to Moses a special country as it exists at a certain time, but revealed to him all the world in all its periods until the last day, i.e., the day of resurrection of the dead and their last judgment.

In a more explicit formulation, this motif is developed in the *Biblical Antiquities*, attributed to Philo,[32] which was composed after the destruction of the Second Temple. This book mentions only briefly that God showed to Moses the promised land, reports in detail that He showed him the hidden places of the cosmos, adds that He revealed to him laws, and concludes with God's announcement that He will bury Moses in peace and that no angel or man will know his sepulchre.

> ...until I shall visit the human generation living at that time (*seculum*). And (then) I will arouse you and your fathers from the land in which you will sleep, and you will be found together and dwell in eternal habitations which have no limit in time (19:10-12).

This text applies the idea of resurrection to Moses in the most comprehensive manner. As Moses' death and burial are limited by the day of resurrection, so is the secrecy of his sepulchre.

The same importance for this ultimate fate of Moses is attributed by Marqah[33] to the Day of Vengeance, defined by him as "the Day of Resurrection for all men...the Day of Recompense for the good and the evil" (IV:12). When Moses stood on Mt. Nebo,[34]

> His Lord exalted him and showed to him the four quarters of the world (not just the promised land!) Great was the joy in Moses' heart when He revealed to him the sequel to the Day of Vengeance, so that he did not fear death" (V:3).

Marqah[35] even adopts the idea that "no one will know his burial place until the Day of Vengeance" (II:12).

In the later midrash, a function analogous to that of resurrection is assumed by the notion of the life in the world to come. Thus in the *Aboth de Rabbi Nathan*,[36]

> The Holy One, blessed be He, said to Moses, "Moses, you have had enough of this world. Your place in the world to come awaits you since the six days of Creation....The Holy One, blessed be He, took the soul of Moses and put it in safekeeping under the Throne of Glory....Not only is the soul of Moses put in safekeeping under the Throne of Glory, but also (all) the souls of the righteous are in safekeeping under the Throne of Glory" (ch. 12, version A).

In this text, the fate of the soul of Moses had become a prototype for the fate of the souls of the righteous in general. The final stage in this development is attested in Midrash *Leqaḥ Tov*,[37] which juxtaposes to the citation of the early midrash: "As he there stands and ministers, he here stands and ministers" and an addition of great interest: "it is taught that the righteous do not die" (*Berakhah* 102). A comparison of *Aboth de Rabbi Nathan* with Midrash *Leqaḥ Tov* is highly instructive. According to the former, Moses died. According to the latter, he did not die. Yet there is nothing really different between these two midrashim except for their formulation; for in any case, the result is that his soul is preserved in the world to come with the souls of all the righteous. This conception neutralizes the opposition between the thesis that Moses died and its antithesis that he ascended to God.

[p. 151] We have suggested that the narrative of the Torah should be interpreted as a denial of two opinions concerning Moses' end: 1) that he ascended to God in the flesh; 2) that he was buried on the top of the mountain. As shown above, the authority of the words of the Torah was not sufficient to uproot the tradition that he did not die.

Less clear is the evidence for the existence of a Jewish tradition which set the place of his burial at the top of the mountain. A midrash of the Roman period leaves the question open whether Moses had been buried above or below. The midrash has been preserved in various versions. Here we quote the version of *Sifre*:[38]

> And already the government of the house of Caesar sent forth and commanded, "go and find the grave of Moses." They went and stood above and saw it below. They went below and saw it above. They divided into two groups, half above and half below. The ones above saw it below and the ones below saw it above. Accordingly, it is said in the Scriptures, "no man knoweth his sepulchre" (§257).

The midrash confounds the plain meaning of the words of the Torah and extracts from them the idea that no man knew whether the grave of Moses was in the valley or on the top of the mountain. This indicates that the author of the midrash neither acquiesced in the Torah's account that Moses was buried in the valley nor dared to contest it outrightly.

The Catena, quoted above (p. 198) goes a step further. This source identifies the place of Moses' burial with that of his disappearance in a cloud. In the light of the parallel sources we may confidently assert that the author located this place on the top of the mountain. Although the Catena stresses that the (exact) location of the burial cannot be established, it clearly presupposes that its area is above and not below.

An explicit statement to this effect is extant in *Memar Marqah*. Marqah[39] states in his enumeration of the ten wonders of Moses:

> The tenth: he was buried by the hand of God on Mt. Nebo and no one will know his burial place till the Day of Vengeance (II:12).

In his description of Moses' death, Marqah[40] depicts this burial in some detail. After Moses' concealment in a cloud,

> The Great Glory took him by his hand, embracing him and walking before him. The great prophet Moses raised his eyes and saw Mt. Gerizim. He prostrated and went down on his face. When he arose from his prostration, he saw the entrance to the cave opened before him....Great was the moment when the great prophet Moses lowered his head and entered the cave. He turned his face to Mt. Gerizim and lay down on the ground looking straight in front of him. God made sleep fall upon him, and his soul departed without difficulty without his knowing (V:3).

The artificial connection of this scene with Mt. Gerizim reflects of course a specifically Samaritan tendency. If we disregard this detail, the general tenor of the text is near to that of the Catena, though Marqah differentiates between the place of concealment and the distant place of the burial in a cave.

However, the belief that Moses' grave is hidden in a cave on Mt. Nebo prodded the propensity to reveal it there. This step was made in Christian tradition. The earliest witness to this tradition is found in the book *Sanctae Silviae Peregrinatio*,[41] whose author visited Israel at the end of the fourth century. She relates that they showed her the grave of Moses inside a church at the very summit of Mt. Nebo. The legend of this church has been transmitted to us in the words of Petrus Iberiensis, who visited the mountain at the end of the fifth century. Here is a summary of his account:[42]

> A shepherd from the town of Nebo who grazed his flock at the top of the mountain saw as in a vision an enormous cave, full of bright light, smelling of spices and glory. Although he was astonished (for he had never seen such a thing at this place) he was encouraged by the Holy Spirit, and taking his life in his hands, he descended into the cave. There he saw a venerable old man whose face shone, emanating grace throughout. The man was resting on something similar to a glowing couch, shining and flashing glory and grace. When he realized that this is the holy Moses, he ran in fear and great joy to the town, and hurried to announce his vision to the townsfolk. The story adds that he was careful to mark the place with a pile of stones, fearing lest the vision disappear. His fear was justified. However, by means of his marker he succeeded in showing the place to the people of Nebo, who believed him and erected a church on the site. The veracity of the shepherd's story was fully confirmed, for all who drew near to this church found healing for body and soul.

It is worth noting that the Franciscan excavations at the site have made it clear that the building of the church should not be dated before the fourth century, and that no other buildings have been found on Mt. Nebo that can be attributed to an earlier period.[43] Thereby, the hypothesis that the Christian church was erected on the site of the sanctuary of the Lord at Nebo, destroyed by Mesha, king of Moab (Mesha inscription 11,14-18), is proven false. Nor can we accept the suggestion of Alt,[44] that it is possible to suppose an historical link between the early sanctuary of the Lord and the Christian church (even though the church was not built on the site of the Israelite sanctuary) since a time-lapse of more than 1300 years separates the two cult places.

More worthy of consideration is the relation of the Samaritan and Christian traditions to the aggaddah in 2 Mac 2: 2-7. The aggaddah refers to the time of the Destruction. Then, it reports, Jeremiah went to the mountain which Moses had climbed to view the inheritance of God and placed the Tabernacle with the holy utensils into a cavernous chamber.

> And some of his followers drew near in order to mark the road, but they could not find it. Now, when Jeremiah came to know this, he blamed them saying, "Unknown shall the spot be until God gather the people again together and mercy come."

The affinity of the narratives about Moses' burial in a cave on Mt. Nebo to this aggaddah are obvious. Especially striking is the similarity of *Memar Marqah*, since Marqah, too, speaks of a cave on Mt. Nebo which will remain secret till the day of the final salvation. [p. 152] Abel[45] even surmises a literary connection between the motif that Jeremiah's followers failed in their attempt to mark the place of the cave and its Christian version that the shepherd succeeded in this attempt. It is, however, improbable that the aggaddah on the Tabernacle should silently presuppose its concealment in Moses' sepulchre and imply that Jeremiah detected this secret place.[46] Second, Maccabees designates Mt. Nebo as the mount from which Moses viewed the Land, not as the place of his burial.

Clearer than the prehistory of the Christian tradition is the reaction of the midrash upon it. Midrash *Leqaḥ Tov*[47] asks, "why do we not know the gravesite of Moses?" It replies, "in order that Israel might not go and place there a sanctuary and sacrifice and make offerings; and in order that the nations of the world might not defile the grave of Moses with their idols and abominations" (*Berakhah* 102). The first part of the answer is perhaps directed to the idea expressed by the Church Father Origen,[48] who claimed that God hid the burial place of Moses so that he might not be worshipped like a god. Presumably Origen derived this idea from a Jewish source. The second part of the answer, however, is a reaction to the Christian cult, i.e., to the church and its statues on Mt. Nebo.

Up to this point we have analyzed the traditions that went further than the Torah in their mythologization of the death of Moses traditions ranging from those that absolutely or reservedly deny his death to those that seek his grave on Mt. Nebo. Now let us describe the development of the biblical motifs that Moses died at the command of God and that God Himself buried him.

The notion that Moses died in accordance with the word of God is given a philosophic formulation by Philo of Alexandria. He opposes the verse that explicitly states that Moses was gathered to his fathers, indicating that his outlook is more mythological than that of the Torah. He continues:

He died by the word of the cause by which the entire world was created, to teach that the glory of a wise man in God's eyes is equal to the glory of the world. For by that word through which He created everything, He raised up to Himself the most perfect of mortals (*De sacr. Abel* 3).

The presentation of the problem differs in the midrash which deals with the question as to whether the Angel of Death had power over Moses as he had over all mortals. The early midrash in *Sifre*[49] definitely denies this in its version:

> At that time God said to the Angel of Death, "Go and bring Me the soul of Moses." He went and stood before him (and said! "Give me your soul"). Moses said to him: "In the place where I dwell you have no right to stand"; he frowned at him, and he went away upon this rebuke. The Angel of Death [p. 153] went back with his words before the Almighty. The Lord said to the Angel of Death, "Go and bring his soul to Me." He went to his dwelling place, searched for him but did not find him. He went to the sea. He said to it, "Have you seen Moses?" It replied, "From the time that he caused Israel to pass through me have I not seen him." He went to the mountains and valleys. He said to them, "Have you seen Moses?" They answered him, "The Lord understands his way. The Lord hid him in the life to come and no creature knows his whereabouts" (§305).

This midrash is composed of two motifs, closely related to each other. 1) The Angel of Death went at the command of the Lord to Moses, but he could not prevail over him, and God Himself took his soul. 2) The Angel of Death, at the command of the Lord, searched for Moses to take up his soul, until he was informed that his Master took up the soul of Moses Himself.[50] The point of agreement between the two motifs is that Moses died, not at the hand of the Angel of Death, who was powerless to carry out the Lord's mission, but rather at the hand of God Himself. The motif of the Angel of Death who failed in his mission comes to its full development in a later midrash, preserved in *Deuteronomy Rabbah* (*Berakhah* X),[51] which states that at first God commanded Gabriel and Michael to take up the soul of Moses, but that they refused to fulfill the mission. Only then did God turn to Sama'el, the leader of the demons, who had already eagerly awaited the moment, and "clothed himself in anger, girded on his sword, wrapped himself with ruthlessness, and went forth to meet Moses." Yet, before he was able to address him, Sama'el was filled with fear; for he found Moses "sitting and writing the Ineffable Name, and his countenance shone like the sun, and he resembled an angel of the Lord of Hosts." In spite of this, he spoke to Moses, saying that the One who created the universe had sent him to take up his soul, as is the lot of all mortals. However, Moses argued against him, saying that he had greater power than any mortal. He listed at length his superhuman traits until Sama'el returned and reported Moses' words to the Almighty. When God reiterated His command to Sama'el, and Sama'el approached Moses a second time, Moses assaulted him with his staff, upon which was inscribed the Ineffable Name, until he fled.

> Thus much did Moses achieve. At the end of a moment, a *bath kol* came forth and said, "The time of your death has come." Moses said before God, "Master of the Universe, remember the day when You revealed Yourself to me in the burning bush, and You said to me, 'Come now therefore, and I will send thee to Pharaoh that thou mayest bring forth My people the children of Israel from Egypt.' Recall the time when I abode on Mt. Sinai for forty days and forty nights. Please do not hand me over to the Angel of Death." A *bath kol* broke forth and said to him, "Do not be afraid. I Myself will attend to you and your burial." At that hour Moses stood up and sanctified himself like the Seraphim, and God came down from the highest heavens to take away the soul of Moses; and with Him were three ministering angels, Michael, Gabriel, and Zagzagel. Michael laid out Moses' bier, Gabriel spread out a fine linen cloth at his bolster, and Zagzagel one at his feet.

The midrash adds [p. 154] God's instruction to Moses as to how he should lie on his bier. It concludes with a dispute between the soul of Moses, which refused to leave the pure body, and God, until "at that moment God kissed[52] him and took away his soul with a kiss of the mouth."

This midrash, which identifies the Angel of Death with Sama'el, the wicked, thus transforms him from a messenger incapable of free will to a power in the heavenly world, who desires from his own nature to do evil. Yet he is not entitled to use this power on his own accord, but in the name of God. And even when he goes on God's errand, his strength fails before the power of Moses, the servant of God.

This daring notion is toned down in the following midrash in *Deuteronomy Rabbah* (*Berakhah* V)[53] in the name of R. Meir. Here, too, the Angel of Death comes to Moses at God's behest, and Moses puts him off twice, but "when he came to Moses a third time he said, 'Seeing that this is from God, I must now submit myself to God's will'." In this midrash as well, Moses has the power to delay the day of his death and be victorious over the Angel of Death. Yet in the end he yields to him because he is the messenger of God.

A complete rejection of all the differences between the death of Moses and the end of the rest of man is reached in the midrash in *Deuteronomy Rabbah*,[54] which maintains simply:

> The Angel of Death does not say, "Seeing that this man is a king, we will permit him another day or two." On that day he shows no respect of persons. ...No man can lodge a claim against him. Despite all the greatness that he enjoyed, when the day of his death came Moses was unable to forestall it. Immediately he said to him, "Behold, thy days approach that thou must die" (*Wayyelekh* III).

In regard to Moses' burial, the development of the tradition becomes most complicated, and one may distinguish in it three trends. 1) God Himself buried Moses, 2) the boldness of this idea is toned down by transferring certain duties in the burial to the angels, and 3) the whole affair is denied. The first trend is represented in its extreme form by Pseudo-Philo's *Biblical Antiquities*,[55] which stresses that God buried Moses with His hands (*per manus suas* 19:16) and that even the angels were ignorant of his gravesite (19:12).

The function of the angels is reduced here to mourning Moses which is emphasized in vehement terms. Moses' burial by God is clearly indicated also by Marqah in his description of Moses' burial on Mt. Nebo, cited above. Moses' reception on the mountain by the angels is here mentioned only in passing.[56] The same stress on God's own attendance to Moses' body is laid in the midrash concerning the bringing of the dead Moses from the portion of Reuben to the portion of Gad, when "he was laid upon the wings of the Shekhinah and the ministering angels said, 'He executed the righteousness of the Lord and His ordinances with Israel' (Deut 33:21), and the Lord said: 'Who will rise up for Me against the evil-doers, etc.'" (Ps 94:16) (*b So-tah* 13b).

The type of midrashim that attribute [p. 155] to the angels the preparation of Moses' litter is represented, e.g., by Midrash *Deuteronomy Rabbah* (*Berakhah* V) discussed above (p. 207) which mentions three of the ministering angels, Michael, Gabriel, and Zagzagel. The motifs in this midrash interweave with the motif of the midrash of the bringing of Moses from Reuben's portion to Gad's portion in the *Yerushalmi Targum* to Deut 34:6. This describes the preparation of Moses' bier by a band of ministering angels: Michael, Gabriel, Metatron, Yofiel, Uriel, and Yefifyah. This is the same bier which Moses was laid upon when he was transferred from the portion of Reuben to the portion of Gad, where God buried him.

The third trend, which has reservations with respect to Moses being buried by the Almighty, is perhaps to be perceived in the cautious formulation of *Pirqe de Rabbi Eliezer*,[57] "Were it not indeed written, it would be impossible to say as is read, 'and He buried him in the valley'" (XVII). The Mishnah (*Sotah* 1:9) goes further and deprives the old tradition of its literal meaning. It quotes the ancient saying, "Whom have we greater than Moses, for none other than the Almighty occupied Himself with him, as it is written, 'And He buried him in the valley'." Then it adds the interpretation (lacking in the Tosephta 4:8), "And not of Moses alone have they spoken thus, but of all the righteous, for it is written, 'And thy righteousness shall go before thee; the glory of the Lord shall gather thee'" (Isa 58:8). Yet even this spiritualization of the mythological motif, which came close to cancelling it out altogether, was not satisfactory to the extreme rationalists, who laid down simply that Moses buried himself (*Numbers R* X).[58]

C. The Assumption of Moses

We have seen that in all the midrashim that recognize the participation of the angels in the burial of Moses, Michael, the guardian angel of Israel, occupies the leading role. One should not ignore the connection between these midrashim and the description of the burial of Moses in the book *The Assumption of Moses*, an apocryphal work from the first century C.E. This book states that God commanded Michael, and him alone, to take care of Moses' burial, meaning that God buried Moses through His messenger, and not Himself. There is, therefore, room to conjecture that the midrashim which report that God buried Moses with the assistance of angels are none other than a compromise between the version that God Himself buried Moses and the version that He buried him through a messenger. Yet, despite the indubitable connection of the description in the book *The Assumption of Moses* to the above-mentioned midrashim, we prefer to treat it separately, since it is the only text that changes the matter of Moses' death into a debate concerning the problem of the two authorities.

The description of Moses' death in *The Assumption of Moses* has not come to us in its original, but is extant only in short quotes, scattered in Christian literature, beginning with the reference to the matter which is found in the Epistle of Jude 9. These fragmentary sources were collected by Charles,[59] who combined them into a continuous story. However, his attempt to reconstruct the thread of the story is not satisfactory at all points, and accordingly we will rely only on his sources. As was stated, it is related in this book that after the death of Moses, God sent Michael to attend to his burial. However, Satan--so the story adds--opposes Michael[60] and argues that he is entitled to Moses' body because he is the lord of matter. [p. 156] To this Michael replies that all of us were created by the Holy Spirit of God, and that God is the Lord over the spirits and all flesh.[61] After his first argument was refuted, Satan bases his request for Moses' body, it seems, on the sin of Adam. Yet, Michael likewise refutes this by noting that Satan himself put into the serpent's mouth the words that enticed Eve and Adam.[62] After Satan exhausts his principal arguments, he begins to villify Moses, and accuses him of murdering the Egyptian. Michael casts aside this villification with the words of Zech 3:2, "The Lord rebuke thee."

The nature of the dispute and the way it proceeds is determined by Satan's first argument. Here he claims lordship over matter, namely, over the body from which the soul has departed. This becomes most clear from Michael's reply. From this claim, and from it alone, can we understand why Satan restricts his demand to the body of Moses, and why he does not request his soul. For one could reach the conclusion from his additional arguments that he was entitled to Moses' soul as well. In his first claim, Satan clearly formulates the view that God has dominion only over the spirit, while matter pertains to Satan's realm exclusively. At the beginning of Satan's statements, the doctrine of dualism is conspicuous in its full degree and in its most principal and acute formulation. It is not sin which brings about the dominion of Satan, but rather his rule over matter parallels the authority of God over the spirit from the time of Creation. Less fundamental is Satan's second argument which is based on Adam's sin. Yet, in this argument too, Satan seeks for himself exclusive power over the bodies of all men. This is not the case with the third argument, in which he accuses Moses of an individual sin. This personal accusation represents Satan in his classic role of prosecutor.

[p. 157] It is apparent from the start that the doctrine of dualism is presented in the mouth of Satan only so that it might be refuted by the words of Michael, the victor in the dispute, and so that it might teach that God is the lord over both spirit and flesh since He is the creator of everything. In addition, it shows that original sin did not bestow upon Satan his own dominion and that even the threat of God's rebuke was sufficient to put him to flight. However, within his polemic against the doctrine of dualism, the author out of necessity incorporates into his story ideas colored by dualism. It is true that Satan suffered decisive failure. Yet the fact is, he dared to go forth of his own accord (unlike Sama'el in the midrash cited above, who acts only at the command of God). In a similar fashion, the author drew from the *Book of Adam and Eve*, entitled Αποκαλύψις Μωυσεως (16ff.), the dualistic story that Satan himself put his words into the mouth of the serpent. But he also removed the sting of the story by changing the words into an argument against Satan. From all of this, we can see the author's struggle with the dualistic doctrines of a crystallizing Gnosticism[63] which permeated the spiritual atmosphere in the Jewish world at the time of the destruction of the Second Temple.

NOTES

1) Deut 34:7 indicates an age of 120 years. This typological figure (cf. Gen 6:3) points perhaps to an additional reason for Moses' death. Even if we disregard this indication, the history of his life makes it clear that he reached a very great age.

2) See, e.g., M. Noth, *Überlieferungsgeschichtliche Studien* (*SKG, Geisteswiss. Klasse* 18/2; Halle, 1943) 31-32.

3) Cf. especially Ibn Ezra *ad loc.*

4) Cf., e.g., M. Pope, *Job* (AB 15; Garden City: Doubleday, 1965) 178-80.

5) Cf. also Job 28:3 which clear befits Divine action.

6) S. E. Loewenstamm, "The Investiture of Levi," *Eretz Israel* 10 (1971) 169-72 (Heb. with Eng. summary, xiv-xv).

7) Thus God demonstrates to the people that Moses acts at His behest. It may even adumbrate that He took part in Moses' action. Cf. Isa 63:12.

8) Contrast: "When your fathers tried Me/proved (!) Me" (Ps 95:8). Here the aetiology of the name Massah and Meribah ("temptation" and "strife") would have required the use of the related verbs nsh and $rîb$. Actually, however, the harsh verb $rîb$ ("strive") has been supplanted by the less offensive word $bḥn$ ("prove"). Cf. also Exod 17:2. Here both verbs nsh and even $rîb$ do appear. But the verb $rîb$ refers to the differences of the people with Moses only.

9) See, e.g., C. H. Cornill, "Beiträge zur Pentateuchkritik," *ZAW* 11 (1891) 20ff.; H. Gressmann, *Moses und seine Zeit* (Göttingen: Vandenhoeck & Ruprecht, 1913) 150ff. Their proposals are entirely different from each other and both unfounded.

10) *Mekhilta d'Rabbi Šim'on ben Yoḥai*, edd. Epstein-Melamed.

11) *Tanḥuma*, ed. S. Buber, Deut, p. 11.

12) *Numbers R.*, ed. M. A. Mirkin, p. 230.

13) *Tanḥuma*, ed. S. Buber, Num, p. 122.

14) *Aboth de Rabbi Nathan*, ed. S. Schechter, pp. 51-52.

15) "All the land" means here the land up to Dan and not the land of Canaan in its entirety. Herein it is made clear that at the time of the formulation of the story, the definition "from Dan to Beersheba" had already supplanted the early

slogan of "the land of Canaan in its entirety (לגבולותיה) which was not used again until the Babylonian exile (Ezek 47:13-21).

16) The Samaritan version and the LXX read ויקברו ("and they buried"). It cannot be determined whether this version hints at the participation of the angels in the burial of Moses or whether a plurality of unspecified men is intended.

17) J. W. Goethe, "Noten und Abhandlungen," in *West-Östlicher Divan*, ed. E. Beutler (Bremen: Schünemann, 1956) 250-53.

18) E. Sellin, *Moses und seine Bedeutung für die Israelitische Religionsgeschichte* (Leipzig, 1922) 43ff.; idem, "Hosea und das Martyrium des Mose," *ZAW* 46 (1928) 26-33.

19) S. Freud, *Moses and Monotheism* (New York: Random House, 1939).

20) A detailed criticism of the various hypotheses dealing with the murder of Moses is set forth by Y. M. Grintz, "Mose," *Yavneh* 2 (1940) 43-70 (a Hebrew review of Freud's book).

21) M. Noth, "Israelitische Stämme zwischen Moab und Ammon," *ZAW* 60 (1944) 19f.

22) Translation by H. St. J. Thackeray, *Josephus* 4 (LCL; Cambridge: Harvard, 1930) 633.

23) *Memar Marqah*, ed. J. Macdonald, BZAW 84 (1963). The text is cited here in his translation unless otherwise indicated.

24) והשגב כוח מאור. Macdonald (202) translates: "and was enveloped like the light (that is extinguished)."

25) Macdonald, 202-03,206. We have reduced Marqah's narrative to its main lines. Actually its structure is more complex. The sentence, "The Glory drew near to him and embraced him" (203), is followed by a long insertion and afterwards taken up again: "The Great Glory took him by his right hand embracing him" (206). The insertion includes three sections: a) Moses' solemn glorification by waters, heaven, earth, fire and cloud. Moses' holy and angel-like character is here strongly stressed; b) The abrupt dry statement that God judges all the human race by death and that nobody can escape this verdict; c) A scene in which God shows to Moses the four quarters of the world and the sequel to the Day of Vengeance. The insertion confirms that Marqah admits Moses' death only after having overcome serious doubts. The first section clearly suggests immortality, the second counterbalances it, the third softens the problem by the idea of resurrection.

26) Quoted by R. H. Charles, *Assumption of Moses* (London: Black, 1897) xlviii.

27) Cf. also Acts 1:9-10.

28) Moses and Elijah are often mentioned together in the midrash. In the New Testament both of them appear to Jesus (Matt 17:1-17). Rev 11:3-6 mentions two witnesses of God to whom He gave power to stop up the sky so that rain may not fall, and power to turn water into blood. It seems that here too Elijah and Moses are intended.

29) *Deuteronomy R.*, ed. M. A. Mirkin, p. 142.

30) This midrash, it seems, is abbreviated from a midrash of the Roman era which is preserved in *Tanḥuma, Va-era* XIX (ed. S. Buber, *Shemot*, p. 341):

> And the Lord said unto Moses, "Stretch forth thine hand toward heaven" (Exod 9:22). This is what scripture says, "He has done whatsoever He pleased" (Ps 115:3). The Holy, blessed be He, said, "The heavens are the heavens of the Lord, but the earth hath He given to the children of men" (Ps 115:16). To what is this similar? To a king that spoke and decreed to the people of Rome that they might not enter Syria and to the people of Syria that they might not enter Rome. Thus the Holy, blessed be He, when He created (the heavenly things said), "the heavens are the heavens of the Lord (but the earth has He given to the children of men)," and when the Holy, blessed be He, sought to give the Torah to Israel, He annulled the first decree and said, "Let the earthly beings rise to the heavenly beings and the heavenly beings descend to the earthly beings and I will be the first to do this." As it is said, "And the Lord came down upon Mt. Sinai" (Exod 19:20), and it is written, "and to Moses He said, 'Come up unto the Lord'" (Exod 24:1).

31) *Sifre Deut*, ed. L. Finkelstein, p. 426.

32) *Pseudo-Philo's Liber Antiquitatum* (ed. G. Kisch; Publications in Medieval Studies, University of Notre Dame 10; Notre Dame, 1949) 165.

33) Macdonald, 182.

34) *Ibid.*, 206.

35) *Ibid.*, 83.

36) *Aboth de Rabbi Nathan*, ed. S. Schechter, p. 50.

37) *Leqaḥ Tov* (Wilna, 1884), Deut, p. 134.

38) *Sifre Deut*, ed. L. Finkelstein, p. 429.

39) Macdonald, 83.

40) *Ibid.*, 206.

41) *Itinera Hierosolymitana* (CSEL 39; Pragae, Vindoboniae, Lipsiae, 1898) 53.

42) R. Raabe, *Petrus der Iberer* (Leipzig, 1895) 85,88.

43) S. J. Saller, *The Memorial of Moses on Mount Nebo* (*Publ. of the Studium Biblicum Franciscanum* 1; Jerusalem, 1941) 44,351.

44) A. Alt, "Ausflüge und Reisen (Nebo)," *PJB* 30 (1934) 28-30.

45) F. M. Abel, "Explorations du Sud-est de la Vallée du Jourdain," *RB* 40 (1931) 378.

46) On the literary connections between the text, concerning the cave on Mt. Nebo, see also M. F. Collins, "The Hidden Vessels in Samaritan Tradition," *JSJ* 3 (1972) 107.

47) *Leqaḥ Tov* (Wilna, 1884), Deut, p. 135.

48) Origenis, *Selecta in Num.*, ed. Migne 12, 578 b.

49) *Sifre Deut*, ed. L. Finkelstein, pp. 326-27.

50) The motif of the search is based upon the praise of Wisdom in Job 28. Note especially the verses,

But wisdom, where shall it be found? And where is the place of understanding? Man knoweth not the price thereof; neither is it found in the land of the living. The deep saith, "It is not in me"; and the sea saith, "It is not with me" (Job 28:12-14).

And more,

Destruction and Death say, "We have heard a rumor thereof with our ears. God understandeth the way thereof, and He knoweth the place thereof."

The reply of the mountains and valleys in the midrash: אלהים הבין דרכו ("God understands his way") echoes the answer of Destruction and Death in the book of Job: אלהים הבין דרכה ("God understands its way"). Compare also the midrash of R. Joshua ha-Levi about the vain search undertaken by Satan when he sought the Torah in the earth, the sea, and also with Moses, a midrash which expounds upon the same verses from the book of Job (*Yalkut Shim'oni*, part II, §594).

L. J. Weinberger ("A Lost Midrash," *Tarbiz* 38 [1969] 285-93 [Heb. with Eng. summary, v]) argues that the motif of His search for Moses is extant also in a lost midrash, reconstructed by him from liturgical and folk poems. Here Jokhebed, Moses' mother, searches for her vanished son. The resemblance is faint. The Angel of Death searches for Moses in order to take his soul. Moses' mother looks for her deceased son, lamenting over him. Nevertheless we concur with Weinberger that even these texts reflect the problems of Moses' death. Cf., e.g., the poem לבי למשה (*ibid.*, p. 287). Here Moses comforts his mother and asserts that no earth and dust cover him, but that his camp is among the camps of the angels.

51) *Deuteronomy R.*, ed. M. A. Mirkin, pp. 58-66.

52) The words עַל פִּי ח' (Deut 34:5) "according to the word of the Lord" have been interpreted "by the mouth of the Lord," i.e., by His kiss. This midrashic exegesis may be the origin of the term מיתח נשיקה ("a death by kiss"), which designates a painless death, especially a death in ripe old age (*b. Berakhot* 8a.; *Mo'ed* 28a; *Baba Bathra* 27a). J. Scheftelowitz (*Die altpersische Religion und das Judentum* [Giessen: Töpelmann, 1920] 159) derives this term from the custom that a person, close to a dying man, kisses him in order to transfer the dying man's soul into his own body at the moment when it departs from its old abode. According to Scheftelowitz, the custom was known among many peoples. Cf. particularly F. Cumont, *Recherches sur le symbolism funéraire des Romains* (BAH 35; Paris: Geuthner, 1942) 119f., who adduces many striking attestations from Roman literature and epigraphy. Nevertheless, Scheftelowitz's proposal is farfetched. The non-Jewish sources do not speak of a kiss by a deity, nor do the Jewish sources ever mention a metempsychosis by the kiss of a man. I am indebted to my friend, Prof. D. Flusser, for drawing my attention to this problem.

53) *Deuteronomy R.*, ed. M. A. Mirkin, p. 152.

54) *Ibid.*, pp. 134-35.

55) *LAB*, edition cited above, n. 32, 165-66.

56) Macdonald, 203,206,208.

57) *Pirke de Rabbi Eliezer*, trans. G. Friedlander (London, 1946) 174.

58) *Numbers R.*, ed. M. A. Mirkin, p. 272.

59) R. H. Charles, *Assumption*, 105-10, q.v. for sources quoted below in nn. 60-62.

60) "When Moses had died on the mountain, the archangel Michael was sent to remove his body. But Satan withstood." (*Scholion ad Epist. Judae* 9). "It is told that Michael attended to the burial of Moses' body while Satan opposed" (*Catena in Epist. Cathol.*)

61) The claim of Satan is handed down in the two sources cited above (n. 60) in the same formula, "To me belongs the body in my capacity as the ruler of matter." Michael's reply is extant in two formulations which complete each other. "All of us are created by His Holy Spirit" (*Acta Synodi Nicaean.* II,20). "This is the Lord of the spirits and all flesh" (*Catena in Epist. Cathol.*).

62) We have no source explicitly testifying to the argument of Satan. However, it can be deduced from the argument of Michael which is preserved by Origen (*De principiis* III:2), who tells us, "And at first in Genesis there is described the fact that the Serpent seduced Eve. Then in the Ascension of Moses, in his dispute with the Devil over Moses' body, Michael

argues that it was "because of the instigation of the Devil that the Serpent induced Adam and Eve to their transgression." This accusation which Michael levels against Satan makes no sense in their dispute over the body of Moses, unless we assume that it comes as a reply to Satan's claim that the body of Moses (and of every man) be due to him because of Adam's sin.

63) On the specific character of the Gnostic dualism in the Assumption of Moses and its comparison with other dualistic doctrines, see D. Flusser, "The Dualism 'Flesh-Spirit' in the Scrolls of the Dead Sea and in the New Testament, *Tarbiz* 27 (1958) 159-65 (Heb.).

THE TESTAMENT OF ABRAHAM AND THE TEXTS CONCERNING MOSES' DEATH

Samuel E. Loewenstamm

A comparison of the Testament of Abraham with the legends concerning the death of Moses hardly calls for justification. The forceful emphasis in the Torah upon the bond which connected these prominent men with God leaves no doubt about their unique affinity to the Divine sphere. It is this affinity which made it difficult to acquiesce in the thought that Abraham and Moses should have suffered death like simple mortals. In a sense, therefore, the legends about their deaths may be considered as answers to analogous questions.

This statement, however, requires qualification. Even in the Bible there exists a deep typological difference between the two men. The patriarch Abraham represents the prototype of a godfearing man favored by the Lord's grace. His image is lacking any superhuman features, and the biblical description of his death is like that of any other human being. Moreover, there is nothing remarkable about his burial. He was merely buried by his sons at a well-known place.

In contradistinction to Abraham, Moses' personality bears clear marks of a superhuman figure. The Torah relates that the Lord's glory was radiating from Moses' face when he descended from God's mountain, and many passages describe the mighty deeds that Moses wrought with God's rod in his hand. It is against this background that the complicated biblical story of Moses' death and burial should be interpreted, as the present writer has tried to demonstrate.[1]

Even this summary characterization of the biblical sources tends to show that the post-biblical legends concerning Moses' death are deeply rooted in ancient myth, whereas no such roots may be ascribed to the treatment of the patriarch's death in the Testament of Abraham.

In the light of this preliminary remark, let us proceed to a succinct scrutiny of this treatise on Abraham's death.[2] The aim of our investigation vindicates its limitation to the main lines of the broad epic picture drawn in the Testament. Its side-issues, such as the speaking tree, the role of Sarah, etc., are of no consequence for a comparison with the texts concerning Moses.

The book is composed of three clearly distinct parts: chapters 1-15 dealing with Michael's mission; chapters 16-20 relating the mission of Death; and the end of chapter 20 depicting Abraham's fate after his decease.

In the first part, God sends Michael to Abraham three times. a) Chs. 1-5: God charges Michael to announce to Abraham the just, His beloved friend, that he has to depart from this vain world, to leave his body and to come to his true Lord. Michael, without gainsay, betakes himself to Abraham, but cannot bring himself to announce to the perfectly virtuous man his death, and therefore he returns to God.

b) Chs. 4-8: God bids Michael go back, and he promises to predict Abraham's death in a dream which Michael is to interpret. Michael complies again, and God sends the dream to Isaac. Michael expounds it to Abraham and announces to him the purpose of his errand. Abraham replies,

> Now I recognize that you are an angel of the Lord and that you have come to take my soul. But I shall not follow you. Anyhow do whatever He orders (ch. 7).

Michael reports to God and asks for guidance.

c) Chs. 8-15: God tells Michael to return to Abraham to remind him of His promises for his posterity and especially of man's common lot to die. Michael complies again, and this time Abraham declares that he will not oppose God's power..."since I have recognized that I am mortal, not immortal." He begs, however, to be shown the world while still in the body. Upon God's order, Michael takes him upon a cloud and shows to him the salvation of the righteous and the perdition of the wicked. But after Michael has brought Abraham back to his home, he meets for a second time with his flat refusal: "I shall not follow you." His new report to God concludes with these words:

> Almighty God, thus he speaks. And I am prevented by pity from taking hold of him since he is from the beginning Your friend and did the best in Your eyes.

And there is no man on earth like him, not even Job the wonderful, and therefore I am prevented from taking hold of him (ch. 15).

It is only now that God imposes the task upon Death,[3] ordering him to approach Abraham in a beautiful appearance and to behave gently to him. At first, Abraham mistakes him for Michael, until Death reveals to him his true nature and tells him that he has come for his holy soul. Abraham replies, "I realize what you say, but I shall not follow you" (ch. 16). After long dialogues in which Death reveals his different forms of appearance and action, he again urges Abraham, "Come on, follow me as the God and Judge of the Universe bids me." Abraham asks for delay. Then Death has recourse to a subterfuge. When Abraham feels faint, Death advises him to improve his health by kissing his interlocutor's hand. Abraham takes this advice and succumbs to Death.

Michael appears again. Accompanied by a host of angels, he wraps the soul into a heavenspun cloth and buries the body. Afterwards he brings the soul with song and praise before God, who orders him to take it to paradise.

The structure of the text is clear. *In the beginning* Abraham does not recognize his visitors, neither Michael nor Death. *In the second phase* he replies to them, "I shall not follow you." *In the third* he asks for delay. The structural differences are restricted to the final phase. Here Michael grants Abraham's request for delay, meets at its end with renewed refusal and desists therefore finally from the performance of his task. In contradistinction to Michael, Death reacts upon Abraham's request for delay by the invention of a gentle scheme to take Abraham's soul without use of force.

Abraham's initial failure to identify his visitors is a retarding epic device, well known from the story of Odysseus' return to his home.[4] The motif is entirely foreign to the concise stories concerning Moses. The influence of these texts on the Testament is restricted to the main line of the narrative.

Abraham's stubborn restiveness is paralleled, in a sense, by Moses' refusals to die. Nevertheless, meaningful differences should be noted. Abraham's laconic declarations, "I shall not follow you," are unsupported by any arguments and at certain stages he even agrees to die and only asks for postponement of the inevitable. In contradistinction, Moses lays a claim on immortality and substantiates his claim in great detail, pointing out the superhuman features of his character. He pleads his case forcefully, whereas Abraham has no real case at all. But precisely the weakness of his position throws into relief the careful and tender regard for him shown by God and His messengers. All of them take into consideration his former merits and do their utmost in order to save the righteous man and beloved of the Lord the bitterness of death. It is true that this intent is not entirely absent in the narrative concerning Moses. Even in the Torah, God softens Moses' death by showing him the promised Land and attending afterwards to his burial, and the midrash that God took Moses' life by a kiss goes a long way in this direction, as does *Memar Marqah*, which strongly underlines the glory which surrounded Moses' painless death. Nonetheless, this moment in the Moses tradition is of accidental character only, whereas in the Testament of Abraham it represents the very essence of the text. The difference can be illustrated by the roles of Michael and Death.

No less than fifteen chapters of the Testament deal with God's attempt to take Abraham's life by the beautiful and graceful archangel Michael. The motif calls for comparison with *Deuteronomy R.*, *Berakhah X*,

> The Holy, blessed be He, said to Gabriel, "Go and bring Moses' soul." He said before Him, "Lord of the World, how can I look at the death of a man whose worth is equally balanced against sixty myriads? How can I look at his death? And a man who has qualities like those, how can I inflict upon him chastisement." And afterwards He sent to Michael saying, "Go and bring Moses' soul." He said before Him, "I was his teacher and he was my pupil. I cannot look at his death."

Hereafter God summons Sama'el who eagerly awaited this order, but Moses puts him off. At the end, God Himself takes Moses' soul.[5] In this midrash the angels decline God's request at the start, and the repugnance of the angels serves the clear purpose of stressing Sama'el's eagerness to take Moses' soul. In the Testament, Michael's broadly depicted errand is a main subject illustrating God's and Michael's tender concern with

Abraham in manifold variations. Thus an incidental feature of one version of the Moses tradition has been transformed into a principal theme of the Testament. So it is Michael, not God, who shows to Abraham the world before his death. In the Testament, God invariably acts by heavenly messengers.

Let us trace the history of this motif. In the Bible, Moses entreats God to be allowed to enter the Land and to see it. God grants only the second half of this request and shows him the Land from a mountain. In post-biblical versions, the interest in the Land is diminishing. Moses is shown from the mountain the whole world till the day of Resurrection, when the dead will become alive and will be judged. A certain inconsistency is obvious. It is hard to grasp how Moses possibly could overlook the whole world from Mt. Nebo. But tradition puts up with this difficulty since the ancient relation about Moses' ascent to the mountain was firmly established. No ancient lore prevented a smooth solution in the case of Abraham. In the Testament, Abraham requests to see the whole inhabited world (οἰκουμένη), which is shown to him while he is riding on a cloud driven by angels. During this drive he sees how men are judged by God in their lifetime and immediately after their death. The idea of resurrection is foreign to the Testament. Nevertheless, the Testament is seemingly influenced by the narratives that Moses, before his death, was shown the world and the ways of divine judgment. Whereas the post-biblical story about Moses can easily be explained as a later stage in the development of biblical tradition, it is clearly impossible to connect the corresponding story in the Testament with any biblical report on Abraham.

Not only Michael's, but even Death's errand is lacking exact parallels. The Angel of Death (or Sama'el) is mentioned in two versions concerning Moses. In one of them he wards Death off and his soul is taken by God. In the other one the Angel of Death takes Moses' soul like that of any ordinary man. Never do we find the motif that Death changes his terrifying image or behaviour when approaching Moses.

Nearer to the traditions concerning Moses is the narrative of Abraham's burial. Even in some of the midrashim which attribute Moses' burial to God, Michael and the angels take an important part in this action, and in the Assumption of Moses it is Michael alone who attends to the burial. Abraham's soul, however, enters paradise, and it is needless to say that this solution does not leave any room for the idea of resurrection. Its next parallel is the midrash in which Moses takes part in the world to come.

To sum up: The traditions concerning Moses' death are more ancient and even more meaningful than their parallels in the Testament of Abraham. Moses' refusal to die should be interpreted against the background of an alternative tradition attributing immortality to him. The same applies to the argument levelled at him that the lot of every man is to die. Abraham's refusals reflect nothing else than man's natural repugnance to death, and it is mainly this natural repugnance which is opposed by the argument that no man can escape death. His reaction that he has now recognized himself to be mortal should not be pressed to mean that he formerly believed in his immortality, since he nowhere pleads such a case. It only points to his readiness to draw consequences from the recognition of his mortality.

Michael's errand is of secondary character. It is perfectly clear that his task does not befit him, and his failure is a foregone conclusion. The motif that God tries to entrust Michael with such a task appears in one of the midrashim concerning Moses, but as a modest secondary embellishment. However, in the Testament of Abraham, it has been enlarged to become the main topic of the book. It is in accordance with the dominant character of this topic that even Death's image has become assimilated to that of Michael, though Death finds at last a considerate way to perform what Michael had declined to do.

NOTES

1) See the previous article.

2) We restrict our discussion to the long recension A. The short recension B omits Abraham's refusal to die.

3) The Testament invariably speaks of θάνατος ('Death'), while the midrash speaks of the 'Angel of Death.' Nevertheless Death appears in the Testament as God's messenger who strictly observes His instructions.

4) Cf. especially Abraham's remark that he recognized Michael when washing his feet because he had done him this service before, when the three men visited him by the oaks of Mamreh (ch. 6). It is hard to grasp why Abraham remembered Michael's feet better than his general appearance. The motif is seemingly an inapt adaptation of the famous scene in which Eurykleia washes Odysseus' feet and recognizes him by his cicatrice, a clear mark of identity (*Odyssey* XIX: 386ff.)

5) No analogous possibility is considered in the Testament, although the idea is not unknown. True, the Sages hold the view that man's soul is taken from him by the Angel of Death. But the question is open to discussion, whether there are extraordinary men whose souls are taken away by God Himself. Many admit such an exception in the case of Moses. The same claim is made in a Baraitha for Abraham, Isaac, Jacob, Moses, Aaron and Miriam (*b. Baba Bathrah* 17a). A still more extreme opinion attributes this privilege even to all Israel as a reward for the acceptance of the Law on Mount Sinai (*Exodus R.* 51:8(6); *Leviticus R.* 18:3).

THE PIERPONT MORGAN FRAGMENTS
OF A COPTIC ENOCH APOCRYPHON

Birger A. Pearson

1. The Fragments

The Coptic fragments presented here in a new transcription and translation were first published by W. E. Crum in 1913.[1] They were part of a collection of papyrus fragments, written in Sahidic Coptic, acquired sometime in 1905-6 by Lord Amherst from a dealer in Luxor, who indicated that they had come from Hou (ancient Diospolis Minor) near the modern city of Nag Hammadi. They were subsequently purchased by J. Pierpont Morgan,[2] and are now preserved in glass in the Pierpont Morgan Library in New York.[3] The Enoch fragments published here are catalogued as: "Pierpont Morgan Library. Coptic Theological Texts 3, fols. 1-9."

---

1. *Theological Texts from Coptic Papyri* (Anecdota Oxoniensia, Semitic Series 12; Oxford, 1913), no. 3, pp. 3-11.

2. Crum, *Theological Texts*, p. v.

3. On a visit to the Pierpont Morgan Library, I received from Mr. William Voelkle, Associate Curator of Mss., some additional information. The papyrus collection was purchased by Mr. Morgan through an agent for ₤8000 in 1912, one year before Morgan's death. The papyri were mounted in glass in the British Museum in 1913. In 1925 they were opened and re-mounted in glass panes, edged with leather, by Charles T. Lamacroft. They were stored in the British Museum until 1929, when they were brought to the Pierpont Morgan Library in New York. In a letter from Mr. Lamacroft dated Nov. 15, 1920, it is stated that the fragments are correctly placed, according to the verification of Mr. Crum. Folio 6 of the Enoch fragments now has a small fragment out of place, and I surmise this occurred when Mr. Lamacroft remounted the papyri in 1925. See

These fragments, consisting of parts of nine leaves from a Coptic codex, comprise the only surviving remnants of an apocryphon devoted to the biblical Enoch, an apocryphon which represents only a portion of what must have been a substantial Egyptian-Christian literature devoted to the antediluvian patriarch.[4] These particular fragments are published here not only because of their intrinsic interest, but also because they contain some important parallels to the Testament of Abraham, with which this volume is chiefly concerned.[5]

---

below, notes to the text, fol. 6r.

4. The Book of Enoch (1 or "Ethiopic" Enoch) circulated in Egypt (at least in part) both in Greek and in Coptic. For the Greek fragments see M. Black, *Apocalypsis Henochi Graece* (PVTG 3; Leiden, 1970). There exists a Sahidic-Coptic fragment from the so-called "Apocalypse of Weeks," containing 1 Enoch 93.3-8; see S. Donadoni, "Un frammento della versione copta del 'Libro di Enoch,'" *Acta Orientalia* (Copenhagen) 25 (1960), 197-202. The Book of the Secrets of Enoch (2 or "Slavonic" Enoch), though now extant only in Slavonic versions, must have been written in Greek in Egypt; see A. Vaillant, *Le Livre des secrets d'Hénoch, texte slave et traduction française* (Paris, 1952). Sahidic-Coptic fragments found at Aswan in 1909 contain meager remnants of an apocryphon apparently devoted to Enoch; see M. Munier, "Mélanges de littérature copte. III.-Manuscrits coptes sa'idiques d'Assouan," *Annales du Service des Antiquites de l'Egypte* 23 (1923), 212-215. The apocryphon represented by these fragments does not seem to be the same as the one with which this article is concerned, but does contain some parallels; on these see below. Finally, in the *Pistis Sophia*, an Egyptian gnostic work, Jesus refers his disciples to mysteries contained in the two "Books of Jeou" which Enoch wrote in Paradise while Jesus was speaking to him out of the Tree of Knowledge and the Tree of Life. See C. Schmidt, ed., *Pistis Sophia* (Coptica 2, Hauniae, 1925), pp. 247 and 349 (Coptic text); cf. G. Horner, tr., *Pistis Sophia* (London, 1924), pp. 123 and 178 (English translation). The two "Books of Ieou" edited by C. Schmidt, though not explicity attributed to Enoch, are probably the books referred to in the *Pistis Sophia*; see C. Schmidt, ed., *Gnostische Schriften in koptischer Sprache aus dem Codex Brucianus* (TU 8; Leipzig, 1892). There are abundant parallels between this gnostic literature and the Hebrew Book of Enoch (3 Enoch), suggesting that such Enoch-Metatron traditions as are contained in 3 Enoch circulated

The surviving fragments are of very poor-quality papyrus (thick and opaque, with rough surfaces), ranging in size from 12.6 cm. (fol. 2) to 15.5 cm. (fol. 1) in height, and from 11.8 cm. (fol. 2) to 18.9 cm. (fol. 1) in width.

The codex from which the surviving folios came was constructed of a number of quires.[6] The folios were probably so arranged that recto pages would show alternately horizontal and vertical fibers. In this way the opened book would have both verso and recto pages showing surface fibers of the same direction, whether vertical or horizontal.[7]

---

in Egypt and were taken over by some gnostic groups there. For 3 Enoch see H. Odeberg, *3 Enoch or the Hebrew Book of Enoch* (Cambridge, 1928); and see Odeberg's comments, pp. 188-191.

5. These fragments have not received much scholarly attention. Th. Lefort reviewed the volume in which our fragments appear, but said nothing at all of the Enoch fragments, concentrating rather on the fragments of the *Life of Pachomius*; see his review in *Muséon* 14 (1913), 323-332. M. R. James devoted a paragraph to the Enoch fragments in his review, and calls the text "a tantalizing piece of a book relating to Enoch," but his remarks add nothing to what Crum had been able to say about the text; see *JTS* 16 (1915), 272-273. O. von Lemm made some valuable suggestions on the text and translation in his *Koptische Miscellen* CXLIII, in the *Bulletin de l'Académie Impériale des Sciences de St. Petersbourg* 8 (1914), pp. 925-927 (r.p.: P. Nagel and K. Kümmel, eds., Oscar von Lemm, *Koptische Miscellen* I-CXLVIII [Leipzig, 1972], pp. 511-513).

6. Fol. 7r bears the number ιΔ on the inside of the top margin, indicating that there were at least 14 quires in the codex. See note to fol. 7r.

7. As is customary in describing a codex (in contrast to a scroll), the "recto" page is the right-hand page of the opened book; the "verso" is the left-hand page. The first page of a book is a recto page; the reverse-side of the same leaf or folio is a verso page.

8. See the examples in Maria Cramer, *Koptische Paläographie* (Wiesbaden, 1964). Crum dates these fragments, along with the other papyri in the same collection, to "about the 7th century." See *Theological Texts*, p. v.

Each of our surviving pages is inscribed in two columns, each column an average of 7.5 cm. wide, and each line consisting of an average of 8 to 10 letters. The hand is a somewhat irregular "Biblical uncial," typical of the 7th-8th centuries.[8] Rudimentary decorations include the marking of a paragraph with an initial letter written in the left margin, and decorated above with a *coronis*: ⟩. The only punctuation mark used is the colon, a raised dot which marks phrases, but it is employed somewhat capriciously.

The fragments are very difficult to read, owing to the poor quality of the papyrus and the fading of the ink. In the case of numerous letters the ink has entirely disappeared. Some traces of such letters have been left, lighter in color than the rest of the papyrus, probably due to a chemical reaction between the original ink and the papyrus. Such traces and very faint traces of ink can be brought out with the aid of ultra-violet light, a device that I employed with good results when I had an opportunity to study the fragments in the Pierpont Morgan Library for two days in May, 1976.

The order of the folios is problematical. Crum ordered the folios as he did in his publication solely on the basis of what he considered to be a logical order according to content, but stated that the sequence was "merely tentative."[9] It is curious that he did not attempt to order the fragments according to their destruction-patterns. Indeed when one combines this kind of physical evidence with a study of the textual content, the sequence of folios can be determined with a high degree of probability.

Study of the destruction-patterns of the folios shows that they fall into two groups, in each of which

---

9. *Theological Texts*, p. 3. He says that "an alternative order might for instance, begin with foll. 2,6,8."

the sequence of folios can easily be determined, i.e. the sequence in which they lay when they were subjected to many centuries of damage from worms and rot. One group consists of fragments from the top-portions of three folios (the top margins are preserved), whose sequence (from the greater to the lesser amount of material preserved) is: fol. 9 →, fol. 1 →, and fol. 7 ↑ .[10] The other group consists of fragments probably from the lower portions of six folios (though no bottom margins are preserved), whose sequence is (from the lesser to the greater amount of material preserved): fol. 2 →, fol. 3 ↑, fol. 5 →, fol. 8 ↑, fol. 6 →, and fol. 4 ↑.

On the basis of textual content, it can easily be seen that fol. 2 contains the opening passage of our apocryphon. In addition, textual content suggests that fol. 9 follows fol. 6. A special problem is posed by fol. 4. In all other cases, when the folios are lined up according to their "profiles" or destruction-patterns, their columns of writing also line up, indicating that the folios were in their original position in the codex when they suffered deterioration. But fol. 4, when arranged according to "profile" with the other folios in its group, shows its columns of writing badly askew. This means that this folio had probably been loose in antiquity, and could have been shoved back into the codex anywhere, not necessarily where it originally belonged. I have accordingly placed this folio in the sequence of pages where I thought it fit best according to textual content, for, in fact, when left in the place assigned to it according to its destruction-pattern, it seems out of place in relation to the other portions of the text.

---

10. I retain the numbering of the folios first proposed by Crum, but of course re-order them. The arrows indicate whether horizontal (→) or vertical (↑) fibers are showing.

I posit the following order of folios (giving fiber directions of the recto pages): Fols. 2 →, 3 ↑ , and 5 → are contiguous. Fol. 4 → fits best, according to content, somewhere after fol. 5, followed by fols. 8 ↑ and 6 →, also contiguous pages. Positing one missing folio, 9 → is next, followed, after another missing folio, by 1 → and 7 ↑ , contiguous folios.[11]

The language of our fragments is pure Sahidic (i.e. the dialect of the Sahidic New Testament). The question as to the original language of the apocryphon cannot be answered with certainty, though I see nothing to indicate that it is necessarily a translation from a Greek original. The presence of Greek "loan-words," of course, is no sign that we are dealing with a Coptic translation from Greek (indeed the term "loan-word" is misleading, for Greek words function in Coptic as Coptic words and are part of the Coptic vocabulary). The Coptic syntax, so far as our fragments allow us to determine, is quite regular, and all Greek words occur in the forms regularly used in Sahidic Coptic (there being no examples of Greek inflection, an indicator of translation-Coptic).[12] Thus, I assume that our text was composed in the Coptic language, specifically, in the Sahidic dialect of upper Egypt.

2. Content

According to the order of the folios adopted here, the opening passage occurs on fol. 2. Somewhat reminis-

---

11. It will be noted that in those cases where we most likely have contiguous folios, the fiber directions alternate in the manner described above, a typical feature of Coptic codices from the 5th century on.

12. Cf. W. Till, *Koptische Grammatik*, 2nd ed. (Leipzig, 1961), sections 76 (substantives and adjectives) and 280 (verbs). Note, also, the peculiar orthography of some of the Greek words in our text, e.g. ⲀⲦⲀⲘⲀⲚⲦⲒⲚⲞⲚ (ἀδαμάντινον), 3r,ii,12: ⲶⲨⲠⲞⲐⲨⲔⲎ (ἀποθήκη), 4r, ii, 12; ⲦⲀⲬⲎ (ταχύ), 7r, i,9. Of course such spellings occur also in Coptic texts that have been translated from

cent of the opening passage of 2 Enoch, the text tells how the Lord received Enoch, son of Jared, into heaven, where he saw "the mysteries that are hidden in the aeons of the Light" (fol. 2 verso, col. i, lines 4-10).[13] I take this as a summary proem; the actual ascent of Enoch was presumably narrated later on in the text (though not in our extant fragments).

We next find Enoch on a mountain, and an angel of God appears to him. The angel is not named (Michael? Gabriel?), but is described as "girded about his loins with a golden Girdle, with a crown of adamant" (fol. 3r, ii,8-12).[14] Enoch is commanded to take a book from the angel's hand and reveal the sacred name in it (fol. 3v). He complies, and finds "three invisible names" in the book (fol. 5r, ii,9-10), those of the Father, Son and Holy Spirit. The angel thereupon instructs Enoch in the mysteries of the Holy Trinity. The three Persons of the Trinity "guide the heaven and the earth" with "a single counsel" (fol. 5v, i,3-7).

Greek and have undergone a history of transmission in Coptic.

13. The use of the term "aeons" does not necessarily imply any "gnostic element" in the text (cf. Crum, *Theological Texts*, p. 4), certainly not a gnostic intentionality. For the use of such "gnostic"-sounding language in the Christian literature of Coptic Egypt, cf. e.g. *Die Bücher der Einsetzung der Erzengel Michael und Gabriel*, ed. C. D. G. Müller (CSCO, Scriptores Coptici 31 [Coptic texts] and 32 [German translation]; Louvain, 1962), *passim*.

14. Michael is regularly presented in Coptic literature as girded with a golden girdle. See C. D. G. Müller, *Die Engellehre der Koptischen Kirche* (Wiesbaden, 1959), p. 18. On the other hand, Gabriel is the "bringer of good tidings" *par excellence* in Coptic literature; *Engellehre*, 36ff. In *The Book of the Installation of the Archangel Gabriel* (Müller, ed. and tr., *Die Bücher*, Gabriel is frequently called "the bringer of good tidings of the aeons of light"; see Coptic text, p. 63 *et passim*, German tr., p. 76 *et passim*. Michael may be considered more likely if we compare 1 Enoch 71:3; but cf. also Gabriel in 2 Enoch 21:3-5.

It seems likely that the final portion of the angel's instructions to Enoch consists of a prophecy of Enoch's translation to heaven and his future role in the judgment: "God will bestow upon you a name more famous than that of any man. You will be taken to heaven in your body, and you will be placed in the midst of the store-house . . ." (fol. 4r, ii,3-12).[15]

After a reference to the previous instruction of the angel on the mountain (fol. 4v, i,5-8), it is stated that Enoch found "three seals" (fol. 4v, i,8-10), and (after a lacuna in the text) "writings" are mentioned (fol. 4v, i,12). There is also mention of a "virgin" (fol. 4v, ii, 6), a possible reference to the Millenium (fol. 4v, ii, 8-10),[16] and (possibly) a mention of punishment in the "abyss" (fol. 4v, ii,12). The context is impossible to reconstruct with certainty, but one is tempted to speculate that Enoch is here encountering written eschatological prophecies attributable to the virgin Sibyl.[17]

In the next extant section, someone (Enoch?) says,

---

15. See above, on the problem of the placement of fol. 4. The word "store-house" is possibly reminiscent of the "store-chambers of blessing that are in heaven," mentioned in 1 Enoch 11:1, but the word in the latter passage is ταμεῖα rather than ἀποθήκη. See further below.

16. The thousand-year reign of Christ on earth is a popular theme in Egyptian Christian literature (cf. Rev 20 in the NT). See on this H. G. Evelyn White, *The Monasteries of the Wadi 'N Natrun*, Part I: New Coptic Texts from the Monastery of Saint Macarius (The Metropolitan Museum of Art Egyptian Expedition; New York, 1926; r.p. 1973), 17f., with reference to fragments from "an apocalyptic gospel" found in the Expedition. The millenial reign is a feature of the Apocalypse of Elijah, with which our Enoch text has some points of contact. See G. Steindorff, *Die Apokalypse des Elias, Eine unbekannte Apokalypse und Bruchstücke des Sophonias-Apokalypse* (TU 17; Leipzig, 1899), p. 106.

17. Two "virgins" are mentioned later in the text, Enoch's sister (Sibyl) and Tabitha. See further below.

"Behold, what is my [   ]¹⁸ becoming, which you
have begotten in her? Behold three times she spoke with
great words" (fol. 8r, ii,5-11). Enoch (?) is then told
that he should go and reveal something in the midst of
his father and mother (fol. 8v, i,4-12).

We then find Enoch outside the bed-chamber of his
virgin sister. His mother is with him and says, "Enoch,
my son, let us go into the bed-chamber, and let us . . ."
(fol. 6r, ii,9-12). His sister hears Enoch's voice, bids
him enter, and they begin to converse (fol. 6v).

It is clear from what follows that Enoch's sister is
no ordinary virgin! She is a prophetess, and there can
be little doubt but that she is none other than the
Sibyl. She tells Enoch that God has chosen him for his
righteousness, and that he shall be taken up in his body
to heaven (fol. 9r). Enoch inquires whether there are
others who shall likewise be taken up, and is told
that Elijah and Tabitha will also be taken up in their
bodies (fol. 9v). It is possible that, in a lost portion
of the text, reference was made to the coming Flood, for
the repopulation of the earth is mentioned in what
remains of that page (fol. 9v). The text breaks off
with the mention of Enoch's son, Methuselah.¹⁹

The last extant portion of the apocryphon deals with
the Judgment. The previous context establishes that
Enoch is being instructed on his future role in the
Judgment by his sister, but the transition to the next
extant passage is difficult to determine. Someone (an
angel? the Son of God?) says (to God?), "If he sees them

---

18. Unfortunately one cannot read ⲤⲰⲚⲈ, "sister"
here.

19. In certain sections of 1 Enoch Methuselah is
the recipient of Enoch's revelations; see especially
1 Enoch 72-91. In the "Melchizedek" section of 2 Enoch
Methuselah is established by God as priest and leader
over the people after the translation of Enoch. See
Vaillant, *Le Livre des secrets d'Hénoch*, pp. 64-69; cf.
also W. Morfill, tr., and R. H. Charles, ed., *The Book
of the Secrets of Enoch* (Oxford, 1896), pp. 85f.

in all their iniquities which they do, he will write them
immediately, and your entire image will go to perdition"
(fol. 1r, i,3-12). This is probably a reference to
Enoch's role as "scribe of righteousness," and the
concern is expressed that he may be too harsh in his
score-keeping! We should understand this passage to
belong either to a dream-vision of Enoch himself, or to
a report by his sister of a vision that she has had of
the heavenly court-room.

The same vision continues with the report of an
archangel putting something on "the balances of righteousness," and bringing "other mighty angels" of a
"fiery" sort (fol. 1v, i,5-12). Mention is made of "the
Son of God seated at the right-hand of his father" (fol.
1v, ii,5-8), and it is probably he who bows down at the
Father's feet, saying, "O my Father, do not . . ." (the
text breaks off here, fol. 1v, ii,8-14).

In the very last extant section, Enoch's sister is
speaking again, instructing Enoch as to his role in the
Judgment. She counsels him not to write down men's sins
too hastily (fol. 7r)! She also tells him about the
"angel of mercy," doubtless the angel Michael. At the
weighing of men's deeds, if the sins outweigh the good
deeds, Michael tips the scale with his rod (fol. 7v)!

How much more material there might have been after
this passage in the original apocryphon cannot, of
course, be determined. Such material as we do have,
however, is of considerable interest from the standpoint
of the relationship between this text and the apocryphal
traditions pertaining to Enoch, on the one hand, and the
relationship of this text to the Testament of Abraham on
the other. These relationships can be established with
reference to the following items: A. The figure of
Enoch; B. Enoch's sister, Sibyl; C. Elijah and Tabitha;
and D. The Judgment.

A. <u>The figure of Enoch</u>. The special character of

Enoch as reflected in our text is largely based upon the older Jewish apocryphal literature. As a special "elect one" (fol. 9r, i,4f.),[20] he is taken bodily into heaven (fol. 2r, i,9; fol. 2v, i,1-3; fol. 4r, ii,8-10; fol. 9r, ii,1-7),[21] and sees the heavenly mysteries (fol. 2v, i, 3ff.).[22] Especially intriguing is the pronouncement of the angel to Enoch concerning a special name: "God will bestow upon you a name more famous than (that of) any man" (fol. 4r, ii,3-7). What name might this be?

In 1 Enoch 70:2 Enoch ascends to heaven in "chariots of the spirit," and we are told that his "name" vanished among those that dwell on earth. This may imply, for the Similitudes of Enoch, that Enoch took over the "name" of the Messiah-Son of Man, though this is not explicitly stated.[23] But it is in 3 Enoch where we find the most intriguing possibility for the interpretation of our passage: the name to be given to Enoch is "Metatron," the Prince of the Presence, the "Lesser YHWH"![24] This would accord well with the role assigned to Enoch in our

---

20. This title is used in the Similitudes of 1 Enoch as an alternative Messianic title for the "Son of Man," with whom Enoch is identified in 1 Enoch 71:14. Enoch-Metatron is called an "elect one" in 3 Enoch 6:3.

21. Derived from Gen 5:24. See e.g. Sir 44:16; 49:14; Jub 4:23; Jant 1.85; and especially the Enoch books, 1-3 Enoch. The store-house mentioned in our text (fol. 4r, ii,11) may be compared not only to 1 Enoch 11:1, but also to 3 Enoch 10:6; Enoch-Metatron is set over "all the treasuries of the palaces of *Araboth* and over all the stores of life that I have in the high heavens," Odeberg, p. 30, where see also his notes.

22. 1-2 Enoch, *passim*.

23. In 1 Enoch 71:14ff. the identification of Enoch with the Son of Man is clearly made: "You are the Son of Man. . . ." R. H. Charles' emendation of the Ethiopic text at this point is not acceptable; cf. *AP* II, p. 237.

24. The identification between Enoch and Metatron is first attested in the Jerusalem Targum, Gen 5:24.

text as a "heavenly scribe,"[25] for Metatron is the "heavenly scribe" *par excellence* in Jewish sources. Thus our text appears to reflect ideas concerning the ascension and exaltation of Enoch already established in the earlier Jewish literature, especially the Similitudes of 1 Enoch and 3 Enoch.[26]

Enoch's most important role in our text is that of the "scribe of righteousness." To be sure, that title does not occur in our text, but Enoch's role as such is clearly delineated (fol. 1r, i,8f.; fol. 7r, i,6ff.; fol. 7v, i,4ff.).[27] This, of course, is part and parcel of the general designation of Enoch as a "scribe" in Jewish apocryphal literature,[28] and the same role is given to Enoch in Coptic Christian literature.[29]

However, our text goes beyond the general designation of Enoch as a "scribe" found in the Jewish apocryphal literature, for it assigns to Enoch the role of scribe *in the Judgment*, and here we are put into close contact with the description of the Judgment in Rec. B of the Greek text of the Testament of Abraham, wherein the "scribe of righteousness, Enoch" is appointed by God to "write down the sins and the righteous deeds of each

---

25. bHag 15a. On Metatron cf. 3 Enoch, *passim*, and Odeberg's discussion, *3 Enoch*, 79ff.

26. This is unusual for a Coptic document, for Coptic literature normally does not assign that exalted role to Enoch. Of course, it should also be stated that Enoch is not mentioned at all in the Talmud, and some of the midrashim even deny that he was translated to heaven. See L. Ginzberg, *The Legends of the Jews*, vol. 5 (Philadelphia, 1925), 156.

27. For the designation, "scribe of righteousness," see 1 Enoch 12:4; 15:1.

28. Cf. "Enoch the scribe," 1 Enoch 12:3; and cf. e.g. Jub 4:17-23; 2 Enoch 23:4ff.; 53:2; 64:5.

29. See e.g. "Enoch, the scribe of righteousness": *Die Bücher der Einsetzung der Erzengel Michael und Gabriel*, pp. 54, 56, 73 (Coptic text). "Enoch the scribe" is invoked as such (or as "Enoch the scribe of righteousness") on Coptic grave stelae. See the Coptic

man" (Rec. B, ch. 11).[30]

B. <u>Enoch's sister, Sibyl</u>. The name of Enoch's virgin sister is not provided in the extant portion of our text, but there can be no doubt about her identity; she is (the) Sibyl. This is borne out not only by the role assigned to Enoch's sister in our text, that of a prophetess, but by the Coptic tradition concerning the Sibyl.[31]

In a remarkable document called "The Book of the Installation of the Archangel Gabriel," the following passage occurs (put into the mouth of Gabriel):

"Moreover I am, O Lord, the one who came to Sibyl (ⲤⲒⲂⲖⲀ) the virgin sister of Enoch the scribe of righteousness. I protected her, and rescued her from the hand of the wicked Devil who desired to do evil to her."[32]

In an equally interesting Coptic text, relating the discovery of the tomb of Christ in Jerusalem by

---

inscriptions edited by H. Thompson in J. E. Quibell, *Excavations at Saqqara*, vol. 4: The Monastery of Apa Jeremias (Cairo, 1912), nos. 233, 295, 304, 329, 340. Such invocations probably reflect the idea of Enoch's role as a scribe in the Judgment. See further below.

30. Enoch has the prerogative of erasing sins as well (fol. 7r, ii,4)! See discussion below on the Judgment.

31. I know of no Jewish apocryphal text which makes this identification. Other names do occur for the sisters of Enoch in Jewish literature; cf. e.g. Ps.-Philo *Ant* 1.14; cf. D. Harrington, ed., *The Hebrew Fragments of Pseudo-Philo* Liber Antiquitatum Biblicarum *Preserved in the* Chronicles of Jeraḥmeel (Texts and Translations 3, Pseudepigrapha Series 3; Missoula, 1974), pp. 10-11.

32. C. D. G. Müller, ed., *Die Bücher*, p. 73 (Coptic text, my translation). I know of no episode in Coptic or other apocryphal literature to which this text refers. For our purposes it is enough to note the identity of Sibla (= Sibyl) as Enoch's sister.

Eudoxia, sister of Constantine,[33] an aged man named Jacob says to Eudoxia,

"Blessed is the chosen race of which Sibyl (ⲥⲓⲃⲩⲗⲗⲁ), the sister of Enoch the scribe, prophesied. . . ."[34]

It is worthy of note that Sibyl is invoked in close proximity with Enoch in numerous Coptic sepulchral inscriptions. The usual form is "Father Enoch, Mother Sibyl" (ⲁⲡⲁ or ⲡⲉⲛⲓⲱⲧ ⲉⲛⲱⲭ, ⲁⲙⲁ or ⲧⲉⲛⲙⲁⲁⲩ ⲥⲓⲃⲩⲗⲗⲁ).[35] This, too, doubtless reflects the tradition in Coptic Christianity that Sibyl is the sister of Enoch.

Finally, Sibyl and Enoch are found together with Elijah and Tabitha in the time of the Antichrist, according to the Arabic version of the *History of Joseph the Carpenter*,[36] but that brings us to the next item in our discussion.

---

33. Unattested in any historically credible source. She is mentioned together with Constantine's mother, Helena, in the Martyrdom of St. George the Diospolite (of Cappadocia), I. Balestri and H. Hyvernat, eds., *Acta Martyrum* II:1 (CSCO 86; Louvain, 1924), p. 261 (Bohairic text); II:2 (CSCO 125; Louvain, 1950), p. 173 (Latin tr.).

34. See F. Rossi, "Transcrizione di tre manoscritti copti del Museo egizio di Torino con traduzione italiana," *Memorie d. Reale Accad. d. Scienze di Torino* 37, ser. 2 (Torino, 1886), p. 106, my tr. The text is reprinted in Rossi's *I papiri copti del Museo egizio di Torino*, vol. 1 (Torino, 1887), fasc. 3, p. 44. The quotation that follows is an expanded paraphrase of part of the "Tiburtine" Sibyl's prophecy of the "sixth generation." For the Greek text see P. J. Alexander, *The Oracle of Baalbek, The Tiburtine Sibyl in Greek Dress* (Washington, 1967), p. 14. See further on the Tiburtine Sibyl below.

35. See J. E. Quibell, *Excavations at Saqqara*, vol. 3 (Cairo, 1909), nos. 1, 5, 12, 23, 26, 29, 30, 31, 32, 43, 44, 48, 50, 53, 54, 59, 62, 65, 76, 82, 120, 150. The forms of the name "Sibyl" vary remarkably: ⲥⲓⲃⲩⲗⲗⲁ and ⲥⲓⲃⲩⲗⲁ are commonest, but ⲥⲓⲃⲗⲉ, ⲥⲓⲃⲏⲗⲗⲁ, ⲥⲓⲃⲗⲗⲁ, and ⲥⲓⲃⲗⲁ also occur. See also *Excavations at Saqqara*, vol. 4 (Cairo, 1912), *passim*. In two inscriptions from Saqqara, nos. 290 and 304, Sibyl is called "the prophetess." It is to be noted that "Sibyl" is a proper name in Coptic traditions. For further references see O. von Lemm, *Koptische Miscellen* XX, (r.p. Leipzig, 1972), pp. 19ff; and O. von Lemm, *Kleine Koptische Studien* I-LVIII, ed. P. Nagel (r.p. Leipzig, 1972), pp. 431, 522.

C. <u>Elijah and Tabitha</u>. In our text, Enoch's sister is represented as telling Enoch that two others will be taken up in their bodies to heaven, Elijah and Tabitha (fol. 9v, i,5f). Here we have to do with an idea that develops out of the "Antichrist" traditions pertaining to the "two witnesses" of Rev. 11:3-12.

In Rev. 11, two witnesses appear to prophesy during the time of the end, are finally put to death by the "beast" (=Antichrist), but are raised up and taken to heaven. In the development of this legend in Christian literature the two witnesses are almost invariably identified as Enoch and Elijah,[37] doubtless on the grounds that these two are singled out in scripture as those "who have not tasted death from their birth."[38]

Enoch and Elijah appear together as the two witnesses in the Apocalypse of Elijah. This apocalypse prophesies that when Elijah and Enoch hear of the appearance of the "Shameless One" (=Antichrist) they will come down to do battle with him and testify against him. He will kill them, and they will lie dead three and a half days in the market-place (cf. Rev. 11:8), but on the fourth day they will rise again to pronounce doom upon the Shameless One.[39]

---

36. See P. Lagarde, *Aegyptiaca* (Goettingen, 1883), p. 37 (Bohairic and Arabic texts), and F. Robinson, *Coptic Apocryphal Gospels* (Texts and Studies 4:2; Cambridge, 1896), p. 229, where the Arabic version is translated: "Who are those four, those of whom thou hast said that the Antichrist shall slay them because of their reproaching? The Saviour answered, They are Henoch, Elias, Schila, and Tabitha." "Schila" is a corruption for "Sibilla," as W. Crum acutely observed; see "Schila und Tabitha," *ZNW* 12 (1911), 352. See further below.

37. See the very valuable treatment by W. Bousset, *The Antichrist Legend*, tr. A. Keane (London, 1896), esp. pp. 203ff.

38. 4 Ez 6:26, with probable reference to Enoch and Elijah. The biblical references are Gen 5:24 (Enoch) and 2 Kgs 2:1-11 (Elijah).

39. Sahidic version, Steindorff, *Apokalypse des Elias*, pp. 124, 126 (Coptic); 125, 127 (German tr.).

This episode is immediately preceded by one in which a virgin named Tabitha is the protagonist. The appearance of the Antichrist is described, and then it is prophesied that the virgin Tabitha will pursue him to Jerusalem, railing at him all the way. Then the Shameless One will kill her, but she will rise again and take up her testimony.[40] At the end of the Apocalypse of Elijah it is prophesied that Elijah and Enoch (but not Tabitha) will come and pursue the "Son of Lawlessness," and kill him. Then Christ the King will come and bring the thousand-year reign upon the earth.[41]

It is clear that the Tabitha episode is modelled upon that of the two witnesses, Enoch and Elijah. In effect she is the third witness although, indeed, her testimony precedes that of Elijah and Enoch.

Who is this Tabitha? There can be no doubt but that this is the woman of Joppa whom Peter raised from the dead, according to Acts 9:36-41.[42] Since her subsequent death is not recorded in Acts, the Christian author or interpolator of the Apocalypse of Elijah assumes that she, like Enoch and Elijah, was taken bodily into heaven.[43]

---

40. Sahidic version, Steindorff, pp. 122, 124 (Coptic); 123, 125 (German tr.); cf. the Achmimic parallel text, Steindorff, pp. 92, 94 (Coptic); 93, 95 (German tr.).

41. Achmimic version, Steindorff, pp. 104, 106 (Coptic); 105, 107 (German tr.); the Sahidic fragments do not contain this concluding passage.

42. Cf. also the v.l. ταβιθα at Mark 5:41, doubtless influenced by Acts 9:40.

43. Cf. Steindorff's note, *Apokalypse des Elias*, p. 92. According to Steindorff, the Apocalypse of Elijah is based upon a pre-Christian Jewish apocalypse reworked and interpolated by Christian editors. The Tabitha episode is such a Christian interpolation; see Steindorff's introduction, p. 19. Recently J. M. Rosenstiehl has challenged this view. According to him, the episode of Tabitha is based upon the Egyptian myth of Tabithet, wife of Horus, but functions in the Apocalypse as an allegorical reference to the Qumran community! See Rosenstiehl, *L'Apocalypse d'Elie, Introduction, Traduction et Notes* (Textes et Etudes pour servir a l'histoire du Judaisme intertestamentaire 1; Paris, 1972), pp. 46, 69, 99. I do not find

As has already been indicated, Tabitha and Sibyl are mentioned as witnesses against the Antichrist, together with Enoch and Elijah, in the Arabic version of the *History of Joseph the Carpenter*.[44] It is probable that the Coptic version, in which only Enoch and Elijah are mentioned, is primary, and that the Arabic version has been expanded on the basis of the Apocalypse of Elijah. I would also venture to assert that the occurrence of Tabitha in our Enoch apocryphon is similarly influenced by the Apocalypse of Elijah.[45]

D. <u>The Judgment</u>. The judgment of men is given prominent treatment at the end of the surviving portion of our apocryphon. First, in a vision given either to Enoch or to his sister, Enoch's role as scribe is mentioned (fol. 1r), and the judgment process itself is described (fol. 1v). Finally, Sibyl counsels Enoch not to write men's sins too quickly (fol. 7r), and describes the work of the "angel of mercy" (fol. 7v). Unfortunately both passages are very fragmentary, and therefore no definitive account of the judgment scenario is possible.

It does seem clear that our document envisions a single on-going, universal (i.e. for everyone), post-mortem judgment,[46] rather than the "Last Judgment" which is a

---

his arguments convincing. Cf. the review of Rosenstiehl's book by A.M. Denis in *Muséon* 86 (1973), 239-241.

44. See above, n. 36.

45. Enoch and Elijah do battle with the Antichrist in the Tiburtine Sibylline Oracle, but despite the fact that the Tiburtine Sibyl shows probable dependence upon the Apocalypse of Elijah, Tabitha does not occur. For the Greek version of the (final) Antichrist episode see Alexander, *The Oracle of Baalbek*, pp. 22 (Greek), 29 (English tr.). For the Latin version see E. Sackur, *Sibyllinische Texte und Forschungen* (Halle, 1898), p. 186. Enoch and Elijah are not mentioned by name in the Oriental versions edited by J. Schleifer, "Die Erzählung der Sibylle," *Denkschr. d. Kaiserlichen Ak. der Wissenschaften, Wien*, Phil. Hist. Kl. 53 (1910), 1-80; see pp. 71-73.

46. This is a feature also of T Abr, as well as of a

more common conception in Christian (including Coptic) literature. The following items are of special import: 1. Enoch is charged with writing down the sins and good deeds of the sons of men (fol. 7r, i). It is feared that all mankind will perish if he sees them in all the iniquities they do (fol. 1r, i). He is thus admonished that, in the course of his duties, he should not write down sins too hastily (fol. 7r, i); indeed he is even told to erase the record in certain cases (fol. 7r, ii). 2. The judgment process is described as a kind of *psychostasia*, wherein the souls (or rather, their good and evil deeds) are weighed in the "balances of righteousness"(fol. 1v, i). The scales are in the charge of an "archangel" (fol. 1v, i,5f.), who is also probably to be identified as the "angel of mercy" (fol. 7v, i,9-11). This angel, if he sees sins (i.e. those of the elect?) outweighing good deeds, will add the weight of his rod to the balances, presumably on the side of the good deeds (fol. 7v, ii).

1. The function of Elijah as scribe in the judgment is a fixture of Egyptian-Christian religion, and the way in which the divine scribe is presented is paradigmatic of that strange combination of hope and fear that is so characteristic of Coptic Christian literature. E.g. in the fragments of another Enoch apocryphon already mentioned,[47] Enoch is similarly admonished:

["Enoch], scribe of [righteousness], do not hasten to write [the sins of the sons] of men, but" (the rest is lost).[48]

---

number of other Jewish apocryphal works; see G. Nickelsburg's remarks in his essay in this volume, p. 35.

47. Munier, "Mélanges," (above, n. 4).

48. Munier, "Mélanges," p. 215, fr. 3r, last 3 lines, my translation of the Coptic: "the sins of the" is also my restoration.

49. See H. R. Hall, *Coptic and Greek Texts of the Christian Period in the British Museum* (London, 1905), pp. 148f., as corrected by O. von Lemm, *Koptische Studien* LIV (r.p. 1972), pp. 50-57, on which my translation is based.

Even in magic the role of Enoch as scribe is feared and manipulated. In one curious magic text inscribed on a wooden tablet there is a striking parallel to Sibyl's admonition to her brother to put his pen down (fol. 7r, i, 6-12). A wounded deer says to Enoch,

"Enoch the scribe, don't stick your pen into your ink until Michael comes from heaven and heals my eye!"[49]

The fear that mankind will not be able to avoid perdition if Enoch sees all the sins they do (fol. 1r, i, 3-12) has an interesting parallel in the Testament of Abraham. In Rec. A of the Greek version, ch. 10, a voice from heaven says to Michael during Abraham's heavenly journey,

"If he (Abraham) sees all those who act in sin, he would destroy the whole creation!"[50]

In our Enoch apocryphon the fear of the righteous patriarch's wrath is (under the influence of TAbr, but "correcting" it?) vested in Enoch, the "scribe of righteousness."

This fear is turned to advantage in the use of a magical curse, addressed as a prayer to God:

"Wreak the vengeance of Enoch upon them! As the blood of Abel cries out against Cain his brother, so the blood of this poor man will cry out until you avenge him against those who have done him this violence! Eloi, Eloi, Lord Sabaoth..."[51]

Cf. also M. Kropp, *Ausgewählte Koptische Zaubertexte* II, no. 18 (pp. 66f.) for a German translation.

50. See M. Stone, tr., *The Testament of Abraham* (Texts and Translations 2, Pseudepigrapha Series 2; Missoula, 1972), p. 24 (text) and 25 (translation). The Greek edition used is that of M. R. James, *The Testament of Abraham* (Texts and Studies 2:2; Cambridge, 1892). Other quotations from T Abr in this article will be from the Stone translation. Note that the wrath of Abraham against sinners is not mentioned in the Coptic version.

51. My translation, from the definitive edition of this text in P. Jernstedt, *Koptskie Teksty Gosudarstvennogo Ermitazha* (Moscow-Leningrad, 1959), no. 70, p. 153, lines 17-22. Cf. also O. von Lemm, *Koptische Miscellen* L (r.p. 1972), pp. 92-102; Kropp, *Ausgewählte Koptische*

The "Vengeance of Enoch," of course, is the punishment that is to follow upon the reading of the record that Enoch compiles of a sinner's evil deeds.

That Enoch, scribe of righteousness, has the authority to erase sins from his account is also indicated in our text (fol. 7r, ii,4). This, too, we find documented elsewhere in Coptic Christian literature. In the *Martyrdom of Apa Anub*, the Savior promises Anub three crowns, and adds this incentive to such as might want to tell Anub's story:

"For every man who will write of your martyrdom and your contest, I shall command Enoch the scribe of righteousness to wipe out of the account-book (χειρόγραφον)[52] all of his sins, and I shall write his name in the Book of Life."[53]

One point needs clarification: Enoch, as we have seen, is the heavenly scribe in the Judgment. But the actual writing of the record is no doubt envisioned as taking place prior to the judgment of the individual, during each person's life-time. Thus Enoch's role in the judgment is not exactly analogous to that of the god Thoth in the Egyptian conception of the judgment scene, for Thoth records the *results* of the weighing of the soul.[54]

Zaubertexte II, no. 70, pp. 232-234, German tr.

52. Cf. Col 2:14.

53. My translation, from the Bohairic text in Balestri and Hyvernat, eds., *Acta Martyrum* (CSCO 43; Paris, 1907), p. 236; Latin tr.: (CSCO 44; Paris 1908), p. 144. There is a possible parallel in ms. E of the shorter version of T Abr, ch. 11. Where the James ed. has (in M. Stone's translation), "And the Lord said to Enoch, 'I will command you to write down the sins of the soul that makes atonement, and it shall enter into life," ms. E has, "And the Lord says to Enoch, 'I am making a sign for you, in order that you write the sins of the soul in the book; and if the soul has received mercy, you will find its sins erased (εὑρήσεις τὰς ἁμαρτίας αὐτῆς ἐξηλειμμένας), and it will enter into life." My translation, from the Greek text in F. Schmidt, "Le Testament d'Abraham" (Diss. Strasbourg, 1971), vol. 2, p. 25. I am grateful to G. Nickelsburg for supplying this reference; Schmidt's work as a

7. Fol. 4 → recto

```
[±6         ]ετ.
[±5         ]ντ[
[±5         ]τ[
[±3      ν]ανογ4
[..]ναϣωπε
[±4      ]ογ ειτε
[±5         ]εcολ
[cλ..].cζαïcoγ
[±5      ]χιν τε4
[±4    ]ε μπα
[±5       ]αα4 ετ
[±5     ]..ν̄..
[±8            ].
```

```
2   πα.[
    ωμ[... πνογ]
4   τε ν[αχαριζε]
    ναk [ν]ογρ[αν]
6   νcοειτ ε[ζογο]
    ερωμε νιμ
8   cενδαϊτk ετ
    πε ζ̄μ πεk
10  c[ω]μα ν̄cε kα
    αk ζ̄ν τμητε
12  [νθ]γποθγkη
    [..]νε ον ϣε[
14  μπε[
        ...[
16  πν̄[
```

8. Fol. 4 ↑ verso

```
[±6         ]τε.
[±7         ]ν̄[
[±5      ].ρπ.
[....]κοc νε
αιντααπαγ
[γ]ελοc ταμο4
εροο4 ζιχμ
πτοο4· α4
ον ϣομτε
ν̄cφραγï[c]
αγω πε[
.γ ν̄cζαï .[
[±7     ]τ.
[±7     ]μc
```

```
    μμ[
2   ζïχ[
    τ̄τ ν[
4   φαγι[οc μπχο]
    εïc τγ.[
6   παρθε[νοc
    χε cα.[
8   ναεϊρ[ε
    ϣο ν̄ρ[ομπε]
10  ζιχμ π[καζ]
    ϣατ̄ν [
12  νογν .[
14
```

Whether or not Enoch was actually envisioned in our document as taking part in the judgment scene itself, the weighing of sins and good-deeds, is not clear from the fragments that remain. If he was, as is probable, then his role would be that of a witness in the judgment, as in the shorter versions of the Testament of Abraham.

In chapter 10 of Rec. B of the Greek version of the Testament of Abraham, and in the parallel section in the Coptic version,[55] Abraham sees a soul brought to judgment, and testimony is given before the judge (Abel, according to the Greek version, God according to the Coptic)[56] by a man reading from a book. This man is simply referred to in the Coptic version as "a gray-haired man" who comes before the judge "with a book in his hand" immediately when the trial begins. In the Greek version the judge calls for the record books only after the soul denies a murder the judge accuses her of having committed:

> The judge then instructed him who writes the records to come, and behold, cherubim bearing two books, and there was an exceedingly large man with them. He had three crowns upon his head and one crown was higher than the other two crowns. The crowns are called the crowns of witness.

---

whole was unavailable to me.

54. Cf. the familiar vignette from the Egyptian *Book of the dead* (ch. 30), showing the heart of the deceased weighed in the balance with *maat* (a feather), with the ibis-headed Thoth recording the result. On the Egyptian background of the weighing of the soul as found in T Abr and, perhaps, in our Enoch fragments, see further below.

55. See G. MacRae's translation in this volume, which is conveniently divided into chapters following the divisions found in James' edition of Rec. B. I do not take account here of the Ethiopic and Arabic versions, which derive from the Coptic.

56. Abel is the judge in Rec. A as well. In contrast, the Coptic version does not mention Abel at all, and underscores the identity of the judge with the words, "God the true judge."

> And the man held a golden pen in his
> hand, and the judge said to him, 'Exhibit
> the sins of this soul.'

In Chapter 11 of the Greek version Abraham asks Michael, "Lord, who is this judge and who is the other one who convicts the sin?" The Coptic version has Abraham ask, "My lord, who is this great gray-haired man with this book in his hand, reminding the judge of these souls?" In both versions[57] Enoch the scribe of righteousness is identified as the one who testifies, and it is stated that God has appointed him to write down all the good and evil deeds that men do.

In my view, the short versions of the Testament of Abraham--and especially the Coptic version--[58] provides us with the key for understanding the role of Enoch in our apocryphon: He has been appointed by God to record the good and evil deeds of all men, and each person's record will be read when he comes to judgment before God, Enoch himself serving as a witness before the bar.[59]

---

57. The Greek version first answers the question about the judge: he is Abel, the first martyr.

58. Although I do not wish to enter the discussion as to which of the versions of T Abr is closest to the original, I tend to think that at crucial points the Coptic version provides us with a more primitive text.

59. In the Coptic Testaments of Isaac and Jacob, which obviously depend upon T Abr, the judgment scene does not occur. Enoch is mentioned in T Is in a list of patriarchs, and his assumption to heaven is mentioned in the Bohairic version. It is noteworthy that he is called "Our father Enoch" (ΠЄΝЄΙѠΤ ЄΝѠΧ), reminiscent of the grave stelae mentioned above. See K.H. Kuhn, "The Sahidic Version of the Testament of Isaac," *JTS* N.S. 8 (1957), p. 231. Cf. also S. Gaselee's translation of the Bohairic version, in G.H. Box, *The Testament of Abraham* (London, 1927), 62-63. For the Bohairic text see I. Guidi, "Il Testamento di Isaaco e il Testamento di Giacobbe," *Rendiconti d. Reale Accademia dei Lincei*, Cl di scienze morali, Storiche, e Philologiche 9 (Rome, 1900), 230. On the priority of the Sahidic version see P. Nagel, "Zur sahidischen Version des Testamentes Isaaks," *Wissenschaftliche Zeitschrift der Martin-Luther-Universität Halle-Wittenberg* 12 (1963), 259-263.

2. In our Enoch fragments the judgment process includes the weighing of sins and good-deeds on a "scale of righteousness." The scale is administered by an angel referred to as "the Archangel" (fol. 1v, i,5) or "the angel of mercy." Both designations belong to the Archangel Michael in Coptic angelology, and I do not hesitate to identify him accordingly.[60]

The idea of a "weighing" of souls (*psychostasia*) or of the deeds of men in a process of judgment occurs in the O.T. and in Jewish literature,[61] and there are analogies in Greek,[62] Iranian, and other literatures.[63] In the ancient Egyptian literature and iconography, of course, the idea is central.[64] Accordingly we might expect to find it as a central concept in Coptic Christianity, whose religious lore is in so many respects derived from that of Pharaonic Egypt. But this, in fact, is not the case. What is even more interesting, however, is that the *psychostasia*, and Michael's role in it, becomes an important symbol in medieval Christianity in the West.[65] To this we shall have to return.

---

60. "The archangel": Müller, *Engellehre*, 8. "Angel of Mercy": *Engellehre*, 18. See especially the *Book of the Installation of the Archangel Michael*, p. 26 (Coptic), 33 (German tr.). This is consistent with his role as advocate and defender of the faithful in Jewish angelology. See e.g. O. Betz, *Der Paraklet* (Leiden, 1963), 63ff. I know of no Jewish texts, however, in which Michael takes part in the weighing of the soul, or the soul's good and bad deeds, in the Judgment. In Coptic Christianity Michael's role as mediator between God and man is so great that he occupies a place analogous to that of Jesus Christ himself in western Christianity. Cf. Müller, *Engellehre*, 4.

61. Job 3:6; Ps 62:9; Prov 16:2; 21:2; 24:12; Dan 5: 27; Pss Sol 5:6; 1 Enoch 41:1; 61:8; 2 Enoch 49:2; 52:15. The most important parallels to our text are 1 Enoch 61:8 and 2 Enoch 52:15. On T Abr and the Apocalypse of Zephaniah see below.

62. See G. McCurdy, "Platonic Orphism in the Testament of Abraham," *JBL* 61 (1942), 218ff.; but the parallels from Greek literature to the judgment scene in T Abr are not real parallels, as Brandon has noted. Cf. S. G. F. Brandon, "The Weighing of the Soul," in J. Kitagawa and C.

The weighing of good and bad deeds on a scale is mentioned in the Coptic Apocalypse of Zephania.[66] This apocalypse, which depicts the fates of the righteous and the damned, features two angels who write down the good deeds of the righteous in a record-book (χειρόγραφον)[67], and an accusing angel (κατήγορος) who similarly keeps a χειρόγραφον of the sins of men.[68] The role of this angel is to "accuse men before the Lord."[69] Thus this angel plays the role of Satan in the O.T.,[70] and one would expect his arch-opponent to be Michael;[71] curiously, Michael is not named in the document. The weighing of good deeds is mentioned in a passage whose context is disturbed, and in

---

Long, eds., *Myths and Symbols: Studies in Honor of Mircea Eliade* (Chicago, 1969), 99.

63. Brandon, "The Weighing of the Soul," 109f.

64. Cf. Brandon, "The Weighing of the Soul," 91-99; cf. also Brandon, *The Judgment of the Dead* (London, 1967), 37-48.

65. See L. Kretzenbacher, *Die Seelenwaage: Zur religiösen Idee vom Jenseitsgericht auf der Schicksalswaage in Hochreligion, Bildkunst und Volksglaube* (Buchreihe des Landesmuseums für Kärnten 4; Klagenfurt, 1958); cf. also Brandon, "The Weighing of the Soul," 100-109.

66. The Sahidic fragment of a Zephaniah apocalypse and the Achmimic fragment of an "unbekannte Apokalypse," as edited by G. Steindorff, *Die Apokalypse des Elias*, most likely belong to the same work, an Apocalypse of Zephaniah. See C. Schmidt, "Der Kolophon des Ms. orient. 7594 des Britischen Museums, Eine Untersuchung zur Elias-Apokalypse," *Sitzungsb. d. Preussischen Akademie der Wiss.*, Phil-Hist. Kl. (Berlin, 1925), 319. This apocalypse is most likely a pre-Christian product of Egyptian Judaism; see Steindorff, *Apokalypse des Elias*, 18f.

67. The same word is used of Enoch's record book; cf. above.

68. *Apokalypse des Elias*, pp. 38, 40 (Coptic), 39, 41 (German tr.).

69. *Ibid.*, pp. 52 (Coptic), 53 (German tr.).

70. See Job 1-2; Zech 3:1ff.

71. Dan 12:1; 3 Bar 11-15 and many other texts. Cf. Betz, *Paraklet*, 63ff. In the NT Jude 9 and Rev 12:7ff. reflect the traditional Jewish view of the struggle between Satan and Michael.

which the text is probably corrupt. The passage runs as follows:

"Now therefore, my sons, this is the contest (ἀγών) where it is necessary that the good-deeds and the wicked-deeds be weighed on a scale."[72]

This passage is followed by a blast on a golden trumpet by a great angel,[73] celebrating the victory over the Accuser:

"For you (sg.) have prevailed over the Accuser, you have escaped the abyss and Amente. You will now ferry over the river, for your name has been inscribed in the Book of the Living."[74]

We turn again to the Testament of Abraham, but this time to Rec. A of the Greek version, for the *psychostasia* scene is absent from Rec. B.[75] In ch. 12 Abraham sees two angels "of fiery appearance" (πύρινοι τῇ ὄψει) driving souls "into the wide gate to destruction." Between the wide gate, leading to destruction, and the narrow gate leading to life, sits a "wondrous man, looking like the sun, like a son of God" on a throne of judgment. Before him stands a table upon which lies a huge book, flanked by an angel on either side holding parchment and ink and a pen, recording the sins and the good deeds. In front of the table is a luminous angel holding a scale in his hand with which to weigh the souls,[76] and on his left there

---

72. *Apokalypse des Elias*, p. 56, my translation, following the suggestion of O. von Lemm, *Koptische Miscellen* CXLII (r.p. 1972), p. 513. Steindorff suggests in a footnote (p. 56) that this passage, with its address to the readers, may be a later gloss. I prefer to see it as an integral part of the apocalypse.

73. Michael is the trumpeter at the Judgment in Coptic Christian texts; see Müller, *Engellehre*, pp. 11, 30.

74. *Apokalypse des Elias*, p. 58, my translation.

75. A "weighing" process may be implied in Rec. B, in ch. 9, wherein Abraham sees a soul whose sins were "of equal weight" (ἰσοζυγούσας) with her (good) works. Cf. also the Coptic version, ch. 9 in MacRae's translation.

76. It is worthy of note that in ch. 12 "souls" are

sits a fiery angel with a trumpet in his hand in which there is fire "for the testing of the sinners."

In ch. 13 Michael identifies the various personages for Abraham: the judge is Abel;[77] the recording angels are left unnamed; the angel holding the scale is the archangel Dokiel,[78] "who weighs the righteous deeds and the sins by the righteousness of God," and the angel wielding the fire of testing is Puruel.[79] We note, too, the absence of Enoch in Rec. A; his place is taken by the two unnamed recording angels, a feature reminiscent of the Apocalypse of Zephaniah.

Another interesting detail in Rec. A, absent from the other versions, is found in ch. 14. Abraham asks about the soul whose sins and good deeds were equal, and Michael replies, "If it could obtain one righteous deed more than its sins, it will go to salvation." Abraham thereupon suggests that he and Michael pray to God in this soul's behalf. Michael agrees, and the soul is taken to paradise. Here, in effect, we see Michael functioning in his role as advocate for the defense and Abraham sharing in it. Nevertheless it is noteworthy that Michael plays no role at all in the judgment scene, unless the unnamed angel recording the good deeds is to be identified as Michael.[80]

---

weighed (ἐξυγίαζεν τὰς ψυχάς), but in ch. 13 "righteous-deeds" and "sins" are weighed. The weighing of "souls" is reminiscent of the weighing of the "heart" in the Egyptian judgment scenes, and the "righteousness of God" mentioned in ch. 13 is reminiscent of Egyptian *maat*, the feather against which the heart is weighed. There can hardly be any doubt as to the influence of Egyptian ideas on T Abr.

77. But his judgment is only the first of three: the second judgment occurs "at the second coming" (of Christ) by the "twelve tribes of Israel"; the final judgment is before God himself. These three judgments are not mentioned at all in the short recension, and probably do not belong to the original version of T Abr.

78. This name does not occur elsewhere. For the etymology see the article by G. Nickelsburg, above, p. 33.

79. Also a hapax. The etymology, from Greek πῦρ, is obvious.

80. Nickelsburg suggests this in his article, p. 44.

The major parallel between Rec. A of the Testament of Abraham and our Enoch apocryphon consists of the metaphor of the weighing of souls (i.e. its good and bad deeds) in a scale. The discrepancy of detail, however, is such that one cannot argue for a direct dependence of the Enoch apocryphon upon the Testament of Abraham. E.g. Abel as judge, the recording angels, Dokiel, Puruel--all these are absent from the Enoch fragments. Of course some of the details in our text are difficult to interpret. E.g. what does "the archangel" put upon the "balances of righteousness" (fol. 1v, i,5-8)? The heart of the person under judgment (as in the Egyptian vignette)? His rod (cf. fol. 7v, ii,10)? A record (χειρόγραφον) of good and/or bad deeds? Or again: who are the "other mighty angels," of a "fiery" kind, that are brought to the scene (fol. 1v, i, 9-12)? Are these angels of testing, like Puruel in the Testament of Abraham? Or are they the "fiery" (πύρινοι) angels of punishment mentioned in the Testament (Rec. A, ch. 12)?[81]

Finally, both in the Testament of Abraham and in our Enoch apocryphon there is a stress on intercession for sinners. As we have seen, Abraham (in Rec. A of T Abr) finally joins Michael in praying for a sinner whose sins and good deeds were equal. In our Enoch fragments the role of "Paraclete" seems to be divided between the Son of God (if that is who it is)[82] who bows down at the feet of his Father in fervent prayer (fol. 1v, ii), and the "angel of mercy" (=Michael) who places his rod on one side of the balances (fol. 7v, ii).

---

81. In T Is and T Jac the punishing angels are called τιμωρισταί. However there is no description of the judgment in either of these testaments. See G. Box, *The Testament of Abraham*, pp. 68f. and 82.

82. In Coptic angelology Michael, rather than Jesus Christ, is usually the advocate for the faithful before the Judgment; see Müller, *Engellehre*, 11. In a homily of Severianos of Ngabal, Michael is described as kneeling before the Father and exhorting him to remember his "image" (εἰκών); see Müller, *Engellehre*, p. 168, and cf. our

The weighting of the scale by the "angel of mercy" is a remarkable motif for which no parallel can be found in the Testament of Abraham, nor--so far as I am aware-- in any other Jewish or Christian apocryphon. It certainly expresses a genuinely Egyptian spirit,[83] and it is therefore surprising that no parallel can be found in Coptic literature. But it is all the more remarkable that the idea shows up in medieval Christianity in the west, first, apparently, in Ireland.[84] The famous sculptured cross of Muiredach at Monasterboice, County Louth, dating from 923, has as one of a series of sacred episodes carved on it a large pair of scales, in one pan of which sits a small human figure. The archangel Michael holds a staff, the butt of which rests on the head of a recumbent devil attempting to pull down the other scale-pan.[85]

The role of Michael in this sculptured monument is quite analogous to the role assigned to him in our Enoch fragments: he comes to the aid of a poor sinner at the judgment, presiding over the weighing process, and ensuring a favorable balance with his rod. The major difference is that it is the devil who wants to weight the scale; in our text it is Michael himself. Otherwise, if we were to inquire as to a literary source for the sculptured scene on the Muiredach cross, our Enoch apocryphon

---

fragments, fol. 1r, i,10; fol. 1v, ii,8ff.

83. Cf. the astute remarks on the Egyptian conceptions concerning the judgment of the dead and the "magical" use of the so-called "negative confession" (*BD*, ch. 125), in S. Morenz, *Egyptian Religion*, tr. A. Keep (Ithaca, 1973), 126-131.

84. Cf. O. Chadwick's remarks about "a vaguely Egyptian ethos about early Irish monasteries and hermitages," in *John Cassian* (Cambridge, 1968), 148.

85. See S. Brandon, "The Weighing of the Soul," 101f. He cites a number of other examples and also discusses T Abr in this connection. Cf. also Brandon, *The Judgment of the Dead*, p. 121, fig. 6, for a representation of the scene on the cross of Muiredach.

would come closer than any extant document. We should
only add that the Apocalypse of Zephaniah, with its motif
of the *psychostasia* as an *agon* between the soul and the
"Kategoros" (=Satan), might be considered as another possible source of influence.

In summary, the Enoch apocryphon represented by the
fragments presented here must have been a most interesting
and unusual text. It is clearly influenced by older apocryphal literature (including Christian apocrypha such as
the Apocalypse of Elijah), but also contains some original
features. It is definitely a Christian product (we have
too little of it left to argue for a Jewish *Grundschrift*),
as is shown by its express mention of the Holy Trinity. I
would assign it to 5th-century Egypt.

As to its relationship to the Testament of Abraham,
it seems definitely to be influenced by Rec. B, but also
shows some lesser degree of influence from Rec. A. If we
had more of this fascinating document to work with, perhaps more could be said.

3. The Text

Some remarks on the following transcription and
translation are in order. It should be remembered that I
am employing Crum's numbering of the folios, though placing them in the order I consider to be more probable. I
supply line-numbering for convenience of reference (Crum
did not number the lines), but it should be said that only
in the cases of folios 9, 1, and 7 do the line numbers
correspond to the lineation of the original pages. In the
cases of the other folios, we do not know how much material has been lost from the tops of the pages.

In the transcription I use a system of word-division
different from that of Crum (following Till's *Koptische
Grammatik* instead). For reasons of space I thought it
best not to render the paragraph incipits according to the

manuscript (with initial letters written into the left margin, decorated with the *coronis*), but I note where these occur in my notes to the text. I have attempted to render the supralinear strokes as they actually appear in the ms. (and omit them when the ms. does so).

In the translation, for reasons of space, I do not indicate the Greek "loanwords" in parentheses as is usually done in editing Coptic texts. I have attempted to make the English translation correspond line-for-line with the Coptic transcription, but this has not always been possible, either because of the differing syntax or for reasons of space.

The following sigla are employed:

A subscript dot indicates that the letter is visually uncertain. Dots on the line outside of brackets indicate letters of which only ink vestiges survive, and which cannot be restored.

[ ] Square brackets indicate a lacuna in the manuscript. Where the text cannot be restored with reasonable probability, the number of missing letters is indicated either with dots or with numbers, e.g. ±7. Brackets in the translation indicate lacunae in the ms. either restored or not, but I do not split English words with brackets, preferring to put whole words either completely in or completely out of brackets, depending on the probability of the reading. All untranslatable material is also put in brackets in the translation.

< > Angular brackets indicate editorial emendations.

{ } Braces indicate editorial cancellation of erroneous additions by the scribe.

( ) Parentheses in the translation indicate material thought necessary for the English sense, but not explicit in the Coptic text.

... Three dots in the translation indicate scant material which, though possibly translatable, is ambiguous. Possibilities for translation are sometimes presented in the notes.

The notes appended at the end present Crum's transcription, where different from mine (though not always indicating every time Crum adds a subscript dot where I do not, or vice versa), and other information pertaining to the ms., the text, and the translation. I do not attempt to indicate where my translation differs from that of Crum, though the differences are frequently substantial.

I should like to render here my thanks to the following: To Prof. George Nickelsburg, for inviting me to contribute this essay, for his patience in waiting for it, and for his suggestions; to Mr. William Voelkle, Associate Curator of Mss, and the staff of the Pierpont Morgan Library in New York, for allowing me to study and to publish these fragments, for generously putting their facilities in the Library at my disposal, and for photographs of the fragments; to the Research Committee of the UCSB Academic Senate, for a subsidy which enabled me to travel to New York to work in the Morgan Library; to Ms. Ruth Beane, my student and research assistant, for help in calligraphy and proof-reading; and finally (but not least!) to Ms. Maelyn Ebert, for her patient and pains-taking work in typing this article in the form in which it appears here.

1. Fol. 2 → recto

```
                                    [ⲧ]ⲛ ⲟⲩⲙ[ⲉ] ⲟⲛ ⲡ̣
                                  2 ⲣⲱⲙⲉ  ⲛ[ⲁⲓ]
                                    ⲕⲁⲓⲟⲥ ⲉⲧ[ⲉ  ⲡⲁⲓ]
[±8        ]ⲁ̣ⲓ                   4 ⲡⲉ ⲓ̈ⲁⲣ[ⲉⲁ   ⲁⲩ]ⲡ̄
[±8        ]ⲉ                       ⲍⲟⲧⲉ  ⲍⲏⲧⲩ  ⲙ̣
[±7        ]ⲁ̇ⲡⲟⲩ                 6 ⲡⲛⲟⲩⲧ[ⲉ]    ϫⲉ
[±7        ]. 2ⲁ                    ⲡⲛⲟⲩⲧⲉ     ⲟ[ⲛ]
[±7        ]ⲡⲉ                    8 ⲉⲣⲉⲛⲉϥ[ⲅⲅⲉ]
[±5       ⲁ]ϥϫⲓ                     ⲗⲟⲥ ⲙⲉ ⲙⲙⲟ[ϥ]
[±7        ]ⲡⲉ                   10 ⲉⲧⲃⲉ  ⲡⲉϥ.[
[±8        ]ⲏ̣                      [ⲙ]ⲛ  ⲡⲉ̣[ϥ
```

2. Fol. 2 ↑ verso

```
ⲁⲩ[ⲁⲛⲁ]ⲗⲁ[ⲙ]
ⲃⲁⲛⲉ   ⲙ̄ⲙⲟϥ  ⲉ                   2
ⲧⲡⲉ·  ⲁⲩⲛⲟⲓ̈   ⲛ̄ⲙ̄
[ⲙⲩⲥⲧⲏ]ⲣⲓⲟⲛ                       4  .[
ⲉⲑⲏⲡ   2ⲛ̄  ⲛⲁⲓ                       ⲉ.[
ⲱⲛ    ⲙⲡϫⲓⲥⲉ                     6  ⲛ̄
ⲁ[ⲩ]ⲱ   ⲛⲛⲟⲩⲥ                        ϫ.[
ⲧⲏⲣⲟⲩ   ⲉⲑⲏⲡ                     8  ⲉⲛ[
[ⲍ]ⲛ  ⲛⲁⲓⲱⲛ  ⲙ̄                       ⲣⲉⲛ[
[ⲡ]ⲟⲩⲟⲉⲓⲛ·   ⲁⲣⲱ                 10  ⲁⲩ[
[...]ⲙⲁ  ⲛⲛ[                          ⲕ[
```

1. Folio 2 recto

                                    Truly, moreover, the
                                 2 righteous man,
                                    that is,
[4 Jared
[feared
[   ] begat him   6 God, for
[   ] under   God's
[8 [angels also]
[   ] he received   loved him
[10 because of his [
[[and his

2. Folio 2 verso
he was
taken up to   2
heaven. He perceived the
[mysteries]   4 [
[that are hidden] in the   [
aeons of the height,   6 [
[and] all the minds   [
that are hidden   8 [
in the aeons of   [
the Light, and   10 he [
[the   ] of the [[

3. Fol. 3↑ recto

```
                                     ⲙⲡ[..].ⲉ[
                              2      2̣ⲟ̣[ⲟ]ⲩ  ⲉϥⲇⲍⲉⲣ[ⲁ]
                                     ⲧϥ̄   ⲍⲓⲭ̄ⲙ̄   ⲡⲧⲟ̣
                              4      ⲟⲩ·  ⲉⲓ̈⟨ⲥ⟩  ⲥⲣⲁ[ⲅ]ⲅⲉ
[±8]           ].                    ⲗⲟⲥ  ⲛ̄[ⲧⲉ]   ⲡⲛ̇[ⲟⲩ]
[±7]           ].ⲧ            6      ⲧⲉ    ⲇϥⲟⲩⲱⲛ[ⲍ̄]
[±7]           ]ⲩⲙⲛ                  ⲛⲇϥ    ⲉⲃⲟⲗ   ⲉ[ϥ]
[±6]           ]ϣⲁⲭⲉ          8      ⲙⲏⲣ   ⲉϫⲛ̣    ⲧ[ⲉϥ]
[±5]           ]ⲡ[.]ⲟ·  ⲁ            ⲧⲡⲉ    ⲛⲟⲩⲙ[ⲟ]
[±6]           ]ⲩⲧⲙ           10     ⲥ̄ⲍ̄   ⲛ̄ⲛⲟⲩⲃ   [ⲉ]
[±7]           ]ⲭⲓ                   ⲣⲉⲟⲩⲕⲗⲟⲙ̣  [ⲛⲁ]
[±7]           ]ⲟⲥ            12     ⲧⲙⲛ̇ⲧ[ⲓⲛⲟⲛ]
                                     [.].[
```

4. Fol. 3→ verso

```
[.]...[....]ⲛⲁ
ϥ ⲇⲉ ⲉⲛⲱⲭ ⲡ                  2
ϣⲏⲣⲉ  ⲛⲓⲁⲣⲉⲇ
[ⲭⲓ  ⲙⲡⲉ]ⲓ̈ⲭⲱ                 4      ⲃ[
ⲱⲙⲉ  ϩⲛ  ⲧⲁϭⲓⲭ                       ⲟⲉⲓ[
[ⲛⲅⲱ]ⲩ  ⲛ̄ϩⲏ                  6      ⲡⲁⲙ[
[ⲧ]ϥ  ⲛⲅⲟⲩⲱⲛϩ̄                       ⲛⲁϣ[
[ⲉ]ⲃⲟⲗ  ⲙ̄ⲡⲣⲁⲛ                8      ⲁ̄ⲧⲡⲉ.[
[ⲡⲉ]ⲇⲉ  ⲉⲛⲱⲭ                         ⲙⲉϩ[
[ⲛ]ⲁϥ  ⲇⲉ  ⲛⲓⲙ                10     ⲛⲧ[
[....].[                             ⲧ̣ϥ̄  [
```

3. Folio 3 recto

[
[
[
[   ] word(s)
[
[
[
[

[
2 day, while he stood
upon the mountain,
4 behold an angel
of God
6 appeared
to him,
8 girded about [his]
loins with a
10 golden girdle, with
a crown [of]
12 adamant
[

4. Folio 3 verso
[said] to
him, "Enoch,
son of Jared,
[take this] book
in my hand
[and read] in
it, and reveal
the name."
Enoch said
[to] him, "Who
[

2
4 [
  [
6 [
  [
8 [
  [
10 and you [
   him (it?) [

5. Fol. 5→ recto

```
                              [.] . . .[
                           2  ⲙⲉ[
[±6]         ]ⲡⲉⲧ           ⲁϥϭⲛ̣ⲧ[ϥ ϫⲉ ⲡ]
[±5]         ]ⲉ  ϩ̇ⲛ         4  ⲣⲁⲛ [ⲙ]ⲡⲉⲡ
[                              ⲛⲁ  ⲉⲧ[ⲟⲩ]ⲁ̇[ⲁⲃ]
[±6]         ]ϫⲉ           6  ⲡⲉϫⲉ  ⲉⲛⲱⲭ
[±6]         ].ⲟⲕ              ⲛⲁϥ ⲇⲉ ⲡⲁ
[±7]         ]ⲕ           8  ϫⲟⲉⲓⲥ  ⲉⲓ̈[ⲥ]  ⲱ̣[ⲟ]
[±5]         ]ⲃ  ⲉⲃⲟⲗ         ⲙ̄ⲛ̄ⲧ   ⲛ̄ⲣⲁⲛ
[±7]         ]ⲉⲧ        10  ⲛ̄ⲁ̇ⲟⲣⲁⲧⲟⲛ̣
[±7]         ]ⲛ              ⲁⲓ̇ϭⲛⲧⲟⲩ  ⲉ[ⲣ]
[±7]         ]..          12  [ⲥ]ⲏⲥ  ϩ̄ⲙ  ⲡϫ̇ⲱ̣
[±8]         ].                ⲱ̣ⲙ[ⲉ
```

6. Fol. 5↑ verso

```
[±6]         ]ⲛ̄[
[±6]         ]ⲟⲩ        2  [.]ⲙ̣[
ϣⲟϫ[ⲛⲉ]  ⲛⲟⲩ              ⲙⲱ̣[
ⲱⲧ  ⲡ[ⲉ]ⲧⲛ̄ⲥⲏ         4  ..[
[ⲧ]ⲟⲩ  ⲛ[ⲧ]ⲟⲟⲩ  ⲥⲉ        ⲣⲱ[
ⲉⲣ  ϩⲙ̄ⲙⲉ  ⲛ̄ⲧ           6  ⲉϫ[
ⲡⲉ  ⲙ̄ⲛ̄  ⲡⲕⲁϩ              ⲧⲏ[
ⲡⲣⲁⲛ  ⲙ̄ⲡⲉⲓ̇ⲱ[ⲧ]         8  ⲙⲉ.[
[ϫ]ⲱϩ  ⲛ̄ⲡⲙⲉϩ              ⲱⲧ[
ϣⲟⲙⲛ̄ⲧ  ⲛ̄.[          10  ⲥⲏϩ[
[.]ⲛ  ⲉⲧϩⲓϫⲛ̄  [             ⲛ̣[
[. . . .]ⲡ[.].[            12  ⲧ[
                              ⲡ̣[
```

5. Folio 5 recto

```
[                          [
[         ] the one who  2 [
[              ] in        he found [it to be the]
[                        4 name [of] the
[                          [Holy] Spirit.
[                        6 Enoch said
[                          to him, "My
[         ] . . .        8 lord, behold
[                          three invisible
[                       10 names
[                          I have found
[                       12 written in the
[                          book [
```

6. Folio 5 verso

```
[
[         ] a            2 [
single counsel             [
which is in              4 [
them. They                 [
guide the                6 [
heaven and the earth.      [
The name of the Father   8 [
[touches] the              [
third [                 10 is written [
which is upon              [
[                       12 [
                           [
```

7. Folio 4 recto
[
[2 my [
[[God]
[   ] good   4 [will bestow]
[   ] will become   upon you a [name]
[   ] whether   6 [more] famous
[   ] to comfort   than (that of) any man.
[   ] write them   8 You will be taken to
[   ] from his   heaven in your
[10 body, and you will
[   ] him (it?)   be placed in the midst
which [12 [of the] store-house
[[   ] . . . [
                                14 [
                                    [
                                16 [

8. Folio 4 verso
[[
[2 upon [
[[
[   ] . . .   4 the holy one [of the
since the angel   Lord], [
had informed him   6 virgin [
about them on   that [
the mountain. He   8 will spend [
found three   thousand [years]
seals,   10 upon the [earth]
and the [except [
   [   ] the writings   12 abyss [
   [
   [14

9. Fol. 8↑ recto

```
[±6        ]ⲙⲟ̣              2   ⲧⲉ.[
[15        ]ⲙ̣ⲏ                  ⲙⲉ[.....]..
[±4       ]ϣ[.]..           4   ϩⲛ̄ .[...]2!
[±4       ]ⲟ̣ⲩ̣  ϩ̄ⲛ              ⲛⲧ[ⲉⲧ]ⲙⲙⲁⲩ
[±7            ].           6   ⲉⲓ̈ⲥ ⲧⲁ[..]ⲉⲧ ϣ[ⲱ]
[±5       ⲉ]ⲛⲱⲭ                 ⲡⲉ ⲛⲟⲩ ⲛ̄ⲧⲁ̣ⲕ
[±6        ]ⲧⲁⲭⲟ           8   ⲭⲡⲟⲥ ⲛ̄ϩⲏ[ⲧⲥ]
[±6        ]ⲣⲁⲛ                 ⲉⲓ̈ⲥ ϣⲟⲙⲛ̄ⲧ ⲛ̣
[±7         ]ⲉ̣            10   ⲥⲟⲡ ⲁ̣ⲥ̣ϣⲁⲭ[ⲉ]
[±7         ]ⲉ̣                  ϩ̄ⲛ ϩⲉⲛⲛⲟ[ⲥ]
                                ⲛ̄ϣⲁⲭⲉ  .2.[
                            12  [.]ⲏⲛ[.].[
```

10. Fol. 8→ verso

```
..[....]ⲡ[
ⲭⲟ[....]ⲙⲉ                  2   ⲡⲟ̣[
ⲉⲣⲉ.[.]ⲙⲙⲉ                      ⲉⲛⲱ[ⲭ
ⲟⲩ⟨ⲩ⟩ⲧⲉ ⲙ̣ⲡⲟⲩⲉⲓ̈            4   ⲙⲛ̄ⲧⲁ̣[
ⲙⲉ ⲉⲣⲟⲥ ⲙⲡⲟⲩ
ⲉⲩⲟⲩⲟⲛϩ̄ⲥ  ⲉⲃⲟⲗ             6   ⲉⲛⲱⲭ ⲡ[ⲁ]
ⲉⲓ̈{ⲉ}ⲙⲏⲧⲉⲓ̈                     ϣⲏⲣⲉ  .[
[ⲛ̄]ϥ̄ⲃⲱⲕ  ⲛϥ̄             8   ⲙ.[
ⲟⲩⲟⲛϩ̄ⲥ  ⲉⲃⲟⲗ                    ⲉⲡⲉ.[
ϩ̄ⲛ ⲧⲙⲏⲧⲉ                  10   ⲛⲁⲩ[
ⲙ̄ⲡⲉⲕⲉⲓ̈ⲱ[ⲧ]                     ⲛ̄ⲁ[
ⲙⲛ̄ ⲧⲉⲕⲙ̣[ⲁⲁⲩ]            12   ⲧⲁ[
[...]ⲭ[                          ⲭ̣[
```

9. Folio 8 recto

[
[
[
[   ] in
[
[   ] Enoch
[   ] judge
[   ] name(s)
[
[

```
     [
  2  [
     in [
  4  of her.
     Behold, what is my [
  6  becoming, which you
     have begotten in [her?]
  8  Behold three
     times she spoke
 10  with great
     words. [
 12  [
```

10. Folio 8 verso
[
[
[   ] true.
Neither was it
known, nor was it
able to be revealed,
except
you go and
reveal it
in the midst
[of] your father
and your [mother]
[

```
  2
     [
  4  Enoch [
     [
  6  Enoch, [my]
     son, [
  8  [
     [
 10  . . . [
     [
 12  [
     [
```

11. Fol. 6 → recto

```
[±8          ]ϣ                    [.].Τ̄[. . .]ΑΤ
[±8          ]π̇·              2   ΕΤ2[. . .]..Χ̣ [Ε]
[±7          ]ϣΝ̄                   ΒΟΛ . . . . . Ο̣
[. . .]Νϣαχε  Ν              4   Μ̄ΠΚΟΙΤΩ̄
[Ν2Ε]λλΗΝ  Μ̄                      Ν̄ΤΠ̇αρθΕ
[. . .]ϹΩΤΜ̄                  6   ΝΟϹ  ΕϹΝΚΟ
[±5      ]. . Χ                    ΤΚ  Ν̄2ΗΤϤ̄
[±5      ]ΪΝΕ                 8   ΠΕΧΑϹ ΝΑϤ Α̣[Ε]
[±6      ]. ΤΑ                    ΕΝΩΧ  ΠΑ
[±6      ]?Ρ̣αϊ̈               10  ϢΗΡΕ  ΜΑΡ[ΟΝ]
[±8      ]Α                       Ε2ΟΥΝ  ΕΠΚ[ΟΙ]
[±8      ]Ε̣                   12  ΤΩΝ  ΝΤΝ̣.[
```

12. Fol. 6 ↑ verso

```
[±5      ].ΝϹ[
Χ̄Ν̣[. . . .]ΑΝΕ              2   ΟΝ[
Κ. . . . .ΝΤ̣ΕΥ
Ν̣[ΟΥ] Ν̣[Τ̄]αϹϹΩ              4   ΤΑΤ. .  ΜΠ̇[Α]
ΤΜ̄  Ε[Τ]ΕΦΩ                      +ΧΙ̣ ΕΚΪΒ[Ε  Ν̄]
ΝΗ  Ν̄ΕΝΩΧ                    6   ΤΝ̄  ΤΑΜΑ[Υ·]
ΠΕϹϹΟΝ  ΠΕ                        Μ̄Ν̄ϢΟ̣[Μ̄]
ΧΑϹ̣  ΝΑϤ  ΧΕ                 8   ΕΤΡΑϤ[
ΕΝΩΧ  ΠΑϹΟ̄                       Ν̄ΚΕΪ[
[2]ΩΝ  Ε2ΟΥΝ                 10  +Χ[
ΕΡΟΪ̇  Ν̄ΤϹΩ[ϢΤ]                   Ν̄[
[Ε]ΒΟΛ  Μ̄ΠΡ[                12   Ν̄[
                                  .[
```

11. Folio 6 recto

```
[                              [
[                           2  which is [
[                              outside [
[         ] the words of    4  the bed-chamber
[the] Greeks                   of the virgin
[                  ] hear   6  in which she was
[                              sleeping.
[                           8  She said to him,
[                              "Enoch, my
[                          10  son, [let us go]
[              ] . . .         into the bed-
[                          12  chamber, and let us [
[
```

12. Folio 6 verso

```
[
[                           2
[         ] at the moment      again [
[when] she heard            4  [    ] I had not yet
[the] voice                    taken the breast [of]
of Enoch,                   6  my [mother.]
her brother, she               It is not [possible]
said to him                 8  for me to [
"Enoch, my brother,            [
[come] in                  10  I [
to me and look,                [
do not [                   12  [
                               [
```

13. Fol. 9 → recto

ⲠⲚⲞⲨⲦⲈ ⲤⲰ
ⲰⲦ ⲈϨⲢⲀⲒ̈ ⲈϪⲰⲔ·
ⲀⲨⲚⲀⲨ ⲈⲢⲞⲔ
ϪⲈ ⲚⲦⲔ ⲞⲨⲤⲰ
ⲦⲠ ⲀⲨⲰ ⲈⲔⲤⲀ
ϨⲎⲨ ⲈⲂⲞⲖ ⲈⲠⲈ
ⲐⲞⲞⲨ Ⲛ[Ⲓ]Ⲙ· ⲠⲈ
ⲀⲀⲨ ϪⲈ [.]ⲈⲒⲀⲨ
ⲀⲚⲞ[. . . .]ⲚⲈⲢ·
Π[. . . . .]. . .

2 ϪⲈ ⲞⲨⲔⲞⲨⲚ [Ⲉ]
  ⲚⲈ ⲤⲈⲚⲀⲀⲚⲀ
  ⲖⲀⲘⲂⲀⲚⲈ ·[
4 Ⲛ ⲢⲰⲘⲈ [ⲈⲦ]
  ⲠⲈ ϨⲘ ⲠⲈϤ[ⲤⲰ]
6 ⲘⲀ ⲈⲒⲘⲎⲦ[ⲈⲒ]
  ⲀⲚ[Ⲟ]Ⲕ· ⲠⲈϪ[ⲀⲤ]
8 ⲚⲀⲨ ϪⲈ Π[ⲈⲚ]
  ϪⲞⲈⲒⲤ ··[
10 [·]· · ·[

14. Fol. 9 ↑ verso

[ⲤⲈ]ⲚⲀϪⲒ̈ Ⲛ[Ⲥ]
[ⲚⲀ]Ⲩ ⲈϨⲢⲀⲒ̈ ⲈⲦ
[ⲠⲈ] ϨⲘ ⲠⲈⲨⲤⲰ
[ⲘⲀ] ⲞⲨⲀ ϪⲈ
[Ϩ]ⲎⲖⲒ̈ⲀⲤ ⲘⲚ
[Ⲕ]ⲈⲞⲨⲈⲒ ϪⲈ ⲦⲀ
[ⲂⲒ]ⲐⲀ Ⲛ[. .]ⲔⲀ
[. .] ⲘⲠⲘⲀ Ⲉ
[.]·Ⲉ Ⲛ2ⲎⲦϤ
·· ⲦⲈ·[

2 ⲈⲒ{Ⲉ}ⲘⲎⲦⲈ⟨Ⲓ⟩ Ⲛ
  ⲠⲖⲀⲤⲤⲈ ⲚⲔⲈ
4 ⲢⲰⲘⲈ ⲚⲐⲈ
  ⲘⲠⲈⲚⲈⲒ̈ⲰⲦ
  ⲀⲀⲘ ⲚϤⲤⲰ
6 ⲢⲤ ⲈⲠⲔⲀϨ
  ⲠⲈϪⲀⲤ ⲚⲀⲨ
8 ϪⲈ [Π]ⲀⲤⲞⲚ Ⲁ
  ⲖⲀ [ⲠⲈ] ⟨Π⟩ⲔⲀⲢⲠⲞⲤ
10 ⲈⲦⲚⲀ[ⲈⲒ] ⲈⲂⲞⲖ
  Ⲛ ϨⲎ[Ⲧ Ⲕ

13. Folio 9 recto
God looked
down upon you,
and he saw you
to be an elect
one, and
removed from
every evil." He
said, "[
[
[

  2

  4

  6

  8

10

Shall they
not take
up [
man [to]
heaven in his
[body] except
[me?" She] said
to him, ["Our]
Lord [
[

14. Folio 9 verso
[Two] will be taken
up to
[heaven] in their bodies,
one
Elijah, and
another Tabitha
[
[   ] the place
where [
[

  2

  4

  6

  8

10

except by
forming another
man like
our father
Adam, and (that) he
inhabit the earth."
She said to him,
"My brother,
⟨Methuselah⟩ [is] ⟨the⟩
fruit that [will come]
forth from [you

15. Fol. 1 → recto

ϫⲉ[
[..]ⲡⲉ̣[
.ⲉⲥⲧⲱ[ⲧ] ⲉⲩ
ϣⲁⲛⲛⲁⲣ ⲉⲣⲟ
ⲟⲩ ⲍⲛ ⲛⲉⲩⲙⲛ̅ⲧ̣
ϣⲁⲩ̣ⲧⲉ ⲧⲏ
ⲣ̣ⲟⲩ ⲉⲩϫⲣⲁⲁⲣ
ⲩⲛⲁⲥ{ⲉ̅}ϫⲁⲓⲥⲟⲩ
ⲛⲧⲉⲩⲛⲟⲩ ⲛ̅
ⲧⲉⲧⲉⲕϩⲓⲕⲱ̅
ⲧⲏⲣⲥ̅ ⲃ[ⲱ]ⲕ ⲉⲡ
ⲧⲁⲕⲟ· ⲁ[ⲗ]ⲗⲁ
ϣⲓⲛ[ⲉ ⲛ̣]ⲧⲟⲩ
ⲛ̅ⲥⲁ̣ [...]ⲙ̣

2 ....[
  ⲉⲩϣⲁ[ⲛ
  .ⲟⲩⲕ ⲉⲩ[
4 ⲛⲟⲩ ⲁⲛ[
  ⲧⲉ· ⲩⲛⲁ[
6 ϫⲉ ⲛⲧⲉⲁ[
  ⲛ̅ⲥⲟⲛⲥ ⲛ̣[
8 ⲧⲉⲩϭⲟⲙ· [
  ⲙⲁ[ⲁ]ϣⲉ ⲍ.[
10 ⲍⲙ̅ ⲡⲕⲟ̣[ⲥⲙⲟⲥ]
   ⲉⲧⲙ̅ⲙⲁ[ⲩ
12 ⲧⲟⲩ ⲉⲡⲧ[ⲏⲣϥ
   ⲡ̣[
14

16. Fol. 1 ↑ verso

[±5   ]....
[±5   ]ⲙ[.]ⲥⲁ.
[...].ⲟⲟ.ⲛ.[
[...].ϥ ⲡⲉ ⲡ
[....]ⲉ ⲙ̅ⲡⲁⲣ
[ⲭⲁⲣ]ⲅⲉⲗⲟⲥ ⲁϥ
[ⲕ]ⲟⲁⲩ ⲉϫⲛ ⲙ̅ⲙⲁ
[ⲁϣ]ⲉ ⲛⲧⲁⲓⲕⲁⲓ
[ⲟⲥ]ⲩⲛⲏ ⲁϥⲉⲓ
[ⲛⲉ] ⲛ̅ⲕⲉⲁⲅⲅⲉ
[ⲗⲟ]ⲥ̣ ⲛϣⲱⲡⲉ
[...]ⲧ̣[.].[.]ϣⲁϩ

2 [±8   ]ⲕ
  [±6   ]ⲩ· ⲉ
  ⲧⲉ [ⲡⲁⲓ] ⲡⲉ ⲡⲣ̣ⲁⲛ
4 ⲙⲡϣⲏⲣⲉ ⲙ̅
  ⲡⲛⲟⲩⲧⲉ ⲉⲩ
6 ⲍⲙⲟⲟⲥ ⲛ̅ⲥⲁ
  ⲟⲩⲛⲁⲙ ⲙ̅ⲡϥ
8 ⲉⲓⲱⲧ· ⲁϥ
  ⲡⲁⲍⲧϥ ⲉϫⲛ̅
10 ⲙ̅ⲡ[ⲁ]ⲧ ⲙ̅ⲡⲉϥ
   ⲉⲓⲱ[ⲧ] ⲉϥϫⲱ
12 ⲙⲙ[ⲟⲥ] ϫⲉ ⲱ̃
   ⲡⲁ[ⲉⲓ]ⲱⲧ ⲙ̅
14 ⲡⲣ̅[

15. Folio 1 recto
[
[
tremble. If he
sees them
in all their
iniquities
which they do,
he will write them
immediately, and
your entire image
will go to
perdition. But
seek rather
for [

2 [
  if he [
4 . . . [
  . . . [
  he will [
6 . . . [
  violence [
8 his power. [
  balances [
10 in that [world]
  [
12 them [completely
  [
14

16. Folio 1 verso
[
[
[
[   ] . . .
[   ] of the arch-
angel. He put
it upon the
balances of righteousness
He brought
other mighty
angels
[   ] fiery

  [
2 [
  [that] is, the name
4 of the Son of
  God
6 seated at
  the right-hand of his
8 Father. He bowed
  down at
10 the feet of his
  Father, saying,
12 "O
  my Father,
14 do not [

17. Fol. 7↑ recto

ⲉⲕϣ[ⲉ] ..[
[....]ϥⲡ̄ ⲛ[ⲟ]
ⲃⲉ ϩⲛ ⲟⲩⲙⲛ̄ⲧ
ⲕⲟ[ⲩ]ⲓ ⲛϩⲏⲧ·
ⲙⲛ̄ ⲟⲩⲙⲛ̄ⲧ
ϣⲁⲩⲧⲉ· ⲛ̄
ⲛⲉⲕⲥⲉϩ ⲛⲉⲩ
ⲛⲟⲃⲉ ⲛ̄ⲥⲱⲟⲩ
ⲧⲁⲭⲏ· ⲁⲗⲗ[ⲁ]
ⲉⲕⲉⲕⲱ ⲙ̄[ⲡ]
ⲕⲁϣ ϩⲓⲭ[ⲙ̄]
ⲡⲕⲁⲗⲁⲙ[ⲟⲣⲓ]
ⲟⲛ .[

2 [.]ϣ[
. ⲡⲉ[...].[
[±5   ]ϣ ⲉⲕ
4 ⲉϥ[ⲟ]ⲧϥ̄ ⲉⲃⲟⲗ
ⲛ̄ⲕⲉⲥⲟⲡ·
6 ⲡⲉϫⲉ ⲉⲛⲱⲭ
ⲛⲁϥ ϫⲉ ⲟⲩⲕ
8 {ⲕ}ⲟⲩⲛ [ⲥⲉ] ⲙ̄ⲡⲉⲡ
ⲛⲟⲩⲧⲉ ⲭ[ⲓ] ⲛ̄ⲟⲩ
10 ⲁⲅⲅⲉ[ⲗ]ⲟⲥ ϩⲛ̄
ⲧⲡⲉ ⲛ̄ϥⲕⲁ
12 [ⲁ]ϥ

18. Fol. 7→ verso

[±8   ].
[.]..[...].ⲩ
[ⲛ]ϣⲟⲣ[ⲡ]
[ⲥ]ϩⲁⲓ̈ ⲛ̄ⲛ̄ⲛ[ⲟ]ⲃⲉ
ⲙⲛ̄ ⲛⲁⲅⲁⲑⲟⲛ
ⲛ̄ⲛϣⲏⲣⲉ ⲛ̄
ⲛ̄ⲣⲱⲙⲉ· ⲥⲉ
ⲛⲁⲭⲁⲣⲓⲍⲉ
ⲛⲁ[ⲩ] ⲙ̄ⲡⲁⲅ
[ⲅ]ⲉⲗⲟ[ⲥ ⲛ̄ⲧ]ⲙⲛ̄ⲧ
ⲁϣⲁⲛⲉϩⲧⲏⲩ
.ⲥ.[..].[..]ⲉⲧ

2 [..ⲛ̄]ⲛⲟⲃ[ⲉ ..]..
[ⲛ̄]ϥϥⲓ [ⲛ̄ⲛⲁ]ⲅⲁ
ⲑⲟⲛ ⲛϥ[ⲧ]ⲁ
4 ⲗⲟⲟⲩ ⲉ[ⲕ]ⲉⲥⲁ
ⲉϥϣⲁⲛⲛⲁⲩ
6 ⲉⲛⲛⲟⲃⲉ ⲉⲩ
ⲥⲱⲕ ⲡⲁⲣⲁ
8 ⲛⲁⲅⲁⲑⲟⲛ
ϣⲁϥϥⲓ̈ ⲙ̄ⲡⲉϥ
10 ϩ[ⲣ]ⲁⲃⲇⲟⲥ ⲉⲧ
[ϩ]ⲛ ⲧⲉϥϭⲓϫ
12 ⲛ[ⲟ]ⲩⲛⲁⲙ ⲛ̄ϥ
ⲧ[ⲁⲗⲟ]ϥ ⲉϫⲛ

17. Folio 7 recto

you [find
[   ] he sin(ned)   2
through
cowardice   4
and
iniquity, you should   6
not write their
sins against them   8
hastily, but
you should put [the]   10
reed on
the pen-holder   12
[

[
[
[   ] you
should erase it
again."
Enoch said
to her,
"Has God, [then],
not taken an
angel in
heaven, and [placed]
[him

18. Folio 7 verso

[
[2
first [
write the sins   4
and the good-deeds
of the sons of   6
men. [They]
will be granted   8
the angel
[of]   10
mercy
[12

[   ] sins [
[and] he takes [the good-
deeds, and he
sets them on the other
side. If he sees
the sins
drawing down (the
balances) more than the
good-deeds, he takes his
rod which is
in his right
hand, and he
[sets] it upon

Notes to the Text

Folio 2 recto, column i, line 4: Crum places this and the other lines in this column one line too far down, in relation to column ii, and reads on line 4:]ⲛ

2r, i,6. Crum:]ⲗⲡⲟⲩ , with ⲭⲡⲟⲩ suggested as an alternative possibility in a note. Read either ⲁⲩ]ⲭⲡⲟⲩ, "he begat him," or ⲁⲩ]ⲭⲡⲟⲩ, "he was begotten."

2r, i,9. Crum:]ⲭⲓ

2r, ii,1. Crum: [·] ⲛⲟⲩ [··] ⲟⲛ He suggests in a note: "presumably 'son of a], or something similar."

2r, ii,4. Crum: ⲁⲩⲡ̄-]

2r, ii,5. Crum: [ⲙ-]

2r, ii,7-9. This construction is difficult, but I follow Crum's translation here.

2r, ii,8. Crum: ⲉⲡⲉⲛⲉⲩ [ⲁⲅⲅⲉ-]

2r, ii,9. Crum: ⲙⲙ [ⲟⲩ]

2r, ii,10. Crum: [ⲉ]ⲧⲃⲉⲡ·· [

2r, ii,11. Crum has nothing for this line.

2v, i,1. Crum: [··ⲁⲛⲁ] ⲗⲁ [ⲙ-]

2v, i,2. Crum: [ⲃ]ⲁⲛⲉ

2v, i,3. Crum: [ⲧ]ⲡⲉ

2v, i,5. Crum: [ⲉ]ⲑⲏ[ⲡ]

2v, i,7. Crum: [ⲁⲣ]ⲱ

2v, i,11. Crum: [···]ⲓⲁ ⲛⲛ [There must have been a definite article in first place on this line.

2v, ii,4. Crum has nothing for this line.

2v, ii,5. Crum: ⲉ [

2v, ii,7. Crum: ⲭ [

2v, ii,8. Read ⲉⲛ[ⲱⲭ "Enoch"?

2v, ii,9. Crum: ⲣⲉ [

2v, ii,10. Crum: ⲁⲥ["she."

2v, ii,11. Crum: ⲡ [

3r. Crum allows the possibility that the top margin is preserved, but although enough space is left on the fragment for 3 lines above the first visibly inscribed line, the surface fibers are virtually all gone. This fragment probably came from the bottom portion of the page; see the Introduction.

3r, i,5. Crum has nothing for this line.

3r, i,6. Crum:]ⲧ

3r, i,8. Perhaps a verb, "spoke."

3r, i,9.   Crum:] ⲁ–
3r, ii,1. Crum: ⲙⲡ [· ·] ⲉ [
3r, ii,2. Crum: ⲟ [·] ⲩ
3r, ii,4. Ms.:   ⲉⲓ
3r, ii,5. Crum: ⲛ̄ [ⲧⲉ ⲡⲛⲟⲩ-]
3r, ii,7. Crum: ⲉⲃⲟ[ⲗ ⲉϥ-]
3r, ii,13. Crum: ?

3v. On this side, too, the surface fibers are missing on the top part of the fragment. There was, contrary to Crum, probably no top margin at this point.

3v, i,1. Crum:] ⲛⲁ
3v, i,2. Crum: ⲥⲁ · ⲉⲛⲱⲭ   A ϥ appears to be written into the left margin.
3v, i,3. Crum: [ⲛⲓ] ⲁⲣⲉⲗ
3v, i,6. Crum: [ⲛⲅ] ⲱ ϥ
3v, i,9. The ⲡ is presumed to have been written in the margin.
3v, i,11. Crum: ?
3v, ii,6. The ⲡ is written in the margin with a *coronis* above it: ⟩
3v, ii,7. Crum: ⲛⲁ[But the tail of the ϥ is visible.

5r. Crum regards this page as the verso side of the folio (with a question mark).

5r, i,3. Crum:] · ⲡ ·
5r, i,5. Crum: ?
5r, i,6. Crum:] ⲉ
5r, i,7. Crum:] ⲟⲕ
5r, i,9. Crum:] ⲉⲃⲟⲗ
5r, i,12 and 13. Crum: ?
5r, ii,1. Crum has nothing for this line.
5r, ii,4-5. The supralinear stroke does not appear over the *nomen sacrum* ⲡⲛⲁ (πνεῦμα).
5r, ii,5. Crum: ⲉⲧ [ⲟⲩⲁⲁⲃ]
5r, ii,6. The ⲡ is written in the margin, with a *coronis* above it.
5r, ii,8. Crum: ⲉⲓ [ⲥ   ϣⲟ-]

5v. Crum regards this page as the recto side of the folio (with a question mark).

5v, i,7. Crum: [ⲡ] ⲉ
5v, i,8. The initial ⲡ is written in the margin.

5v, i,9. Crum: [·]ⲱϩ He translates the word, "is written," (with a question mark), as though the word were ⲤⲎϨ.

5v, i,12. Crum has nothing for this line.

5v, ii,2. Crum has nothing for this line.

5v, ii,3. Crum: ⲘⲎ[He places this and the other lines in this column two lines too high in relation to relation to column i.

5v, ii,4. Crum: ?

5v, ii5. Crum: ⲣ·[

5v, ii,8. Crum: ⲘⲈ[

5v, ii.9. Crum: ⲱ[

5v, ii,10. Crum: ⲤⲎ[

4r. It is not certain where folio 4 fits in relation to the other folios, nor is it certain which is the recto page and which the verso. See the Introduction. Crum regards this as the recto page.

4r, i,1. Crum places this line and the others in this column one line too far down in relation to column ii, and reads:]ⲈⲦ[

4r, i,4. Crum:]ⲀⲚⲞⲨⲰ

4r, i,5. Crum:]ⲀⲨⲰⲠⲈ

4r, i,8: Crum does not restore the word ⲤⲞⲖⲤⲖ "comfort."

4r, i,12. Crum:]ⲠⲚ̄ⲦⲨ̄

4r, i,13. Crum: ?

4r, ii,6. Crum: Ⲉ[ϨⲞⲨ-]

4r, ii,8. The Ⲥ is written in the margin, with a coronis above it.

4r, ii,12. [Ⲛⲉ]ⲨⲠⲞⲐⲨⲔⲎ So also Crum. This is probably a scribal error for ⲚⲦⲀⲠⲞⲐⲎⲔⲎ, and the word is translated accordingly. Ⲁ cannot be read in the ms.

4r, ii,13. Crum: [··]ⲦⲈ ⲞⲨⲤⲒⲈ

4r, ii,14. Crum:]Ⲡ[

4r, ii,15-16. Crum has nothing for these lines.

4v, i,3. Crum:]ⲣⲠ·

4v, i,4. Crum:]ⲔⲞⲤ Ⲛⲯ̄—

4v, i,6. Crum: [ⲄⲈ]ⲖⲞⲤ

4v, i,9. Crum: ⲰⲞⲘ[Ⲧ]Ⲉ

4v, i,12. Crum: [Ⲟ]Ⲩ·ⲚⲤϨⲀⲒ̈ The visible trace of the first letter looks more like Ⲁ

4v, i,13. Crum:]Ⲧ

4v, ii,1. Crum: ⲱⲙ[

4v, ii,3. Crum: [.]ⲧ̄ⲛ[

4v, ii,4. Crum: ⲫⲟⲅ[ⲓⲟⲥ

4v, ii,5. Crum: ⲉⲓ̈ⲥ ⲧⲩ̄.[

4v, ii,6. Crum: ⲡⲁⲣⲑ[ⲉⲛⲟⲥ

4v, ii,7. Crum: ⲭⲉⲥ.[

4v, ii,8-9. Read ⲙ̄ⲡ̄]/ϣⲟ or ⲛ̄ⲧ̄]/ϣⲟ "the thousand years"? Crum inexplicably translates ϣⲟ ⲛ̄ⲣ[ⲟⲙⲡⲉ] "hundred [years]."

4v, ii,10. Crum: ⲟ̈ⲓ̈ⲁⲙ[ⲡ ⲕⲁϩ]

4v, ii,12. Crum: ⲛⲟⲩ..[

8r. Crum regards this as the verso page.

8r, i,5. Crum has nothing for this line.

8r, i,6. Crum:]ϩⲛ̄—

8r, i,7. Crum has nothing for this line.

8r, i,8. Crum: ⲉⲛ]ⲱⲭ

8r, ii,1. Crum: ·ⲉ[

8r, ii,2. Crum: ⲙⲉ[

8r, ii,3. Crum: ϩⲛ̄[····]ϩⲓ

8r, ii,11. Crum: ⲕϩ·[

8r, ii,12. Crum: [.]ϩⲛ··ⲱ[

8v. Crum regards this as the recto page.

8v, i,1. Crum:]ⲡ[

8v, i,2. Crum: only]ⲙⲉ

8v, i,3. Crum: ⲉⲣⲉ[····]ⲙⲙⲉ

8v, i,4. Crum: ⲟⲛⲧⲉ ⲙ[ⲡ̄]ⲟⲩⲉⲓ ⲟⲛⲧⲉ , written in the ms., is obviously a scribal error for ⲟⲩⲧⲉ.

8v, i,10. Crum: [ϩ]ⲛ̄ⲧⲙⲏⲧⲉ

8v, i,11. Crum: [ⲙ]ⲡⲉⲕⲉⲓⲱ

8v, i,12. Crum: [ⲧ] ⲙⲛⲧⲉⲕⲙ[ⲁⲁⲩ]

8v, ii,5. Crum: ?

8v, ii,7. Crum: ϣⲏⲣⲉ[

8v, ii,8. Crum: ⲙ[

8v, ii,9. Crum: ⲉⲡⲉ[

8v, ii,10. Either "for them" or a form of the verb, "to see."

6r, i,1. Crum places this line and the others in this column one line too far up in relation to column ii, and reads:]ⲱ[

6r, i,5. Crum disregards the lacuna at the beginning of the line, reading Νωαχε Ν—

6r, i,8. Crum:].Χ

6r, i,10. Crum:]Τα‐

6r, i,11. Crum: ς]ραϊ

6r, ii,1-3. The material at the end of these lines is on a small fragment which is now attached to the wrong position on the other side of the main fragment. Since the smaller fragment was in the right place when Crum made his transcription, I assume the wrong placement occurred when the fragments were remounted in 1925. See the Introduction. The proper placement of the small fragment can easily be ascertained by a study of the fibers, and by comparison with the destruction-pattern on the contiguous folio, 8r.

6r, ii,1. Crum: only]αc

6r, ii,2. Crum: ιες [····]π

6r, ii,8. The initial π is written in the margin, with a *coronis* above it.

6r, ii,12. Crum: ΝΤΝ[

6v, i,2-4. See note to 6r, ii,1-3.

6v, i,1. Crum places this line and the others in this column one line too far down in relation to column ii, and reads: [···]Νc

6v, i,2. Crum: ΧΝ[··]αΝε

6v, i,3. Crum: Κ···Ντεγ

6v, i,4. Crum: Ν[ογ ΝΤ]α ccω‐

6v, i,8. The initial Χ is written in the margin.

6v, ii,4. Crum: +απ·· Μπ[

6v, ii,5. Crum: +Χ[ι]

6v, ii,13. Crum has nothing for this line.

9r. The top margin is preserved.

9r, i,1. The first-perfect prefix α- undoubtedly occured on the preceding line.

9r, i,8. The initial Χ is written in the margin.

9r, i,10. Crum: ?

9r, ii,1. The initial Χ is written in the left margin. Crum does not provide for another letter after ογκογΝ

9r, ii,2. Crum: πο···αΝ[α‐]

9r, ii,3. Crum: λαΜβαΝε[

9r, ii,8. The initial Ν is written in the margin, with a *coronis* above it. Crum reads: Να[γ] χε[

9r, ii,9.   Crum: [ⲭ]ⲟⲉⲓⲥ ·· [

9r, ii,10. Crum has nothing for this line.

9v. The top margin is preserved.

9v, i,1.   Crum: [··] ⲛⲁⲭⲓ

9v, i,9.   Crum:]ⲉ ⲛ?ⲏ[ⲧ]ϥ̄

9v, i,10.   Crum:]ⲧⲉⲧ[

9v, ii,1.   Ms.: ⲉⲓⲉⲙⲏⲧⲉ which Crum prints.

9v, ii,2.   Crum: ⲡⲗⲁⲥⲥⲉ ⲛⲕ[ⲉ-]

9v, ii,4.   Crum: ⲙⲡⲉⲛⲉⲓ ⲱ[ⲧ]

9v, ii,7.   The initial ⲡ is written in the margin.

   9v, ii,8-9. As suggested by Crum in a note, it is assumed that ⲙⲁⲑⲟⲩⲥ has been erroneously omitted from the name ⲙⲁⲑⲟⲩⲥⲁⲗⲁ

9v, ii,9.   Crum: ⲗⲁ[·ⲡ]ⲕⲁⲣⲡⲟⲥ

9v, ii,10. Crum: ⲉⲧⲛ[ⲁⲉⲓ ⲉ]ⲃⲟⲗ

9v, ii,11. Crum: ⲛ̄?[ⲏⲧⲕ

   1r. The top margin is preserved. Crum regards this as the verso page.

1r, i,1.   Crum: [·]ⲉ[

1r, i,3.   Crum: [·] ⲥⲧⲱ[ⲧ ⲉ]ϥ—

1r, i,10.   Crum: ⲧⲉⲧⲉⲕ[?]ⲓ ⲕⲱ̄

1r, i,12.   Crum: [ⲁⲗ]ⲗⲁ

1r, i,13.   Crum: ⲱ̄ⲓⲛ[ⲉ·]ⲧ ⲡ· He suggests ⲛ]ⲧⲟϥ in a footnote.

   1r, i,14. Crum suggests in a note: ⲛⲥⲁ[ⲟⲩⲣⲱ]ⲙ[ⲉ] "for a man," i.e. "to mitigate the severity of the recording angel." I understand the recording to be done by Enoch himself. See the Introduction.

1r, ii,1.   Crum: ?ⲣ[

1r, ii,2.   Crum: ⲉϥ[

1r, ii,3.   Crum: [·]ⲟⲩⲕ ⲉϥ[It is not possible to read ⲙⲟⲩⲕ "perish."

1r, ii,4.   Crum: ⲛⲟⲩ·ⲁⲛ

1r, ii,6.   Crum: ⲭⲉⲛⲟ[

1r, ii,7.   Crum: ⲛⲥⲟⲛⲥ·[

1r, ii,9.   Crum: ⲙ[·]ⲱⲉ?[

1r, ii,10. Crum does not restore ⲕⲟⲥⲙⲟⲥ

1r, ii,11. Crum: ⲉ[·]ⲙⲙⲁ[

1r, ii,12. Crum: [·]ⲩⲉⲡ[

1r, ii,13. Crum has nothing for this line.

1v. The top margin is preserved. Crum regards this as the recto page.

1v, i,1-4. Crum has nothing for these lines.

1v, i,12. Crum:]o [N] ⲱⲁϩ

1v, ii,3. Crum: ⲧ[ⲉⲡⲁⲓ]ⲡⲉ ⲡⲣ[ⲁⲛ]

1v, ii,4. Crum: [ⲙ̄-]

1v, ii,10. The ⲧ is written over part of a ⲙ, which the scribe apparently began to write.

1v, ii,11. Crum: ⲉⲓ[ⲱⲧ]

1v, ii,13. Crum: ⲡⲁ[ⲉⲓⲱ]ⲧ

1v, ii,14. Crum: ⲡⲣ[...]ⲙⲡⲩ   There is no trace of the last three letters read by Crum on the fragment now. Perhaps a small piece broke off here subsequent to his transcription and is now lost.

7r. The top margin is preserved, and the numeral /ⲗ (14) occurs in the top margin at the inside, even with the left margin. Since this numeral occurs on the inside of the page it must be taken to indicate the quire number rather than the page number. Thus this page is the first of the fourteenth quire. So also Crum, but he allows for the possibility of taking this page as a verso page, with the numeral therefore in the proper position for a page number.

7r, i,1. Crum: ⲉⲕ? [ⲉ

7r, i,4. Crum: ⲕⲟⲩ[ⲓ]

7r, i,13. Crum: ⲟⲛ ⲥ[

7r, ii,1. Crum has nothing for this line. The tail of a ⲱ is visible.

7r, ii,2. Crum: ·ⲡⲉ [

7r, ii,3. Crum: [ⲉⲕ-]

7r, ii,6. The ⲡ is written in the margin, with a *coronis* above it.

7r, ii,8. Crum: ⲕⲟⲩⲛ [·ⲙ]ⲡⲉⲡ-

7r, ii,9. Crum: ⲛⲟⲩⲧⲉ [+] ⲛ̄ⲟⲩ- O. von Lemm suggests [ⲭⲓ] instead of [+]; *Koptische Miscellen* CXLIII, p. 512.

7r, ii,10. Crum: ⲁⲅⲅⲉ[ⲗⲟ]ⲥ

7r, ii,11. Crum: ⲧⲡ[ⲉ]

7v. The top margin is preserved.

7v, i,1-2. Crum: ?

7v, i,8. Crum: ⲛⲁⲭ[ⲁⲣ]ⲓⲍⲉ

7v, i,9. Crum: ⲛⲁ[ⲕ] "thou shalt be granted..."

7v, i,12. Crum: ⲥ[...]ⲉⲧ[·]

7v, ii,1.   Crum: [..N]ṄO[ΒЄ
7v, ii,3.   Crum: N[YT]Ạ —
7v, ii,11. Crum: [2 N]
7v, ii,12. Crum: [NO]YNⱭM

THE JUDGMENT SCENE IN THE COPTIC APOCALYPSE OF PAUL

George MacRae

The brief and rather fragmentary Apocalypse of Paul contained in Nag Hammadi Codex V (17,20--24,9) includes a scene of the judgment of souls in heaven which offers an interesting parallel to that in the Testament of Abraham, more specifically the Coptic version of the shorter recension. The Coptic Apocalypse of Paul is not related to the Greek work of the same name, though the latter also contains a rather elaborate judgment scene. The two scenes have little in common, and that of the Greek work does not directly reflect the Abraham tradition. The Nag Hammadi Apocalypse builds on the tradition of 2 Cor 12:2 to portray the ascent of Paul, led by a Holy Spirit and accompanied by the Twelve Apostles, from the third to the tenth heaven. The Gnostic character of the work is revealed in the portrayal of an "old man" enthroned in the seventh heaven as a hostile figure who attempts to block Paul's further ascent; this seems clearly to imply a negative view of the God of the Old Testament.

The relevant passage for comparing the judgment scene is 20,5--22,13. In the fourth heaven Paul witnesses the scene of the judgment of a single soul, and in the fifth he sees angels driving the souls. It is possible that the latter is a trace of the two ways or gates scene in the T Abr, although there is no specific mention of two gates. Almost certainly the scene in the fourth heaven depends on the judgment scene in T Abr or on a source common to both works, for it mentions details (e. g. the "book") found in T Abr which have no functional significance in the Apocalypse. Among the main points of contact between the two, comparing especially the Coptic version of T Abr, are the following: the role of the angels, the whipping of the soul, the singling out of one soul, the soul's protest, the mention of the book, three witnesses who speak in turn, the charge of murder, the mention of night by the third witness, the casting down of the soul. In both scenes there is a tendency to assign a time to the witnesses, though the times do not coincide. The divine judge of T Abr is replaced by the toll-collector (τελώνης) of the fourth heaven.

It is not possible to determine the date and original provenance of the Apocalypse of Paul. The MS comes from Upper Egypt and should be dated along with the bulk of the Nag Hammadi library to the mid-fourth century. If the document originated in Egypt, its resemblance to the Coptic version of T Abr may have some significance for an Egyptian tradition.

The following translation is an original one made from a text prepared by the Coptic Gnostic Library Project of the Institute for Antiquity and Christianity, Claremont. Reconstructions of lacunae are represented by the use of square brackets. Greek loanwords in Coptic have not been retained in the translation. The text and other translations may be found in the following works:

The Facsimile Edition of the Nag Hammadi Codices. Codex V (Leiden: Brill, 1975).

A. Böhlig and P. Labib, *Koptisch-gnostische Apokalypsen aus Codex V von Nag Hammadi* (Halle-Wittenburg, 1963) 15-26.

W. R. Murdock, *The Apocalypse of Paul from Nag Hammadi* (Dissertation, School of Theology at Claremont, 1968).

R. Kasser, "Bibliothèque gnostique VII: L'Apocalypse de Paul," *Revue de théologie et de Philosophie* 19 (1969) 259-263.

TRANSLATION (20,5--22,13)

But in the fourth heaven I saw angels resembling gods in race, and I saw the angels bringing a soul[1] out of the land of the dead.[2] They placed it at the gate of the fourth heaven. And the angels were whipping it. The soul spoke saying: "What sin was it that I committed in the world?"

The toll-collector who dwells in[3] the fourth heaven replied saying: "It was not right to commit all those lawless deeds that are in the world of the dead."[2]

The soul replied saying: "Bring witnesses! Let them [show] you in what body[4] I committed lawless deeds. [Do you wish][5] to bring a book [to read from]?"

And the three witnesses came. The first spoke saying: "Was I [not in] the body the second hour [   ]?[6] I rose up against you until [you fell][7] into anger [and rage] and envy."

And the second spoke saying: "Was I not in the world? And I entered at the fifth hour, and I saw you and desired you. And behold, then, now I charge you with the murders you committed."

The third spoke saying: "Did I not come to you at the twelfth hour of the day when the sun was about to set? I gave you darkness until you should accomplish your sins."

When the soul heard these things, it gazed downward in sorrow. And then it gazed upward. It was cast down. The soul that had been cast down [went] to [a] body which had been prepared [for it. And] behold [its] witnesses were finished.

[Then I gazed] upward and [saw the] Spirit saying [to me]: "Paul, come! [Proceed toward] me!" Then as I [went], the gate opened, [and] I went up to the fifth [heaven]. And I saw my fellow apostles [going with me] while the Spirit accompanied us.

And I saw a great angel in the fifth heaven holding an iron rod in his hand. There were three other angels with him, and I stared into their faces. But they were rivalling[8] each other, with whips in their hands, goading the souls on to the judgment.

But I went with the Spirit and the gate opened for me. Then we went up to the sixth heaven.

NOTES

[1] The passage is confused as it stands: the phrase κατὰ γένος is out of place and there is at least one dittography. The translation adopts the simplest rearrangements, first proposed by H.-M. Schenke.

[2] The phrase "of the dead" might also be translated "of mortals."

[3] The phrase "dwells in" might also be translated "sits at."

[4] The phrase "in what body (σῶμα)" is obscure; it would be possible to translate "against what person."

⁵ Instead of "[Do you wish]" it is also possible to reconstruct the imperative "[Please]"; the former is preferable, however, because it fills the lacuna better.

⁶ Perhaps one should reconstruct "of the day," as in the case of the third witness, or "of morning."

⁷ Instead of "[you fell]" it is also possible to reconstruct "[you were found]."

⁸ The Greek ἐρίζειν suggests a word play referring to the Erinyes of Greek mythology.

SUMMARY AND PROSPECTS FOR FUTURE WORK

George W.E. Nickelsburg, Jr.

This concluding section will be both reflective and prospective. Where do the papers in this volume leave us in our study of T Abr? In what directions do they point us? These questions will be raised within the context of the broader current discussion of T Abr and, to a limited degree, will be directed to aspects of that discussion. Since the individual papers in this volume sometimes bear on more than one issue, my comments are arranged topically.

The Recensional Problem

Francis Schmidt contends that the most important question in the current discussion is: Which is the older of the two recensions of the T Abr? (pp. 65f.). Robert Kraft responds: " . . . many aspects of the current discussions [of the recensional problem] are simply premature, whether or not they ultimately prove to have been accurate" (p. 137).

Kraft's most sweeping criticism of the proposed solutions to the recensional problem is that they presume undemonstrated models for the manner in which the two recensions developed (pp. 127-29). Should a given model be invalid, the arguments constructed on it would collapse. The criticism is sound. Moreover, the long history of attempts to solve the Synoptic Problem in the gospels provides sufficient warning to would-be literary detectives.

Inductive study of the texts might eliminate some of Kraft's suggested models. His list may be simplified into three types of models:

    a) linear dependence (#'s 1,2,4,5a)
    b) dependence on a common original (#'s 3,5b,6-9)
    c) dependence on various individual traditions (#'s 10-12)

The last of these types is, perhaps, the least likely. Separate dependence on various individual traditions is highly unlikely if one can demonstrate that both recensions contain the following: a very similar plot line; similar elements in that plot; differing corresponding elements which require the context of that plot; elements in one recension with no counterpart in the other which also require the context of that plot. It should be noted that the elimination of this specific type of model would remove Kraft's principal objection to Schmidt's ordering of the recensions (p. 130).

The location of "primitive" elements is the chief criterion for deciding between type a) and type b). Consistent discovery of such elements in one or the other recension would be evidence for the priority of that recension. Discovery of a fair spread of such elements in both recensions would support a hypothesis of dependence on a common original (an occasional such element might indicate contamination from the oral tradition). However, as Kraft indicates, our problem is in establishing criteria for "primitivity." The logical pitfall is that one may beg the question and *assume* that certain forms of the tradition must be more primitive than others. One need not and ought not demand one's own version of consistency or coherence from an ancient author (so Kraft, p. 129). A later author may give new consistency, coherence, and logic to received materials, as almost every solution of the Synoptic Problem maintains. Whether priority is indicated when such consistency is *of the essence* in one recension and totally lacking with respect to the same elements or narrative sequences in the other recension (so my paper, p. 92) is a question to which Kraft does not address himself.

The most promising avenues toward a solution of the recensional problem involve, according to Kraft, the working back from the Christian contexts in which T Abr was copied and preserved. He suggests two approaches: a) the refinement of linguistic criteria (pp. 133-35); b) the study of the thought worlds of the copyists and compilers (pp. 135-37). A possible entree into these thought worlds is provided by two documents reproduced in part in this volume: the Coptic Enoch Apocryphon and the Coptic Apocalypse of Paul. Both stem from Christian circles that knew either T Abr or traditions common to it.

Most obviously related to the recensional problem is the Coptic Enoch Apocryphon published by Birger Pearson, who notes similarities to unique features of both the short and long recensions (pp. 243-55). The fragmentary state of the papyrus makes firm conclusions difficult. Did the author have direct knowledge of both recensions or of a short recension judgment scene with a *psychostasia*, or did he have indirect knowledge of one or both of these? In any event, it is clear that we are in the presence of Christian circles that knew and utilized traditions that we otherwise know from T Abr.

George MacRae has noted similarities between the Coptic Apocalypse of Paul and the short recension of T Abr, specifically the Coptic version (pp. 285f.). In this connection, we should also note the similarities between T Abr and the Greek Apocalypse of Paul, observed already by M.R. James, who concluded that the short recension of T Abr drew on the Greek Apocalypse of Paul.[1] It is beyond the scope of this summary to discuss possible connections between the Coptic and Greek Apocalypses of Paul. Scholars with access to the whole of the Coptic Apocalypse maintain that the two works are not related.[2] However, given the similarities between T Abr and both Apocalypses (though the same parallels to T Abr do not, for the most part, occur in both Apocalypses), the relationship between the two Apocalypses could perhaps be profitably reexamined. Conversely, parallels between the Coptic Apocalypse and T Abr call for reexamination of James' thesis. What any or all of this might contribute to an understanding of the recensional problem in T Abr remains to be seen.

---

[1] For this conclusion, see James, *Testament* (1895) 49. For his discussion, see *ibid.*, 20-29, 44-49. For the Greek text of Apoc. Paul, see K. von Tischendorf, *Apocalypses Apocryphae* (Hildesheim: Olms, 1966 reprint) 34-69. For an English translation, see H. Duensing, "Apocalypse of Paul," *New Testament Apocrypha* (eds. E. Hennecke and W. Schneemelcher; Philadelphia: Westminster, 1964) 755-98.

[2] H. Ch. Puech, "Les nouveaux écrits gnostiques découverts en Haute-Egypte," *Coptic Studies in Honor of Walter Ewing Crum* = *Bulletin of Byzantine Institute* 2 (1950) 134f., cited by H. Duensing, "Apocalypse" 759; and G. MacRae, above, p. 285. In a brief note to me, Prof. MacRae refers to James' discussion and allows that "my statement that Greek Apoc Paul shows no direct connection with T Abr [may be] too sweeping," though he does not accept James' specific thesis of dependence.

The similarities between T Abr and the *midrashim* on the death of Moses also have a potential bearing on the recensional problem. The motif of Moses' continual refusal to die, which is of the essence in these *midrashim*, also structures the narrative in the long recension, but it is lacking in the short recension (so also Loewenstamm, p. 225, n. 2). Loewenstamm argues that the traditions in question were originally Mosaic rather than Abrahamic. If one accepts this view, one must ask which is more reasonable: that Mosaic motifs have been transformed into a story about Abraham; or that these motifs have restructured an already existent story about Abraham, which had elements parallel to the Mosaic story, but functioning in a totally different way. Although the motif of continual refusal to die is essential to the structure of both the Moses *midrashim* and the long recension, we should not overlook certain parallels between the Moses material and the *short* recension. According to the version of the story in *Deuteronomy R.*, *Berakah* X, Moses appearance is like the sun, like an angel (cf. short recension 13:10 in Grk. ms. E and Slavonic, below, p. 324). When Moses sees Sammael approach, he trembles (cf. short recension 13:4: James 117.17f.). The opening words of chs. 1 and 13 of the short recension parallel almost *verbatim* the Greek of Deut 31:14, the passage under which the Moses midrash is placed as commentary in *Deuteronomy Rabbah*.[3] This evidence might support a hypothesis of common dependence of our long and short recensions on a *Vorlage* in which Moses motifs were more explicit (one might also argue that the story is being revised toward a Moses tradition that is implicit). However one answers these questions, these data should be considered in discussions of the recensional problem. Non-Abraham traditions are, of course, not of the same value as texts of the recensions of T Abr, but they should be studied in this connection.

Thus while a precise and certain answer to the recensional question may elude us presently, avenues of research are open to us. Robert Kraft has suggested some new approaches. Primary sources not previously discussed in this context may

---

[3] It is at least noteworthy that the reading closest to Deuteronomy occurs not in our best Grk. ms. E and its affiliate, the Slav. P, but in the Grk. A D.

provide new imput. The specific arguments and counterarguments in the first three papers above and in Anitra Kolenkow's paper (pp. 149f., n. 1) have not been dealt with by Kraft (p. 127) and may warrant careful scrutiny. Along with all of this, we shall be helped by closer examination of the various facets and aspects of each of the recensions. They are, after all, the texts before us. To the extent that we know them better, we shall have a better chance to learn more of their relationship to one another and to any putative archetype of the story.

Genre and Structure

The paradox of the genre of T Abr is well known: although the book has many of the features of Jewish Testaments, it is not formally a Testament. Indeed, it clearly presumes that Abraham never made a testament. If we wish to solve the genre question, we must approach the writing as a whole, taking its various parts into consideration and attempting to see the rationale which interrelates them.

Francis Schmidt took such an approach to the short recension in his dissertation, employing explicitly structuralist categories. In his view, the book redefines the categories of life and death. This redefinition is explicit in Isaac's dream. Moreover, in his trip through heaven, Abraham sees souls passing to "life." Finally, the action of the story describes how Abraham is taken from this world and its pseudo-life to the life that really counts--eternal life. In my review of his dissertation, I have raised some questions about this interpretation (p. 16), but his interpretation should be studied more closely.

In the present volume, Anitra Kolenkow and I have sought a holistic explanation of the long recension, and we have arrived at conclusions which may, with some refinement, bring us closer to an understanding of our author's intention. My approach has been to analyse the structure of the plot and to attempt to distill from it in a single sentence the author's point: the moment of death, and its inevitable consummation, are in the hands of the sovereign God, and there is none who can resist (p. 87). In coming to this conclusion, I saw as the

constant in the whole of the book the struggle between God and
Abraham: God's command; Abraham's refusals; God's ultimate
triumph, the transition to which takes place in the shift from
Part One to the parallel Part Two. What was lacking in my paper
was an attempt to integrate into this structure the obviously
parenetic intention of the chariot ride sequence (which I
discussed in my 1972 paper, pp. 24-26).

The author's parenetic intention is central to Anitra
Kolenkow's analysis of the long recension. Our author wishes
to preach against a sin generally not recognized as such: the
desire of the righteous to destroy sinners. The chariot ride
sequence shows up the sinfulness of this attitude and assures
us that Abraham did repent of the sin. Moreover, Death is seen
as an opponent of God, carrying out precisely the activity for
which Abraham is blamed, but to no effect; for God's mercy
excuses from post-morten judgment those who have suffered an
untimely death. This explanation has the virtue of relating
the parenesis of the chariot ride sequence to a broader context
than I had seen in either of my papers (though I note the parallel between chs. 10 and the end of 17). If we are looking
for a holistic solution, however, this explanation does not
quite cover all the evidence; for it deals only with chs. 9-20.
Chs. 1-8 function mainly as prologue and setting. Nor do they
fit into Kolenkow's generic category, "the story that uses the
sins of the righteous to teach" (pp. 147f.).

The explanations which Kolenkow and I have proposed coincide on the centrality of Death. The content of the parenesis
in the long recension centers on death itself, and not on other
subjects discussed in a deathbed situation--an important distinction from the corpus of Testaments. More specifically, our
writing treats the *timing* of death. God chides Abraham for
calling down sudden death upon sinners who have no chance to
repent. He desires that people have this chance. Untimely
death, when it does happen, is itself the judgment. In the
action of our story, God reverses the two instances of untimely
death (chs. 14,18). Related to this is the matter of unexpected
death (παραλόγως / ος , 19-20: James 102.20-27). The contrast
between the 72 deaths and the one death that has its fitting
hour is reminiscent of ch. 11 and the imbalance between the

many who are destroyed[4] and the few who are saved. In the context of ch. 10, the point would be the following : death is unexpected and hence it is untimely for the many who do not repent and are destroyed in the judgment. In the case of those who do not have an opportunity for repentence (e.g., those ones whom Abraham "destroyed"), there is no further recompense.

Kolenkow has shown the parenetic intention of this theology: it is sinful and contrary to the expressed (in Scripture) will of God to desire, invoke, or effect the death of the sinner who has not had the chance to repent. The use of the figure of Abraham makes the point more explicit: this is a warning to the "righteous" who have such intentions against the "sinners"-- the categories and the sentiments are all too well known in contemporary Jewish literature.[5]

The whole of chs. 1-20 provide a context for the author's parenesis. On the one hand, Abraham's calling down death upon the sinners when their time is not up is the more culpable in view of his own refusal to accept death when *his* time has arrived. The author's structuring of his plot has an even broader contextual function. It tells us about the nature of death. It is inevitable ἀπαραίτητον, 1: James 77.10). Abraham lost the struggle to evade it. Its timing is set in the heavenly courtroom. Death is God's agent. (Only when this timing coincides with the lack of opportunity to repent is there no judgment.) Both Abraham's refusal to die and his calling down of death on sinners constitute human meddling in heavenly affairs. Finally, there is perhaps a warning. Death is unexpected. God made an exception with Abraham. When the Patriarch refused, God took him unexpectedly (hence the irony of Abraham's question) by a ruse. To Abraham also came the uncertain (ἄδηλον) end of life (1: James 77:11). Even the righteous must be prepared.

If we have come any closer to a holistic interpretation of T Abr, we have still not answered the genre question, which involves, by definition, a comparison with other works of the

---

[4] The terms, ἀπόλλυμι, ἀπώλεια, occur in T Abr in their technical meaning of destruction *qua* punishment and not just any sort of death.

[5] Cf., e.g. Pss Sol, Enoch 92-105.

same kind. Kolenkow refers to the genre of "works which use the failings of the righteous to teach." But is this a genre, or is it a common usage of a given theme in several different types of literature which are more properly called genres because of their common, identifiable formal characteristics (e.g., Testaments)?

Sources, Motifs, and Traditions

Since James' initial publication, scholars have suggested possible sources for the materials in T Abr. Kohler was the first to amass the Jewish parallels. More recently Delcor has added the evidence of the Targum Neophyti. Schmidt has taken note of parallels in Essene literature; however, his primary contribution has been to compile in great detail parallel materials from the history of non-Jewish religions (mainly Iranian, Greek, and Egyptian). These treatments of T Abr raise a number of questions, not all of them applicable to each of these discussions.

A first question relates to the labels applied to particular motifs and traditions. Many cited parallels from non-Jewish sources are sufficiently close to T Abr to justify a theory of substantive relationship. But what is the nature of the relationship? Does a parallel in Iranian sources necessarily prove derivation from Iran? Do we know enough about Mediterranean and Mesopotamian culture and myth to determine what is uniquely Iranian and what may have been part of a much broader cultural and mythic expression?

A second question is related to the first. What can we learn from our sources about the historical context in which these ideas were transmitted and modified? The history of ideas is a first step, but where possible, we should ask about the factors and conditions reflected in these ideas and the traditions that carry them. Robert Kraft has called for a similar inquiry into the context of the transmission of the whole of T Abr (pp. 135-37). In the present context, we may ask: what can we know about the hellenistic, syncretistic circles that gave rise to T Abr and its kin? What was the rationale and what was the justification (if such was needed) for this mix of ideas?

A final question relates to the sharing of common traditions within the Jewish community itself. Can we determine the interrelationship of the various manifestations of the tradition? What can we learn about the contexts in which these traditions arose? Delcor suggests that certain motifs in T Abr derive from the scriptural interpretation in the Palestinian Targum. In one case, the latter is derived from a Septuagintal translation of the Hebrew (see above, pp. 10f., 17). Are the Targum and the Greek Bible prior, or does T Abr witness to an oral tradition reflected also in the translations? Is the form of the tradition in T Abr always secondary to, and explicable on the basis of these translations?

Provenance

Francis Schmidt places the origin of the short recension in Palestine and the origin of the long recension in Egypt, the latter on the basis of Egyptian ideas in that recension. Delcor indicates an Egyptian setting for both recensions and argues that Palestinian ideas present in T Abr had migrated to Egypt. Robert Kraft agrees that the "Palestinian" or "Egyptian" character of a tradition is of little help in locating the geographical origin of the document in which it is found (pp. 129f.; see also my comment above, pp. 15f.). The papers in this volume add a little to our knowledge about the geographical locations of the two recensions. The Coptic Apocalypse of Paul and the Coptic Enoch Apocryphon offer additional documentation of the presence of the short recension in Egypt. Moreover, certain of the details in the Enoch Apocryphon (and a related Coptic Enoch fragment) suggest knowledge of a form of the judgment scene of the short recension closer to that preserved in Grk. ms. E and the Slavonic than in the Boharic version (cf. Pearson above, p. 246 and n. 53, with Slav. 11:9-11 [below, p. 322] and Coptic ch. 11 [below, p. 335]). This may suggest the presence in Egypt of a form of the short recension fuller than the Coptic. The Enoch Apocryphon probably indicates direct or indirect knowledge of the long recension. On the other hand, we have noted the close connections between the long "Egyptianized" recension and the rabbinic stories about Moses' death.

The hypothesis of an Essene (or Essene-related, i.e., Therapeutic) origin has continued to appear since the time of Kohler, though not always on the same grounds. However, the evidence does not seem conclusive. On the one hand, it remains to be demonstrated that we are in the presence of *uniquely* Essene ideas (see above, pp. 16,19). On the other hand, T Abr lacks certain key Essene ideas. This has led Schmidt to suggest that T Abr is the product of a popular Essenism, intended to gain converts (*Testament* 2, 120). Of such, however, we know very little. On similar grounds, Delcor suggests a Therapeutic origin (*Testament* 72f.). This argument bears closer scrutiny, but again our sources are meager, and some of them are no more surely Therapeutic than T Abr. Perhaps the quest for a specific religious milieu is the product of our desire to know more than we really can, and of an outdated and oversimplified view of sectarian Judaism.

A Final Note

Our study has pursued only certain areas of inquiry. Others remain open. What is the relationship between T Abr and the Apocalypse of Abraham? If we are to study the place of T Abr in early Christianity, we must do so also within the context of the triad of Testaments. Can we learn anything about the context of the short recension from the Testaments of Isaac and Jacob? Finally, new and better data will doubtless be supplied by the publication of new texts. F. Schmidt and J. Smit Sibinga are working on an edition of the Greek, based on a larger number of texts. Gaguine mentions a number of unpublished Ethiopic texts. M. Weber will publish a fifth century Sahidic text (see below, p. 337). This ensemble of texts will provide a firmer base for future studies.

APPENDICES

THE CHURCH SLAVONIC TESTAMENT OF ABRAHAM

Donald S. Cooper and Harry B. Weber

INTRODUCTION

A. *Language and Provenance of the Translation*

The oldest representatives of the Slavic translation of the short recension of the Testament of Abraham are written in a language customarily referred to as *Church Slavonic*. The term *Old Church Slavonic* is usually reserved for the language of a group of South Slavic manuscripts written in or around the eleventh century, which are copies of translations, primarily from Greek literature, made over the period subsequent to the first reduction to writing of the Slavic dialects of Macedonia and Bulgaria, during the period after the call of Saints Cyril and Methodius to Moravia in 862.[1] The Slavic dialects of Macedonia and Bulgaria at this time differed little, and the term *Old Church Slavonic* is applied to them jointly. This language was used during the middle ages as a literary or church language not only throughout the areas corresponding to modern Yugoslavia and Bulgaria, but with the conversion of the Eastern Slavs, it came to be used as a literary language also in Russia. The term *Church Slavonic* is used to refer to this literary language, both in its earliest Old Church Slavonic form, and in its development as a literary language in these areas.

As the living Slavic languages progressively diverged more from Old Church Slavonic, their linguistic peculiarities came to be reflected in later copies of Church Slavonic texts, primarily in their orthography. Church Slavonic manuscripts

---

[1] On the historical background, see F. Dvornik, *Byzantine Missions among the Slavs* (New Brunswick: Rutgers Univ. Press, 1970). Nicolaas van Wijk gives an overview of the development of the Church Slavonic textual and linguistic tradition in his *Geschichte der altkirchenslavischen Sprache* (Berlin: de Gruyter, 1931) 1-23. The fullest treatment is still Vatroslav Jagić, *Entstehungsgeschichte der Kirchenslavischen Sprache* (2nd ed.; Berlin, 1913).

showing certain orthographic traits characteristic of the Bulgarian area are customarily referred to as *Middle Bulgarian*. Church Slavonic manuscripts showing certain orthographic traits characteristic of texts copied in the East Slavic area are referred to as *Russian Church Slavonic*. Serbian Church Slavonic texts, like those above, are written in the older version of the cyrillic alphabet, while those written in the Croatian area are written in a version of the earliest Slavic alphabet known as glagolitic.

The Church Slavonic translation of the Testament of Abraham was probably made somewhere within the areas of modern Yugoslavia and Bulgaria or adjacent Slavic speaking areas, where Church Slavonic served as a common literary language. No systematic study of the morphology, syntax, and vocabulary of the Slavic text has so far been made, but certain linguistic details indicate that the translation was probably made not later than the tenth century. The textual tradition of Church Slavonic texts is not generally a learned one in which archaic forms could be restored by a learned scribe, except in rare cases where a text was copied in an area where the spoken language retained these forms. Thus an approximate index of the age of the Church Slavonic translation of T Abr is furnished by its preservation, primarily in P (see below), of a number of correct morphological and syntactic usages which are already archaic and occur side by side with younger usages in OCS manuscripts copied in the eleventh century.[2] Such phenomena are: the correct use of the supine; archaic aorist forms; third person dual verbal desinences in -*te*;[3] the short nom. sing. masc. pronoun "this"; the gen. sing. in -*e* from nouns of the consonantal declension; and the use of the prepositionless locative. These linguistic facts suggest that the translation was probably made not later than the tenth century, a period in which numerous translations of Greek religious literature into Church Slavonic were made in the Slavic cultural centers which

---

[2] A. Vaillant, *Manuel du vieux slave* (2nd ed.; Paris, 1964) I, and P. Diels, *Altkirchenslavische Grammatik* (Heidelberg, 1932) I.

[3] Already noted by E. Turdeanu, "Notes sur la tradition littéraire du Testament d'Abraham," *Studi bizantini e neoellenici a cura di Silvio Giuseppe Mercati* 9 (Rome, 1957) 409.

then flourished both in Macedonia and in eastern Bulgaria. Thus the Church Slavonic translation bears indirect witness to the textual complexion of a short recension of T Abr current in the Byzantine area in the tenth century.

F. Schmidt contends that the Church Slavonic text is closest to Greek ms. E.[4] Our comparison of the Church Slavonic text with the Greek texts collected by Schmidt does indicate an especially close relationship to E. Nonetheless, there also exist affinities to other mss. of the short recension. A systematic comparison of the text of the first two chapters of the Church Slavonic version with the readings of the Greek mss. of the short recension collected by Schmidt indicated the following examples of agreement between the Church Slavonic text and Greek mss. other than E.

1:1	were completed]	*eplērōthēsan* F *eplērounto* B G *ēggisan* A D E	
	archangel]	*archaggelon* F om A E	
2	and]	*kai* B C D F G om E	
	go out of]	*exeleusē* A C *exerchomenos ex-* *eleusei* E *exeleusetai* D different text B F G	
2:1	found him]	*heuren auton* A B C D F G *synēntēsen de autou (sic!)* E	
	with his ploughmen]	*emprosthen tōn arotriōtōn* C *eggista tōn boōn eis arotriasmon* E	
	for]	*gar* A C D F *de* B E	
	very]	*pany* B F G om A C D E	
4	I am a traveller] *poreuomenos tēn hodon* was translated as if it were a predicate (anarthrous) substantivized part. phrase	*stratiōtēs eimi kai poreuomenos tēn hodon emathon peri tēs philanthrōpias sou,* etc. C *philanthrōpos* (+ *ei sy* A D) A D E	
6	Let us go to my house]	*hina apelthōmen en tō oikō mou* A *hina apelthontes en tō o. hēmōn* E	
7	Lord elder]	*timie pater* B F G *adelphe* D om rel.	
9	showed me]	*hypedeixe moi* B G *apedeixen me* F *eipe(n) moi* A C D E	

---

[4] F. Schmidt, *Le Testament d'Abraham* (1971) 1. 29-33.

It should be noted, however, that these agreements are of quite varying significance. In 2:1, e.g., "found him" preserves an old reading against a stylistic innovation in E, while in 1:2, "go out of" agrees in error with A C D in eliminating a Semiticism,[5] the pleonastic participle in *exerchomenos exeleusei*, preserved in E. Other agreements link the Church Slavonic text with the innovations of the group B F G. Similar considerations need to be applied in relation to the grouping of the Church Slavonic texts with E on the basis of textual agreements, since it is agreement in error rather than agreement in readings which establishes affiliation of texts, and the above examples alone suffice to indicate that the relationships involved are more complex than the simple grouping of the Church Slavonic texts with E would indicate.

B. *Manuscripts*

There exist a number of copies of the Church Slavonic version of T Abr, most of which are either late or fragmentary. The most complete list of published texts has been assembled by Turdeanu in his valuable study of the Slavic tradition of the text.[6] The following list is based on that of Turdeanu, with the addition of some information from Schmidt's list of publications,[7] and some additions from other sources.

East Slavic Sources

1. Russian Church Slavonic text of the 16th century (hereafter T), fol. 2r-10v of ms. no. 730 of the Troicko-Sergieva Lavra, published by N.S. Tikhonravov, *Pamjatniki otrechennoj russkoj literatury* I (Sanktpeterburg, 1863; Repr. Slavistic Printings and Reprintings The Hague: Mouton, 1970) 79-90.

2. Ukrainian ms. of Uzgorod, 18th century, published by Ivan Franko, *Apokriphy i legendy* 4 (L'vov, 1906) 104-108.

---

[5]*Ibid.* 35; cf. F. Blass and A. Debrunner, *A Greek Grammar of the New Testament and Other Early Christian Literature* (transl. R.W. Funk; Chicago, 1961) 218. Examples from the LXX are listed by Martin Johannessohn, *Der Gebrauch der Kasus und der Präpositionen in der Septuaginta* (Diss. Berlin, 1910) 1. 57.

[6]Turdeanu, "Notes" 405-10.

[7]Schmidt, *Testament* 1. 6-9.

South Slavic Sources

1. Middle Bulgarian text of the 13th or 14th century (hereafter P), Moscow Public Library no. 27 (collection of P.I. Sevast'janov), fol. 1r-6r, edited by G. Polívka, "Die apokryphische Erzählung vom Tode Abrahams," *Archiv für Slavische Philologie* 18 (1896) 118-125, and by N.S. Tikhonravov, "Apokrificheskie skazanija," in *Sbornik otdelenija russkogo jazyka i slovesnosti Imperatorskoj Akademii Nauk* 58 (1894), pp. 1-8 of supplement (hereafter P'). The MS was described by A.E. Viktorov in *Sobranie rukopisej P.I. Sevast'janova* (Moscow, 1881) 63ff., and by I.I. Sreznevskij in *Drevnije slavjanskije pamjatniki jusovago pis'ma* (Sanktpeterburg, 1868) 72f.

2. Seventeenth century MS published as *Tikveshki rŭkopis*, edited by N.A. Nachov in *Sbornik za narodni umotvorenija, nauka, iknizhnina* 8 (Sofia, 1892) 411-413. Reprinted by B. Angelov and M. Genov in *Stara bŭlgarska literatura* (Sofia, 1922) 194-96.

3. Bulgarian text of the 16th century, published by B. Petriceicu-Hasdeu in *Cărtile poporane ale Românilor în secolul XVI* (Bucarest, 1879) 189-94.

4. Fragment from 1520 of štokavian (Serbo-Croatian) origin, published by Vatroslav Jagić in *Arkiv za povjestnicu jugoslavensku* 9 (1868) 83-91. Reprinted by M. Rešetar in *Zbornik za istoriju, jezik, i književnost srpskog naroda* 15 (1926) 57-59.

5. Croatian fragment in the glagolitic alphabet, from 1468, published by V. Jagić together with the štokavian fragment above, and reprinted in V. Jagić, *Prilozi k historiji književnosti naroda Hrvatskoga i Srbskoga* (Zagreb, 1868) 25-27.

6. Croatian text published by R. Strohal in *Stare hrvatske apokrifne priče i legende* (Bjelovar, 1917) 57-60.

7. Unpublished Croatian glagolitic text in the Bodleian Library; cf. Marin Tadin, "Glagolitic Manuscripts in the Bodleian Library, Oxford," *Oxford Slavonic Papers* 5 (1954) 141.

8. Serbian MS of Mt. Athos, from 15th century, edited by P.A. Lavrov in *Apokrificheskie teksty* (Sankpeterburg, 1899) 78-81; reprinted from *Sbornik otdelenija russkogo jazyka i slovesnosti Imperatorskoj Akademii Nauk*, 67 (Sanktpeterburg).

Other unpublished texts are listed by A.I. Jacimirskij in his *Bibliograficheskij obzor apokrifov v juzhnoslavjanskoj i russkoj pis'mennosti* (Petrograd, 1921) 1. 95-99.

C. *The Present English Translation*

The English translation which is presented here is based on those two manuscripts which most closely represent the earliest Church Slavonic translation of this work. The main part

of the present translation has been made from the thirteenth or
fourteenth century manuscript (P), in Middle Bulgarian orthography, published by Polívka in 1896. His edition has been
collated against that of Tikhonravov (P'), and all disagreements of these editions which are significant for the establish-
ment of the text have been noted. Lacunae in Polívka's edition
of P, which have been filled in from Tikhonravov's edition of
the same manuscript (P'), have been enclosed in brackets ⌐ ⌐.
The first four chapters and the beginning of the fifth were
lost from this manuscript, and there are occasional other lacunae in the text. It is not possible to determine from Polívka's
edition whether these latter result from physical defects in
the manuscript or from scribal error. The missing sections of
the text are here supplied from the sixteenth-century manuscript (T), in Russian Church Slavonic orthography, published
by Tikhonravov in 1863. This text goes back to the same original translation as P, but contains some variant readings which
are the result of development within the Church Slavonic textual tradition, as well as a certain number of readings which
appear to preserve the original Church Slavonic translation in
passages corrupted in P. However, it also contains some variants which indicate revision on the basis of a Greek text
different from that on which P is based.

Polívka inserted in his text in parenthesis a certain number of readings from T in order to fill what he considered to
be gaps, and sometimes he added other conjectural material in
identical parentheses. His additions from T have generally
been retained here within brackets ⌐ ⌐, and in a few cases
other such additions have been made where comparison with the
Greek texts indicated that they were called for. Polívka's
conjectural material has been omitted. However, the present
translation does not note all deviations of T from P. Rather
the object of the translation has been to present the text of
P and to reject or emend apparently corrupt readings of P,
primarily on the basis of whether they seemed plausibly related
to the readings of the Greek texts collected by Schmidt. The
evidence of T has, however, been regularly consulted and has
usually been cited where questions arose as to the correctness
of the text of P. Wherever the reading of P or P' has not been
accepted, it has been cited in the corresponding footnote.

307

The present translation has been made with the intent of producing a text which would be maximally useful for comparison with the existing Greek texts. Thus the original word-order has been preserved so far as possible, and critical comparison of the Church Slavonic texts with the Greek ones has been based first on E, and then on comparison of the readings of the other texts of the short recension in Schmidt's dissertation. Comparison of the critical sigla employed will make clear the detail of this procedure. The English translation has been made fairly literalistic in order to permit the most direct possible retroversion to Greek. Old Church Slavonic has a grammatical structure very much like that of Greek, and the Slavic translators usually translated in a fairly literalistic manner, which often permits exact retroversion from the Church Slavonic to the Greek text. The use of an English intermediary permits reproduction of the *sense* of the Church Slavonic text, but does not always permit reproduction of its structure: e.g., there was no definite or indefinite article in Church Slavonic, and verbal prefixes comparable to those of Greek or Latin are used routinely, but could not always be reproduced in the English text. Furthermore, in regard to some details of the translation involving detailed analysis of syntactic categories such as tense and aspect, it must be recognized that syntax is the least developed area of our knowledge of Old Church Slavonic, and sometimes it is not possible to specify the exact grammatical value of some forms or constructions as precisely as those of Hellenistic Greek.

Verse numbers in the present translation are those used by F. Schmidt in his edition of Greek texts (*Testament* 2).

In the present version, the text of T was translated by Harry B. Weber and edited by Donald S. Cooper. The text of P was translated by Donald S. Cooper, who also supplied the introduction and notes.

D. *Sigla and Abbreviations in the Apparatus*

SIGLA

( )	addition by translator to clarify sense
(( ))	suggested deletion of material present in the ms.
[p.]	beginning of page in edition
< >	conjectural emendation
ⲅ ⲅ	Reading of Slav. ms. T
г ⸍	Reading of Slav. ms. P'
† †	Apparent reading of (corrupt?) Greek original underlying Ch. Sl. translation, but not attested in any extant Greek ms.
+	adds
1°, 2°,	etc. first, second, etc., occurrence of given word in verse.
. . .	lacuna or apparent omission in the ms.
=	equals, is the equivalent of
word---word	comment or variant on the two words and all words between them

ABBREVIATIONS

abbrev.	abbreviation		loc.	locative
abs.	absolute		masc.	masculine
acc.	accusative		ms.	manuscript
act.	active		neut.	neuter
adj.	adjective		nom.	nominative
aor.	aorist		obj.	object
Ch. Sl.	Church Slavonic		om	omit(s)
dat.	dative		part.	participle, participial
diff. rel.	*different reliqui*		pass.	passive
dir.	direct		pl.	plural
ed.	edition		prep.	preposition
fem.	feminine		pres.	present
gen.	genitive		pron.	pronoun
Gk	reading of all Greek mss. of short rec. of T Abr		rdg.	reading
impf.	imperfect		refl.	reflexive
impv.	imperative		rel.	relative
inst.	instrumental		sing.	singular
lit.	literally		transl.	translation
			vb.	verb

WORKS CITED

Blass-Debrunner-Funk	F. Blass and A. Debrunner, *A Greek Grammar of the New Testament and Other Early Christian Literature* (Transl. R.W. Funk; Chicago, 1961)
Diels, *Grammatik*	Paul Diels, *Altkirchenslavische Grammatik* (Heidelberg, 1932) I
Lampe, *Lexicon*	G.W.H. Lampe, *A Patristic Greek Lexicon* (Oxford, 1961-68)
Schmidt, *Testament*	Francis Schmidt, *Le Testament d'Abraham* (Diss. Strassbourg, 1971) I-II
Schwyzer, *Grammatik*	Eduard Schwyzer, *Griechische Grammatik* (Munich, 1958-71) I-IV
Turner, *Grammer*	James Hope Moulton, *A Grammar of New Testament Greek*, Volume II, *Syntax*, by Nigel Turner (Edinburgh, 1963)

MANUSCRIPTS CITED

Greek (Cited after Schmidt, *Testament* II):

A   Paris, Bibliothèque Nationale, Fonds grec 1613

B   Paris, Bibliothèque Nationale, Supplément grec 162

C   Vienna, Cod. Histor. gr. 126

D   Milan, Ambrosian Greek codex 259 (D 92 sup.)

E   Milan, Ambrosian Greek ms. 405 (G 63 sup.)

F   Météores, Bibliothèque de la Métamorphose 382

G   London, British Museum, Add. 10014

Church Slavonic (see above, pp. 304f.)

P   Moscow Public Library, no. 27 (collection of P.I. Sevast'janov), fol. 1r-6r, ed. G. Polivka

P'   *idem.*, edited by N.S. Tikhonravov

T   Moscow, ms. no. 730 of the Troicko-Sergieva Lavra, fol. 2r-10v

TRANSLATION

⟨ABOUT THE REVELATION REVEALED TO OUR FATHER ABRAHAM BY THE ARCHISTRATEGOS MICHAEL ABOUT HIS TESTAMENT AND ABOUT (HIS) DEATH

1:1 When the days were completed for Abraham to ⟨be presented⟩ ((and)) the Lord said to Michael the archangel, "Michael." And he said, "Behold, here I am, Lord." And the Lord said, 2 "Arise and go to Abraham and say to him, 'You shall go out of this life 3 before you go out of this world.'"

2:1 And Michael went to Abraham, and found him sitting by his ploughmen, for he was very old and gray. 2 And Michael kissed him with the love for God, but Abraham not knowing who it was. And he said to him, 3 "Where are you from, man going along the road?" 4 Michael answered him, "I am a traveler." And Abraham said to him, 5 "Stay by me a little, until ⟨I⟩ send for (your) pack animal. 6 Let us go to my house, for it is toward evening, so that having eaten, you may rest, so that an animal may not meet you and you be frightened." 7 And Michael asked Abraham, "Tell me, lord elder, what is your name, before we arrive at your house?" 8 Abraham answered and said to him, "My parents made for me the name [p.80] Avra. And once the Lord said to me, 'Rise, go out from (your) own land and away from (your) own kinsfolk and go into the land

---

The translation follows T (reprint, pp. 79-81) from the title to 5:2a, and P from 5:2b to the end. The beginning of the pages in the respective editions are noted in brackets [ ].

1:1 be presented] *parastēnai* E   die T, which can be derived from the Ch. Sl. transl. of *parastēnai* by the omission of two letters.

2 you---out] *lit.* it will be to you to go out. Elsewhere this construction may indicate necessity.

2:2 for God] The prep. has varied senses.   om Gk. : was] *lit.* is

5 I send] T substitutes one (wrong) letter for the correct 1st sing. desinence of the verb "send." Emended after Gk.

6 having eaten] *lit.* having fed yourself. By missegmentation, the last letter of the part. has become incorporated with the following refl. pron., producing "fed all."   om Gk.

2:8-3:3   311

into which I shall command you, and do not disobey.'   9 And
thus I went into the land which the Lord showed me, saying,
'Henceforth your name will not be called Avra, but let your
name become Abraham.'"   10 And Michael answered and said to
him, "Permit me, lord, for I am a guest †at the house of a man
beloved by you† . For I heard that he, having gone, drove in a
calf and slaughtered (it) when you were my host at his house."
11 And thus therefore conversing with each other Abraham and
the angel, and having arisen, they set off. While they were
walking,   12 Abraham called two Damascenes, Elizar's sons,
his home-born slaves, slave children. And he said to them, "Go
and bring the pack animals, that we may seat on them this weary
man."   13 But Michael answered, "Do not trouble your slave
child; let us walk there, enjoying ourselves."

3:2 And they came near the river and found a large tree
standing on the way, having 320 branches like a very beautiful
birch.   3 And they heard a voice saying from the branches
†to them†, "Holy one, bring the notification to him to whom you

---

8 Avra] Usual form of the name in Ch. Sl. is Avraamŭ :
and 5°---disobey] om Gk.   The clause may belong with the
beginning of v. 9 if it is related to E's reading there ēkousa
de autou.

10 I---guest] epixenoumai A C D E   xenizomai B G
xenizōmen F.   T has an abbrev. which usually stands for nom.
sing. "Lord," but apparently here stands for "guest" :
†at---you†] Text of T represents a misreading of the abbrev.
ПНР (from E's rdg. pater anthrōpōn memelēmenōn) as the elided
prep. para (most probably in an uncial text).   Ch. Sl. text
corresponds to *par'anthrōpō memelēmenō (soi) :   When---
house] lit. you being by hospitality (lodging) to me by him
(at his house). T is unclear and may be corrupt.   aggelois
xenizomenois en tō oikō sou hopōs euphranthōsin E   the same
with minor variants A C D   om B F G

11 set off] = eporeuthēsan A

12 his---children] An alternative rdg. through the insertion of one letter would be "the slave children of his home-
born slave (fem.)" :   that---man] scribal error for "that
this weary man may seat himself upon them," involving the
change of three letters. The nom. case of the original subject is retained, confirming kathisē A D E :   slave child]
unexpected dat. instead of gen.-acc.

3:2 tree] The Ch. Sl. word elsewhere translates both
dendron and drys.

3 †to them†] = *autois   itacistic for autēs E :
bring] impv., one letter different from pres. act. part., correctly translating enegkas E. With this correction, T agrees
with hagios ho tēn phasin enegkas E

have been sent." 4 And having heard the voice, Abraham was frightened and hid the mystery in his heart, saying, "What will this mystery be to you (pl.)?" 5 And when therefore they came into his house, ((and)) Abraham said to his slave children, "Go to the herd and drive in small cattle and slaughter and cook (them) quickly, that we may eat and drink. For (there is) gladness for me today." 6 And the servants, as Abraham commanded them, quickly prepared food. Abraham summoned his son, saying thus to his son, "Dear Isaac, having stood up, fill a handbasin of water, that I may wash the feet of this guest who is lodging with us. 7 For I think in my mind that it is the last time for me to full the handbasin and to wash the feet of anyone who is a guest in our house." 8 And Isaac, having heard his father speaking, ((and)) weeping brought the handbasin. And he said, 9 "Lord father, what is it that you said, that 'it is the last time for me [p. 81] to wash the feet of this man lodging with me'?" 10 And Abraham having seen Isaac weeping, he too began to weep greatly. And the angel, having seen him weeping, he also began to weep with them. 11 And Michael's tears fell, they became like stones.

4:1 And also Sarah, having heard their weeping, <being> in the bedchamber, having come out, said to Abraham, "What is this, lords, which you beweep?" 2 Abraham answered and said, "There is nothing evil. And go into your chamber, do your work, lest you trouble the guest." 3 And Sarah went away, preparing for them <the midday meal>. And the sun came

---

5 small cattle] Like *thremmata* Gk., the Ch. Sl. word refers to goats and sheep.

7 anyone---guest] substantivized part. corresponding to *xenizomenou* A B C D E G, with no counterpart to preceding *anthrōpou* : in our house] *lit.* by us = *pros hēmas* B C D E G

10 having seen 1° 2°] In ed. of T, the part. suffix is carried over to the following word as a superscript.

11 stones] The desinence of the noun is omitted in T.

4:1 being] The gen. pl. desinence of the part. found in T arose by addition of two letters to the correct translation of *ousa* A C D E (assimilation to "their").

3 the midday meal] T ("both") omits the two final letters of word which in other texts translates both *to ariston* E and *ton deipnon* A C (*tou deipnou* B F G)

to the West. The archangel Michael went out and went up to the heavens before the Lord God to worship, 5 for when the sun has set, the angels of God worship. And the same one worships first, and thus all the angels in order. 6 And all the angels departed to their places. 7 And Michael said to God, "Lord, do you command (me) to speak before your glory?" 8 And the Lord said, "Speak, Michael." 9 And the archangel said, "You sent me, Lord, to Abraham your servant. In departing from the world his soul (must) go out of (infin.) (his) body. 10 But I did not dare to †reveal† to him the word, for he is your friend and a just man, receiving strangers. 11 I beg you, Lord, send the memory of death to Abraham, that it may enter into his heart and he himself may understand (it). 12 And let him not hear (it) from me, for (it is) a great speech to say to him that he must go away from this world." 14 Then said the Lord to the archangel, "Michael, go to Abraham, lodge with him, 15 and those things which you see them eating at his house, you also eat with them. And where he rests, you too rest there with him. 16 I shall impose for Isaac the memory of death in a dream on his heart."

5:1 And the archangel came to Abraham and was found being a guest at his house. And Abraham received him with joy just as (he did) the others. And he prepared the evening meal. And they ate and drank and made merry. 2 And Abraham ordered his son Isaac to spread a bed for the man^m [p. 118] guest, that

---

5 has set] part. construction in T = Greek gen. abs. in B F G : in order] *or* according to rank om Gk.

9 his soul---body] *lit.* to his soul to go out of his body, construction as noted in 1:2 above

10 †reveal†] T probably translates *ekphanein* rather than *ekphanai* of A C E.

12 speech to say] conflate rdg. of *ho logos* E, *eipein* A C D : he---away] *lit.* to him it is to go away

13 om T

15 them eating] substantivized part. : at his house] *lit.* by him; similarly in 4:14

16 I shall impose] personal desinence omitted

5:1 was---house] Reading of T was possibly (but not certainly) derived through scribal errors from correct Ch. Sl. transl. of *kai heuren auton hetoimasanta* E.

he might rest. And having lit a candle, he fastened (it) to the candlestick. 3 And Isaac did so. And Abraham said, "Have you done as I said to you?" And Isaac said, "Yes, lord." And Abraham and Michael went in to sleep. 4 And Isaac said, "Command me, father, that I also should lie down with you (dual)." 5 And Abraham said to Isaac, "Child, go into your chamber and rest, let us not <burden> the guest." 6 And Isaac went, he did not disobey his father, and lay down to sleep.

6:1 At the seventh hour of the night, Isaac arose and came to the door, where these ones were lying, and said, "Father, open the door to me, that I may look at your old-age, before they ⌈take⌉ you from me." 2 Having arisen, Abraham opened, and he ⌈came⌉ into the chamber and hung himself on the neck of (his) own father, w⌈eeping⌉ and kissing him. 3 Abraham also began to weep ⌈with him⌉. And ⌈having se⌉en him weeping, Michael also began to w⌈ee⌉p with them. 4 And having heard, Sarah, who was in her chamber, came ⌈to the door, w⌉here they were weeping, and asked ⌈him, 5 "Lord⌉ Abraham, what happened to you (pl.), that ⌈you (pl.) ⟨⟨who⟩⟩ are weeping t⌉hus this night? Has someone ⌈brought news⌉ to you about your nephew Lot, ⌈that he has died, or⌉ something bad has happened to him?" 6 ⌈Michael⌉ a⌈nswered and said,⌉ "No, Sarah...not..." ⌈And

---

2 he fastened] aor., formally the same as impv. sing.

3 went] sing. instead of dual

5 let---burden] *lit.* let us not acquire, error of one letter from correct translation of *mē* (+ *pote* A C D) *epibareis* (-*rys* B E F) *genōmetha* Gk. Ch. Sl. text could also reflect *mēpote* and be translated as "lest we..."

6:1 look at] Ch. Sl. vb. preceded by acc. refl. pron., which is not usual with it : take] initial letters of a word meaning simply "take" P   hasten away T

3 with---seen] P' includes one more letter before the lacuna than P, which implies the omission of "with him" in ms.

5 you---thus] In P' one more letter is read after the lacuna than in P, indicating that the ms. cannot have agreed exactly with the text of T.

6 not] The text in P is incomplete, and T is different. The prefix preserved in P would agree with the correct translation of the vb. in *ouk enegka* (-*kan* A   -*ken* D) *phasin peri Lōt* A C D E :

Sarahⁿ, having hⁿeard the distinction of speech, also understood that Michael's speech was [p. 119] distinct from all speeches of men living on earth, by its quietnessⁿ, and his speech was glorious.   7 And she said to Abraham, "How do you cry, a guest having taken shelter with us,   8 or how did you burst into tears when this light was shining in our house? There is joy on today's day."   9 Abraham said, "How do you know that this man is God's?"   10 Sarah answered and said, "I have understood that he is one of those three men who ate beneath the oak of Mamre, when <you>, having gone out to the field, drove in a calf and slaughtered (it),   11 and we ate with them in our house."   12 And Aⁿbraⁿham said, "In truth you have understood this well.   13 For ⌜I⌝, when I was washing his feet, understood in .... that they are the same feet which I washed then also beneath the oak of Mamre. And when he wanted to ⌜d⌝eliver Lot from Sodom, they told me a ⌜secret⌝."

7:1 Abraham said to Michael,   2 "Explain to me, ⌜lord, who you areⁿ." Michael said to Abraham, "I aⁿm the archangel Michaelⁿ." Abraham said, "Then tell me, <why> ⌜have you comeⁿ?"

---

distinction] T omits last letter of word translating *diaphoran* E, so that it becomes finite vb., "distinguished" :   was 2°] part. construction equivalent to gen. abs.

7 taken shelter] part. in instrumental sing. instead of dat. found in T with another vb., which formation would correctly translate gen. abs. *eiselthontos tou anthrōpou* Gk.

8 burst into tears] one inchoative vb. P

9 is] P has pres. part. in agreement with acc. "this man," obj. of vb. "know."

10 who ate] past part. P

13 For I] one letter of Ch. Sl. "I" from T's rdg., "I also therefore"   *hoti kagō* A C D E :   .... omission in P T   *en tē kardia mou* A C D E   P' has appropriate space; ms. evidently unreadable. In both P and P', the omission is followed by a vowel-letter which would be correct as the last letter of the translation of the Greek phrase :   he wanted] 3rd sing. aor. of "want," probably error for late 3rd pl. impf. form of "walk, go," translating *hypagontes* A D E

7:2 Explain] appear T   *delōson* E   *eipe* A B C D F :   why] *ti* Gk. = "why"   P has gen. sing. of "what" but omits prep. "for" necessary to translate Gk.   T agrees in sense with P, but not in form.

3 And Michael said, "Your son Isaac ⌐will tell you.⌐ 4 And⌐ Abraham ⌐said⌐, "My son, tell me, ⌐child, what sort of dream vision did you have⌐?" 5 Isaac said, "I saw in ⌐a dream myself as the sun and moon, and a crown⌐ was on my head, 6 ⌐and lo, a great man⌐, ⌐shining⌐ down from the heavens li⌐ke light, called the father of li⌐ght. 7 And he took the sun from my head and left the ⌐rays⌐ on me. 8 And I began to weep, saying, 'Do not take away the glory of my head and light of my house and my glory.' 9 And the sun began to weep, and the stars, saying, 'Do not take away the light of our strength.' 10 The radiant man answered, he said to me, 'Do not weep that I have taken away the light of your house, for it is going away from lowness to height, 11 and from ⌐narrowness⌐ to space, and from darkness to light.' 12 And I said to him, 'I beseech you, lord, take also the rays with him.' 13 And he said to me, 'Neither do the rays shine at this hour, until [p. 120] the twelve hours of the day are finished, that they may take all the rays of their own gleam. 14 †As Moses was saying I saw a radiant man and the sun, my father, ascending to heaven†." 16 And having answered, Michael

---

4 what---have] T, *lit.* what to you dream (sleep) vision. P' reads two more letters than P at the end of this lacuna, indicating that the ms. cannot have agreed exactly with the text of T.

6 shining] T = *lampōn* Gk. was taken P, orthographic error for "shining" : like] P' has one letter of a different word at the beginning of "like."

7 rays] T = *tas aktinas* A C D E (om B F) moon P, orthographic error for "rays."

8 began to weep] P, one inchoative vb.

11 narrowness] *or* constraint T *stenochōrias* C E (*-rian* A *-rion* D) om B F sleep P, orthographic error for "narrowness"

13 that---gleam] P, which could also be read "that all the rays may take their own gleam." "their own gleam" is probably a scribal orthographic error for "that ((also)) all the rays may be taken on high" T, which corresponds to *hina holas tas aktinas labōsin anō* E

14 †As---heaven†] *sic!* P (P' omits one letter in "radiant," producing "man of light") "As Moses was saying, I saw a radiant man (and) the sun being my father T a shared corruption; cf. *kai heōs entautha legōn ho phōteinos anthrōpos, eidon kai ton hēlion tou oikou mou anabainonta eis tous ouranous* E (A B C D F differ in details.

15 om PT

said, "In truth it is thus. The sun, Isaac, is your father, and he will be taken up to the heavens, 17 and his body will remain on eart ⌜h⌝ until eight thousand years are completed. Then all flesh will ar ⌜i⌝ se. 18 And now, Abraham, order your house and complete your management." 19 And Abraham said to Michael, "I pray you, my lord, if I shall go out of the body, ((but)) I would like to ⌜go⌝ up with the body, that I might see all the works of the Lord, which he has done in heaven and on earth, before my transl ⌜at⌝ ion." 20 And having answered, Michael said, "It is improper for me to do this on my own, but let me go and speak to the Father about this, in order that if he orders me, then I will tell you all things."

8:1 And Michael went up to the heavens and stood before the Father and spoke about Abraham. 2 And having answered, the Lord said to Michael, "Go and take Abraham with the body, and tell him all things. And do for him whatever he tells you, for he is my friend." 3 And Michael came and took Abraham with the body on clouds and bore him to the river called Ocean. 4 And having looked, Abraham saw two gates, one small and the other large, 5 and between the two gates a man was sitting on a throne of great glory, and a numerous crowd of angels around him. 6 And this man was weeping and laughing, and the weeping outdoing the laughter. 7 And Abraham said to Michael, "Who is this, lord, ((both)) he who is sitting on the throne between the two gates and with such glory, and the numerous crowd of angels stands in front of him; and he

---

19 would like] T   P reads *lit.* wanted, which could be derived from T by omission of four letters, but could also be read as an impf. and thus a correct literalistic translation of modal *ēthelon* A D, "I would like" (Blass-Debrunner-Funk, *Grammar* 181f. §359) :   translation] Ch. Sl. word is most often used of death, not of linguistic translation, but may have a range of meaning similar to Greek *metastasis*.

20 but---go] "let" not "permit," but probably translating hortative subjunctive *alla* (+ *as* B F) *apelthō* A B F (cf. N. Turner, *Grammar* 94) :   in order that] *or* and

8:3 Ocean] *Okriani̯* P   *Okianŭ* T

7 both---sitting] The rel. clause translates a substantivized pres. part.   P' omits "both" :   such] The adj. in P usually has the sense of "such great."

is weeping and laughing, but the weeping is sevenfold greater than the laughter?" 8 And Michael said to Abraham, "Do you not know him?" 9 And Abraham said, "I do not know, lord." 10 ⌜And Michael said⌝, "Do you see the two gates, both the great one and small one? 11 These two are the ones leading to life ⌜and to death. The narrow one is the one leading to life⌝, and the broad gate, to destruction. 12 This ⌜ma⌝n also is Adam, the first man whom G⌜od made. 13 And he led him to⌝ this place to see all the souls comi⌜ng o⌝ut of the body, for all are from him. 15 And [p. 121] when ⌜you see⌝ (him) laughing, understand that he ⌜sees⌝ the soul⌜s⌝ led into life. 14 If <you see him> beginning to weep, understand that ⌜he sees sou⌝ls being led to destruction. 16 And there ⌜fore⌝ weeping ⌜over⌝ comes laughter. understan⌜d that⌝ he sees the ⌜gre⌝ater part of the world...to destruction, and for that reason, ⌜we⌝eping over ⌜comes⌝ laughter sevenfold."

9:1 Ab⌜raham⌝ said ⌜to⌝ Michael, "And can they not ⌜go through⌝ the narrow gate, and can they not go into life?" And Michael said, "Yes, ... not." 2 And Abraham began to weep, saying therefore, "⌜Woe is me, what⌝ ⌜shall I do, 3 for I am⌝

---

11 ones leading] substantivized part. : narrow one] substantivized adj.

13 all the souls] In the orthography of P this could easily have been altered, by the change of one letter, from the correct translation of *pasan* (*pasa* A) *psychēn* Gk. : all 2°] P fem. in agreement with "souls" T masc. as *pantes* A C D E (*pantas* B F as acc. subj. of inf.)

14 if you see him] *ean oun theōrēs auton klaionta* E (minor variants A C D) om. P P' has first two letters of "you see" T corrupt : beginning to weep] one inchoative vb. P weeping P'

16 ...] om P T *theōrei to perisson tou kosmou apagomenon dia tēs pylēs tēs apagousēs eis tēn apōleian* E (similar A C D)

9:1 And ---life] Ch. Sl. text is almost certainly a corruption of the correct translation of *kai ho mē dynamenos eiselthein dia tēs stenēs pylēs, ou (pōs* A) *dynatai eiselthein eis tēn zōēn* A C D. "can they not" 1° is an orthographic error from a late part. form with sing. altered to pl. in "they" 2° : ...] omission in P yes, you (sing.) can T

2 began to weep] inchoative vb. : therefore] last letter omitted in P : woe is me] *lit.* woe to me

⌐a¬ person who is⌐¬ ⌐heavy¬ ⌐of body¬, and I will not be able to enter there ⌐into the narrow¬ gate, ⌐for¬ they are not able to go into i⌐t except chi¬ldren who are about ten years old."
4 And Michael sa⌐id to him¬, "You alone will go in and a⌐¬ll simi⌐lar to you, but many from the world go thro⌐ugh the wide¬ gate to destruction." 5 While ⌐Abra¬ham was stan⌐ding¬, at that hour, lo an angel drove ⌐60,000 souls, but¬ was carrying ⌐one¬ <soul> in his hands. And he drove ⌐the 60,000 <souls> in¬to the gate leading to destruction. 6 A⌐braham¬ said, "Are all <these> going to destruction?" Mich⌐ael¬ said ⌐to Abra¬ham, 7 "Let us go, let us seek in ⌐those¬ souls. ⌐If¬ we find a worthy soul, we will le⌐ad it into li¬fe." 8 And having gone ⌐out¬, they sought and did not fi⌐nd in those souls one wor¬thy of life, except ⌐that which¬ the angel was ⌐hold¬ing in his hands. For he found ⌐her¬ sins ⌐equal¬ with ⌐her just works¬. And he leads her neither ... nor into life, but <leads> her to a pla⌐ce which is in¬ the middle. 9 But these ones they lead to destruction.

---

3 who is] Rel. clause for pres. part. T : into it] with different segmentation, could be read "within," but cf. *eiselthein en aute* E : who are about] *lit.* as being

4 and 2°] om. P'

5 While---standing] temporal clause for part. construction = Greek gen. abs. : one] T, inst. sing. for acc. sing. *mian de psychēn* E. The desinences are confused in the reverse direction already in much older texts (Diels, *Grammatik* 175), so that the form is probably hypercorrect. : soul] last two letters of word corresponding to "soul" preserved in P : souls 2°] T, loc. sing. masc. or neut. of pron. "that," probably by error for gen. pl. "souls"(*tōn psychōn* E), an error more likely in a glagolitic than in a cyrillic ms.

6 all these] T *houtoi pantes* A B C D F P reads "and also" for "these," a substitution of one letter

7 we will lead] Personal desinence of vb. omitted

8 her just works] T = *tōn agathōn ergōn autēs* E. The word means "(behavior in accordance with) law (divine or civil), truth." P has inst. pl. "just" with no head-word : ...] omission of text corresponding to *en mochthō* A C D E *ep apōleia (-as* emend. Schmidt) B *eis apōleian* F P has one letter which could be the last letter of "to destruction" : leads 2°] P omits two letters, transforming the form into "having led." T has a substitution of one letter in "led" (producing an impossible form) : place] last three letters omitted in P word omitted in T

10 ⌐And Abraham said⌐ to Michael, "These souls which ⌐the angel⌐ [p. 122] is driving--is that the one who takes (them) out or <not>?"   11 ⌐And⌐ having answered, ⌐Michae⌐l said, "Death is leading them to the pla⌐ce⌐ of judgment, ⌐in order that⌐ the judge ⌐may ju⌐dge them."

10:1 Abraham said to Mich⌐ael, "I desire⌐ ⌐that you should lead me ⌐to⌐ the place of judgment⌐ ⌐that I may see ho⌐ ⌐w⌐ the judge judges."   2 And then Michael . . . Abraham and led him to the place, where ⌐paradise is⌐.   3 When they reached the place where the judge was,   4 ⌐he heard a sou⌐l howling in torments, crying ⌐and saying, "H⌐ave mercy on me, Lord."   5 And the judge said, "How sha⌐ll I have me⌐rcy on you, and you have not <had mercy> on your own daughter, but arose against the fruit of your own womb and ⌐destroyed yourself⌐?"   6 She answered and said, "Murder did not happen by my agency, but she has slandered me."   7 And the judge said to bring the memoir of the report.   8 And lo, a cherubim (sing. sense) carrying two books. There was with him a very large man, having on his head three crowns.   9 And one crown was taller

---

10 the one---out] substantivized part.   *ho pherōn* E : or not] or another P T *ē ou* A C D E   om B F   The reading of T and P is based on an orthographic error in a common archetype.

10:2 ...] Then Michael said to Abraham, "Let us (*or* we shall) go, Abraham, where paradise is" T   Closest to P is *tote Michaēl epoiēsen tēn nephelēn analabein ton Abraam kai apagageinai (sic! eisēgagen* D) *auton* C :   to---is]   *en topō ho estin paradeisos ek merous autou*   E

4 have mercy] Phrase = sing. Ch. Sl vb. as in *eleeson* Gk.

5 had mercy] P has only the prefix of the vb. attested in v. 4 translating the same Greek vb.   T has "done mercy," the same expression as in Lk. 1:72 :   yourself]   om P *autēn* B E F   different rdg. A C D   T has refl. pron. "yourself" (gender and person unmarked). The extension of the 3rd person refl. pron. to all persons and the vacillation of *heaut- / aut-* in late Greek texts explain the confusion (E. Schwyzer, *Grammatik* 2. 193; Blass-Debrunner-Funk, *Grammar* 148.

6 by my agency] lit. "from me" here and in v. 12

7 bring] Schmidt (*Testament* 2.23) translates this into *elthein*, which is read by A C F :   report *or* text, written communication, *etc*.

than the other. And they summoned this man to witness.
10 And this man was holding in (his) hand a golden pen. And the judge said to the man, "Expose the sin of this soul."
11 And the man having opened one book of those carried by the cherubim (sing.), ((and)) he sought the sin of that soul.
12 <That man> having answered ((and)) said, "Oh wretched soul, how do you say that 'murder did not happen by my agency'?"
13 Have you not, soul, after the death of your husband, committed adultery with the husband of your daughter?" 14 And he exposed her other sins to her, which she had done at any hour.
15 The soul, having heard these things, cried out saying, "Woe is me! For I forgot all the sins, but these did not forget them." [p. 123] 16 And also the servants <of wrath> took her and tormented her.

11:1 Having answered, Abraham said to Michael, "Lord, who is this judge? And who is he who speaks judgment? For does the judge not judge, besides him who speaks judgment?"
2 Michael said to Abraham, "Do you see the judge? This is Abel who was tormented first. 3 And this one who speaks

---

9 this] two letters omitted in P   which man they called to witness T

11 those carried] substantivized pres. pass. part. : that] does not imply Greek pron., but is introduced for anaphoric Greek article.

12 that man] T, as above, pron. replaces an anaphoric article   *kai apokritheis ho anēr eipen* E   Abraham P : and] *sic!* P T

14 And he exposed] *lit.* and exposing

15 Woe is me] *lit.* woe to me

16 of wrath] fiery P   angering T   P preserves the derived adj. formation, T, the stem of the adj. attested elsewhere in Ch. Sl. as a correct transl. of *tēs orgēs* C D E

11:1 he---judgment] substantivized part. Ch. Sl. word so translated here and below more generally means "reply, answer," but in one OCS text, it translates *apophainomai* precisely in this sense :   For---judgment] closest Greek reading is *hoti ou krinei prin ho apophainomenos anorthōsē* E

2 was tormented] P' has the first letter of the refl. pron. omitted in P, but present in T.   *ho...martyrēsas* Gk. is translated in the sense of martyrdom by torture

3 And---judgment] substantivized part. exactly translating *houtos de ho apophainomenos* E :

judgment is Enoch your father; this one is the teacher of heaven and scribe of righteousness.   4 And the Lord sᵉnt him hither, that he might write the lawless deeds and ⌜right⌝eous deeds of everyone."   5 And Abraham said to Michael, "Can Enoch carry the part of the souls, or speak judgment to all souls?"   6 Michael said, "If he speaks judgment wrongly, they do not permit him. And Enoch does not speak judgment on his own,   7 but the Lord (is) the one speaking judgment. If it is (necessary) to write, it is entrusted to Enoch. 8 For Enoch prayed the Lord saying, 'I do not want to speak judgment to the souls, so that I may not be oppressive to anyone.'   9 The Lord said to Enoch, 'I give you the freedom, that you write the sins of men in the book.   10 If the soul will be <shown mercy>, you will find its sins erased and it will enter into life.   11 If the soul will not be <shown mercy>, you will find its sins written, and they will lead it into torment.'"

12:1 After he saw the place of the judge, the cloud carried ⌜him⌝ to the firmament.   2 And Abraham, having looked down at the earth, saw a man committing adultery with a married woman.   3 And Abraham said to Michael, "Do you see this

---

this one] Single pron. "this" in substantival function : teacher---righteousness] Both adnominal genitives in E (*ho didaskalos tou ouranou kai grammateus tēs dikaiosynēs*) are correctly translated by denominative adjectives in P

    4   lawless deeds] *lit.* lawlessnesses: righteous deeds] *lit.* righteousnesses, justices :   of everyone] *lit.* of whomever

    6   permit] *lit.* "give" in a well-established special usage

    8   oppressive] *lit.* heavy

    9   give---freedom] *or* "consent," on the assumption that the text of P is altered by one letter from a phrase which elsewhere translates *syneudokeō* in this sense :   of men] denominative adj. which does not indicate number of "men"

    10,11   shown mercy] merciful P, probably by incorrect resolution of abbrev. of pass. part. of vb. "show mercy." T has "show mercy" in both cases in slightly different rdgs. *kai ean hē psychē eleēthē* (v. 10)   *ean de hē psychē mē eleēthē* (v. 11)   E   diff. rel.

    12:1   he---place] *lit.* vision of the place

12:3-13:1

lawlessness? May fire come down from the heavens and eat him up." 4 At that hour, fire came down from the heavens and ate him up. 5 The Lord said to Michael, "Just as Abraham says, listen to him, for he is my friend." 6 And Abraham, having looked again, saw on the earth others slandering. 7 And Abraham said, "May the earth burst asunder with them and may it consume them alive." 8 Just as Abraham said, the earth consumed them. 9 Abraham, having looked again, saw certain ones going into the [p. 124] desert to commit murder. 10 And Abraham said to Michael, "Do you see the lawlessness of these ones? ((Order)) May beasts come from the desert, may they destroy them." 11 At that hour beasts came from the desert and ate them up. 12 The Lord said to Michael, "Return Abraham back to earth, do not allow him to go around the whole earth, which I made; for he does not have mercy on anyone, for he has not made them. 13 And perhaps they will turn from their sins and repent and be saved." 14 At that hour Michael returned Abraham. 15 And when Sarah died, 16 Abraham buried her.

13:1 And when the days of Abraham were shortene͞d, ͞((and)) the Lord said to Michael͞, " <Let Death not dare> to

---

9 certain ones] Single pron. in substantival function : going] desinence omitted in P

10 these ones] sing. pron. in substantival function : order] And he ordered T. The addition of the vb. makes it possible to read "Order that beasts should come from the desert that they might destroy them." The vb. is an addition within the Slavic textual tradition, since the syntactic ambiguity does not exist in Gk.

11 them] an extra vowel-letter in P could be an extra "them" in the accus.

12 Return] *lit.* turn : allow] *lit.* give.

13 turn] *or* be turned

14 returned] *lit.* turned

13:1 Let---dare] until Death dares P And does Death not dare T. Both rdgs. probably arose through the addition of different particles to the translation of a text such as *ou mē* (*ou* D) *tolmēsē (-sei* D + *ho* D) *thanatos* (+ *tou* C) *eggisai autō* (*-tou* D om A) *tou exenegkein tēn psychēn* A C D, with the omission of *ou*, as in F, i.e., "Let Death not dare..."

approach him, so as to take his soul, for he is my friend. 2 But go, beautify Death with much beauty and send (her) to Abraham, that he may see her with (his) own eyes." 3 And Michael beautified Death and sent her to Abraham. 4 And Abraham, having seen that Death approached him, began to fear greatly. 5 And Abraham said to Death, "I pray you, tell me who you are, and go away from me; 6 for since I saw that you had come to me, my soul was troubled within me. 7 And I am not worthy of you, for you are a great spirit, but I (am) flesh and blood. Because of this I cannot bear your glory; 8 for I see your beauty, that it is not from this world." 9 Death said to Abraham, "I say to you, in all creation which God has created, one like you was not found. 10 For I have searched in angels and in men and in powers and in thrones and in dominions and in all things living upon earth and in waters, and one like you was not found." 11 And Abraham said to Death, "You purely lied, for I see your beauty, that it is not from this world." 12 And Death said, "Do you think that this beauty is mine, or I can become so beautiful to every man?" 13 And Abraham said to her, "Then whose is this

---

2 go] *lit.* having gone :   her] In Ch. Sl., death is of fem. gender

4 that---approached] rel. clause for past act. part. modifying "death" :   began to fear] one inchoative vb.

6 that---come] *lit.* past act. part. modifying "you," dir. obj. of "saw"   so also T.   On the basis of *aph hou gar se etheasamēn kathēmenon eggista mou* A C (closest to P sim. rel.), we judge the original Ch. Sl. rdg. to have been "sit down near," which would differ by two letters from the attested rdg.

7 great] P T   *hypsēlon pneuma* A C D E (different rdg. B F)   The words "great" and "high" in Ch. Sl. have the same first and last two letters and the same number of letters. Thus the attested Ch. Sl. rdg. is probably a scribal error : bear] *meaning* suffer, endure *rather than* carry

9,10 one like] substantivized adj.

10 things living] substantivized pres. part.

11 purely lied] lied T.   Probably to be emended to "Why did you lie?" cf. *(dia ti* D   *pos* A) *etolmēsas pseusasthai* A D E   *ti pseudai se* B (*-de se* F), which should be read as *ti pseudesai* (Blass-Debrunner-Funk, *Grammar* 45 §87). In the Ch. Sl. text, the suggested rdg. requires a change of two letters. The Greek pres. is treated as historical, which is translated by an aor. as usual.

beauty?" 14 Death said to [p. 125] Abraham, "There is no one more rotten than I." So Abraham said, "Show me yourself, who you are." 15 Death said, "I am the bitter name; I am weeping; I am the destruction of everyone." 16 Abraham said to her, "Who are you?" Death said, "I am Death, who parts souls from bodies." 17 Abraham said to her, "Are you Death? Can you effect for all that their souls go out of (their) bodies?" 18 And Death said to Abraham, "Do you think that this beauty is mine, or I show myself thus to all? 19 But if then someone is righteous, they <having taken from him> all righteousness, make a crown and place (it) on my head, and I go to him with such submission and righteousness. 20 If someone is a sinner, I come to him with great rot, and they make his sins a crown, and place (it) on my head, and with great terror I trouble him very much."

14:1 And Abraham said to her, "Show me your rottenness." 2 And Death took off ⌜the righteousness of Abraham⌝ from

---

Gk. 15 everyone] *or* everything   *egō eimi hē ptōsis pantōn*

16 who parts] rel. clause for attributive part. in P

17 effect] *lit.* do : that---bodies] *lit.* that for them souls go out of bodies

18 Do---mine] *lit.* Do you think this beauty being mine?

19 having---righteousness] agreeing best is *pros auton lambanousin holēn tēn dikaiosynēn* E.   T agrees with emended text. In P, the omission of one letter has changed "having taken from him" to dat. sing. masc. of past act. part. : from him] dat. P   *pros auton* E :   place (it)] text of P can be divided to read either "they place (it)" or "I place it" :   submission] *en pithanotē* <*ti*> E (other texts incompatible with P) is translated here not in its usual act. sense of "persuasiveness" or "plausibility," but in a sense corresponding to *pithanos* in the pass. sense of "obedient, docile," as in Xen. *Cyr.* 2.2.10; *Oec.* 13.9

20 with 1°] *or* as   *en megalē saprotēti* A D E *e. m. sapriā* F : place (it)] same ambiguity as in v. 19

herself and showed him (her) own rottenness. ⟨And thus⟩ she showed...for she had heads,   3 which had snakes' faces-- for this reason, many die through asps--   4 and other heads, which had swords--for this reason, many die from the sword. And ⌜some⌝ had fire.   5 On the same day, seven sons of Abraham died from terror of Death. And Abraham prayed to God, and he resurrected them all.   6 And Abraham, as in a dream, gave over (his) own soul, And the hosts of the Lord came blessing the friend of God, and they carried his soul to rest, glorifying the supreme God.   7 And Isaac buried Abraham, (his) own father, near (his) own mother, glorifying the supreme God, to whom is glory into ages of ages. Amen.

14:2 And thus]   and that one P, by omission of two letters from correct transl. of *houtōs de* E.   T agrees with conjecture in sense, but has a different word in place of "and"

3 snakes'] denominative possessive adj. without indication of number of corresponding adnominal gen.   *prosōpa drakontōn* D E F   *prosōpon drakontos* A

3,4 for this reason] *lit.* because of this

4 swords] *or* spears. Elsewhere in Ch. Sl. this word translates Greek *logchē* and *rhomphaia* and Latin *gladius* and *lancea*.:   some] P' in agreement with T as to pron. stem, but not gender and number.   both P (The editors read one letter differently)   Gk. omit sentence.

6 dream] *or* sleep   *hōs en oneirois* Gk. :   hosts] *lit.* forces   *ēlthon de harmata kyriō tō theō* E *(sic!* Schmidt emends to *kyriou tou theou)*   *kai idou harma tou theou* C diff. rel.   "forces" of P translates *armata* in the medieval Greek sense of "bands of troops" (Lampe, *Lexicon* s.v. *arma*) then the angels of the heavenly hosts came   T

THE COPTIC TESTAMENT OF ABRAHAM

George MacRae

The importance of the Coptic versions of the Testament of Abraham, which are at the origin of the tradition continued in the Arabic and Ethiopic versions, lies not only in the antiquity of the MSS but in the peculiar features of the narrative which in a sense mediate between the long and short recensions of the Greek.[1] The purpose of the present translation is to permit the reader who lacks access to the Bohairic to make comparisons based on the contents of the story.

The basis of this translation is the Bohairic version, which survives in a single MS, Vatican Coptic 61, dated 962, f.148^V-163^V, published by I. Guidi in 1900.[2] In addition, a Sahidic papyrus MS in the collection of the University of Cologne, for which a fifth-century date has been proposed, contains substantial fragments of the work.[3] The Sahidic is to be published by M. Weber and was not consulted in the preparation of the following translation. According to F. Schmidt, the Sahidic version is very close in content to the Bohairic except for a few details in the concluding episode of the story. A German translation of the Guidi text was published by E. Andersson in 1903,[4] and a French translation by M. Chaine was posthumously published in 1973.[5] The present translator has profited from consulting both of these.

The Vatican MS also contains the Testaments of Isaac and Jacob, and the (pseudo-) Athanasian preface indicates that in the Coptic tradition (and its derivatives) the three testaments were regarded as a single work.[6] I have included a translation of the preface below, though it must be regarded as secondary to the T Abr itself. The chapter divisions are not of course in the MS. I have introduced them in imitation of the chapter divisions of the short recension in the edition of M. R. James in order to facilitate comparison.[7] It will be observed that in many instances there is very little correspondence in the length of chapters between the Greek and the Coptic. For those who wish to consult the Bohairic, I have also included in square brackets the folio numbers of the MS.

The translation is for the most part literal rather than a rendering into idiomatic English. For example, the various Coptic expressions for death such as "departure from the body" are distinguished in the translation. I have not regarded it as useful to include in parentheses the Greek loanwords in the Coptic, but in one or two cases they are mentioned in the notes. I have made no effort in the brief notes to record every dialectal variation or apparent misprint; only a few instances are mentioned which might affect the translation. The occasional words in parentheses are supplied by the translator to bring out the meaning more clearly.

TRANSLATION

[f.148b] This is the departure from the body of our holy fathers, the three patriarchs Abraham and Isaac and Jacob Israel. Abraham left the body on the 28th of the month of Mesore, Isaac also on the 28th, and Jacob too on the 28th of this same month of Mesore. And they were taken to the heavens with glory and honor.

This is what our holy father Abba Athanasius, Archbishop of Alexandria and apostolic successor in Alexandria,[8] declared. This is what he found in ancient books of our holy fathers the apostles. In God's peace, amen.

Listen to me attentively, O people who love Christ, and I will tell you of the life and the departure from the body of our holy fathers the patriarchs Abraham and Isaac and Jacob. This is what I found in the ancient books of our holy fathers the apostles, I your father Athanasius, [f.149a] for the benefit of everyone who will listen to them to glorify God.

I. It happened that when the days of our father Abraham the patriarch drew near, God sent to him Michael the holy archangel to tell him of the decree of his departure from the body.

II. Now Abraham was in the field. The archangel Michael appeared to him and said to him: "Hail, great man Abraham!" Abraham replied and said to the archangel Michael: "Hail indeed, my lord brother!" The patriarch Abraham said to the archangel Michael: "Where have you come from, or where are you going, walking alone in this desert? Watch out, my brother, take heed to yourself lest a beast frighten you in the field."

Afterwards Abraham said to Eleazer his servant: "Hasten! [f.149^b] Go into the city. Bring me a mule so that we may have this stranger mount it lest perhaps he has grown weary from the journey."

Michael said to Abraham: "Do not send for an animal nor bring it for me. But let us rise and let us walk together in the field and converse with each other."

III. They arose and walked together until they arrived under a tree that had three branches, a tamarisk in its species. They heard a voice. It came from one of the branches like a wind, crying out three times saying: "Holy, holy, holy is he whom the messenger is visiting." When Abraham heard this, a great fear suddenly came upon him.

When they arrived in the city, they went into Abraham's house. Abraham said to his son Isaac: [f.150^a] "My son Isaac, hasten! Bring the basin of water that we may wash the feet of this stranger who has visited us. For my heart tells me that this is the last time that your father will put water into a basin to wash the feet of a stranger who visits him. I tell you, O my beloved son Isaac, this is the last time that you will see your aged, good father."

Isaac wept saying: "My father Abraham, what is this saying filled with grief and tears which I hear from you as you say, 'This is the last time,' my good father?"

Abraham said to his son Isaac: "I myself do not know what has happened to me. For from the time this man has visited me my heart has made a leap within me."

[f.150^b] Then Abraham said to his servant: "Hurry! Go to the sheep and all the cattle, whether sheep or goats or calves. Bring us three of each kind by species. Slaughter them and cook them, that I may rejoice with this stranger who has visited us before I depart to that place where I must be forever." Abraham's servant departed and did as he had been told.

IV. While they were making preparation, Michael went out of the house of Abraham on a pretext.[9] He flew up[10] to the heavens. He bowed before God and entreated him, speaking thus: "I entreat your goodness and I glorify your mercy that you cause the remembrance of death to prick the heart of Abraham so that he realizes himself that he is about to go forth from the body, and that you [f.151^a] cause Isaac his son to see him in a vision. For I am not able to tell him this word of bitterness, full of tears and grief, that he is about to go forth from the body, because he is your friend. Moreover I visited him, I with you and Gabriel, and he treated us with great kindness. Moreover because he is hospitality (itself) for strangers and the holy ones, this is why I cannot tell him this word that is bitter and harsh."[11]

The Lord over all answered and said to Michael: "O Michael, my faithful servant, rise, fly to Abraham, and everything he eats, pretend as though you are eating it with him, and where he sleeps, you sleep there too. Do not be disobedient to him in anything, for he is my friend, and also because I visited him at the tree of Mamre."

V. Now when the Savior had said this to Michael, he came again on a pretext. [f.151^b] He entered Abraham's house and began to eat. And Abraham ate with Michael and Isaac his son. And during the meal Abraham said to his son Isaac: "Hasten, my son, and prepare a bed so that this stranger who has visited us may rest."

Isaac said to his father: "My father, I too am coming with you to sleep this night."

Abraham said: "Let us not trouble this stranger. Go into your chamber and sleep." And Abraham slept with Michael, while his son Isaac slept in his chamber.

VI. Now it happened when midnight came that Isaac got up, frightened out of sleep. He went to the door of his father's chamber and knocked, cried out, and wept saying: [f.152^a] "My father Abraham, rise and open the door for your son Isaac, that I may come in and embrace you and be filled with (your presence) this (one) more time before you depart from me."

Immediately Abraham rose in great fright and opened the door for his son Isaac. And Isaac ran toward his father and kissed him. They embraced each other and wept mightily so that Michael himself also wept with them when he saw them so grieved. When Rebecca heard this, she and her maidservants, she rose and went to the door of the chamber where Abraham slept. She heard them weeping bitterly. She opened the door and ran in in fright. She said to Abraham: "My lord father Abraham, has my lord Isaac perhaps died [f.152^b] that you weep so?" But when she saw Michael also weeping, she turned and said: "No, it is not Isaac who has died. There, I see Isaac grieving with his father." She said to Michael, who had the form of a man: "I ask you, O man, where have you come from? Or where are you going? O man, have you perhaps brought my lord Abraham news of his brother Lot, that he has been taken prisoner, he and his sons?"

Michael answered and said to Rebecca: "O Rebecca, nurse of the righteous, I have not brought news of Lot nor of any of his sons. For the Lord watches over him. Wherever he goes no evil will befall him, for he is an honored race."

Rebecca answered: "Blessed are you when you go in and go out."[12] [f.153^a] For she had known his voice[13] from (the time of) her fathers and her husbands.[14] And she said to Abraham: "Why do you weep while the holy one is with you?"

Abraham answered: "How do you know, O my daughter, that this man is a holy one?"

Rebecca answered saying: "Unless I am wrong in my heart, O my father, this is one of the three men who visited you under the tree of Mamre, those for whom you prepared a feast."

And Abraham spoke to her thus: "Truly, O my daughter, from the very time I washed his feet I knew that he was one of those who were hastening to Sodom. But let us ask him, 'Why have you come here?'"

VII. Abraham spoke and said to the archangel Michael, who had the form of a man: "For what matter have you come here, O my brother?"

Michael said to him: "Isaac your [f.153^b] son will tell you what he has seen."

Abraham said to Isaac: "What have you seen, O my beloved Isaac?"

And Rebecca too grasped Isaac weeping and begged him speaking thus: "My lord Isaac, tell us what you have seen. Instruct us. Do not hide anything from us."

Isaac said to them: "My tongue is not suited for me to tell what I have seen. But listen to me and I will tell you everything that I saw. It happened to me in my chamber as I was sleeping alone that I saw a vision in the middle of the night. Lo, the sun and the moon and the stars formed a crown above my head. Then I saw a man of light who had come out of the heavens, one who is called the father of all lights. He took away the sun that was over my head, and the moon wept before the man [f.154^a] of light saying: 'The light that was in my house has been taken away. For when I am powerless the sun gives me power so that I become new again.' And the stars also wept in this single weeping and the sun also spoke before the man of light: 'If you are going to take me away, then wait for me to gather my rays, for I do not want to leave them behind.' After this, O my sister Rebecca, I looked to my right and saw that sun resembling my father Abraham and the moon resembling my mother Sarah. And the stars too were like all my servants, and they all were weeping. And I myself was weeping with them over my father Abraham because he was to be taken away from me. The man of light spoke and said to me: 'Do not weep, Isaac, over Abraham your father because he is going to be removed. [f.154^b] For he will be taken away from a narrow place and taken to the broad one, he will be taken away from poverty and received into wealth, he will be taken away from servitude and received into freedom.' When I had seen these things, I came before the door of the chamber, my heart frightening me. There, I have told you what I saw."

The archangel Michael spoke: "What have you seen? Repeat (it) to us in your (own) words, O my son, and it will happen truly." Then all knew that Abraham was going to go forth from the body, and they wept greatly.

The patriarch spoke and said to Michael: "If this is the will of God or he has determined thus for me, I will not speak in opposition. Only I ask you, my lord, to console your servant and take him [f.155^a] up to the heavens before I go forth from the body."

Michael said to Abraham: "This matter is not mine (to grant) but my Lord's. I shall ask the Lord on your behalf. If he commands me, I shall take you up with delight and joy."

VIII. Then Michael went out of Abraham's house and flew up to the heavens. He prayed to the Father for Abraham that he might command him to take him up to the heavens. The Father said, speaking with the archangel Michael: "Obey Abraham in everything that he tells you. Bring him up to the heavens in his body first. Teach him everything he desires. See that you fully satisfy him, for he is my friend."

Then the archangel Michael withdrew from before the Lord. He mounted a cloud with Abraham. It drew them to the regions of the Ocean and raised them up to the heavens in glory.

[f.155^b] I, Abraham, saw a gate there, a large one and a small one. I saw a man wearing white garments, seated at the two gates weeping, and sometimes he laughed. But his tears were much more frequent than his laughter, about eleven times (more). I said to Michael: "What are these two gates, this large one and this small one?"

Michael said to me: "This is the gate that leads to life, and to death. You see this large and broad gate; this is the one that leads to death. You see also this small gate; this is the one that leads to life. You see this man seated between them; this is Adam the first man, whom God placed here to see all the souls that go forth from the body passing before him. [f.156^a] You have also seen that his tears are greater than his laughter since he sees the evil deeds of all the souls that go forth from the body passing before him, for thousands are those that go into the gate of perdition, but few are those that go into the gate of life."

IX. After this I looked and saw crowds of souls, myriads in number; their angels going behind them, they went into the gate of perdition. Michael said to me: "Come, let us seek among these souls and see if we shall find that one which is worthy for me to take it into the life of the Lord."

Abraham and Michael both sought among the souls, (but) they did not find that one which was worthy among them except one single soul whose sins equalled its good deeds. It was taken[15] into life, [f.156^b] but the rest of the souls were all taken into the gate of perdition. Michael said: "Woe to these, woe to these, for they are sinners who have not been able to enter into life."

And I, Abraham, spoke: "I am a man who also leads his existence in a body that is heavy. For I know that it is not possible for anyone to enter into that narrow gate, which is (the gate) of life, except for a few who are twelve years old and those who have guarded themselves from sin."

The archangel Michael said to me: "Do not be afraid, O

Abraham; you and those who will come after you, those who will be like you--you will enter into eternal life."

I said to the holy archangel Michael: "My lord, as for all these souls that go forth from the body, is it Death who [f.157^a] brings them forth or is it their angel?"

The archangel Michael said to me: "Do not be afraid, O Abraham, you and those who will be like you, for it is Death who brings them forth from the body."

I said to the holy archangel Michael: "How many souls come forth each day from the whole world, and how many souls are born?"

The archangel Michael said to me: "Do you think, O Abraham, that it is these souls alone that come forth from the body in the whole world each day, O Abraham?"

I said to the archangel Michael: "Instruct me, for indeed I do not know."

The archangel Michael said to me: "Listen and I shall teach you how many souls therefore come forth from the body each day in the whole world, whether in the daytime or at night: ninety-nine thousand and ninety-nine hundred."

X. And while [f.157^b] Michael the archangel was telling me this, lo, a soul was brought, surrounded like a robber. It was said: "Let the judge give judgment on this soul."

The judge said: "Let her deeds be read to her; her deeds are written."[16]

Immediately a gray-haired man came forth from the veil with a book in his hand, and he began to read all the sins of that soul right up to the evil she had done. That soul anguished before the judge, speaking thus: "None of these things ever came from me." For the soul thought to herself that there would be no recollection of all the things she had done.

God the true judge said to her: "Is there lying here where there is no lying?"

That soul began to speak: "My Lord, [f.158^a] none of these things ever came from me."

The judge said to her: "Do you wish that the deeds you have done should convict you now one by one and that they all be recalled to you?"

The judge made a sign with his eyes. Immediately they

stood before her like witnesses. The first said to her: "Look at me, O soul. Is it not you who rose up and spoke with your daughter's husband in an evil plot: 'Rise and lie with me and take the place of my husband'--until you rose up against your own daughter and killed her and took her husband from her."

As soon as the miserable soul heard this, she wept saying: "Woe is me, woe is me with my lawless deeds. Whither shall I flee? For I thought to myself that no one knew what I had done. [f.158b] Behold, now I am convicted."

The second witness stood and accused her saying: "Look at me, O soul. Am I not the one who stands at the time when those of heaven and those of earth sing praise? Instead of extending your hands and praying to God, you did not even remember the name of God, but you were (involved) in eating and drinking and all your exceedingly evil desires."

The third witness stood before her saying: "Look at me, O soul, and recognize me. Am I not the one who is appointed over the thanksgiving?"[17] And the angels and archangels and Cherubim and Seraphim all wept over the race of men. The witness said to her: "You used to go out at night and do abominable things."

When the soul heard this, she wept saying: [f.159a] "It is enough for me, O true judge, to convict me. I know that I have no word to say." Immediately her mouth was shut. She was cast down to the depth of hell.

XI. I said to the holy archangel Michael: "My lord, who is this great gray-haired man with this book in his hand, reminding the judge of these souls?"

The archangel Michael said to me: "This is Enoch, the scribe of righteousness. God saw that he was trustworthy and appointed him to write down all the good deeds and evil deeds that men do."

XII. When Abraham had seen these things, the holy archangel Michael brought him to his house. He slept on his bed to die like all men, as the Lord had determined for him. [f.159b] And Abraham summoned all his menservants and maidservants. He gave them the document of their freedom and made a great feast for the poor on that day.

XIII. When his departure from the body drew near, God said to Michael: "My chosen one, I do not wish Death to frighten Abraham when he comes forth from the body, for he is my friend. But adorn him when he comes to him so that his soul will not be frightened of him." Michael adorned Death according to the works of Abraham and sent him to him.

Death entered and lay down at the side of Abraham as he slept. When he touched his body, he shuddered, his body trembled, and his soul leaped within him, wishing to go forth from the body. [f.160^a] Abraham said to him: "Who are you (who appear) in this manner? For from the moment I saw you my body and my soul and all my members shuddered within me, and my soul trembled, wishing to go forth from it. But who are you (who appear) in this manner? I do not know.[18] Are you not a great angel of the Father, since you are in such beauty and in this great honor? That is why I could not bear your brilliance. But at the time when the angels will come to me, I will have more strength so that my flesh will become strong and my soul will rejoice within me. But when you came to me, my flesh dissolved and likewise my soul too trembled within me. I beseech you, therefore, tell me who you are. Little by little, lo, my eyes have become darkened. I do not know those who surround me. [f.160^b] Little by little my sensation wishes to despise its receptacle and to abandon its receptacle.[19] Little by little my understanding becomes ignorant. Now then, see, my tongue has become ignorant and small and cold when you came to me. Little by little my breath has grown light in me and has come near to being quenched. Now also my soul has come leaping within me wishing to go forth from my members."

And Abraham wept exceedingly and called out in great fear and great clamor for his son Isaac saying: "Draw near to me, O my son, to see if you may recognize the one who is visiting my bed, the one of whom I am frightened. For I have become an old man; my eyes have become darkened. For this reason I did not recognize him."

Isaac drew near to [f.161^a] his father. He kissed his mouth and said to him: "My father Abraham, I see no one beside you. Why do you weep and shudder? Tell me your thought, O my father."

Abraham said to him: "My son Isaac, your father is going forth from the body like everyone; he will depart never to return."

Isaac wept and said to his father: "Woe to me. As you depart, you leave me and I will become an orphan. Where shall I find another father like you?"

Abraham said to him: "Do not weep, O my son Isaac, and do not be frightened. You have the Lord. He will protect you until the day when you go forth from the body."

And Abraham turned to the one who lay by his side and said to him: "Tell me openly who you are or what is your name." [f.161^b]

Death said to him: "Hear my name which is bitter. I am the origin of grief. I am the one who--if I take him away he does not return again. I am the one who causes fright to everyone. I am the one who brings grief upon a mother and I take from her her children who surround her. I am Death, O Abraham, who takes away every man."

Abraham said to Death: "Are you Death, though you are so beautiful? How can you wish to make a man fear when you come after him in this beauty?"

Death said to Abraham: "Do you think I come after every man in this fashion? No, O Abraham, but only the righteous; I come after them in this beauty. But the sinners I go after in all my ugliness so as to frighten them when I take them out of the body."

Abraham said to Death: "Does the beauty of such beauty surround you?"[20]

[f.162^a] Death said to Abraham: "This beauty is yours. In accordance with the deeds of each one, I clothe myself with them in order to come after them."

XIV. Abraham said to Death: "Show yourself in your (true) appearance and form that I may see you."

Death said to Abraham: "Let your servants remain outside the door of the chamber lest they see me and all die. For no one has ever seen my form and lived."

Abraham said to Death: "Is it indeed possible for anyone to die before his limit of life and his time?

Death said to Abraham: "Yes, as a result of the great wounds and pestilences which God sends upon the lands and the cities because of their sins. When he is angry with them, he sends us (saying): 'Carry off their souls as you wish.' We both go forth, I, Death, [f.162^b] and my son whom I begot from the filth of matter. I named him Prilimos because he comes from the filth of everything.[21] We both go forth full of wrath; we smite from beginning to end. Whoever approaches us on every path, we spare neither small nor great. We have no shame over a gray-haired man. We do not spare a youth. We have no mercy for a child who feeds on his mother's milk. We do not spare a bride nor a bridegroom, but we snatch them from their bridechamber. My son Prilymos gives sickness; my own task is to take them out of the body."

When he had said this, he began to reveal his form and he stripped himself of all his beauty. He had a multitude of heads, some with serpent[22] faces, others casting forth fire, [f.163a] so that eighteen of Abraham's servants fell down and died as a result of fear of him. But the rest fell on their face. The shadow of Death covered them until Michael came and raised up the servants of Abraham and stood them upright, and Death withdrew with those who were his own to go to his (own) places.

And the archangel Michael took the soul of Abraham and wrapped it in linen cloths and placed it on a chariot of light. Armies of angels went before it until his soul was received into the resting-places in the third heaven. He rejoiced with all the righteous.

The patriarch Abraham left the body on the 28th of the month of Mesore, being one hundred seventy years old. Isaac wept for his father and prepared him for burial with great honor. He took him [f.163b] and buried him in the tomb of his mother Sarah, which he had bought from the sons of Heth. Sixty days were spent in weeping for Abraham. After the mourning Isaac went into his house and said to his servants: "See, my father has set you free. You yourselves arise and do the works of freedom so that freedom will be yours."

And Isaac also abounded in works of his piety,[23] believing in the God of his father Abraham and glorifying the Father and the Son and the Holy Spirit, who proceeds from him. All glory and all honor and all adoration is due to the Father with him and the Holy Spirit, giver of life and consubstantial with him, now and at all times and forever and ever. Amen.

The life of our father the patriarch Abraham is ended. His holy blessing be with all our people forever. Amen.

NOTES

[1] See the articles of G. W. E. Nickelsburg, Jr. and F. Schmidt in the present volume, and also M. Delcor, *Le Testament d'Abraham* (Studia in Veteris Testamenti Pseudepigrapha 2; Leiden: Brill, 1973) 23-24.

[2] "Il testo copto del Testamento di Abramo," *Rendiconti della Reale Accademia dei Lincei, Classe di scienze morali, storiche e filologiche*, Serie Quinta, 9 (1900) 157-180.

[3] See F. Schmidt, *Le Testament d'Abraham: introduction, édition de la recension courte, traduction et notes* (unpublished dissertation; Strasbourg, 1971) 17-19; Delcor, *Le Testament d'Abraham*, 17.

[4] "Abraham's Vermächtnis aus dem Koptischen übersetzt," *Spinx* 6 (1903) 220-236.

[5] In Delcor, *Le Testament d'Abraham*, 186-198.

[6] On the authenticity of this preface see Schmidt, *Le Testament d'Abraham*, 15-17.

[7] M. R. James, *The Testament of Abraham* (Texts and Studies II, 2; Cambridge: Cambridge University Press, 1892). The text is conveniently reprinted with translation in M. E. Stone, *The Testament of Abraham: The Greek Recensions* (Texts and Translations 2, Pseudepigrapha Series 2; Missoula: SBL, 1972).

[8] The Coptic (Greek) words, in apposition with Athanasius, are not entirely clear: ⲡⲓⲁⲡⲟⲥⲧⲟⲗⲓⲕⲟⲥ ⲡⲓⲁⲗⲉⲝⲁⲛⲇⲣⲉⲁⲥ. One might have expected a reference to the apostolic origin of the see of ⲣⲁⲕⲟϯ itself.

[9] Here and at the beginning of chap. V the Coptic phrase translated "on a pretext" (with Chaine) is ϧⲉⲛ ⲟⲩϩⲱⲃ.

[10] The Bohairic ⲉϧⲣⲏⲓ can only be a mistake for ⲉⲉⲣⲏⲓ.

[11] Literally: "that is bitter and it is harsh." The present form ⲩⲛⲁⲱⲧ may, however, be a mistake for the relative ⲉⲑⲛⲁⲱⲧ.

[12] Or possibly (Chaine): "at your arrival and at your departure."

[13] Chaine translates ⲥⲙⲏ as "renown" rather than "voice"; this would be possible if the underlying Greek were φήμη rather than φωνή. In the Greek long recension, chap. VI Sarah apparently recognizes Michael on the strength of his speech.

[14] Plural sic.

15 Or possibly: "they took it."

16 Literally: "Let them read to her among (from among?) her deeds. Lo, her deeds are written."

17 Greek εὐχαριστία.

18 Or perhaps (Andersson): "I do not know who you are..."

19 The word translated "receptacle" (i.e. the body?) is ⲇⲁⲙⲓⲟⲛ, which I take to be Greek ταμιεῖον although in all other instances the form is ⲧⲁⲙⲓⲟⲛ. Andersson in translating "göttliche Kraft" apparently understands the word as δαιμόνιον.

20 Translated literally; apparently the meaning is: "Does such great beauty belong to you?"

21 The name Ⲡⲣⲓⲗⲓⲙⲟⲥ, a few lines below Ⲡⲣⲓⲁⲩⲙⲟⲥ, contains a play on the word for "filth," λῦμα, here ⲗⲩⲙⲙⲁ.

22 Emending ⲛⲉⲃⲟⲩⲍⲓ to ⲛⲉⲍⲃⲟⲩⲓ.

23 Or: "divine worship," Coptic ⲙⲉⲧϣⲁⲙϣⲉⲛⲟⲩⲧ̅.

www.ingramcontent.com/pod-product-compliance
Lightning Source LLC
Chambersburg PA
CBHW021117300426
44113CB00006B/176